RUSSIAN AND EAST EUROPEAN STUDIES

Andrew Malozemoff, *Russian Far Eastern Policy, 1881–1904. With Special Emphasis on the Causes of the Russo-Japanese War*

TSARIST RUSSIA
AND BALKAN NATIONALISM

RUSSIAN AND EAST EUROPEAN STUDIES

Tsarist Russia and Balkan Nationalism

RUSSIAN INFLUENCE IN THE INTERNAL AFFAIRS OF BULGARIA AND SERBIA, 1879-1886

Charles Jelavich

UNIVERSITY OF CALIFORNIA PRESS

BERKELEY AND LOS ANGELES · 1958

8 4 5 6 5
3 2 7. 4 7
J 4 8 t

University of California Press
Berkeley and Los Angeles, California

Cambridge University Press
London, England

© 1958 by the Regents of the University of California
Library of Congress Catalogue Card Number: 58–12830

FOR

BARBARA

PREFACE

"IF RUSSIA comes to liberate, she will be received with great sympathy; but if she comes to rule, she will find many enemies," wrote Liuben Karavelov, one of Bulgaria's most distinguished authors, in 1870. His words were a clear expression of the most important single rule which determined the relations of the Balkan peoples to the Russian government in the seven years after the Congress of Berlin.

The purpose of this study is to examine to what extent this principle was followed, and how Russian policy, based primarily on considerations of Russian interests as a European great power, came into intense conflict with Bulgarian nationalism, but, in contrast, won the sympathy of the Serbian people, who deeply resented the domination of Austria-Hungary. The emphasis will be placed chiefly on the relations of Russia with Bulgaria and Serbia; no attempt will be made to cover in detail the general European aspects of the events described.

In this study of Russo-Bulgarian and Russo-Serbian relations, the reader will perhaps be struck by the similarity of the events of the 'eighties to those of the decade after the Second World War. A note of caution must be sounded, however, for the two periods can be compared only superficially. In the years covered by this study, the question of Bulgaria and the Straits was one of the problems which dominated Russian diplomacy. Although Russia engaged in controversies with Britain over the central Asian territories and with China over Kuldja, these issues were regarded as being of lesser importance than Bulgaria and the Straits. In their relations with the Bulgarian people, the Russian officials were dealing with a nation of primary political significance, an autonomous state which enjoyed considerable freedom of action in international affairs, which Bulgaria does not have today. Despite the fact that Bulgaria was recognized at the Congress of Berlin as falling within the Russian sphere of influence, the Bulgarian leaders, as events were to prove, retained the means of blocking Russian domination. Unlike the situation today, when the Soviet Union stands as the only great military power in the area, the tsarist government was faced with the constant and formidable opposition of Great Britain, Austria-Hungary, and Germany. Moreover, Russian policy after the Congress of Berlin was strictly defensive. In any controversy with Russia the Bulgarian statesmen could expect positive support from Russia's opponents; consequently the Russian government always had to take into consideration the possible actions of other powers. Serbia at this time was under Austro-Hungarian, not Russian, domination.

At present, in contrast, Bulgaria as a nation has been relegated to a position of minor importance, a satellite state in an area controlled by the Communist party. No great power has taken the place of the dismembered Dual Monarchy or the defeated German Empire on whom the small Balkan and central European states could depend as an effective balance against Russia. In a sense Jugoslavia is now in the position occupied by Bulgaria in the 'eighties, but the similarities are again more apparent than real.

Comparisons can be drawn between the present and the past on the role of ideology in the relations between the states. In her associations with the Balkan Slavs in the nineteenth century, Russia used the principles of Orthodoxy, conservatism, and Slavic brotherhood, and in the twentieth century communism and Slavic kinship, but the practical effects were totally different in the two periods. In 1878–1879, after the liberation of Bulgaria from Ottoman control, Russia did not attempt to impose upon the nation a system of government in conformity with that in St. Petersburg. In fact, the Bulgarian constitution drafted by Russian officials and subsequently sponsored by the Russian government not only established the form of government preferred by the Bulgarian people themselves but also granted constitutional rights to the Bulgars which Russia denied to her own citizens. Moreover, although the offices of the Orthodox church were used where possible to influence opinions, and the close racial and linguistic bonds between Russia and Bulgaria were exploited to the maximum, nothing in the nature of a modern propaganda campaign was organized or envisaged.

A study of the relations between Russia, Bulgaria, and Serbia in the nineteenth century demonstrates the great changes that have occurred in international relations since the First World War. In the last century the Balkans, the proverbial powder keg of Europe, were used as the classic illustration of an area dominated by anarchism, intrigue, political assassination, revolution, and warfare. The period of the 'eighties was certainly one of the most eventful in the history of that peninsula, yet the only war, the Serbo-Bulgarian, lasted two weeks and resulted in few casualties. And the great "atrocity" of the decade, the abduction of the prince of Bulgaria, Alexander of Battenberg, in retrospect reads like an incident in a light opera. Perhaps, then, the only valid generalization that can be made is that, although on the surface the declarations and actions of individuals of today and those of the 'eighties may appear to follow a roughly similar course, in recent years there has been an intensification of the latent aspects of the earlier era—the use of terror, of subversion, of naked force, and of despotic rule.

As the Bulgarian government turned away from Russia, it looked increasingly for advice and guidance to Russia's adversaries, Austria-

Hungary and Great Britain. Hence the Russian demands and the Bulgarian reaction received full coverage in the diplomatic reports. In Serbia, King Milan was often more frank in imparting his views to the Habsburg representatives than to his own ministers. The British and Austrian archives contain numerous accounts based on the conversations of N. K. Giers, Russian foreign minister from 1882 to 1895, who was remarkably candid in expressing his views. Both the British and Austrian representatives trusted and admired him, although they feared that his moderate and peaceful advice would not always prevail with the tsar.

This work is based mainly on unpublished material from Great Britain and Austria. The political dispatches from the British foreign office found in the Public Record Office and the similar sources in the Austrian Haus-, Hof-, und Staatsarchiv were excellent for the specific events discussed.

The great difficulty in preparing a study of Russian foreign policy is, of course, the scarcity of Russian documentary materials. The author was fortunate, however, in having access to the correspondence of Giers. Although the collection is incomplete, certain sections proved especially valuable for the subject under consideration. Of foremost importance was the correspondence with A. P. Davydov, A. G. Jomini, A. E. Vlangali, and I. A. Zinoviev.

Of the published material on the subject, C. E. Black's authoritative work, *The Establishment of Constitutional Government in Bulgaria,* has been used for the political background. E. C. Corti's biography of Alexander of Battenberg, based on the prince's correspondence, was the chief source for the views of the young ruler. Anyone who has used Slobodan Jovanović's monumental studies on Serbian history will appreciate the debt owed to him by any writer in the field. Simeon Radev's two volumes covering the formation of the Bulgarian state are an indispensable source for the internal history of Bulgaria. S. Skazkin's work on the Dreikaiserbund remains the best study of that subject and of Russo-Bulgarian relations to 1883. The author's debt to these five writers is reflected throughout the following pages. Mention should also be made of the recently published four-volume diary of D. A. Miliutin, and the work of I. V. Koz'menko on the Bulgarian constitution.

In the transliteration of Slavic names the Library of Congress system has been used, with certain exceptions. Where a name is familiar to the English reader in another spelling or under a different system of transliteration, that form has been adopted: Bulgariia (not B"lgariia), Tyrnovo (not T"rnovo), Ignatiev (not Ignat'ev), Kaulbars (not Kaul'bars). For those in the Russian service with non-Russian names, the form familiar in the West and that found in the majority of the diplomatic dispatches has been used: Giers (not Girs), Jomini (not Zhomini), and so on. Specific dates are cited according to both the Julian and Gregorian calendars, a difference of twelve days in the nineteenth century. The dates in the footnotes are those found in the source. To save space in the footnotes, St. Petersburg is abbreviated (St. P.).

The manuscript was completed and submitted in January, 1956: published material which has become available after this date has not been incorporated in the text.

It is a pleasure to be able to acknowledge the generous help I have received in the preparation of this book. My first obligation is to the late Professor Robert J. Kerner, who gave me constant encouragement, advice, and guidance throughout my research. I have profited from my discussions on diplomatic history with Professor Raymond J. Sontag. My other colleagues, Professors Oleg A. Maslenikov, C. Bickford O'Brien, and Nicholas V. Riasanovsky read the entire manuscript and offered very detailed criticisms and suggestions, all of which were most helpful. I benefited from the general comments of Professors Walter Galenson and Julian Towster. Professor Myron F. Brightfield gave me professional advice and criticism in the writing of the work. None of these individuals, of course, is responsible for the presentation and conclusions, which are my own.

I wish to convey my warmest thanks to Mr. Serge Giers for permitting me to use the papers of his grandfather. His understanding of my needs facilitated my research considerably. I want also to express my appreciation to the staff of the British Museum, of the Public Record Office, especially to Mr. E. Kenneth Timings, and of the Haus-, Hof-, und Staatsarchiv, where Dr. Gebhard Rath placed at my disposal all the materials I requested, even though some of the physical difficulties of the war period had not been overcome.

I am grateful for the financial support of the Institute of Slavic Studies, the Institute of East Asiatic Studies, and the Institute of Social Sciences, University of California, Berkeley. Miss Genevieve Rogers gave me expert editorial help. Mr. Harold Kirkpatrick read the manuscript, offered important suggestions, and prepared the index. Mrs. Celia Wakefield typed the work, and Mr. Thomas Akawie prepared the map.

Only I can appreciate fully the contributions which my wife made in every phase of the preparation of this work. Therefore, the dedication is a token gesture for all that she has done and meant.

C. J.

CONTENTS

ABBREVIATIONS USED IN FOOTNOTES

UNPUBLISHED MATERIALS

FO: Great Britain. Public Record Office, Political Despatches.
HHS: Austria-Hungary. Haus-, Hof-, und Staatsarchiv, Politisches Archiv.
NKG: Private Correspondence of Nikolai Karlovich Giers.

PRINTED MATERIALS

GOVERNMENT DOCUMENTS

AP: Great Britain. *Accounts and Papers* (Blue Books), XCVIII (1881); LXXXII
(1883); LXXV:1 (1886), LXXV:2 (1886); XCI:1 (1887); XCI:2
(1887).
Avantiury: P. Pavlovich, ed. *Avantiury Russkogo Tsarizma v Bolgarii.* Moscow,
1935.
BD: Pancho Dorev, ed. *Dokumenti za Bulgarskata Istoriia: Dokumenti iz Turskitie
Durzhavni Arkhivi, 1863–1909.* Sofia, 1942.
DDF: France. *Documents diplomatiques français,* 1ʳᵉ serie, Vols. III–VI.
GP: Germany. *Die grosse Politik der europäischen Kabinette, 1871–1914,* Vols.
III–VI.

SECONDARY MATERIALS

Black: C. E. Black. *The Establishment of Constitutional Government in Bulgaria.*
Princeton, 1943.
Corti, *Alexander:* E. C. Corti. *Leben und Lieben Alexanders von Battenberg.* Graz,
Salzburg, Vienna, 1950.
Corti, *DTD:* E. C. Corti. *The Downfall of Three Dynasties.* London, 1934.
Goriainov, "Razryv": S. M. Goriainov, "Razryv Rossii s Bolgariei v 1886 godu,"
Istoricheskii Viestnik, CXLVII (1917).
Jovanović, *Milan:* Slobodan Jovanović. *Vlada Milana Obrenovića.* Belgrade, 1934.
Koch: A. Koch. *Prince Alexander of Battenberg.* London, 1887.
Miliutin: P. A. Zaionchkovskii, ed. *Dnevnik D. A. Miliutina, 1878–1882.* Moscow,
1950.
Radev: Simeon Radev. *Stroitelite na Suvremenenna Bulgariia.* Sofia, 1911.
Skazkin: S. Skazkin. *Konets Avstro-Russko-Germanskogo Soiuza.* Moscow, 1928.
Staal: A. Meyendorf. *Correspondance diplomatique de M. de Staal.* Paris, 1929.

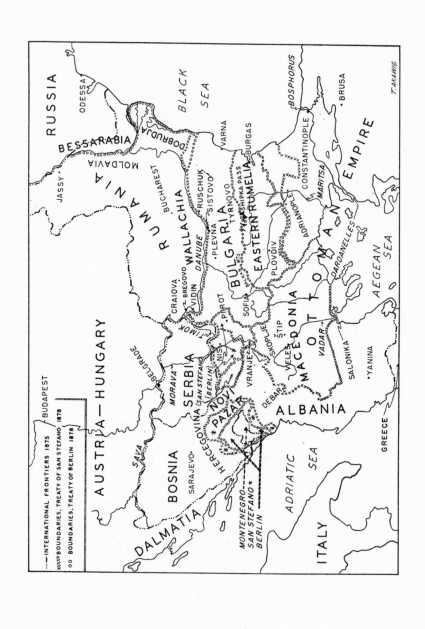

I

INTRODUCTION
RUSSIA'S NEAR EASTERN POLICY

IN THE DECADE after the Congress of Berlin, Russian policy in Europe was dominated by three considerations: avoidance of diplomatic isolation, security at the Straits, and protection of the Russian position in Bulgaria, the one positive gain of the Russo-Turkish War. Although Russia, through the Three Emperors' Alliance, had attained the coveted position of being one of three in the European complex of five great powers, the disaster of her Bulgarian policy is a remarkable illustration of the inability of the Russian government to maintain control in an area where it enjoyed prestige and power.

Even though, in the years under consideration, Russia made advances in the Middle East, the Balkan problem was the center of Russian diplomacy. By constant supervision of the destiny of the new Bulgarian state, Russia hoped to secure a strong advance post toward the Straits and at the same time offer a point of attraction to the other Slavs of the Balkan Peninsula. Her interests were thus primarily those of a great power, but in pursuing her aims she hoped to play upon the Panslav sympathies of the Bulgarian people and thereby exploit her role as the liberator of the Slavic peoples from foreign oppression. Since Bulgarian nationalism could, in 1878, still be considered as synonymous with certain Panslav aspirations, every opportunity existed for the accomplishment of the Russian program in Bulgaria.

In her relations with all the Balkan peoples, Russia enjoyed great advantages which were not shared by the other major powers. Although the dissolution of the Ottoman Empire and the resultant division of its widespread lands had been a vital concern of the major European states for well over one hundred and fifty years, the great powers had been unable to agree upon the principle by which the dying empire should be partitioned, or if, indeed, it should be partitioned at all.

Two general bases of territorial division were recognized: the balance of power and nationalism. Each had its adherents and each at one time was used as the justification for depriving Turkey of her lands. The chief claimants under the first principle were the Habsburg empire, Great Britain, and Russia, although Italy, Germany, and France all at one time or another gained thereby. It was, however, the principle of nationalism which finally obtained general acceptance. Here two pos-

[1]

sible interpretations existed. The individual Balkan states could be
allowed to develop as independent units in free coöperation or competition with one another—or they could become satellites of the great
powers.

Of the two powers with primary interests in the Balkans, Russia and
the Habsburg empire, the latter had the most to gain by a simple division of Ottoman territory. It was difficult for Austria, herself a hetero-
geneous state, to benefit from the application of national principles to
the Balkan lands. Since the majority of her population were of Slavic
origin, the formation of free Slavic states outside her borders could only
menace her existence. When, after 1866, Austria was excluded from
further participation in German affairs and, in the same period, found
herself unable to embark upon the overseas ventures of the Atlantic
powers, the Balkan Peninsula became the only field open to imperial
expansion. The dream of a great empire stretching from Vienna through
the western half of the Balkan Peninsula to Salonika was exceedingly
attractive.

In the movement southeast the monarchy had certain positive assets.
The first, and that which in the end proved most important, was predominant military power on the scene. Second, Austria-Hungary could
hold out to the Slavic peoples of the free states and the Ottoman territories the attractions of western civilization, although Vienna was
faced with competition from Paris as the real center of the "West."
Third, the monarchy could offer great economic advantages. It had the
capital with which to develop the Balkan lands, which were natural
market areas and sources of raw materials for the industrial states.

Against these favorable elements, however, were the grave disadvantages under which Austrian policy labored. After the Ausgleich of
1867, Vienna had constantly to consider Magyar opinion, which in its
relations with the Slavic inhabitants of the monarchy proved extremely
shortsighted and in the end prevented the evolution of the Habsburg
empire into an organization acceptable to the majority of its peoples.
Jealous of their privileged position, the Magyar politicians fought bitterly against any increase in the Slavic element in the state, but at the
same time they agitated for the extension of Habsburg power in the
Balkans, even at the cost of a war with Russia. Habsburg diplomacy
was thus hampered by the fact that it could not make use of Slavic
nationalism except in a negative sense. With no "natural ties" in the
Balkan Peninsula, the empire was forced to rely primarily on force
and diplomacy. Therefore, in her relations with the Balkan lands,

Austria stood for outright annexation of territory, as in the case of Bosnia-Hercegovina, or the reduction of the Balkan states to vassaldom, as witnessed by her treaty with Serbia in 1881.

Russia, in contrast, could exploit all avenues of approach to gain predominant influence in the Balkans. On the basis of Russian national interest and power politics, the chief goal in the Balkan Peninsula was control over the Straits and Constantinople, the "key" to Russia's back door. Despite all the turns of Russian policy in the nineteenth century, this objective remained constant. In Russian foreign relations all Balkan interests were subordinated to the problem of the Straits.

Parallel to this aim, which was primarily military and strategic, ran the Panslav ideal of the unity of the Slavic, Orthodox people against the encroachments of the west, as represented in particular by the German states. On this ground Russia could gain much support from the Balkan peoples, who had been conditioned to religious and ideological struggles by centuries of Moslem rule. The principal agency which Russia could employ in this regard was the Orthodox church. Through it Russia could reach down to the roots of Slavic national feeling and to the individual Slavic peasant.

Both principles—balance of power and nationalism—were thus of benefit to Russia. She could accept the idea of partition and annexation because she was strong enough to insist that she receive a fair portion; she could support the creation of the little states because she could expect that they would turn to her as the major Slavic and Orthodox power. On the basis of Slavdom and Orthodoxy, she attracted Serbia, Bulgaria, and Montenegro; on the basis of Orthodoxy alone, Rumania and Greece came within her orbit. The major check to the extension of Russian power thus came not from the natural conditions of the area but from the fear of the great powers of the menace to their interests in Russian expansion in the Balkans.

Certainly, it was the pressure of the great powers that forced Russia to make her fateful choice of Bulgaria over Serbia during the eastern crisis of 1875–1878. Although, in the past, Russian policy had been to support all the Orthodox peoples of the Balkans against both the Turks and the Austrians, Russia recognized after the Crimean War that such commitments were too widespread. Of the lands under Turkish control, those inhabited by the Bulgarian people were of principal importance because of their strategic position in regard to the Straits. Thus, although Russian opinion retained a strong sympathy for Serbian national aims, the Russian government through its support of the establishment of the Bulgarian exarchate in the 1870's gave a clear indication that Russian national interests rather than Panslav sentiments would in the end determine Russian policy.

Unfortunately, this position was not clearly realized in Belgrade. Throughout the Bosnian crisis of 1875 the Serbs continued to look to Russia for protection and material assistance. When they went to war with the Ottoman Empire in 1876, they did so primarily as a result of Russian unofficial, if not official, encouragement. It appeared logical to them that Russia would render assistance, because in their opinion Serbian aims coincided with Russian national interests.

Despite the fact that large sections of the Russian public would gladly have undertaken the support of both Slavic, Orthodox peoples, the Russian government was well aware that it could not act unilaterally. Faced with the probability of war with Turkey, Russia knew that she would have to compensate the Habsburg empire, whose interests centered in Bosnia-Hercegovina and Serbia. Russia could not make an agreement with her chief competitor in the Balkans without sacrificing Serbia. The sentimental and cultural ties between Serbia and Russia in no sense outweighed the strategic importance of Bulgaria. If Russia did not gain Austrian acquiescence, she faced the danger of the formation of a hostile European coalition which would prevent even the liberation of the Bulgarian lands. Recognizing that the achievement of a limited program was better than none, Russia accepted the necessity of the sacrifice of Serbia, and in July, 1876, signed the Reichstadt agreement.

The terms agreed upon by A. M. Gorchakov and J. Andrassy, the Russian and Austrian foreign ministers, respectively, provided for the possibility that Serbia and Montenegro, with whom the Bulgarians had joined in the war against the Ottoman Empire, would emerge triumphant. Should this occur, it was agreed that Bulgaria, Rumelia, and Albania would be erected into autonomous or independent states. However—and this was to prove most important in the future—under no condition should a large Slavic state be created. Serbia and Montenegro were to be allowed a common frontier in the Sanjak of Novi Pazar. On the fate of Bosnia-Hercegovina, a disagreement later arose on exactly what had been decided. Andrassy was under the impression that he had been given the right to annex both provinces, whereas Gorchakov claimed that he had consented to an Austrian annexation of only the northern part of Bosnia. Finally, Russia was to be allowed to regain the Bessarabian territory that she had lost in 1856, which would again bring her frontiers to the Danube. In 1877 these terms were incorporated in the Treaty of Budapest, thereby permitting Russia to go to war against the Ottoman Empire.[1]

When the Russian army finally achieved victory in 1878, the Russian public hailed the event with intense enthusiasm. The century-old dream of expelling the Turks from the Balkans was on the verge of success; Russia now appeared to have the power to grasp the key to her back door—the Straits. The Russian military gains and the public's support of them were exploited to the maximum by N. P. Ignatiev, Russian ambassador at Constantinople, who incorporated the hopes and aspirations of Russian opinion, particularly of the Panslav elements, in the terms of the Treaty of San Stefano.

The principal and most controversial provisions of the treaty concerned the creation of the so-called Greater Bulgaria, whose boundaries satisfied the desires of even the most ardent Bulgarian nationalists. Roughly speaking, all of present-day Bulgaria was included, together with a crucial extension into Macedonia and eastern Albania. Although Salonika was reserved for the Greeks, Bulgaria was given a frontage on the Aegean Sea which cut off the port city from the Greek mainland. The new Bulgarian state was to be autonomous, to have its own prince, its own administrative statute, and a national militia, and all Turkish troops were to be evacuated. In order to guarantee a successful initiation of the administration of the state and, incidentally, to ensure Russian control, a Russian commission was to be appointed to advise and supervise the government for two years; a Russian army of occupation was to remain for the same period. The extent of the frontiers of the San Stefano Bulgaria and the control of the administration of the country would have guaranteed Russian domination of the Straits and would have sealed off the latter area from the European continent. The Austrian drive toward the Aegean would thereby have been blocked and a Russian army would have been encamped a short distance from the Straits. Even though the treaty provided that the other two Slavic states, Serbia and Montenegro, would be recognized as independent and receive additional territory, their interests were completely subordinated to those of Bulgaria. Although a Panslav, Ignatiev considered the interests of Russian strategy ahead of those of a united Slavdom.[2]

With regard to the Straits, the treaty in its final form stated that the

---

[1] A complete discussion of the negotiations for and the terms of the Reichstadt and Budapest agreements is found in Sumner, *Russia and the Balkans, 1870–1880*, pp. 155–176, 229–254, 583–588; Pribram, *The Secret Treaties of Austria-Hungary, 1879–1914*, II, 188–203; "Reikhshtadt," *Krasnyi Arkhiv*, I (1922), 36–61; Langer, *European Alliances and Alignments, 1871–1890*, pp. 91–93, 113–114.

[2] For a fuller discussion of the San Stefano treaty see Sumner, *op. cit.*, pp. 399–424, 627–636; Hertslet, *The Map of Europe by Treaty*, IV, 2672–2696.

waters were to remain open in time of peace and war to merchant ships "of neutral states arriving from or bound to Russian ports." The provision was a defeat for Ignatiev, who during the preliminary negotiations had supported two strong proposals. First, although the sultan was to continue to uphold the general principle that the Straits were closed to warships of other nations, Russia was to receive the unique right of sending ten warships a year through the area. They would sail individually and not be allowed to stop in the Bosphorus. Second, a secret provision was to be signed providing that, should war break out, Russia and Turkey would immediately conclude a defensive alliance by which the Russians would render all the military support necessary to enable the sultan to block passage through, or seizure of, the Straits by another power. From the point of view of Russian interests, such an agreement would be almost the equivalent of actual physical possession of the area. Realizing its international implications, the Russian foreign office prevented the incorporation of this stipulation in the final treaty.[3]

In the negotiation of the treaty, Ignatiev had worked on the assumption that the Balkan problems resulting from the Russo-Turkish War could be settled on a bilateral basis between St. Petersburg and Constantinople. In this combination, Russia held all the high cards; it was to be expected that the Ottoman Empire would yield to the demands of the greater power. Although the Russian foreign office greatly desired to settle the eastern question in as favorable a manner as possible, the officials realized that the maximum program could not be attained all at one time. When the British government protested against Ignatiev's intended solution of the Straits problem, the Russian government assured the British that it regarded the issue as an international one which could not be settled by unilateral or bilateral action. Ignatiev was then given the appropriate instructions.

Although the British objections to the Straits terms were accepted, the final treaty still contained the provision for a Bulgaria whose boundaries clearly violated the Reichstadt and Budapest agreements with the Habsburg monarchy. As could be expected, once the terms of the treaty were announced, Andrassy immediately protested against Russia's unilateral breach of the previous agreement. Andrassy clearly recognized that the implementation of San Stefano would be a death blow to Austrian influence in the Balkans. Not only had the Reichstadt agreement been violated in the creation of a large Slavic state, but Austrian demands for compensation in Bosnia-Hercegovina had been

---

[3] Sumner, *op. cit.*, pp. 408–409.

ignored. Joined by Great Britain, who likewise could not permit an upset of the relative balance of strength in the eastern Mediterranean, the Austrian government delivered a strong protest. Confronted with her two chief opponents, Russia had the alternative of accepting a modification of the treaty or of going to war. Since Russia had barely succeeded in defeating the decrepit Ottoman Empire, a new war would be certain disaster. Unable to accept the risk of a forceful solution, Russia was compelled to submit the Treaty of San Stefano to a conference of the powers at Berlin.

Thus, in 1878, under the chairmanship of Bismarck, the second great congress of the nineteenth century was held in a German capital. Although much of the preliminary work had been done before the opening of the sessions, the earlier decisions were not accepted without discussion and alteration. The delegates were concerned primarily with the thorny Bulgarian problem. At San Stefano, Russia had awarded Bulgaria the maximum boundaries and had provided the most favorable circumstances for Russian influence in the new state. Her goal at the conference was therefore to salvage as much as possible of the original treaty. Confronted with the united opposition of Austria and Great Britain, Russia was forced to accede to the dismemberment of her Bulgaria. First, the Macedonian lands were restored to the sovereignty of the sultan, which removed the Russian obstacle to Austrian expansion southward. Second, Bulgaria was deprived of access to the Aegean Sea, a circumstance which was to the interest of Great Britain. Third, the remaining Bulgarian territories were divided into two separate states, Bulgaria and Eastern Rumelia, with the Balkan mountains generally as the dividing line.

Even this last provision became a matter of dispute between Russia and Great Britain. The latter claimed that the line of the Balkan mountains ran north of the Sanjak of Sofia and, consequently, that area should be included in Eastern Rumelia. The Russians, in contrast, maintained that the mountains ran southward and that Sofia belonged within the Bulgarian state. The real point at issue was that the state which included Sofia would hold the territory through which the railroad line from Constantinople to Vienna was to run, and would dominate the Maritsa Valley also. It was recognized at the congress that the autonomous Bulgaria would be a Russian satellite. The Russian view on the disposal of Sofia was finally accepted, but only after Russia had given up its claim that the Mesta and Struma valleys of Macedonia should be included in Bulgaria and Rumelia.[4]

---

[4] An excellent analysis of the Berlin settlement is given in Sumner, *op. cit.*, pp.

Once the territorial divisions had been settled, the congress considered the type of administration that was to be provided for the two Bulgarian provinces. For Bulgaria proper the powers accepted the provisions of the Treaty of San Stefano that the state was to be an autonomous principality ruled by a prince elected by the Bulgars, but not a member of any of the reigning families of the great powers. The stipulation in the treaty which provided for a Russian advisory commission and a military occupation for two years came under Austrian and British attack, and the period of occupation was eventually reduced to nine months.

The administration of Eastern Rumelia, in contrast to that of Bulgaria, was firmly removed from Russian control. The province was to be run by a governor-general appointed by the sultan with the consent of the great powers. A joint European commission, rather than a Russian one, was to supervise the administration. All Russian troops were to evacuate the territory within nine months. The principal dispute, however, concerned the conditions under which Turkish troops might reenter Eastern Rumelia. Russia feared that such an occurrence might lead to further bloodshed and might even embroil her in a new war with the Ottoman Empire. She preferred to have the local inhabitants organize their own militia and police; these national organizations might eventually become the center of a movement for union with Bulgaria. The congress finally agreed that internal order in Rumelia would be maintained by "a native gendarmerie assisted by a local militia," whose officers would be appointed by the sultan. If internal disorders occurred, the use of Turkish forces—and these could under no condition be irregulars—would have to be justified to the representatives of the great powers at Constantinople. Turkish troops were to be used only in the frontier fortifications.[5]

Although the other matters discussed at Berlin were not so explosive as the Bulgarian problem, they were of almost equal importance for Balkan diplomacy. The status of Bosnia-Hercegovina, which had been the subject of much previous correspondence, was settled quickly when Russia agreed to Austrian occupation and administration. The fate of the Sanjak of Novi Pazar was less easily resolved. Because of its potential military and commercial value, the Russians were reluctant to allow Austria to garrison the area. Austria wished not only to prevent Serbia and Montenegro from achieving a common frontier, but also to keep

425–553, 658–669. See also Hertslet, *op. cit.*, IV, 2729–2799; Medlicott, *The Congress of Berlin and After*, hereafter cited as Medlicott, *Berlin;* Rupp, *A Wavering Friendship: Russia and Austria, 1876–1878;* and Stojanović, *The Great Powers and the Balkans, 1875–1878.*

[5] Sumner, *op. cit.*, pp. 518–529.

open the route for commercial expansion southward. Russia agreed to accept the Austrian view only in face of the threat that the monarchy might oppose the Russian recovery of the Bessarabian lands.[6]

The other small Balkan states received territorial gains, but not in proportion to those enjoyed by Austria, Russia, and Bulgaria. Both Montenegro and Serbia were recognized as independent. Although they were forced to surrender land acquired under the Treaty of San Stefano, Montenegro succeeded in retaining access to the Adriatic. In the settlements of the Serbian frontiers, Russia preferred to give areas claimed by Serbia and Bulgaria to the latter, a policy which was to have repercussions in future Balkan events. Rumania received her independence, but the simultaneous loss of southern Bessarabia was bitterly resented, despite the acquisition of Dobrudja as compensation.

The last and most important general question taken up by the congress concerned the Straits. Although the Treaty of San Stefano had contained no drastic provisions in this regard, the Russian claims to areas in eastern Turkey, in particular the seaport of Batum, led Britain to advance the argument that the *status quo* in the Black Sea, and thus also at the Straits, had been altered, especially if Russia were to use Batum as a naval base. After much discussion, Russia yielded some of the territory acquired under the Treaty of San Stefano, and agreed that Batum should be "essentially" a commercial port, not a naval base.

Nevertheless, Britain, who in the separate Cyprus Convention had agreed to defend the sultan's Asiatic territories against further encroachments in return for the right to occupy and administer the island of Cyprus, did not consider her interests sufficiently protected. Lord Salisbury informed the delegates at the congress that the obligations of Great Britain "relating to the closing of the Straits do not go further than an engagement with the sultan to respect in this matter His Majesty's independent determinations in conformity with the spirit of the existing treaties." To this the Russian government could only reply that "in their opinion, the principle of the closing of the Straits is a European principle, and that the stipulations concluded in this respect in 1841, 1856, and 1871, confirmed at present by the Treaty of Berlin, are binding on the part of all the powers in accordance with the spirit and letter of the existing treaties, not only as regards the Sultan but also as regards all the powers signatory to these transactions."

In the succeeding years Russian policy was to be strongly influenced by the apprehension aroused by the British pronouncement on the

---

[6] *Ibid.*, pp. 529–532.

Straits. To the Russian foreign office it now appeared as if Britain had
served notice that, should conditions warrant it, the British fleet would
be free to sail into the Straits or to seize control of them without regard
to international commitments.[7]

Not only was Russia forced to submit to the destruction of her Bulgarian program at the Congress of Berlin, but her other Balkan interests were seriously jeopardized. At San Stefano the Russian government had permitted Ignatiev to compromise Russian relations with the
Balkan states in exchange for one major victory in the form of a greater
Bulgaria. If the latter could have been maintained, the gamble would
have been worth taking, but to gamble and lose only served to disclose
Russian intentions to the other great powers, and at the same time to
alienate those Balkan states who relied on Russian support of their own
aspirations. In other words, Russia had shown herself ready to sacrifice
her century-old connections with the Serbs, Rumanians, and Greeks in
return for a permanent and definite influence among the newly liberated
Bulgarian people. From a military-strategic point of view the choice
was sound, since Russia could more easily defend her interests at the
Straits from Bulgaria than from Rumania, Serbia, or Greece. Politically, however, serious repercussions were soon felt in the latter states,
who considered themselves betrayed by Russia's championship of the
Bulgarian claims.

The grievances of the Rumanian government concerned not only the
erection of a dominant Bulgarian state but also the loss of Bessarabia.
Russia felt that the return of the territory to her possession was essential
both because of the Russian element in the Bessarabian population and
because control of the area would give Russia a voice in solving the
problem of the navigation of the Danube. The loss of southern Bessarabia in the Crimean War had been a blow to Russian national pride.
Although the Russian annexation of the territory can be well understood on the basis of strategy and power, the action violated a previous
agreement. Before the commencement of the Russo-Turkish War, Russia
had agreed to protect Rumanian territorial integrity in return for the
right of Russian troops to use Rumanian soil from which to attack
Turkey. Once the fighting had begun, Rumanian soldiers fought side by
side with the Russians against the Turks. Although Rumania at the end
of the war did receive her independence and the territory of Dobrudja,
she regarded these as inadequate compensation for the loss of the

---

[7] The statements made by the two delegates are found in Hertslet, *op. cit.*, IV,
2727–2728. Russia's general views on the Straits problem are given in Goriainov,
Le Bosphore et les Dardanelles, pp. 340–387, and *La question d'orient à la veille du
traité de Berlin.*

Bessarabian lands in violation of the convention with Russia. Russia was determined to keep the territory regardless of the effects on Russo-Rumanian relations. The bitterness engendered by the Russian action contributed to the decision of Rumania to orient her policy toward Austria. In 1883 a firm alliance was signed between the Habsburg monarchy and Rumania directed against Russia. This treaty was certainly one of the direct consequences for Russia of the Treaty of Berlin.[8]

Russian relations with Greece were based largely on the complicated Macedonian problem. When the Ottoman Empire agreed to the establishment of the Bulgarian exarchate, the sultan's firman was so worded as to permit the Slavic peoples of Macedonia to join the exarchate. Naturally, any such extension of the authority of the exarch over the Balkan Slavs would be at the expense of the Greek patriarchate. Initially, Russia had hoped that the problem of religious jurisdiction could be solved to the satisfaction of both the Greeks and the Bulgars. When this proved impossible, Ignatiev threw all his weight behind the Bulgars, and in 1872 the Greek patriarch declared the Bulgars schismatic.

Previously, one of the principal assets of Russia in the Balkans had been the unity of the Orthodox church, but now this was shattered. The problem was further complicated by the fact that the Greek patriarchate in the nineteenth century had become an instrument of Greek nationalism; now the exarchate was to become the tool of Bulgarian nationalism. Instead of common Orthodox unity against Ottoman power, the two ecclesiastical organizations turned to bitter factional warfare in Macedonia, which became the center of the struggle for land and power. When the San Stefano boundaries were announced, the Greeks at once protested. Not only did the new Bulgarian state include Macedonian lands claimed by Greece, but also it was given indisputably Greek lands, and Salonika was cut off from the Greek mainland. Like Rumania, the Greek government thereafter realized that it had little to expect from Russia.[9]

It is, however, the reaction of Serbia rather than that of Greece or Rumania that is of prime importance, because, like the Bulgarians, the Serbians had traditionally turned to Russia for aid and protection. The first indication to Serbia that Russia might shift to the unique sponsorship of Bulgarian nationalism had been the creation of the exarchate.

---

[8] Sumner, *op. cit.*, pp. 569–570.
[9] Stavrianos, "L'institution de l'Exarcat bulgare: son influence sur les relations interbalkaniques," *Les Balkans*, XI, 56–69; Grim, "K Istorii Russko-Bolgarskikh Otnoshenii," *Novyi Vostok*, V (1924), 69–70; Arnaudov, *Eksarkh Iosif i Bulgarskata Kulturna Borba sled Suzdavaneto na Eksarkhiiata*, I, 51–130.

When the Serbs objected that the conditions excluded Serbian religious activity in Macedonia, they were informed by the Russians that the exarchate was a Slavic matter and not exclusively Bulgarian. It would benefit all the Slavs and not just one element.[10] The Serbs accepted this explanation with misgivings. The Russians were soon to show not only that they did not intend to protect Serbian religious interests, but also that they were prepared to sacrifice Serbia's national program. In the Reichstadt and Budapest agreements, Russia had indicated her attitude toward the aspirations of Serbia. Although she was sympathetic to the Serbian desire for independence, she wished to use the South Slav territories of Bosnia and Hercegovina as compensation to Austria for Russian gains in Bulgaria.

San Stefano was an even greater blow to Serbian claims. After the Russo-Turkish armistice in 1878, the Serbian government informed Russia of its desire to acquire the Sanjak of Novi Pazar, Old Serbia, and a part of Macedonia, including Skoplje, Veles, Debar, and Štip. Serbia also wished to annex Vidin, which is on the Danube at the point where Serbia and Bulgaria meet. Although the Macedonian territories had a large Serbian population, Ignatiev rejected the Serbian claims and believed that even Niš, a predominantly Serbian town, should go to Bulgaria. In the Treaty of San Stefano, Serbia gained only her independence and the Niš enclave. Other territories claimed by Serbia, some of which had been conquered by her troops, had been incorporated into the San Stefano Bulgaria. The formation of a greater Bulgaria, together with the expected Austrian occupation of Bosnia-Hercegovina and possibly the Sanjak of Novi Pazar, would have doomed Serbia to existence as a small and impotent state. More Serbs would have inhabited lands outside the principality than within. The Treaty of San Stefano was thus as damaging to the Serbian position as to that of Austria-Hungary and Britain.[11]

From the point of view of Russian policy, the abandonment of Serbia was logical. Russia was making peace not on the basis of Balkan nationalism or the "Slavic idea" but on that of the balance of power and national interest. N. K. Giers, director of the Asiatic department of the ministry of foreign affairs, bluntly told the Serbian delegate sent to Russia during the negotiations for the peace of San Stefano that "the interests of Russia came first, then came those of Bulgaria, and only after them came Serbia's; but that there were occasions on which Bul-

[10] Jovan M. Jovanović, *Južna Srbija od Kraja XVIII Veka do Oslobodjenja*, pp. 65–69.
[11] Jovanović, *Milan*, II, 195–205.

garian interests stood on equal footing with the Russian."[12] The Russian foreign office realized that if Russia wished to dominate in Bulgaria, Austria would have to receive compensation in the western Balkans. Russia thus had no wish to strengthen Serbia, since it appeared inevitable that she would fall under Habsburg influence. Serbian nationalism and even independence had to be sacrificed in the interests of Russian policy dictated by the situation at the Straits.

The Congress of Berlin provided the final demonstration of the hopelessness of the Serbian position. Not only did Serbia fail to gain significant additions of territory; she was forced by Russian policy to become a vassal state to Austria-Hungary. P. A. Shuvalov instructed the Serbian delegates to coöperate with the monarchy and not to do anything without the latter's consent. In return for supporting the Serbian claims to Pirot and Vranje, Austria was able to extract important railroad and commercial concessions from the now isolated Serbia. Despite her acquiescence to the Habsburg desires, Serbia gained only approximately fifty square kilometers more land than she had been given by the Treaty of San Stefano. She did not receive Novi Pazar, Skoplje, Veles, Debar, and Štip in Macedonia; and she was forced to see Bosnia-Hercegovina placed firmly under Austrian control. Thereafter, Austria-Hungary was able to exploit the position she had gained in Serbia to bind the Serbian economy firmly to that of the Dual Monarchy and to negotiate a treaty which signified the political vassalage of the Serbian nation. Austria-Hungary was thereby able to direct Serbian national aspirations away from Bosnia-Hercegovina toward Macedonia, which led eventually to a costly fratricidal war between the two Slavic states over the territory.[13]

As a result of the Congress of Berlin, Russia had been isolated diplomatically. Now she was faced by a new threat at the Straits. Moreover, she had lost the support and sympathy of the Serbian, Greek, and Rumanian governments. These states had gained their independence from Turkish rule largely through Russian military efforts, but the policy of the support of the San Stefano Bulgaria had broken the bonds of sympathy which united them with Russia. Each of these states had aspirations which were thwarted by the creation of the new Bulgaria; each knew that it needed the support of the great powers to obtain its desires. Since Russia now stood behind Bulgaria, the little states naturally looked to the Russian adversaries, Great Britain and Austria-

---

[12] *Ibid.*, pp. 199–200.
[13] *Ibid.*, pp. 206–214.

Hungary. Greece turned to the great sea power; Rumania and Serbia became client states of the Dual Monarchy.

In a letter to Giers from Berlin, Gorchakov reflected the disappointment of the Russian delegation over the results of the conference:

The treaty of peace will be signed tomorrow. I do not envy him [Shuvalov] being the carrier of that sad publication and I only regret having had to put my signature on such a transaction. I doubt that it has more vitality than the leaves that fall. Moreover, everything depends on the policy that the emperor will adopt for the future, and if, as in 1856, we return to the system of *recueillement*. For my part, I admit that I did not expect this page at the conclusion of my physical or political life, which cannot be very far away. All that I ask is that I have consecrated all my efforts in safeguarding as much as possible the dignity of the emperor and Russia.[14]

In spite of the obvious setbacks which Russia had suffered, she had nevertheless made definite gains. Although the San Stefano Bulgaria had been divided into an autonomous principality in the north and a province under a Christian governor in the south, few believed that the two areas could be kept separated indefinitely. Certainly, the lesson of the Rumanian principalities would not be lost on the Bulgars. Since Russia was mainly responsible for the achievement of Bulgarian autonomy, she could hope to enjoy tremendous popularity in the country. Her prestige, together with the fact that Russian predominance in Bulgaria had received the tacit recognition of the great powers, signified that, with the unification of the two Bulgarias, she would have accomplished a large part of her objective of San Stefano. If she kept the sympathy of the Bulgarian people, maintained her dominant position in the administration of the country, and led the movement for national unification, she would have acquired a military base within striking distance of the Straits.

Whereas Bulgaria was the Russian outpost in the eastern Balkans, Montenegro served the same purpose in the west. At Berlin, the independence of Montenegro was recognized and she received an outlet on the Adriatic. Montenegro remained the most faithful ally of Russia in the Balkans. Although the principality did not have the strategic value of Bulgaria, Russia could use Montenegro as a base from which to operate against Austrian penetration southward and to interfere in Serbian and Austro-Hungarian domestic politics.

The drastic weakening of Ottoman power after the Russo-Turkish War was also in the Russian interest. The empire was saddled with a

---

[14] Gorchakov to Giers, *NKG*, Berlin, June 30, 1878. The disillusionment of Baron Jomini, senior adviser to the foreign minister, is reflected in Jomini to Giers, *NKG*, Berlin, June 27 and July 2, 1878.

war indemnity which it could not hope to meet, and what little prestige it had previously enjoyed was lost. Areas of strategic and military importance for the defense of the empire had passed into other hands. The possessions in the Balkans had been greatly reduced, and the Turkish capital was open to attack. Eastern Turkey was exposed to Russian invasion from the newly acquired lands. Russia no longer had to regard the Ottoman Empire as a military threat.

It was in consideration of these advantages that Giers wrote to A. G. Jomini, senior adviser to the foreign minister, concerning the reception of the treaty in St. Petersburg:

[A. I.] Nelidov is right in telling you that the efforts of our plenipotentiaries to bring the work of the congress to a good result are appreciated here in high circles. The impossibility of obtaining more is recognized and, provided that an agreement is reached on the question of Batum, they will be perfectly satisfied—and indeed with reason, for what war can be compared with this one for results? The independence of three principalities, the creation of one Bulgaria, only tributary, and another autonomous,—no more rayah and so many other things. My God! would we not have treated as mad anyone who would have dreamed of such a result two years ago. And all that with the sanction of Europe.[15]

The Russian gains at Berlin, significant as they were, were discounted by the more influential elements of the Russian public and press. The Panslav groups, which had been so active and so loud in their demand for and support of the war, could see only total defeat at the conference table. Led by Ivan S. Aksakov, one of the most influential Russian writers, the Panslavs mercilessly denounced the dismemberment of Greater Bulgaria, which to them signified the loss of Russian domination of Constantinople and the Straits area. Equally unforgivable in their eyes was the abandonment of the Slavic provinces of Bosnia and Hercegovina to Catholic, German Austria. Although England and Austria-Hungary bore the brunt of their attacks, the Russian diplomats were not spared. They were judged completely incompetent—the dupes of London and Vienna. Even the tsar was swept along by the popular indignation.[16]

The swell of discontent reflected not only the dissatisfaction of the nation with the peace at Berlin but also its uneasiness with regard to internal conditions. The reforms of Alexander II had been far from a

---

[15] Giers to Jomini, *NKG*, St. P., June 23/July 5, 1878.

[16] Three recent works on Slavophilism and Panslavism are Riasanovsky, *Russia and the West in the Teachings of the Slavophiles*, Petrovich, *The Emergence of Russian Panslavism, 1856–1870*, and Kohn, *Panslavism: Its History and Ideology*. See also Sumner's concise discussion, *op. cit.*, pp. 56–80. Aksakov's views on the Slavic problem are best expressed in *Slavianskii Vopros'*. A valuable work on the Russian press is Grüning, *Die russische öffentliche Meinung und ihre Stellung zu den Grossmächten, 1878–1894*.

success. Instead of alleviating the manifold internal problems, the reforms had too often raised false hopes and led to new difficulties. The war had been a tremendous financial strain on the Russian treasury, which was hard pressed to find new sources of income to meet the increasing costs of government. The disillusionment of the Russians caused many to look for a revolutionary and radical solution of their nation's problems. The increase of underground activity and violence added to the instability within the state. When considering the foreign policy of Russia in the period after the Congress of Berlin, it is of utmost importance to keep in mind the extreme financial disorder of the empire and the rising tide of revolutionary activity.

Within the Russian government the foreign office naturally bore the chief weight of the public recriminations against the peace and, indeed, that department was in an unfortunate situation. Gorchakov, chancellor and foreign minister, was an octogenarian, frequently ill and increasingly unable to fulfill the functions of high office. He had enjoyed an illustrious career after the Crimean War, when he had led Russia out of isolation and had secured the abrogation of the 1856 clauses regarding the Black Sea defenses. By 1878 his failing powers left the foreign office without real direction. Adventurers such as Ignatiev were thus able to gain great influence in the formulation of Russian policy. At the Congress of Berlin, Gorchakov played an ignominious role. He frequently undid the constructive work of Shuvalov or inadvertently divulged Russian strategy too soon. When he met defeat on a problem, he would blame a subordinate. If an issue was bound to result in a Russian setback, he made certain that others handled it. Despite the obvious incapacity of his minister, Alexander II refused to retire him. Thus, during the crucial years after the Congress of Berlin, Russian policy was not directed by the titular head of the foreign office.[17]

With the growing incapacity of Gorchakov, the duties of the minister fell increasingly upon the shoulders of his subordinate, Giers, who did not enjoy the prestige of the position.[18] Although Giers did not receive the title of office until 1882, he functioned as foreign minister after 1878, but under grave handicaps. A career diplomat, he had served in posts within the Ottoman Empire, in Moldavia, Wallachia, Constantinople, and Egypt, and later in Persia, Switzerland, and Sweden. In 1875 he was brought back to St. Petersburg as assistant to the minister

[17] Sumner, *op. cit.*, pp. 501–503.
[18] For a description of Giers' career see von Erdmann, *Nikolai Karlovich Giers, russischer Aussenminister, 1882–1895;* "Nikolai Karlovich Giers," *Brokgauz-Efron Entsiklopedicheskii Slovar'*, XVI (1893), 761; *Ocherk Istorii Ministerstva Inostrannykh Diel, 1802–1902*, pp. 169–182.

of foreign affairs and as director of the Asiatic department. In character, Giers was well suited to serve under the self-centered Prince Gorchakov. Mild and conciliatory in manner, Giers throughout his career
excelled in the virtues of compromise and moderation. Although often
hard pressed by the Panslav tendencies of sections of the Russian public
and by Alexander III, Giers was able to imprint his pattern of diplomacy on Russian policy. Unlike many, he held an extremely realistic
view of the limitations of the Russian position. He realized that an adventurous policy was impossible for a militarily weak and economically
unstable nation. Security in Europe and at the Straits became and remained the cornerstone of his policy. Until 1890 an alliance with Germany, first with and then without Austria-Hungary, became the basis
of his diplomacy; thereafter he concluded the agreement with France.

Unfortunately, Giers had to depend entirely upon the favor of the
tsars under whom he served. Since he had no popular support from
either the Russian public or the aristocracy, his position was often
challenged. His chief handicaps were the Swedish origin of his family
and his Protestant faith. His background, together with his firm espousal of friendship with Germany, made him a natural target for the
Russian nationalists. Moreover, he had married the Moldavian Olga
Cantacuzene, a niece of Prince Gorchakov. Although the close family
alliance which was thereby effected with the Russian foreign minister
aided Giers in his subsequent career, it intensified the non-Russian
character of his establishment. Lacking a personal fortune and excluded
from the upper circles of the Russian aristocracy, Giers in 1878 occupied a position of little more than a clerk or a secretary to the tsar.[19]

In international relations, the Russian public after 1878 naturally
sought a scapegoat outside their own country. The Russian press designated Austria-Hungary and Britain as the culprits in the Russian failures, but by 1879 Germany had been added to the list of those responsible. By the summer of 1879 a full-scale press war had been inaugurated
between Germany and Russia. The recent economic steps which Germany had taken against Russian agricultural exports added fuel to the

---

[19] In an undated memorandum in *NKG* Jomini reports that when Gorchakov told
the tsar that he was too old to continue as foreign minister, the emperor said he
could not retire him: someone with a Russian name should be minister. Prince
Lobanov-Rostovskii, adviser to Gorchakov, was regarded as a candidate for the post,
but the tsar considered him too *"paresseux."* Miliutin (III, 160, 163, 164, 170, 182,
206) discusses the frequent difficulties experienced by the government because
Gorchakov was retained as foreign minister. Perhaps the best description of the
Gorchakov-Giers relationship is in Schweinitz, *Denkwürdigkeiten*, II, 166: "[Gor-
chakov] behält seine 40,000 Rubel und 100 Zimmer, reist ins Ausland und liest Ro-
mane, und Giers fährt fort zu arbeiten ohne Rang, Gehaltszulage und passendes
Quartier."

fire. The obvious fact that, on the various commissions established to work out the final details of the Berlin settlement, Germany frequently voted with Austria-Hungary and Britain was added proof to the Russian public of German hostility.[20] The diplomatic isolation of Russia, evident at Berlin, was now complete. Even Germany, whose chancellor had claimed to be an "honest broker," had now openly joined the opposition.

Not only was Russia without allies, but her opponents were obviously united in their efforts to thwart her every move. Although there was no formal alliance between Britain and Austria-Hungary, they acted together against Russia. Moreover, the Dual Monarchy was soon approached by Germany. The attacks upon Germany in the Russian press, the concentration of Russian troops on the German borders, and other apparently menacing circumstances caused Bismarck to review the entire situation.[21] The Russian army was weak, and Bismarck did not fear a Russian military attack, but he was apprehensive that a Russian diplomatic offensive might lead to the isolation of Germany. A Russian-Austrian-French alliance would leave Germany without allies and faced with the possibility of war on three fronts.

To forestall such an eventuality and to end the threat to Germany's southern front, Bismarck now set to work to obtain an alliance with the Dual Monarchy which would be a guaranty of peace on the continent and would also prevent the Dual Monarchy from seeking to disrupt the recently unified German Empire. The basis of the alliance was to be a defensive pact directed against Russia. When the idea was presented to Andrassy, he received it warmly. The principal objection came from Emperor William, who at first would not even consider an alliance against his nephew the tsar, with whom he had the most cordial relations. When all efforts at persuasion had failed, Alexander II provided Bismarck with just the ammunition he needed. The tsar, prone to emotional outbursts, in August, 1879, wrote his uncle a letter without consulting any of his advisers. He bared all his grievances against the Germans, especially Bismarck, and concluded with the comment that the results of German actions "may be disastrous for both countries." Bismarck could not lose the opportunity of exploiting this veiled threat of war for his own policy. In October, 1879, he at last obtained the kaiser's consent to the Dual Alliance. This treaty in its final form provided that if either power were attacked by Russia, the two German states would act jointly. If Russia supported the attack of a third power, that is,

[20] Sumner, *op. cit.*, p. 558.
[21] Miliutin, III, 162, 166–167.

France or Italy, on either Germany or Austria, the two German states would support each other. The agreement, defensive in nature, became the cornerstone of German and Austrian policy until the First World War.[22]

Popular indignation against Germany was felt throughout Russian society, but many in responsible positions saw that the mounting trend could result only in disaster for Russia. The lessons of the Crimean War—to avoid isolation and to gain the maximum security in the Black Sea area—were still valid. While the press continued to heap abuse on the Germans, the leading members of the Russian government commenced a series of meetings in which they reviewed the entire diplomatic scene. They realized that allies would have to be found and that the British threat to the Straits, as made clear by Salisbury's declaration at the Congress of Berlin, would have to be met. The discussions on the ultimate direction of Russian policy were influenced primarily by the opinions of three men: N. K. Giers; D. A. Miliutin, minister of war; and P. A. Saburov, Russian minister to Athens from 1870 to 1879, and subsequently ambassador to Berlin. The final decision was made by Alexander II, but on the recommendation of his chief advisers.

In the minds of these men the threat from Britain overshadowed all other considerations. British policy was judged aggressive not only at the Straits but also in the Middle East, as was evidenced by the recent British declaration at Berlin and by the activities in Afghanistan. Great Britain was firmly entrenched in Egypt and had recently occupied Cyprus. If the Ottoman Empire should crumble rapidly, Britain was in an excellent position to seize the vital, strategic areas of that state to the detriment of Russian interests. The British threat had become more serious since close coöperation had been established between Britain and the Habsburg empire. Austrian policy had been able to achieve real gains in the past years without firing a shot. The Russian program for the Balkan Slavs had been blocked and severely crippled; Bosnia-Hercegovina had been acquired at no cost whatsoever. Russia feared that the Dual Monarchy would now launch an active program of expansion southward through Serbia to the Aegean. There she would join hands with Great Britain. The union of the strongest naval power with a formidable land power would signify the end of Russian attempts to dominate the Balkans and the Straits.

The only remedy for the deplorable condition of Russian diplomacy was an ally to neutralize the British-Austrian combination. An obvious

[22] Windelband, *Bismarck und die europäischen Grossmächten, 1879–1885*, pp. 66–89; Langer, *op. cit.*, pp. 171–185; Miliutin, III, 155–159; Pribram, *op. cit.*, I, 18–31.

partner was France, but this republican state had few admirers in Russian official circles. Moreover, France could render little effective assistance to Russia at the Straits because of her distance from the area and her military weakness. Italy did not have the resources or strength to qualify as a partner. Austro-Russian hostility in the Balkans ruled out an alliance in that direction.

Only one possible choice remained—Germany—despite the fact that the Russian press had now turned its full force against that country and its chancellor. The advantages to be gained from a German alliance were obvious and immense. In case of a Russo-Austrian war, Germany could localize the conflict by threatening to come to the aid of Russia if Austria were joined by another power, notably England. If the more probable conflict arose, that of Russia and Britain over the Straits or the Middle East, Germany could neutralize Austria. The Russian government believed that it could deal with Britain, but not Britain in alliance with another power.[23]

The most ardent advocate of an agreement with Germany was Saburov, who played the principal role in the negotiations which culminated in the signing of the Dreikaiserbund of 1881. In July, 1879, Saburov discussed Russo-German relations in detail with Bismarck at Kissingen. On the basis of these conversations he drew up a memorandum which was submitted to Alexander II. In the discussions on the subject in succeeding months, Saburov remained the champion of a German alliance, but one conceived in a limited sense. In contrast to Giers and Miliutin, Saburov was not so obsessed with the defeat at Berlin and the economic and military weaknesses which resulted from the Russo-Turkish War. Therefore he advocated for Russia a much more extensive and ambitious foreign policy than that envisioned by the other responsible officials in the Russian government. In his mind the Straits remained the center of Russian policy. "This key alone," he wrote, "will be able to give us complete security on our southern frontiers. A single fortification at the mouth of the Bosphorus will take for us the place of a fleet, of an army, and of a whole line of fortresses necessary today to maintain our coasts on the Black Sea in a state of defense."[24] Until Russia could obtain actual physical control, he advocated the negotiation of a Russo-Turkish understanding for the joint defense of the area. Russia, he argued, had opposed Ottoman power in Europe; she had no quarrel with the empire in Asia. Now that Turkey had virtually been

[23] Skazkin, pp. 103–114; Miliutin, III, 154, 158–160, 164, 166–170, 173; Nolde, *L'alliance franco-russe*, pp. 237–248; Simpson, *The Saburov Memoirs*, pp. 72–77, 82–83; Jomini to Giers, *NKG*, Sept. 9, Sept. 17, 1879.
[24] Simpson, *op. cit.*, pp. 88–89; Saburov, "Besedy P. A. Saburova s kn. Bismarkom v 1879 g.," *Krasnyi Arkhiv*, I (1922), 62–91.

excluded from Europe, it might be well to take the opportunity afforded by British championship of reform in Turkey to regain influence in Constantinople. Russia should aid Turkey in resisting British pressure and in return receive the right to make a joint agreement for the defense of the Straits.[25]

As a supplement to Russian policy at the Straits, Saburov advocated the adoption of an openly aggressive policy in central Asia. Russia could thereby pose a threat to the British position in India and exploit the difficulties in Afghanistan. If Britain should threaten the Straits, Russia could move in central Asia. Saburov proposed that Russia build up her Black Sea fleet in order that Russian troops might be swiftly dispatched to the Straits should an emergency arise.[26]

In this program one of the purposes of the Russian alliance with Germany was to prevent the formation of a European coalition, led by Britain, against Russia. As the partner of Russia, Saburov expected Germany to neutralize Austria. With Germany and Austria thus provided for, Russia could deal with Britain alone. In negotiating with Germany, Saburov strongly opposed any discussion of the Straits. He pointed out that Germany did not have the physical means of aiding Russia in the area, and he feared that the issue would complicate the conversations.[27]

Leading the opposition to Saburov's conception of Russian policy were Miliutin and Giers. Miliutin had distinguished himself as leader of the liberal faction in Russia which desired the continuation of the reform program. He had been responsible for the army reforms which were a part of the Great Reforms. His position in the government had become increasingly strong, and by 1878 he was the most powerful single minister. Zaionchkovskii states that "no decision was taken by the tsar without prior consultation with Miliutin."[28] His influence was so great in foreign affairs that he overshadowed the officials of that ministry. Although Bismarck and the German government regarded him as the arch-Germanophobe in Russia, Miliutin in no way shared the opinions of the extremists among the Panslavs.[29] In fact, no one worked more earnestly toward the conclusion of the agreement with Germany than did Miliutin once the policy had been adopted.

As minister of war Miliutin was in a far better position than Saburov

---

[25] Simpson, *op. cit.*, pp. 50–109. In his memoirs Saburov has omitted the views which he expressed in November, 1879, concerning his plans for Turkey, the Straits, and the Middle East. These are found in Skazkin, pp. 110–111, 122–127.

[26] Skazkin, p. 127.

[27] Miliutin, III, 183, 186, 188, 191–192.

[28] *Ibid.*, I, 51; Skazkin, p. 127.

[29] Bismarck to Kaiser Wilhelm, *GP*, III, no. 447, Gastein, Aug. 24, 1879; Miliutin, III, 157–160, 234.

to assess the Russian military potential accurately. Opposing the ambitious plans of the adventurous diplomat, Miliutin advocated a policy of peace and conciliation in the Near and Middle East as well as in Europe. Although he agreed that Russia needed security at the Straits and that Germany was the only possible ally, he differed with Saburov on the immediate aims of Russian policy and on the purpose for which the German alliance should be designed: Germany was needed as an ally to block the formation of a coalition, but the issue of the Straits must be an integral part of the pact. If this vital portion were not included, the alliance would be of little value. British occupation of the Straits was, in Miliutin's opinion, an immediate danger. Should this happen, Russia could do little, since the Black Sea fleet which was intended to transport troops to the Straits would take more than two or three years to complete. He would have preferred to have obtained the promise of material aid from Germany for the defense of the Straits, but he realized that this was not possible or practical. He therefore argued that Germany should be asked to support the principle of the closure of the Straits as an international obligation in opposition to the Salisbury declaration of 1878. He wished Germany to join with Russia in cautioning the Turks against opening the Straits to the British. Germany was further to exert pressure on Turkey not to send troops into Rumelia, although this action was allowed under the Treaty of Berlin.[30]

Miliutin was equally emphatic in his opposition to Saburov's program in central Asia. Russia, he believed, was in no position to undertake an open aggressive struggle with Britain. A policy of peace and agreement was to be sought in this area as elsewhere.[31]

Although Giers differed with Miliutin on certain aspects of the Balkan problem, he shared the war minister's view on the Russian international position. He too recognized that Russia could not assume wide commitments.[32] The program of Giers and Miliutin was that finally accepted by Alexander II. The German alliance was to be negotiated in order to serve a dual purpose: to prevent the formation of a hostile coalition and to secure support for Russia in her interpretation of the Straits agreements. The treaty would thereby close the major loopholes

---

[30] Miliutin, III, 173, 183, 186, 188; Skazkin, pp. 127–128. Miliutin advocated a Balkan confederation as a solution for the problems of the area. Miliutin, III, 275–277; IV, 20, 162 n. 14; Skazkin, pp. 143–145.

[31] Miliutin, III, 197–198.

[32] Giers' views are expressed in Giers to Jomini, *NKG*, Aug. 20, 21, 27; Sept. 4/16, 6/18, 11, 13, 20, 25, 27; Oct. 25, 26, 30; Nov. 1, 2, 6, 8, 13, 20, 1879. See also Skazkin, pp. 120–122; Miliutin, III, 173, 182–183, 186, 192.

in the Russian defenses and allow the nation a period of peace in which
to repair the damage of the late war and to deal with the pressing problem of internal reform.

Saburov returned to Berlin in January, 1880, armed with new instructions and with added status as Russian ambassador to Germany.
Bismarck found himself in an enviable position. The Dual Alliance had
not estranged Russia, but, instead, enabled Germany to manipulate two
powers. To Bismarck the Straits and the Balkans were of secondary
importance in comparison with the danger to Germany from France.
If Russian neutrality could be assured in case of a Franco-German war,
Germany had little to fear in the west.

A second danger, however, existed for German policy in Europe. An
alliance with Russia alone would not guarantee against the outbreak of
an Austro-Russian war over the Balkans. Bismarck had previously
made it clear that he considered the existence of Austria-Hungary as
a great power vital to the security of the German Empire. If it were
necessary to choose between the Dual Monarchy and Russia, Germany
would always side with the former. The Russian proposals now gave
Bismarck the opportunity of avoiding such a choice in the succeeding
years. He thus moved to secure a rapprochement between Vienna and
St. Petersburg. He rejected the overtures for a bilateral treaty, arguing
that if Vienna learned of the existence of the agreement she might turn
to France or even seek to win Russia from Germany. Germany would
consider an agreement with Russia only if Austria were included.
Russia, desperate for an ally, was forced to accede.[33]

Whereas Germany and Russia were able to reach a general agreement
on the principal points at issue between them, Austria and Russia
proved antagonistic. Heinrich von Haymerle, who had replaced Andrassy, was a cautious and suspicious statesman. It was difficult for him
to envision an alliance with Russia in view of the hostility of the Russian press toward Germany and the actions of the Russian agents in the
Balkans after the Congress of Berlin. Haymerle would have much preferred to secure Britain rather than Russia as an ally. He feared that
an agreement with Russia would result in the enmity of Britain and
the end of Anglo-Austrian coöperation in the Balkans. More important,
the Austrian government began to suspect that it was being displaced by
Russia as the principal ally of Germany. Consequently, Haymerle at
first strongly resisted the proposals for the establishment of the Three
Emperors' Alliance. It was not until the spring of 1880, when the con-

---

[33] Windelband, *op. cit.*, pp. 93–123; Skazkin, pp. 132–172; Langer, *op. cit.*, pp.
192–200.

servative ministry of Disraeli was replaced by the liberal ministry of the Austrophobe Gladstone, that Haymerle was forced to reappraise Austrian policy.[34]

Although Haymerle then agreed to enter into negotiations with Russia, he never could put complete trust in any agreement which Russia signed. He could see only intrigue, deceit, and dishonesty emanating from St. Petersburg. He felt that Austrian interests would be secure only if he could obtain Russian approval for certain basic concessions in the Balkans. He wanted Russia to acquiesce not only to the eventual annexation of Bosnia-Hercegovina but also to that of the Sanjak of Novi Pazar. He wished complete assurance that the frontiers of Rumelia would not be extended southward toward Constantinople or westward into Macedonia. The latter move would jeopardize Austrian plans for a railroad to Salonika. Bulgarian propaganda in Macedonia, which was aimed at preparing the inhabitants for the eventual restoration of the San Stefano Bulgaria, was to cease. Russia was to refrain from giving any encouragement to a Bulgarian-Rumelian movement for unification; she was not to sponsor political organizations or movements in the Balkans which were directed against the interests of the Dual Monarchy, and Rumania was to be secured from any Russian threat.

Besides the political concessions, Haymerle added economic stipulations. Russia was to do nothing to hinder the construction of the Vienna-Constantinople railroad, but rather was to use her influence in Sofia and Belgrade to persuade the governments concerned to abide by the provisions of the Berlin treaty relative to the railroads. Serbia was to be induced to come to an agreement with Austria on commercial matters. Finally, Haymerle was against any guaranty being given to Russia on the Straits question.

These points represented the maximum Austrian program. Their acceptance would have assured Habsburg predominance in the peninsula. The Russian government in opposing the Austrian demands was adamant that Russia receive protection at the Straits and that Austrian influence in the Balkans be kept within the limits defined by the Treaty of Berlin. It was thus left to Bismarck to effect a compromise between Vienna and St. Petersburg.[35]

The arguments which Bismarck used to convince Haymerle were highly realistic. An alliance with Russia would prevent a Franco-Rus-

---

[34] Langer, *op. cit.*, pp. 200–204.

[35] Reuss to Bismarck, *GP*, III, no. 520, Vienna, Dec. 18, 1880; Bismarck to Reuss, *GP*, III, no. 521, Friedrichsruh, Dec. 22, 1880; Reuss to Bismarck, *GP*, III, no. 522, Vienna, Dec. 25, 1880; Simpson, *op. cit.*, pp. 144–154, 163–170; Skazkin, pp. 148–155; Windelband, *op. cit.*, pp. 124–136.

sian agreement against Germany or an Italo-Russian move against the Dual Monarchy. If the Dreikaiserbund were established, Russia would not be able to alter the *status quo* in the Balkans without the consent of the two German states. In regard to the Straits, Bismarck correctly stated that Russia was asking for nothing more than Austria had supported in the past, namely, the closure of the Straits on the basis of international treaty.

Bismarck himself supported the idea which both the Russians and the Austrians had previously considered and rejected: the division of the Balkans into spheres of influence. If Russia had accepted the proposal, it would have meant that she agreed to abandon to Austria the Slavic lands of Serbia, Bosnia-Hercegovina, the Sanjak of Novi Pazar, and Montenegro. Although she had consented to the Austrian occupation of Bosnia-Hercegovina and had tacitly agreed that Serbia would fall under Austrian control, she did not by any means intend to surrender forever her influence among the western Slavs. The Russian ties with Montenegro in particular had been and were still proving useful for Russian policy.

Austria-Hungary was opposed to the division on similar grounds; she had no intention of surrendering the advantages she held in the eastern Balkans. The Treaty of Berlin had provided that the new Bulgarian state would have to undertake the railroad commitments entered into by the sultan with the Habsburg empire. After the construction of the vital Bulgarian link in the Vienna-Constantinople line, the Austrian government hoped to exert economic and political influence in the entire area served by the railroad. The Russian government knew that Russian business could never compete with the western firms.[36] Russia had "nothing to buy or sell" in the Balkans, whereas the Habsburg empire and Germany needed the raw material of the area and had the manufactured goods to offer in exchange.

Since both Russia and Austria-Hungary felt that they had more to gain by leaving to the future the ultimate disposal of the Balkan area, the final agreement reached between the three powers was little more than a reaffirmation of the division agreed upon at Berlin. Austria-Hungary remained predominant in Bosnia-Hercegovina and Serbia; Russia, in Bulgaria and Eastern Rumelia.

The final treaty signed in June, 1881, gained for Russia the major objectives established by Giers and Miliutin. Specifically, Germany and Austria-Hungary agreed to support the closure of the Straits on the basis of international control; Turkey was to make no exception to this

---

[36] Jomini to Giers, *NKG*, Nov. 4, 1880.

principle. If she did, the three powers would inform her that she had put herself "in a state of war toward the injured party," and had "deprived herself henceforth of the benefits of the security assured to her territorial *status quo* by the Treaty of Berlin." Russia no longer needed to fear British opposition in the Near and Middle East or the building of a hostile coalition; she was one of three on the European continent.

In return for these advantages, Russia made certain concessions to her allies. Germany secured Russian neutrality in case of a Franco-German war. Austria-Hungary received the assurance that, in the event of a renewed Russo-Turkish war, an agreement would be reached "as to the results of the war." In other words, Russia could not make any changes in the *status quo* relative to the Ottoman Empire without consulting her allies. The exceptions to this rule were covered in a protocol and are of great importance for this study.

The two major alterations in the Treaty of Berlin provided for in the agreement of 1881 gave equal advantage to Austria-Hungary and Russia. In the first place, Austria received recognition of her right to annex Bosnia-Hercegovina, but not the Sanjak of Novi Pazar, when she deemed annexation "opportune." In the second place, Russia obtained Austrian agreement to the union of the two Bulgarias, but only if this action took place "by force of circumstances." Russia was not actively to promote agitation for union. Furthermore, she agreed to join her allies in preventing Bulgarian action to acquire Macedonia. In regard to Rumelia, Russia obtained one more concession. Since the Treaty of Berlin gave the Ottoman Empire the right to defend Eastern Rumelia, the Russian government was constantly plagued by the fear that the reappearance of Turkish troops in Rumelia would lead to fighting between the Turks and the Bulgars, and eventually force Russian intervention.[37] In 1880 Bismarck had supported the Russian position and had exerted pressure on the sultan not to send troops to the area. The terms of the Dreikaiserbund contained a further stipulation that the three signatory powers agreed that the occupation of Rumelia or the garrisoning of the Balkan mountains was "full of danger for the general peace" and that they would use "their efforts to dissuade the Porte from such an enterprise." Simultaneously, it was urged that Bulgaria and Rumelia should not provoke the sultan "by attacks emanating from their territory." The rivalry of Russia and Austria-Hungary

---

[37] Russia's concern over the possible return of Turkish troops to Rumelia was evident in all the negotiations leading to the Dreikaiserbund. The private letters of E. P. Novikov, Russia's ambassador in Turkey, to Giers, *NKG,* clearly reflect Russia's apprehensions during the difficult days of 1880. See also Jomini to Giers, *NKG,* St. P., May 23, Sept. 14, Sept. 23, 1879.

in the Balkans had thus been adjusted by an even trade. In the future, Russia could hope to obtain the union of the Bulgarias; Austria-Hungary, the annexation of Bosnia-Hercegovina. Both powers would thereby make concrete gains, but the balance of power in the area would not be upset.[38]

The Dreikaiserbund agreement set the pattern for Russian diplomacy in Europe and the Near East until 1887. The Black Sea coast of Russia was protected by the agreement relative to the Straits; her frontiers in Europe were secured by the very existence of the alliance. Her dominant position in Bulgaria was assured of German support, although at the cost of abandoning Serbia to Austrian influence. The basic conditions had thus been created for a policy of retrenchment and the *status quo*. Because of its depleted military resources and weak financial condition, this was the only policy which the Russian government could follow. The few changes that had been provided for—the union of the Bulgarias and the annexation of Bosnia-Hercegovina—were destined for the future. Russia had no desire to hasten even the first step in the re-creation of the San Stefano Bulgaria. In the next few years the Russian government hoped to be allowed to build up its army and deal with the multitude of internal problems which had arisen.

The good faith of the Russian government and its intense desire to make the agreement function are demonstrated by its treatment of the Serbian government. The firm manner in which Russia brushed aside all appeals for help from Belgrade indicates how willing she was to forego the Panslav enthusiasms of the previous decade. In 1880, when Austria was negotiating the terms of the railroad and commercial treaties with Serbia, the Serbian government under Jovan Ristić appealed to Russia for aid in combating the more excessive of the Austrian demands. Since the negotiations for the Dreikaiserbund were then in progress, the Russian government refused to take part in the affair.[39] An excellent illustration of the official Russian attitude is contained in the following letter of A. G. Jomini to Giers concerning the Austrian commercial exploitation of Serbia:

However, I admit that I share the opinion expressed by [D. A.] Kapnist to [J.] Marinović, that is, that it is not at all to the interest of Serbia to refuse because of national pride the advantages that can be gained for her material progress from Austrian exploitation. It will result in a development of her wealth, whereas a fight with that formidable neighbor, even on an industrial and commercial basis, would cut the export trade short. The only precaution to take is (1) not to allow an Austrian regency to be established in Serbia under the pretext of railroads, (2) to

---

[38] The terms of the Dreikaiserbund are in Pribram, *op. cit.*, I, 36–49.
[39] Jomini to Giers, *NKG*, Sept. 12, Nov. 2, 1880; also one undated [1880?] letter.

profit from the increasing prosperity which would result from Austrian tutelage and to increase the *effective* forces of the country in view of the final crisis which will one day decide the destinies of all Eastern Europe.[40]

In the acceptance of the Dreikaiserbund agreement, Russia in no sense abandoned for all time her claim to leadership in the Slavic world. The policy of peace and the *status quo* was the short-term policy inaugurated in order that Russia might deal with her domestic problems and reëstablish her international position. The complete re-formation of the San Stefano Bulgaria and the expulsion of Austrian influence from the South Slav lands remained a long-term Russian objective whose implementation was to be postponed indefinitely. The Russian press and the Russian public might still think in terms of the Slavic idea and rise in anger at any apparent loss of "Slavic" prestige before a "German" advance, but the Russian government itself adhered to the policy of the Dreikaiserbund for the entire period in which the treaty was in effect.

Russian policy in 1878 and 1881 was based on classic principles of nineteenth-century diplomacy. Balkan populations and territories were traded in such a manner that Russia and Austria-Hungary received a proportionate increase in power and position. Only for Bulgaria was the dangerous question of Balkan nationalism raised, and there the national ideals of Greece and Serbia were sacrificed in the interests of the Russian protégé. Yet it was this very issue of Balkan nationalism which was to determine the success or failure of Russian policy in the Near East. In the four major Balkan areas with which this study is concerned—Bulgaria, Eastern Rumelia, Serbia, and Macedonia—a dangerous and unstable situation had been created by the very terms of the treaties through which Russia had hoped to assure peace and tranquillity in the Near East.

In 1878 the situation in Bulgaria seemed ideal for Russian interests. Russia, fostering Bulgarian national passion, had led the war for liberation against the Ottoman Empire. The Russian army in Bulgaria was looked upon as an instrument of liberation; in their gratitude the Bulgarian people would have preferred a Russian official as their prince. A unique relationship had been established between Russia and liberated Bulgaria: Bulgaria was not an autonomous state in the true sense, but a Russian client within the Russian sphere of influence. Russia sorely needed Bulgaria as her land base in the Balkans, both as a protection for her interests at the Straits and as a balance against Austrian

---

[40] *Ibid.*, Sept. 3, 1880.

influence in the western Balkans. The great difficulty of holding a state in close association without actual physical occupation had yet to be solved. Bulgarian nationalism, which hitherto had advanced hand in glove with the increase in Russian influence in the Near East, had yet to meet the test of peace. In the struggle against the common Ottoman foe, it was not difficult for the Bulgarians to accept dictation from Russian officers or officials. Whether this relationship could be maintained in the future had still to be determined.

In Serbia, however, Russian policy conflicted with Serbian nationalism. A Slavic, Orthodox nation having strong historic ties with Russia had been delivered into the hands of a German power. The danger for Russia lay in the intensity of Serbian feeling. In the past the Serbian people had made great sacrifices to obtain their independence from Ottoman rule; it appeared doubtful whether they would accept the policy of the *status quo* which the Dreikaiserbund agreement forced upon them. A Serbian move in any direction, whether agitation in Bosnia-Hercegovina or fostering insurrection in Macedonia, would undo the work of the Russian diplomats and reopen the entire eastern question.

Russia had most to fear, however, from the confused situation in Macedonia,[41] where, under Ottoman rule, the struggle of the Greeks, Serbs, and Bulgars among themselves and against their Moslem rulers continued with intensity and violence. Here the three major orthodox ecclesiastical organizations, the patriarchate of Constantinople, the Bulgarian exarchate, and the Serbian metropolitanate, waged continual warfare for the extension of the power of their co-religionists and their nationality. Neither Austria-Hungary nor Russia had wished to deal with the details of this problem in 1881. Russia hoped that by force of circumstances the entire territory would fall eventually to a re-created San Stefano Bulgaria; Austria-Hungary wanted control of the western portion, since it lay on the road to Salonika. For the Balkan nationalities, however, it remained the one territory open to national expansion. The rivalries of the three states concerned—Bulgaria, Greece, and Serbia—which ultimately involved their great power patrons, could not be expected to remain long suppressed.

Despite the dangers inherent in the situation, Russia by 1881 had been successful in her major policy aims. Her great opportunity for the future lay in the use which she could make of her privileged position in Bulgaria. Her predominance in that country gave her not only military

[41] *Ibid.*, Aug. 20, Sept. 4, 1880.

advantages but also the opportunity of demonstrating her abilities in the guidance of the Balkan peoples. The establishment of the autonomous principality had been her one great achievement at the Congress of Berlin. It remained to be seen whether she could develop her relations with that country so that it would henceforth be a stronghold of Russian power in the Balkans.

II

AUTOCRATIC RUSSIA SPONSORS A CONSTITUTIONAL REGIME IN BULGARIA

Since the Congress of Berlin had destroyed the Greater Bulgaria of the Treaty of San Stefano, Russia was forced to concentrate her attention on the more limited area of the new Bulgaria, which the great powers had conceded was within her sphere of influence. Russia realized that whatever chance she might have of reuniting the San Stefano lands would be determined mainly by developments in the autonomous northern principality. If Sofia became the capital of a strong, prosperous, and well-administered state, a major step would have been taken toward the reëstablishment of the divided nation.

In order to achieve this goal, Russia had to carry through four measures. The first called for the adoption of a constitution by the principality before the withdrawal of the Russian forces. This step would prevent political and administrative dislocation and chaos, and would serve also to remove any pretext for British, Austro-Hungarian, or Turkish intervention in the internal affairs of the principality. Second, it was mandatory that the Bulgars immediately elect a prince as a stabilizing element in the infant state. Third, Russia wished to train and arm the Bulgars, especially those in Eastern Rumelia, in order that they might act as a deterrent to any Anglo-Turkish attempt to bring about the return of Turkish troops to the southern province. If the latter event occurred, the probability of a new war was great. Such a conflict, it was believed in St. Petersburg, would bring nothing but disaster to Russia. Fourth, the Russian government wanted the administrative agencies of the new state, provided for by the constitution, to start functioning before the Russian troops left the country. Perhaps the greatest obstacle to the achievement of the Russian objectives was the time factor; Russia had only nine months to carry out her plan according to the stipulations of the Treaty of Berlin.

Of the four measures, the formulation and adoption of a constitution was of primary importance. The Russian government immediately set to work to devise a constitution which could be submitted to the Bulgarian people. Although the possibility of an autonomous government for Bulgaria had been discussed, no detailed plan of administration had been drawn up. Various plans for an autonomous Bulgaria had been proposed by the Bulgarians in exile in the 1860's. In 1867 the

Russian government had suggested to the great powers that Christians living within the Ottoman Empire be given administrative autonomy, but the proposal was rejected. In 1876–1877, in the agreements with Austria, Russia again contemplated the possibility of a Bulgarian state. Gorchakov even received a memorandum from a group of Bulgars who advocated the establishment of a constitutional monarchy for their co-nationals.[1]

However, it was only in the Treaty of San Stefano that the Russian government gave any indication of the precise type of administration which it wished to see adopted by Bulgaria. Article VI stated that Bulgaria was to be an autonomous tributary principality. Article VII provided that the prince "be freely elected" by the people, but prior to this "an assembly of Bulgarian notables . . . under the superintendence of an Imperial Russian commissioner, and in the presence of an Ottoman commissioner" should formulate an organic statute for the principality on the basis of the statute adopted for Moldavia and Wallachia in 1831.[2] In April, 1878, the Russian government directed General A. M. Dondukov-Korsakov, Russian imperial commissioner in Bulgaria, who was to be most concerned with the formulation and implementation of the Bulgarian constitution, to work out a document in line with the Règlement Organique, the Russian-sponsored statute introduced in 1831 for the administrative organization of the Danubian principalities.[3] Before any serious action could be taken, the Congress of Berlin forced the Russian government to reconsider its plans.

Unlike the Treaty of San Stefano, the Berlin accord made no provision for an imperial Russian commission to supervise the adoption of a constitution, nor was any particular statute designated as the model for the future Bulgarian administration. Nevertheless, Russia on her own initiative was determined to carry out her earlier intentions. Since the great powers had admitted that the reduced Bulgaria was within the Russian orbit, the Russian government wished to make sure that a successful and friendly regime would hold power in Sofia. Russia was particularly anxious that the Bulgarians, who had no previous experience in constitutional government, should at least be provided with a draft which they could consider. Therefore, on June 24/July 6, the Russian foreign office dispatched to Dondukov-Korsakov new in-

---

[1] Koz'menko, "Pervonachal'nye Proekty Tyrnovskoi Konstitutsii," *Osvobozhdenie Bolgarii ot Turetskogo Iga*, pp. 226–231. Hereafter cited as Koz'menko, "Proekty." See also Burmov, *Bulgarski Revoliutsionen Tsentralen Komitet, 1868–1877*, and Kosev, *Novaia Istoriia Bolgarii*, pp. 308–377.

[2] Hertslet, *The Map of Europe by Treaty*, IV, 2679–2681.

[3] Koz'menko, "Proekty," pp. 232–233.

structions which stressed the need for prompt action so that a constitution could be adopted and a prince selected before the evacuation of the Russian troops.[4] In the succeeding months the necessity for speed was emphasized at every opportunity. Dondukov, working under pressure, was able to consult with only a small group of Bulgars before sending his proposals to St. Petersburg.

To assist him in his work, Dondukov appointed S. I. Luk'ianov, chief of the legal division of the occupation and adviser to the minister of justice and to himself. The two men decided to ignore the earlier instructions concerning the Règlement Organique. They substituted the Serbian and Rumanian constitutions, whose provisions they considered more appropriate to the needs of the Bulgarians. Moreover, as Dondukov correctly informed the foreign office, the 1831 statute was not applicable in Bulgaria, since it stated that the ruler and the members of the assembly were to be boiars. Five centuries of direct Ottoman rule had bereft Bulgaria of a class of landed aristocracy. Neither the Russian foreign office nor the ministry of war protested this decision.[5] It should be noted that in later years, when the Bulgarian constitution proved a source of embarrassment to the Russian government, Dondukov was blamed for providing Bulgaria with a liberal document. However, all his decisions were approved or directly altered by the officials in St. Petersburg; they, not the general, were responsible for the type of government instituted in Bulgaria.

Despite the changes made in the previous instructions, the constitution which Dondukov dispatched to St. Petersburg in November, 1878, was, as he correctly concluded, conservative in principle and operation. The prominent Bulgars whom Dondukov had been able to consult had wished to curtail the powers of the prince, since the Treaty of Berlin stipulated that he was to be chosen from a non-Bulgarian family. They had also wished to have a senate composed of the leading Bulgarian officials. Their views, however, were ignored. Instead, the document proposed by the Russian general granted the prince extensive executive and legislative powers. He had the right to demand that his proposals be accepted or rejected in their entirety without amendments. He appointed all ministers, who were responsible jointly to himself and the assembly. The latter body was to be composed of members of the church hierarchy, government officials, and other prominent citizens. The people as a whole received the guaranty of certain basic civil rights such as equality before the law, inviolability of property and person,

---

[4] *Ibid.*, pp. 233–234.
[5] *Ibid.*, pp. 234–236.

and freedom of the press. Freedom of assembly was curtailed because Dondukov did not want any "intriguing" to take place.[6]

When the general's proposals arrived in Russia, Giers gave them his immediate attention, but his suggestions were of only a minor editorial nature. He then asked A. A. Mel'nikov, vice-director of the Asiatic department, to examine the document carefully. The one major revision proposed by the foreign office concerned the position of the Bulgarian church. In the initial proposal it was stated that the church was to be under the control of the Holy Synod and the joint minister of foreign affairs and religion. In the revised text the name of the secular official was omitted. Instead, the church was to be administered by the exarch or, in his absence, by the Holy Synod in accordance with the church laws. The church was also to be in communion with the ecumenical patriarchate. Whereas the first draft had contained the implication that the jurisdiction of the church was confined to the northern principality, the second clearly indicated that it extended over all the Bulgarians. Although the Treaty of Berlin had destroyed Bulgaria's political unity, Russia was determined to keep all the Bulgars together through their church as a step toward eventual political reunification. In addition, Russia wished to mediate the differences which had developed when the exarchate was created at the expense of the patriarchate in 1870. Orthodox unity was vital for the achievement of Russian political and military goals in the Balkans.[7]

Although the Russian foreign office in its commentary on the proposed constitution tended to emphasize the power of the prince, Miliutin, who saw the draft next, was in favor of increasing the part played by the elected representatives. He was convinced that the success or failure of the Russian plans in Bulgaria would depend upon popular support rather than on the foreign prince who had yet to be chosen.[8]

After these men had made their views known, the tsar appointed a committee of five to examine the statute. The chairman was Prince S. N. Urusov, chief of the Second Chancery. Two of his advisers, N. D. Miagov and F. A. Brun, together with A. A. Mel'nikov and A. D. Gradovskii, one of the most eminent professors of law in Russia, were the other members. The committee deliberated only eleven days, December 11/23 to December 22/January 3, since speed was essential. Using the Serbian

---

[6] *Ibid.*, pp. 236–238; Koz'menko, "Peterburgskii Proekt Tyrnovskoi Konstitutsii 1879 goda," *Istoricheskii Arkhiv*, IV, 190–191, 196–219. Hereafter cited as Koz'menko, "Peterburgskii Proekt."

[7] Koz'menko, "Proekty," pp. 241–243; Koz'menko, "Peterburgskii Proekt," pp. 219–226.

[8] Koz'menko, "Proekty," p. 243; Koz'menko, "Peterburgskii Proekt," pp. 226–228.

and Rumanian constitutions as guides, the group made a number of minor editorial revisions of the proposed articles.

The chief action of the committee, however, was to shift the real power in the government from the right to the center. The man responsible for this basic change was Gradovskii,[9] who argued that no Bulgarian who had participated in the Russian occupation and administration of the principality should be allowed to take part in the assembly which selected the prince and approved the constitution. Direct Russian influence in the formation of the new government was to be kept at an absolute minimum. Gradovskii attacked and succeeded in having altered the major provisions of the text. Instead of a two-house assembly, in which the composition of the lower house would be determined by the upper, a unicameral system was substituted. This assembly was given the right not only to approve or disapprove measures but also to amend them. Its members were to be chosen by a direct system of voting; otherwise, Gradovskii argued, the prince through his appointive powers would dominate the legislative branch of government. The assembly was to have a financial hold over the prince, since its approval of the yearly budget was necessary. In addition to these liberal provisions, the committee adopted the principle of freedom of the press and association, with the limitation that if public meetings took place outdoors, the group was to be subject to police control.[10]

The committeemen, with the exception of Gradovskii, were not of liberal but of conservative sympathies. Yet they and the tsar approved a constitution that granted concessions which the Russian people themselves did not enjoy. The reason for this is explained by the Soviet historian I. V. Koz'menko, who examined this phase of the constitutional problem on the basis of the published and unpublished evidence available in Russia. He found that Miliutin's influence in governmental circles was decisive. The minister of war argued that the Bulgarian constitution could not be more conservative than those of the neighboring states or the organic statute being formulated by an international commission for Rumelia. It was incumbent upon Russia, in her own interests, to raise her prestige among the Bulgars. She had liberated Bulgaria and henceforth she must prove that she favored the government desired by the Bulgarian people. Popular support was important, because, as Miliutin judged the situation, Bulgarian nationalism had

---

[9] Contrary to earlier views, recent research in Russia has shown that Gradovskii had a prominent role in the drafting of the document. Koz'menko, "Proekty," pp. 243–250; see also Koz'menko, "Peterburgskii Proekt," p. 184 nn. 2, 3, pp. 184–188.

[10] The minutes of the deliberations are published in Koz'menko, "Peterburgskii Proekt," pp. 228–301.

reached the aggressive, dynamic stage. Russia had to associate herself with the forces of action and not work against them. The union of Bulgaria and Rumelia was inevitable; all indications were that it would be effected by Bulgaria rather than by Rumelia. Russia thus had to take the necessary steps to secure the maximum advantages from this union. In other words, Russia could not ignore either the domestic conditions in Bulgaria or the influence of the neighboring states of the principality for the sake of maintaining strongly conservative principles of government.[11]

Once the approval of the tsar was obtained, Giers returned the draft to Dondukov with two further suggestions. First, he emphasized the need of stressing the autocephalous character of the Bulgarian church, but also its subordination to Constantinople in the realm of dogma. Second, he insisted that the word "vassal" be incorporated somewhere in the constitution in order to avoid unnecessary difficulties with the Porte. The insertion of this term would clearly indicate that Bulgaria was still considered under the suzerainty of the sultan. Officials in St. Petersburg were apprehensive that the British were trying to commit the Turks to some rash action which would reopen the entire Balkan problem. Giers wanted to avoid friction, especially since Anglo-Russian tension in the Near and Middle East was still acute.[12]

The Russians were keenly aware of the tension within Bulgaria. Bulgarians in both provinces were deeply disappointed in the Treaty of Berlin. They denounced its provisions bitterly and continuously. Meetings were held throughout the Bulgarian lands demanding the restoration of the union. The sentiments of the populace were eloquently expressed by the eighty-two-year-old former Exarch Antim, who with tears in his eyes exclaimed, "Our head, our arms and legs are cut off and it is demanded that we constitute a living body!" Most of the Bulgars believed that their participation in the impending deliberations would signify tacit acceptance of the Berlin agreement. When rumors began to circulate that Russia was not going to evacuate her troops on schedule, these reports increased Bulgarian determination not to accept the proposed separation. These developments alarmed Miliutin. He was certain that the British and Austrians would believe that Russia had provoked the Bulgarian demonstrations. He consequently informed Dondukov that he should categorically assure the Bulgars that Russia intended to fulfill the terms of the Berlin treaty. More than a month passed before Dondukov was able to convince the Bulgars on this point.

[11] Koz'menko, "Proekty," pp. 250–252.
[12] *Ibid.*, p. 253.

It was only with the greatest reluctance that they finally assembled in Tyrnovo on February 10/22, 1879, to start the discussions on the constitution.[13]

In providing the Bulgars with the draft of a constitution the Russian government sought primarily to give them a document whose provisions they could debate. Although Russia naturally expected to influence the form of government to be adopted, she did not intend to exert any particular pressure to ensure the acceptance of her point of view. Giers, on December 27, 1878/January 8, 1879, wrote to Dondukov that he should grant the assembly *"complete* freedom" to express its views and reach its own decisions, and that he should do all he could to resolve any apparently irreconcilable arguments, and, in general, render all assistance possible.[14] Russian policy throughout the debates remained that of noninterference with the discussion of the provisions of the new constitution.

For the first two weeks the delegates did not even consider the constitution, but discussed the injustices imposed upon them at Berlin and the statement which should be presented to the great powers. After this initial delay, serious work began, but the debates on the 166 separate articles of the draft took time. With each passing day the officials in St. Petersburg became more alarmed that the constitution would not be adopted and a prince selected before their troops were withdrawn. Dondukov received numerous telegrams and letters urging him to hasten the proceedings of the Tyrnovo assembly.[15] This action was the major pressure exerted by the Russians, not to influence its decisions but to ensure the establishment of a constitutional order within the time limit. Miliutin could foresee only political chaos in Bulgaria if a stable regime were not established before Russia was forced to withdraw.

In their anxiety for a swift conclusion to the debates the Russian government did not give full weight to the difficulties of Bulgarian domestic politics. Of the 231 deputies sent to the constitutional assembly, only 89 were elected, and these on the basis of one representative for every 10,000 males. The other representatives were appointed from the church hierarchy and the prominent men of the local communities. Since the group reflected the division of interests in the nation, there was no unanimity of opinion or action. Immediately the delegates found themselves separated into two camps, which eventually

[13] *Ibid.,* pp. 254–256; Miliutin, III, 115; Vasiliev, "Bor'ba Bolgarskogo Naroda protiv Reshenii Berlinskago Kongressa 1878 goda," *Voprosy Istorii,* Aug., 1955, pp. 119–130.
[14] Koz'menko, "Proekty," p. 256 n. 5.
[15] *Ibid.,* pp. 258–259.

were labeled the Conservative and Liberal parties. The distinction was based primarily on their differing views regarding the division of power between the executive and legislative branches of the government.

The Liberals, led by the young "intellectuals," advocated the supremacy of the legislative over the executive branch. There were many able orators and popular leaders in this group. They exploited the Bulgars' distrust of the executive branch, which they associated with the despotic rule of the sultans. This party was overwhelmingly supported by the electorate. The Conservatives, who were definitely in the minority, did not believe that the electorate was politically mature enough to allow a dominant legislature. Instead, they supported the granting of greater power to the executive, who would guide and educate his subjects through the initial years of independence.[16]

During the discussions the Conservatives sought, among other things, to enact controls over the press and to provide for a senate which would serve as a counterweight to the national assembly. The Liberals, nevertheless, were able to dominate the proceedings, and eventually their views became embodied in the Tyrnovo constitution, which was adopted in April, 1879. The final draft differed from the Russian proposals in many details; the most important was the shift in emphasis farther to the left. The Russian text, because of the influence of Gradovskii and Miliutin, had in its final form been more liberal than the original draft of Dondukov, and the Tyrnovo document continued this shift of power. The popularly elected assembly was now given the means of attaining dominance in the new state.[17]

Since much of the history of Bulgaria in the period under study involves the clash between the executive and the legislative branches, it is important to consider the division of power. The prince as the head of the state was commander-in-chief of the army and was responsible for relations with foreign powers and the negotiation of treaties. He appointed and dismissed cabinet members. He convened and adjourned the national assembly, which he also had the privilege of proroguing or dissolving. However, he could prorogue it for only two months; if he dissolved it, a new election would have to be held within two months and the representatives reconvened within four months of the time of dissolution. The prince shared a number of powers with the national assembly. One article stated that "the legislative power resides in the prince and in the national representation." Another added that "the initiative in legislation belongs to the prince and the national assembly."

---

[16] Black, pp. 123–124.

[17] The Russian draft of the constitution is found in Koz'menko, "Peterburgskii Proekt," pp. 301–322; the provisions finally adopted are in Black, pp. 291–309.

Although the prince appointed and dismissed the ministers, they were "responsible to the prince and to the national assembly collectively for whatever measures they [took] in common, and individually for the administration of the department entrusted to him."[18]

Despite the powers delegated to the prince, the framers of the Tyrnovo constitution wished to make sure that the real power lay with the elected representatives. The national assembly, whose members were chosen by universal manhood suffrage on the basis of one representative for every 10,000 individuals of both sexes, held the final control through its right of examining all legislation and approving the annual budget. There was only one exception to the yearly submission of the budget: "should an immediate necessity of expenditure, not admitting of delay, occur at a time when the national assembly cannot be convened." Then the budget of the preceding year would remain in force. Even this action would have to be approved at the next meeting of the assembly. The constitution provided that "no law may be enacted, extended, modified, or annulled until it has been examined and passed by the national assembly, which alone has the right of its authorized interpretation." If the prince initiated legislation, the assembly had the right to "modify, amend, or correct the bills submitted to it." The major privilege denied to the assembly was the right to amend the constitution, which was reserved to the Grand National Assembly, chosen on the basis of two representatives for every 10,000 inhabitants.

Because of the haste in which it was drawn up and the inexperience of the Bulgarian legislators, the Tyrnovo constitution left much to be desired. The danger for the future lay in the ambiguity of many of the articles. Although it was the intention of the representatives to secure the control of the national assembly, loopholes were left which an ambitious prince could exploit to his own advantage. The interpretation to be placed on the provisions of the constitution was a matter which would have to be worked out in the succeeding years.

It is evident that Russia had allowed the Bulgarians wide latitude in the selection of the form of constitutional government. A draft document had been provided, but no attempt had been made to prevent its alteration, and that in a direction not entirely to Russia's advantage. In the choice of a ruler, the next problem that the assembly had to consider, it was Russia, with the concurrence of the great powers, and not the Bulgarian assembly, that made the decision.

Because of the liberal nature of the Bulgarian constitution, the character and abilities of the first ruler of Bulgaria would largely de-

---

[18] See articles 9, 108, 111, 122, 141, 144, 153.

termine the success or failure of the new regime. He had to be a prince
who understood constitutional government and who could work with
and through political parties. The number of candidates available was
extremely limited because of the provisions contained in both the
treaties of San Stefano and Berlin that no member of the reigning
dynasties of the great European powers would be permitted to hold the
office. Hence the candidates were from the lesser states, such as
Montenegro, Rumania, and Denmark, and the princely families of
Germany. The standard by which each eligible prince was judged was
his acceptability as an individual to the great powers rather than his
ability to govern the Bulgarian people under the Tyrnovo constitution.
The candidate finally chosen, Alexander of Battenberg, possessed
the attributes which were considered necessary to the future prince
of Bulgaria. A. P. Davydov, Russia's first diplomatic representative to
Bulgaria, described Alexander's qualifications in the following terms:

> I believe that the best candidate, I will say more, the only possible one is Prince
> Battenberg. He is related to our Imperial Family, he has the support of the two
> great German courts...he fought for the independence of Bulgaria and he is
> young enough to adjust himself to the hard task which awaits him and to identify
> himself with the country which will entrust its destinies to him.[19]

A closer study of his background, however, raises grave doubts concerning the wisdom of the choice in view of the Bulgarian political
situation and the prince's training and background. Alexander of Battenberg was born in 1857, the second son of Prince Alexander of Hesse.
His father occupied a prominent position in European society which he
used to further the fortunes of his children. He held the rank of general in the Austrian army, thereby establishing close connections with
the Habsburgs. His sister had married Tsar Alexander II, thus ensuring
an intimate association with the Russian royal family. Priding himself
on his diplomatic abilities, Alexander of Hesse sought to promote
closer relations between St. Petersburg and Vienna. Perhaps it was
with this in mind that he named his second son Alexander Joseph after
the baby's godfathers, Tsar Alexander and the venerable ninety-year-
old Austrian field marshal, Joseph Radetsky.[20]

Prince Alexander was educated in Germany, where his training was

---

[19] Davydov to Giers, *NKG*, Sofia, Dec. 25, 1878/Jan. 6, 1879. The prince's biographer, Corti, *Alexander*, p. 52, described the young man as "A favorite nephew of the
tsar, related to the English ruling house, a German prince, the son of an Austrian
general, closely connected with Russia by virtue of his participation in the campaign
of 1877–78 and yet not a Russian, his choice gave the impression of a concession to
Beaconsfield, a compliment to Bismarck, and a favor to Austria, and at the same
time it seemed to deliver an irresolute tool in the hands of Russia."

[20] Corti, *DTD*, p. 94.

primarily in military service. He became a member of the cadet corps and then entered the Hessian dragoons. Later he was made a lieutenant in the Prussian Gardes du Corps. His military training proved to his advantage when Russia became involved in war with the Ottoman Empire. Alexander of Hesse saw this as an excellent opportunity to promote the fortunes of his twenty-year-old son at the court of the tsar. Hence, after the young prince had obtained the approval of the kaiser for a German officer to join the Russian forces, he left for St. Petersburg. His reception in the Russian capital was very cordial, for the empress was his aunt. He described his visit in glowing terms: "Altogether I am so touched by the kindness and graciousness with which I am overwhelmed that every minute I am becoming more Russian even than I was before. . . . Everybody treats me as a member of the family, they call me by my Christian name and kiss me and expect me to do the same."[21]

From the sober but relaxed atmosphere of St. Petersburg, Alexander departed for the mountains and plains of Bulgaria, where an uncontrolled slaughter was taking place. The devastation and loss of life impressed the young officer deeply. The war was his first real opportunity to work with and to observe the Russians closely. While he was with the army his name was first suggested as a possible candidate for the Bulgarian throne. Since the Hesse family was in financial difficulties and no other more profitable career appeared open to his son, Alexander of Hesse "was anxious that his son should be a candidate." When Alexander of Hesse expressed this hope to his brother-in-law the tsar, Alexander II replied that he would "never" wish his nephew to have such a difficult position.[22] Nevertheless, Alexander continued to press his son's candidature. In August, 1878, he tried to influence the tsar through the empress, but Alexander II remained unenthusiastic, commenting, "Of course, if they decide on him I shall say nothing against it. But in his own and his father's interests I certainly do not covet it for him."[23] Thereafter, however, the tsar's sentiments gradually changed. On November 9/21, 1878, Miliutin noted in his diary that the tsar was now leaning toward Alexander of Battenberg.[24]

When the news of the prince's candidature reached Bulgaria, the reaction was unfavorable. Many Bulgars were suspicious of him because of his German background. Even more hostile views were expressed by the Russian officials in Bulgaria, who were of predominantly Panslav

[21] *Ibid.*, p. 230.
[22] *Ibid.*, p. 247.
[23] *Ibid.*, p. 251.
[24] Miliutin, III, 103.

sympathies. The Bulgarian people themselves openly advocated a Russian candidate, either Count Ignatiev or Prince Dondukov-Korsakov, both of whom were very popular in the principality. If neither of these men was available, they wished no prince at all. In fact, it was argued that even a Russian candidate should not be considered, since this would be a tacit recognition of the Berlin settlement. Others argued that the question was entirely academic, since Russia would not carry out her declaration to evacuate the Bulgarian lands. In view of these sentiments and the unsettled conditions in Bulgaria, the Russian government was obliged categorically to express its views and name a candidate. By March, 1879, the tsar finally gave his consent to the choice of Alexander of Battenberg.[25]

On April 17/29, 1879, the tsar's birthday, a telegram arrived in St. Petersburg from Dondukov, who, as Miliutin remarked, with his characteristic "cleverness" had urged the Bulgars to elect their prince on this day. "On our instructions," continued Miliutin, Alexander of Battenberg had been unanimously elected. The tsar received the news with evident satisfaction, but not the prince's aunt, the empress. In 1878 she had stated, "I should be wretched to think of one of my sons being in so difficult a position." When she heard of the election, she expressed great concern because she had "little faith in the durability and happy future of this new state."[26]

Thus Alexander of Battenberg became prince of Bulgaria at the age of twenty-two. A handsome young man who impressed all with his vigor and enthusiasm, he yet lacked perhaps the most essential qualifications for his position. His past training had been exclusively military: he received orders and executed them or gave orders and expected them to be obeyed. He had had no experience in diplomacy or civil administration. His chief asset was his close family ties with the tsar. Since Russia was to assume the dominant position in Bulgarian policy, it was hoped that the liaison between the prince and the Russian court would lessen conflicts. Unfortunately, Alexander of Battenberg came to Bulgaria with hostile feelings toward Russia and a refusal to recognize the realities of the situation.

The prince's dislike for the Russians stemmed in part from his experience with the Russian army in the Russo-Turkish War. The favorable impression which he had received when he first arrived on Russian soil changed radically when he joined the Russian army in Bulgaria. After his rigorous military training in Germany, he was bound to be

---

[25] Koz'menko, "Proekty," pp. 254–256, 259; Miliutin, III, 131–136.
[26] Miliutin, III, 138; Corti, *DTD*, p. 251.

highly critical of the Russians. Writing to his father on November 13, 1877, he commented:

Such hair-raising things happened daily that if I had simply reported the bare facts, everyone would have regarded them as the exaggerations of a pro-Turk. You have no idea (1) of the levity with which the High Command does its work; (2) of the disorder *within* the army and *behind* the army; (3) of the robbery that goes on in the commissariat. The letter would be too long. But if you like I can give you the most extraordinary *proofs* on each individual point. Things are really so bad that it is a mercy we have only the Turks against us—all would have been lost long ago if we had had any other enemy.

But enough of this vexatious theme. How gladly would I—unlike the Press—write nothing but good of the Russians! It is unfortunately impossible, and no one is sorrier about it than Your Sandro.[27]

His criticisms were in the main directed to the echelons above the rank of major. The officers and soldiers below he described as "splendid." Unfortunately, when he became the ruler of Bulgaria he dealt primarily with the senior Russian representatives, whose abilities and qualities he held in contempt.

Alexander's dislike for the Russians was again evidenced after he was elected prince. Before leaving Hesse for Bulgaria, he received, to his dismay, an invitation from the tsar to visit Russia. The grand duke of Hesse, writing to Queen Victoria on April 26/May 8, 1879, assured her that the prince "is *not Russian* in heart, and that he is *not* inclined to act as Russia's tool [marionette]." Alexander did not wish to go to Russia; he realized that it was "too natural that people will say he is gone to get his instructions, and he is altogether likely to be regarded as a Russian vassal." But, the grand duke continued "He yielded at length, simply to avoid appearing ungrateful, since he and his family owe so much to the Emperor's kindness."[28] In analyzing this episode, Corti wrote, "This communication was not an ordinary matter of courtesy, but really expressed Alexander of Battenberg's inmost feelings, in which the germ of the final issue of the young prince's Bulgarian adventure lay concealed."[29]

If Alexander felt this way about Russia, the question immediately arises: why had the tsar approved his election? The evidence now available concerning the prince's views is contained in the letters he wrote to his father, and these, of course, the Russians did not see. The Russian court and government took it for granted that for personal and dynastic reasons the prince would be compelled to follow their advice,

---

[27] Corti, *DTD*, pp. 235–236.
[28] Buckle, ed., *The Letters of Queen Victoria*, 2d ser., III, 16–17. Hereafter cited as Buckle, *Victoria*. See also Giers to Jomini, *NKG*, Livadia, May 1/13, 1879.
[29] Corti, *DTD*, p. 257.

or at least not work actively against their interests. Shuvalov best described the situation to Salisbury when he said of Alexander that, "as
he was poor, and was nothing but a lieutenant, he might look upon the
Principality of Bulgaria as a promotion."[30] The Russian government
expected to be able to keep close supervision over the prince, his policies,
and his associates through the Russian civil and military advisers who
would remain in Sofia. Moreover, since Alexander had no personal fortune, he would be dependent on Russia for financial assistance. Alexander's position seemed to place him under Russian control, and he had
not yet given evidence of his determination to rule independently.

Not only did Alexander show increasing signs of dislike for the Russians, but there are indications that he was not particularly fond of his
future subjects. His unfavorable opinion of the Bulgars was expressed
before he had any idea that he would someday be their prince. During
the war of 1877 he was appalled by the way "the Bulgars hurl themselves upon the Turks, murder them, plunder and burn everything,"
once they were certain that the Russian army was near. On June 26/
July 8, 1878, he wrote to his brother, "The country is simply magnifi-
cent, but the Bulgars are just as fiendish as the Turks."[31] Again, in the
spring of 1879, after his election, he showed his feeling toward his subjects. When he was asked to visit Russia, it was proposed that a
Bulgarian delegation greet him there as the new ruler. Alexander, however, did not want to take part in the ceremony. Concerning this episode
the grand duke of Hesse wrote to Queen Victoria, "If it can be done
without being glaringly rude, he [Alexander] will refuse to receive the
Bulgarian deputation at Livadia." However, he was not able to avoid
meeting the group.[32]

Although Alexander of Hesse was largely responsible for obtaining
the Bulgarian throne for his son, he too was concerned with the future.
He finally concurred with the sentiments the tsar had expressed, and
noted in his diary for May 27/June 8, 1879, that "the poor boy will have
to sacrifice his youth to the arduous task." His son's position was complicated by the Tyrnovo constitution, which he described as being "more
democratic than any other in the monarchist world." He evaluated it
as "an incredibly clumsy piece of work, very democratic in tendency,
and full of gaps." He was certain that the constitution would make it
"impossible" for his son to rule.[33] The views of the father were shared
by the son. Alexander never willingly accepted the limitations which it

---

[30] Buckle, *Victoria*, III, 6.
[31] Corti, *DTD*, pp. 231–232.
[32] Buckle, *Victoria*, III, 16–17; Miliutin, III, 142; Giers to Jomini, *NKG*, Livadia,
May 15, May 19, 1879.
[33] Corti, *DTD*, p. 256.

placed on his power, nor did he agree with the basic ideas behind its stipulations. Educated in a monarchist world, his ideas and sentiments remained authoritarian. He came to regard the Tyrnovo constitution as a Russian-sponsored document whose sole purpose was to curb his power. He wished to be the ruler of Bulgaria in reality as well as in name.

By June 24/July 6, 1879, when Alexander finally arrived in Bulgaria, Russia had completed the two major tasks undertaken in Bulgaria after the Congress of Berlin. Bulgaria now had a constitution and a prince. Within these accomplishments lay the germ of the conflicts which were to develop both within Bulgaria and between Bulgaria and Russia. The tsarist government, which had the major responsibility for Bulgarian politics, had allowed the Bulgars to adopt a liberal constitution. Simultaneously a headstrong prince was placed in charge of the new state—a prince who was determined both to reign in his own country and to resist outside dictation. Russian policy called for the maintenance of stable, peaceful conditions within the principality; Russian strategic interests demanded that the ruler and his subjects remain attracted to St. Petersburg.

The beginning of Alexander's reign in Bulgaria was not auspicious. He came from Europe by sea, stopping first at Constantinople to pay his respects to his sovereign the sultan. While there he had an acute attack of indigestion. Before he landed at Varna he had a spell of seasickness, and it was only with the greatest effort that he was able to acknowledge the greeting of the large crowd which had assembled to welcome him. Still in a weakened condition, he was compelled to make a brief tour of his new country before settling in Sofia on June 28/July 10.[34]

The new prince had a difficult task before him in administering the reduced Bulgarian state. First, the division of the Bulgarian lands into Bulgaria and Eastern Rumelia was entirely artificial and had been dictated by the needs of great power politics. No one knew how long the situation could be maintained. The Bulgars not only were carrying on agitation and propaganda, but also were organizing and arming themselves for a forceful solution to the problem. These groups, motivated by strong passions, could make the position of the prince untenable. If he tried to suppress them, he would arouse the animosity of his subjects. If he ignored or encouraged them, he would be subjected to heavy pressure from the great states. The interest of the major powers in Bulgaria constituted the second difficulty that was to beset the growth

---

[34] *Ibid.*, pp. 257–258; Corti, *Alexander*, p. 65.

of the new nation. Political and military events in Bulgaria, which was situated strategically on the road to the east, involved not only Russia but also Austria-Hungary and Britain. Although Bulgaria was recognized as being within Russia's sphere of influence, the two opposing powers never relinquished their efforts to combat Russian activities. Even though Alexander of Battenberg was a Russian appointee, his real sympathies remained with his German background and his English relations. The third series of problems which faced Alexander concerned domestic affairs. Bulgaria was a backward agricultural state. The devastation during the Russo-Turkish War had intensified her manifold economic problems. On the level of domestic politics, Bulgaria sorely needed a ruler who could guide her toward becoming a modern state both politically and economically.

In carrying out his first task, the selection of ministers, Alexander gave clear evidence of his attitude toward the constitution. When he took his oath of office, he promised to work for the "welfare and the prosperity of the principality." In his mind this phrase took precedence over the actual articles of the constitution. From the beginning he felt that he alone had the right to judge what was to the best interest of the nation; he considered that the Tyrnovo constitution was an obstacle to Bulgaria's fruitful development. Among the Bulgars, only the Conservatives shared his views, but they were the minority party. The constitution had been the work of the Liberals and their policies had the backing of the electorate. However, Alexander was free to appoint whom he wished to the ministry without the confirmation of the national assembly. His Russian and Bulgarian advisers urged that the first ministry should be a coalition of Conservatives and Liberals. Reluctantly he agreed, but after some delay, bickering, and deliberations he reversed himself and entrusted to F. S. Burmov, a Conservative, the formation of the first ministry of the autonomous Bulgaria.[35]

The prince's decision was regarded as a direct challenge to the Liberals. He had in effect served notice on them that, in spite of their political predominance, he would carry on his administration without them. His opinion of the majority party is reflected in a letter to his father justifying his actions.

I could do nothing else. I am too anxious to prove to Europe and to the country itself that with my advent Bulgaria has become a monarchy ... and that not only will I not protect Nihilists, but I shall pursue them with fire and sword. Can you

---

[35] Black, pp. 156–158; Matveev, "Bolgariia i Vostochnaia Rumeliia posle Berlinskago Kongressa," *Istoricheskii Viestnik*, XXIV (1886), 584–593; Parensov, "V Bolgarii," *Russkaia Starina*, CXXV (1906), 510.

believe it when I tell you that in the few days I have been here I have aged by *ten years?*[36]

Alexander came into conflict also with Russian policy, or to be more precise, Russian officialdom. Although the Treaty of Berlin provided for the withdrawal of Russian troops from Bulgaria, it was expected that the Russians would remain in Bulgaria to advise and guide the young nation in the difficult task of self-administration. In military matters in particular, Russia was anxious to have her influence prevail; a friendly Bulgarian army, organized and equipped by Russia, was needed to defend the vital Near Eastern front. The development of the Bulgarian army would be the responsibility of the Bulgarian minister of war. On the basis of the constitution Alexander could choose his ministers, but in reality he was obliged to consult the tsar in the appointment of the minister of war, who for the next six years was a Russian officer. In the first cabinet this position was held by P. D. Parensov, a thirty-six-year-old major general in the Russian army.

Like Alexander himself, Parensov had few qualifications for his position. He had served in the Russian army in various capacities and had taken part in the Russo-Turkish War. Afterwards he had acted as assistant to Dondukov-Korsakov. He was fortunate in his personal connections; Giers was his uncle and Miliutin was satisfied with his work. Keenly aware of Russian interests in Bulgaria and, in particular, of the role that the Bulgarian army was supposed to play in Russian strategy, he believed it his task to guarantee that nothing should jeopardize the aims of his nation. These, he believed, could best be achieved by supporting the Bulgarian constitution. Since he belonged to the Panslav anti-German faction, he looked upon the election of Alexander of Battenberg with misgivings. He was particularly suspicious of the personal advisers whom the prince had brought with him from Germany. These two factors, his desire to uphold the constitution and his anti-German sentiments, soon brought Parensov into direct opposition with the prince.[37] The antagonism between the Russian representative and the German prince established a pattern which was to remain until the expulsion of the latter from Bulgaria.

The conflict between Bulgaria and Russia was expressed in terms of the personal dislikes and prejudices of the individuals concerned. The first of the quarrels, on the relatively minor issue of Alexander's title, revealed the major obstacle to smooth relations between Alexander and

---

[36] Corti, *DTD*, p. 258.
[37] Parensov, *op. cit.*, CI, 113–115; Skazkin, p. 227.

the agents of his patron state. The differences between the general and
the prince came to the fore the same day, July 5/17, that Alexander
designated Burmov as minister-president. That night the prince gave
a dinner in honor of his ministers. Afterward Parensov observed Alexander in conversation with the other ministers, who subsequently informed the general that the prince was disturbed by the provision in
the constitution which stated that Alexander was to be addressed as
"Excellency" (*Svetlost*), whereas by birth he deserved the title "Highness" (*Vysochestvo*). Therefore, he had requested the ministers to
address him as "Highness" and they had agreed. Parensov, nevertheless,
refused. If the constitution provided the title "Excellency," he would
use that term until the constitution had been properly amended. Under
no condition would he sanction a violation of the constitution. When
it was pointed out that dissent meant that the cabinet was divided, he
answered that he would resign before yielding. Finally a compromise
was reached. Parensov and the army would use the term "Excellency"
in all correspondence in Bulgarian, but in correspondence and conversations conducted in French, "Altesse" would be substituted.[38]

The solution was not a happy one. Instead of pacifying Alexander,
it made him more irritated because, as he complained, "Only the army
calls me Excellency, whereas everyone else Highness."[39] Parensov would
not yield, since he believed that the German prince was seeking to
establish a precedent for the future violation of the constitution. Even
more important than the personal affront to Alexander was the fact that
the Liberals seized upon the incident to demonstrate to the electorate
how the prince treated the constitution. Subsequently, a liaison developed between Parensov and the Liberals which the latter used to
embarrass the prince by exploiting Russian prestige among the Bulgars.
Alexander blamed the Russian government for permitting Parensov to
become the rallying point for attacks against him. Parensov's attitude
signified that in effect the minister of war was a Liberal, whereas the
remainder of the cabinet were Conservatives.[40]

The conflict over the title determined the future relations of the
prince and the general. While the European press and segments of
the Russian press criticized Parensov for his stand, the attitude of the
Russian government was ambiguous. When, in September, 1879,
Parensov went to St. Petersburg, he discussed the matter with both
Giers and Miliutin. Giers advised, "My friend, why not satisfy him?
Why not call him Highness?" But on the previous day Parensov had

---

[38] Parensov, *op. cit.*, CI, 378–381.
[39] *Ibid.*, CXXV, 281.
[40] Black, pp. 159–160.

seen Miliutin, who called the problem "nonsense" and sanctioned the general's conduct. The contradictory advice amazed Parensov. The affair was not resolved until after Parensov had been recalled to Russia in the spring of 1880.[41]

After this incident, Alexander's dislike for the Russians in Bulgaria continued to increase. From his point of view Bulgaria was "flooded" with Russian nationals. Besides the Russian military personnel who were in the country to train the Bulgarian army, the foreign office had sent consuls, vice-consuls, and large staffs to all the prominent Bulgarian cities. Numbers of businessmen had come after the war seeking to profit from the development and exploitation of Bulgaria's resources and markets. "All the scum of Russia has taken refuge here and has tainted the whole country," Alexander wrote.[42] Thus, immediately after his arrival in Sofia, Alexander had turned against his patron state. As Corti wrote, "Within the first three weeks the Prince had come into conflict with all the Russian officials in Bulgaria, and was obliged to appeal to the tsar." In a few months Alexander had developed "a violent hatred of all that was Russian. Whenever anything happened he saw the hand of Russia."[43]

Prince Alexander felt isolated among the Bulgars. No bonds of sympathy or common interest yet existed to unite him with his people.[44] Faced with a situation repellent to his character, Alexander sought ways to improve his position, which he believed could be done only by strengthening his authority through a change in the constitution: by legislative means, by the suspension of the constitution, or by a *coup d'état*. The first two courses were impossible of realization, since the Liberal party in control of the assembly would never consent to the modification of the constitution by legal means. The third would involve the use of force and the aid of the army, but the army was under the command of General Parensov and took orders from him. It was in this sphere that Alexander realized that he must effect a change.

As Bulgarian minister of war, General Parensov occupied an ambiguous position. In theory he was responsible to the prince and the national assembly, but in fact his loyalties remained with Russia and

---

[41] Parensov, *op. cit.*, CXXV, 521–522. In January, 1880, prior to Alexander's departure for Russia, General Parensov, as senior officer at a dinner, was required to address the prince. When the prince spoke to him in Bulgarian, Parensov became so confused that he unintentionally called Alexander "Your Highness." Thereupon Alexander threw his arms around the general and kissed him. However, the assembled group thought it a prearranged affair between the two. Parensov, *op. cit.*, CXXXIII, 261–263.

[42] Corti, *DTD*, p. 258.

[43] *Ibid.*, p. 258.

[44] *Ibid.*, p. 259.

what he conceived as her interests. From the evidence available it appears that Parensov was never given clear instructions by the Russian government. In September, 1879, after three months as minister, he still did not know how Russia expected him to act in his dual role of Russian citizen and Bulgarian official. He did not know whether he should follow his fellow ministers if the Conservative government fell or was asked to resign by the prince. Nor had he been told what authority he had over the other Russian officers in the Bulgarian service. Once, after Parensov gave an order to a Russian officer, the latter retorted, "What does the Russian government think about this?"[45] When the general was in Russia in September, Alexander II informed him that he would receive his orders from Miliutin, but that he was responsible to the tsar for the Russian officers in Bulgaria. The general was to inform these officers that, although they were members of the Bulgarian army, at the same time "each one of them is a *carrier of the Russian name.*" The tsar concluded by informing the general to continue serving as he had been. Most of Parensov's correspondence was with Miliutin, who maintained that Russia should not interfere in Bulgarian internal affairs. When, on another occasion, Parensov sought his advice, Miliutin telegraphed that "he should not forget that he is the minister of the Bulgarian principality." Contradictory instructions did not ease Parensov's duties.[46]

The Russian general ran into technical difficulties with the army. If it were to be modeled after the Russian forces it would need the best equipment and the best training cadre, but Parensov was forced to rely mostly on captured Turkish material because Russia herself did not have sufficient supplies. The training cadre was a more complicated matter. To staff it Parensov needed well-qualified and able men, who were available only while the Russian army remained in Bulgaria. Once the evacuation commenced, most of the officers and noncommissioned personnel returned to Russia. Volunteers had to be recruited and these proved to be of low quality—able to carry on routine duties but lacking in imagination, initiative, and organizational ability. Parensov reported that he personally knew of officers, disqualified by the Russian army, who had now received assignments in Bulgaria. Little attention was paid to an officer's previous training when assignments were made. A cavalry officer might be assigned to an infantry unit, or a squad leader might be placed in charge of a company. In September, 1879, Parensov was forced to appeal to the tsar for aid,

[45] Parensov, *op. cit.*, CXXV, 283–285.
[46] *Ibid.*, p. 525; Miliutin, III, 232.

which he received in October when additional noncommissioned officers landed at Varna.[47]

The difficulties which Parensov experienced in organizing the Bulgarian army were evident to the prince. He frequently told the minister, "We [in Germany] always did it differently." Alexander would have preferred to use the Prussian system as the model for his army, but this was just what Parensov would not tolerate. German influence was to be kept out of the military establishment at all costs. Count Khevenhüller, Austrian diplomatic agent in Sofia, increased the general's suspicions when he tried to induce Parensov not to organize a Bulgarian army, but only a militia. He argued that an army would be expensive and unnecessary and that it was contrary to the Treaty of Berlin. These events were occurring in the summer of 1879, before Russia had taken the first step toward a rapprochement with Germany, and when the peak of the great wave of anti-German feeling was sweeping Russia.[48]

Despite the minister of war's anti-German sentiments, Alexander continued to press for changes in the Russian system. He observed, for instance, that the ceremony connected with the changing of the palace guard was not like the German. More serious was his demand that Prussian and Austrian officers be introduced into the military service, an action that would have been greatly to his interests, since it could be assumed that these men would be personally loyal to Alexander. Through his control of the foreign officers, the prince might in time be able to achieve the actual command of his army. Parensov objected vigorously that these suggestions reflected on the abilities of the Russian army and that their implementation would be a violation of the constitution. The constitution did in fact state that Bulgarian subjects alone could hold civil and military positions and that foreigners could be employed in public service only if the national assembly approved each appointment.

In November, 1879, the conflict between the prince and Parensov reached a critical stage. Alexander demanded that the general accept the appointment of a Lieutenant Köller, a German officer, and at the same time make plans to receive additional foreigners. Rather than yield, Parensov threatened to resign, a tactic he frequently employed, since it frightened the prince, who was not yet ready to defy the tsar's representative. Alexander finally made another proposal. If Parensov would agree to accept Lieutenant Köller and one other officer, then the

[47] Parensov, *op. cit.*, CI, 112–121; CXXV, 72–73, 275, 282–283, 523–526.
[48] *Ibid.*, CXXV, 278–279; CXXXII, 609.

prince promised never again to bring up the matter of foreign officers. Parensov finally decided that two foreign officers could do no harm to Russian interests.[49]

During the crisis Parensov sought the advice of his chief, Miliutin. The reply was received only after the general had already agreed that two foreign officers would be accepted. Miliutin informed Parensov that his personal opinion was that foreign officers should be kept out of the Bulgarian army, but "he could not give official instructions to him *as the minister* of the Bulgarian prince, *responsible to the constitutional order*. It would be extremely unsatisfactory for the Russian government to interfere in the internal affairs of Bulgaria." Parensov interpreted this to signify Miliutin's approval of his adhering to the constitution and the policy which he had hitherto followed.[50]

The compromise solution did not end the friction between the prince and the war minister. Alexander now determined to ask the tsar for Parensov's recall. His decision had come not only as a result of their differences over the prince's title and the army, but also because of Parensov's refusal to coöperate with the prince in action against the Tyrnovo constitution. Since the intervention of the army could be expected in any governmental crisis, the struggle for the control of the military establishment was intimately connected with the constitutional question.

By September, 1879, the third month of his reign, the prince had become convinced that he could not rule with the constitution, and "was already considering a *coup d'état*."[51] The constitution, besides limiting his authority, enabled the Liberals to block the work of the Conservative ministry. Although the prince could not rely on Parensov for assistance, he did find encouragement in the advice of the Russian consul general in Sofia, A. P. Davydov. The relations of this official with the prince and his co-national Parensov illustrate the carelessness with which the Russian government selected its representatives in the principality. Whereas General Parensov, backed by Miliutin, believed that Russian interests could best be served through the development of a strong, efficient army, the support of the Liberal party, and the maintenance of the constitution, Davydov, in contrast, scorned the Liberal party and the constitution. He was convinced that it was to Russia's advantage to support Conservative party rule and to sanction the prince's endeavors to alter the constitution. His views were closer to the opinion of Giers than to those of Miliutin.

[49] *Ibid.*, CXXXII, 606–613.
[50] *Ibid.*, CXXXII, 618–619.
[51] Corti, *DTD*, p. 259; Miliutin, III, 166.

Thus the two principal Russian agents in Bulgaria supported conflicting programs, and neither was enthusiastic about his position in Bulgaria. Parensov admitted that when he was first offered the post of Bulgarian minister of war, he was reluctant to accept it. Then he began to consider what his future would be if he returned to Russia. He could not have his former army post, which had already been assigned to someone else. "Fate could send me God only knows where," he wrote.[52] Under these conditions he decided to remain in Sofia and eventually he became reconciled to his duties.

Davydov, on the contrary, never ceased in his efforts to obtain a transfer. Most of his service had been in the west, and he strongly resented his assignment to Bulgaria, which he regarded as a primitive and hostile country. Almost from the first day of his arrival in the principality, he pleaded for recall or another assignment. It is revealing to read Davydov's private letters to Giers concerning the Bulgarian situation and his reaction to it. As the political controversies became more heated in 1879, the Russian consul became increasingly desirous of leaving the country. In March and April, when the debate on the constitution was in progress, he wrote to Giers that he would prefer a post in the west even though it was a demotion, rather than remain in the east. In June, when he went on leave to Vienna, he wrote that after only five days away from the Balkan Peninsula he felt better. In August, when the quarrel between Alexander and Parensov attracted attention, Davydov wrote that he would "go willingly no matter where and in no matter what capacity rather than stay here." In October he declared himself ready to leave the service rather than remain in Bulgaria. By November he had become desperate and begged Giers to recall him unless "you wish me to lose my head completely."[53]

It seems incredible that Giers retained Davydov in his position in view of the latter's disgust with the situation in Sofia. Yet Davydov continued to hold the key diplomatic post in the Balkans during the crucial formative year of the Bulgarian state. The Russian officials themselves had stressed that it was of the utmost importance that the new government function with the minimum of friction and the maximum of harmony and efficiency. The hostility which developed between Davydov and Parensov, who together would determine the success or failure of the Russian activities in Bulgaria, was disastrous for Russia. It is to Davydov's credit that he foresaw the impending difficulties and,

---

[52] Parensov, *op. cit.*, CI, 113–116.
[53] Davydov to Giers, *NKG*, Tyrnovo, March 27/April 8; *ibid.*, Bucharest, April 20/May 12; *ibid.*, Vienna, May 27/June 8; *ibid.*, Sofia, Aug. 19/31, Oct. 7/19, Nov. 6/18, 1879; Gorchakov to Giers, *NKG*, Baden, Sept. 3/15, 1878.

in April, 1879, advised his government that one person should be made responsible for Russian policy. His suggestion was ignored.[54]

Davydov was strong in his condemnation of the constitution. He had been in Bulgaria at the time of its adoption. In a letter to Giers in April, 1879, he pronounced the judgment that "the constitution is worth absolutely nothing." He condemned all its liberal features.[55] After the election of the prince, Davydov again wrote to Giers and stated that, although he did not know Alexander's views, still, "if he considers that a constitution is good only to be violated, he will be very satisfied with that which they will give him, for it is absolutely good only for that."[56] Just before Alexander arrived in Bulgaria, Davydov wrote, "The fact is that I have the greatest apprehension for the future of the principality; what I fear are the first years, and I do not know how to deplore enough that we have started the country on the constitutional road."[57] Once Davydov learned of Alexander's views, the two became close collaborators. In fact, it was probably from the advice and support of Davydov that Alexander gained courage to explore the possibility of abrogating the constitution.

Alexander realized that it was necessary to solicit the support of the tsar before initiating measures to change the constitution. Although the prince blamed the Russian government for most of his problems in Bulgaria, he still held his uncle in great esteem and appreciated the assistance he had given to the Battenberg family. Alexander hoped to find the Russian court sympathetic toward him because of his difficulties with the liberal Tyrnovo constitution. In September, 1879, he wrote to St. Petersburg explaining the reasons for his inability to continue under the existing circumstances. Upon receipt of the letter, the tsar consulted Miliutin and Giers.[58] In addition to the information provided by the prince, the Russian officials had a report from Colonel A. A. Shepelev, aide-de-camp to the prince. Unlike Parensov and Davydov, who were extremists, Shepelev was gifted with unusual tact and understanding. His reports testify that he was singularly devoid of the emotionalism and petty vanities which characterized so many of the Russian representatives in Bulgaria. He stands out as one of the most able Russian officials in Bulgaria in the decade after the Congress of Berlin.

Shepelev's relationship to the prince enabled him to keep in close touch with the latter's thoughts and opinions. He had warned Alexan-

---

[54] Davydov to Giers, *NKG*, Tyrnovo, April 18/30, 1879.
[55] *Ibid.*, April 9/21, 1879.
[56] *Ibid.*, April 18/30, 1879.
[57] *Ibid.*, May 27/June 8, 1879.
[58] Miliutin, III, 165–166; Skazkin, p. 228; Corti, *Alexander*, p. 45; Jomini to Giers, *NKG*, Oct. 17, 1879.

der at the beginning of his reign that Bulgaria had few experienced men for the administration of the state. He advised that Bulgaria's first government should be a coalition of Conservatives and Liberals in order that the country might have a stable government in its formative years and that party conflicts would be postponed until a later date. Shepelev acted as an unofficial informant for Miliutin, who learned more about Bulgarian events from the colonel than from Parensov. In his relations with Alexander, Shepelev did what he could to prevent the prince from taking sudden or drastic measures. When, however, the prince could not be dissuaded from his determination to force a change in the constitution, Shepelev sent a detailed report to Miliutin which arrived simultaneously with Alexander's letter to the tsar.

Shepelev advised the Russian government not to fear the continuation of liberal power in Bulgaria. He described the Conservatives as the better educated group who supported the Treaty of Berlin, which the Liberals opposed. The latter party, Shepelev continued, was not truly radical. Although the Liberals wished to overthrow the Conservative ministry, it was only with the intention of replacing them in office. In matters of national interest, the Liberals were as capable of correct action as the Conservatives. In the struggle between the two political factions, Shepelev believed the prince should hold himself above party politics and appoint his ministers from the group which commanded popular support. Alexander was young, prone to act independently, and lacked the ability to handle people. He should not have caused a crisis over the question of his title immediately after taking office, but should have induced some member of the national assembly to suggest an amendment to the constitution. In view of these circumstances, Shepelev advised Russia to reject the prince's proposal. If Russia acquiesced, the Bulgars would accuse her of having acted hastily and dishonestly when she approved the document. The moment for drastic action had not yet come; Alexander should be advised to adhere to the constitution.[59]

After Miliutin, Dondukov-Korsakov, and Giers had read both Alexander's and Shepelev's letters, they all recommended that the colonel's advice should be followed. The tsar, although agreeing with his ministers, did not wish to make a decision until he had received a report from Davydov also. The opinions of the latter are not available, but the tsar's decision is. He admitted that the constitution might have been adopted without sufficient deliberation and that some of its provisions were far from ideal, but legal methods for amending it were

---

[59] Parensov, *op. cit.*, CXXV, 509–518.

available. He therefore cautioned his nephew not to act abruptly and advised him to be loyal to the constitution, since "it had been solemnly accepted."[60]

In view of the emperor's decision, Alexander had no choice but to abstain from further action against the constitution. He and his ministers went ahead with plans for the election to the national assembly. When the results were tabulated, only thirty of the one hundred seventy elected members could be relied upon to support the Conservative ministry. The ministers realized that it was hopeless to try to rule the country in the face of such formidable opposition in the national assembly. In order to avoid a vote of censure they advised Alexander not to call the assembly into session. They even advanced the idea that Parensov should use the army to back a temporary suspension of the constitution. Alexander rejected these suggestions and the assembly finally convened on October 21/November 2, 1879.[61]

The opposition to be expected from the assembly became apparent at once. In his opening address the prince expressed his gratitude to the tsar-liberator without specific reference to Russia. When Parensov queried him about this, he replied, "I adore the tsar, but Russia is not for me." The assembly immediately censured Alexander for his obvious indiscretion. In its reply to the prince's speech the assembly used the title "Your Excellency" instead of "Highness." Alexander was then advised that, subsequently, with the convening of each new assembly, he should express his love and devotion to Alexander II and the Russian people in order to strengthen the bonds between the two nations. The assembly criticized the Conservative ministry for seeking to rule outside the constitutional limits. It was obvious that the address had but one purpose—to remind the prince that under the Tyrnovo constitution the legislative and not the executive branch of the government was dominant. The assembly next elected Petko Karavelov, a leading Liberal, as its president. By this step it underscored its lack of confidence in the Conservative leadership.[62]

The Conservative ministers, recognizing the assembly's vote of no confidence, offered their resignations, but Alexander refused to accept them. In a detailed report to Miliutin, Shepelev discussed the prince's reactions to the impasse. When Alexander told Shepelev that the tsar would want to strengthen the power of the Conservatives and would eventually approve the measures necessary to ensure the executive authority, Shepelev repeated his previous advice that a coalition min-

---

[60] Skazkin, p. 229 n. 1; Miliutin, III, 166.
[61] Black, pp. 164–165; Parensov, *op. cit.*, CXXVI, 71–72.
[62] Parensov, *op. cit.*, CXXVI, 329–340; Miliutin, III, 178–179.

istry be formed, since the majority of the Bulgarian people supported the Liberals. The alternative, the dissolution of the assembly, appeared highly dangerous. If this happened, "God help Bulgaria," Shepelev concluded.[63]

Since no other practical solution seemed possible, Alexander finally decided to follow Shepelev's counsel. He agreed to entrust to Karavelov the formation of a coalition ministry which was to include at least two of the former Conservative ministers. However, the prince made two conditions. First, he would not accept the assembly's reply to his speech until it addressed him as "Highness." Second, the assembly had to withdraw its suggestion that he express his gratitude to the tsar and the Russian people when each new assembly was convened. After these stipulations were rejected, Alexander took the only course open to him and dissolved the assembly on November 27/December 9.[64]

In order to make certain that no outbreaks would occur, Alexander on November 24/December 6 had sent a note to Parensov "to take *secret* measures to ensure that general order not be destroyed." The nature of this request disturbed Parensov, since Alexander had just informed him of the intention of introducing German officers into the army. On the day that the assembly was dissolved, Alexander met with Parensov and discussed the admission of Lieutenant Köller and of other foreign officers into the army. When Parensov objected that the proposed action was unconstitutional, Alexander replied that, since the assembly had been dissolved, the constitution was not in force. The general pointed out that the constitution could be abrogated only by the Grand National Assembly, which had adopted it, or by the use of force. Parensov thereupon offered his resignation. Alexander would gladly have been rid of his minister of war, but he did not wish to offend the tsar. Nevertheless, both Alexander and Parensov recognized that the parting of the ways had come. The general wrote that he knew he had "crossed the Rubicon." Alexander was convinced that Parensov would have to be dismissed, but in a manner which would not be interpreted as open defiance of Russia.[65]

Throughout his conflicts with Parensov and the assembly, Alexander received constant and vigorous encouragement from Davydov, whose disdain for the constitution and the Liberals had been increased by the events of the recent months. In May he had clearly stated his feelings concerning the majority party: "My position vis-à-vis a radical ministry or even the radical members of a mixed ministry would be extremely false; it would not be less false vis-à-vis some Russians with whom I am

[63] Parensov, *op. cit.*, CXXVI, 70–78.
[64] *Ibid.*, CXXVI, 335–340; CXXXI, 442–443; Miliutin, III, 183.
[65] Parensov, *op. cit.*, CXXXII, 603, 613; CXXXIII, 257.

not in agreement; the prince would not find in me the support which he has a right to expect, and our influence would suffer."[66]

After the overwhelming victory of the Liberals in the fall elections, Davydov conceded that the party was well organized and popular, but he refused to admit that its policies were correct. Although he was willing to consider a mixed ministry, he was strongly opposed to an exclusively Liberal government. A *coup d'état* against the constitution, he believed, was the only solution for the Bulgarian political dilemma. He considered that the legal means for modifying the constitution were impractical. The debates and deliberations connected with such a change would only increase the prevalent unrest and uncertainty. The overthrow of the constitution, however, would have to be accomplished with the blessing of the tsar. Otherwise, the Liberals would spread the rumor that it was the result of Austrian machinations, and that "the most precious gift" that Russia had bestowed on the principality had been taken away through foreign influence. In a letter to Giers, Davydov admitted that many Russian officials in Bulgaria, as well as the Liberals, considered him "a traitor or an imbecile" who supported the Austrian interests. He argued with his opponents that "the constitution is an absurdity in theory and an insanity in practice; ... it is precisely because of that that it is our duty to save this country from the consequences of a mistake that we have committed."[67]

Motivated by sentiments akin to those of Russia's chief diplomatic agent, Alexander decided to appeal to the tsar again. This time Shepelev delivered the message. Although indicating that he had not given up hope of ruling with the Conservative party, the prince asked the tsar personally to intervene to achieve the abolition of the Tyrnovo constitution and the substitution of a new charter. If the tsar would not lend his aid, the prince would have to proceed alone.

Miliutin in his diary commented extensively on the events which followed. As could be expected, the Russian minister of war blamed Davydov for the Bulgarian impasse. The latter, wrote Miliutin in a somewhat sarcastic tone, "true to his role as a diplomat," abetted the prince's inclination toward autocratic rule. Moreover, Davydov had joined the Austrian representatives in urging Alexander to dissolve the assembly. Thus diplomatic intrigue together with the Germanic tendencies of the prince had resulted in the present situation. Miliutin was particularly disturbed by the methods Davydov proposed to use in a *coup d'état* against the constitution. The Russian consul had urged the

---

[66] Davydov to Giers, *NKG*, Bucharest, April 30/May 12, 1879.
[67] *Ibid.*, Sofia, Nov. 6/18, Nov. 20/Dec. 2, 1879.

prince to carry out the action from Russia. He was to go to St. Petersburg and from there send an order to the Bulgars to alter the constitution. "Could one think of anything more unpleasant, especially on the part of a Russian diplomat," commented Miliutin. He was pleased that Shepelev was able to obtain an audience with the tsar in order to present the other side of the picture.[68]

On December 11/23 Giers and Miliutin met with the emperor to consider the Bulgarian situation. Although Giers was aware of the "contradictions and absurdities" in Davydov's views, he remained under his influence and appeared willing to sanction the use of force to effect a *coup d'état*. Miliutin, in contrast, argued on behalf of the constitution, and his view was upheld by the tsar, who had been prepared by his meeting with Shepelev. Miliutin and Giers, aided by Baron Jomini, drafted the answer to be sent in the tsar's name.[69]

The reply was worded in a manner which clearly indicated the tsar's wishes but at the same time left the responsibility for the final decision to the prince. The letter was designed to appeal to Alexander personally and to make him feel that he was culturally and intellectually superior to his subjects. He was advised to move cautiously in order not to offend the pride of the Bulgarians, and to use extreme measures only as a last resort. The constitution had been set up according to the provisions of the Treaty of Berlin. If the tsar supported the abrogation of the Tyrnovo constitution, the action would expose him "to the accusation of exercising illegal intervention in the affairs of the Principality." The solution to the problem was to be found not in a *coup d'état* but "in legitimate channels and with the greatest possible discretion."

Through ignorance and inexperience, the tsar's letter continued, the Bulgarian people had been led astray by influential men—an obvious reference to the Liberals. The prince and those whom he could trust should seek to reëducate and reorient the electorate. "If in this propaganda for reason and for the public weal the authority of my name, my advice, and the sentiments of gratitude of the Bulgarian people to Russia can be of any assistance to you, you have full discretion to make use of them." If, in spite of the prince's efforts, the Bulgars did not reform but instead inclined toward "anarchical tendencies," then they deserved the ill will of Europe.

As a practical measure the tsar suggested holding another election for representatives to the assembly. The prince should try to persuade the new body to alter the constitution in those parts where "experience

---

[68] Miliutin, III, 189–190; Matveev, *op. cit.*, XXIV, 595.
[69] Miliutin, III, 190–191.

has proved it to be unworkable." If this step failed, Alexander should dissolve the assembly and "appeal to the country by convoking a general meeting, at which you can propose a new constitution revised with the necessary maturity and in accordance with the experience that has been acquired." The tsar concluded by saying that the ultimate decision rested with the prince, but the Russian suggestions would "give more time for reflection and persuasion." The tsar assured the prince of his best wishes and placed his "moral assistance" at the prince's disposal. "Given time, everything will settle itself," he prophesied, "and the conservative elements which are present in an agricultural people, though sorely tried, are industrious and resistant, and will come to the fore again in the end."[70]

Again Alexander could do nothing but follow this advice. He had, however, gained one advantage: Alexander II had conceded that if the assembly, which had still to be elected, failed to act, he could proceed with more drastic measures. As Skazkin wrote, Russia had in reality provided the prince with a plan for the overthrow of the constitution. To offset this gain, Alexander lost his most loyal and powerful supporter. Miliutin noted in his diary on December 15/27 that one result of the tsar's decision to uphold the constitutional order was that Davydov would have to be replaced.[71]

Although the Russian consul admired the prince, he was delighted to leave Bulgaria. When he arrived in Bucharest, on his way home, he wrote with joy to Giers, "I am finally out of that galley. All that I ask is that no one will ever mention the word Bulgaria to me." In a final analysis of conditions in the principality, he expressed confidence in the prince, "the only good card that Bulgaria holds," praised his "calm, his judgment, and his good sense," and compared him to Leopold I of Belgium. Nevertheless, Davydov was convinced that Bulgaria could be saved from disaster only by a modification of the constitution. As a climax to his bitter experiences in Sofia, Davydov reported that his trunk with all his official papers had been stolen between Sofia and Ruschuk.[72]

Before he left the country, Davydov had been confident that if elections were held and if the tsar permitted his name to be used freely in the campaign, a Conservative victory would be guaranteed. But when Alexander, in accordance with the tsar's suggestion, ordered new elections to be held, on January 13/25, 1880, the Liberals again emerged triumphant, and the new assembly was to be under their control. The prince realized that Parensov would oppose any plans he might make

[70] Corti, *DTD*, pp. 372–374; Skazkin, p. 230.
[71] Skazkin, p. 231; Miliutin, III, 191.
[72] Davydov to Giers, *NKG*, Bucharest, Jan. 28/Feb. 8, 1880.

for the strengthening of his powers. When he heard of the recall of Davydov, he blamed the general for this too. Consequently, he determined to go to St. Petersburg to plead his case personally and seek the dismissal of the minister.

Before he could leave Bulgaria, Alexander was required by the constitution to appoint a regent for the period of his absence. Unexpectedly, Parensov was his choice for the post. Parensov was flattered and pleased that he, a thirty-six-year-old major general, had been selected to be the head of a principality, even if only for a short time. But he was not prepared to accept the conditions attached to his appointment. Davydov informed him that Alexander was determined to abolish the constitution and that he would not return to Bulgaria under the existing circumstances. Therefore, the prince would send Parensov orders from St. Petersburg to suspend the constitution and place the country under a regime in which the prince would have unlimited powers for seven years. When Parensov asked what he was to do if the nation disagreed, Davydov replied that he should use bayonets to enforce the decision. Parensov naturally reacted violently to the proposal. Only if the tsar ordered it would he carry out such a plan; otherwise he would use the army to defend the constitution. Having failed to secure the coöperation of the general, Alexander appointed Bishop Kliment as regent and, accompanied by Davydov, left for Russia.[73]

The imminent arrival of the prince in Russia caused much concern. Miliutin was particularly anxious, since Davydov's reports, especially his last, had made a favorable impression on the tsar. On February 2/14, 1880, Alexander II ordered Miliutin, Giers, and Dondukov-Korsakov again to review the Bulgarian situation. Giers continued to defend Davydov's position, but Dondukov could foresee only harm to Russian interests if a forceful *coup d'état* were effected. They decided to wait for a personal report from Shepelev, who arrived in St. Petersburg on February 4/16. When the three officials met with Shepelev, Miliutin again "quarreled with Giers, who could not liberate himself from the influence of the false views of Davydov." Giers believed that Alexander should be advised only to remain within legal limits. The others felt that specific guidance should be given to the prince because it was necessary to "divert him from the various harmful and unprofitable tendencies and enterprises." Since agreement could not be reached, it was decided that Giers should meet with Alexander to find out exactly what the prince desired.[74]

---

[73] Parensov, *op. cit.*, CXXXIII, 263–268.
[74] Miliutin, III, 209–210, 213.

In his conversations with both Giers and Miliutin, Alexander made a favorable impression. To Giers he denied that he wished to effect a *coup d'état* or to introduce German officers into the army, and reaffirmed his devotion to Russia. In the subsequent meeting with Miliutin, on February 15/27, Alexander maintained the same tone of moderation. He objected to the title "Excellency," which only the military in Bulgaria used in addressing him; the European and even the Russian diplomats called him "Highness." He complained bitterly about Parensov's behavior and said he could no longer keep him in office. In his diary Miliutin commented that if even half of what he had heard were true, Parensov was indeed prejudiced and lacking in tact. The Russian minister admitted that although the prince was young and inexperienced, he was in a difficult position because of the party quarrels and "the intellectual backwardness of the people." The next day Miliutin reported to the tsar on his conversation with the prince. At this meeting Alexander II decided to approve the use of the term "Highness" by the Russian military personnel without waiting for a constitutional amendment. As a result of this decision, Parensov was recalled. Having accomplished his first goal, the prince now turned to the constitutional problem.[75]

In December, 1879, he had written to his father that "the worse the Russians make it for me, the firmer I shall be,"[76] but this confidence was soon dispelled. Although the prince had a complete plan for a new constitution "in his pocket," neither Giers nor Miliutin could offer him any encouragement; the tsar had not altered the opinion he had expressed in November,[77] in spite of the intervention of Alexander of Hesse on his son's behalf. Disillusioned and dispirited, the prince realized that he would still have to rule with the constitution, but at least Parensov would not be there to defend it with "16,000 bayonets."

On March 20/April 1, less than a year after he had been elected prince, Alexander returned to Sofia from St. Petersburg. Four problems had faced him: the question of his title, the control of the army, the bitter Liberal-Conservative party strife, and the constitutional limitations on his powers. Only in the controversy concerning his title had he achieved the results he desired, but the year had not been totally lost. He had gained immeasurably in experience and wisdom. Moreover, he felt sure that if he continued to be unable to rule with the constitution, the tsar would sanction more drastic measures to strengthen his powers.

---

[75] *Ibid.*, pp. 216, 220; Parensov, *op. cit.*, CXXXIV, 20–26.
[76] Corti, *DTD*, p. 263.
[77] Miliutin, III, 226–229.

For Russia the first year of Bulgarian self-administration had revealed the contradictions in the Russian attitude toward the principality. Certainly, the basic dilemma in Bulgarian politics for the succeeding decade arose from the nature of the government established at this time under Russian sponsorship. First, Russia had allowed the Bulgarian representatives to adopt the form of constitutional government they preferred. The Tyrnovo constitution and the rise to legislative dominance of the Liberal party followed. Second, the Bulgarian prince was determined that neither Russia nor the political parties should impose their demands upon him. The duality of the nature of the Bulgarian government—authoritarian as embodied in the person of the prince, and liberal as expressed by the Tyrnovo constitution and the power of the Liberal party—made the smooth functioning of Bulgarian administration impossible. The logical arbiter between the two groups was the Russian government, which, however, desired to stay aloof from the conflicts in Bulgarian political life. Aside from the Bulgarian military establishment or foreign affairs in general, the Russian government did not formulate a clear policy in regard to its aims within Bulgaria. Problems were met as they arose; interference was limited to the recall of representatives whose personal policies were disavowed and to the advice to Alexander to adhere to the constitution.

The lack of a clearly defined policy on individual Bulgarian internal issues meant that the Russian agents in Bulgaria had no guidance in these matters. Because of the nature of the Russian position in Bulgaria, it would have been difficult for these men to have remained apart from the controversies even if they had been so inclined. Being without instructions, they naturally followed their own predilections. The duality within the Russian government was thus reflected in the opposing activities of Parensov and Davydov. Despite the obvious harm done to Russian influence in Bulgaria by their quarrels, no attempt was made to ensure unity of action between the Russian diplomatic and military agents in Sofia. The pattern of conflict between prince and legislature, Russian consul and Russian military representative, remained constant throughout the period under study.

Although the first year of Bulgarian independence had been difficult, Russian prestige was high, and the Bulgarian people still thought well of the "tsar-liberator." The prince, though strongly anti-Russian, admired and respected his uncle, Alexander II. Bulgaria was still in fact and in natural inclination within the Russian orbit.

III

THE RUSSO-BULGARIAN CONTROVERSY OVER THE RAILROADS AND THE CONSTITUTION

DURING the second year of Russo-Bulgarian relations, the policy of Russia remained that of professed noninterference in Bulgarian internal affairs. Two problems, however, arose which eventually forced the Russian government to take a stand in Bulgarian domestic matters. The first, the Bulgarian railroads, whose construction had been provided for in the Treaty of Berlin, became a source of friction and misunderstanding. The second, the change in the constitution, marked a shift in the attitude of the Russian government toward the balance of political power in Bulgaria.

On March 24/April 5, 1880, Dragan Tsankov was selected as leader of the newly formed Liberal government, apparently because he was the least offensive candidate. He immediately displayed his tact by addressing the prince as "Highness," thus ending that source of controversy. Petko Karavelov, the most influential member of the Liberal party, was given the post of minister of finance and, in addition, acquired the important position of party leader in the assembly.

The only other significant member of the government was the minister of war, K. G. Ernrot, one of the most controversial figures in Russian dealings with the Bulgars. A Finn who had risen in the Russian military service, General Ernrot was an able officer of conservative tendencies and a strong will. When he was recommended to Alexander, the latter decided that, before his selection was finally determined, the general should agree to certain basic points. In a number of discussions between the two, the prince demanded in effect that Ernrot agree to be simply an instrument of his will and obey his commands as he would those of the tsar. Ernrot, however, refused to accept these stipulations, despite the fact that the tsar himself felt that the Bulgarian minister of war, even if Russian in nationality, should follow the dictates of the prince. When Miliutin heard of Alexander's demands, he described them as "childish," and remarked that he personally would not serve under such conditions. Alexander finally modified his stand, so that the general would take the office, and requested the tsar to appoint him minister of war.[1] Thus, at the time of Ernrot's appointment, it appeared that he

---

[1] Corti, *Alexander*, pp. 81–82; Black, p. 181; Hajek, *Bulgariens Befreiung und staatliche Entwicklung unter seinem ersten Fürsten*, pp. 174–175.

would occupy a strong and independent position in the Bulgarian cabinet.[2]

When Alexander was in St. Petersburg negotiating with Ernrot, the Russian government sent instructions to A. M. Kumani, who replaced Davydov as consul general in Sofia. These reaffirmed Russia's previous decision to advise the prince to continue to rule constitutionally and not to employ any drastic means to strengthen his position. Although Kumani did not share the views of his predecessor, Davydov, that force should be used to change the constitution, he was not convinced of the value of that document as an instrument of government. On February 17/29 Kumani had reported to the Russian government that the Bulgarian constitution was a hastily concocted "magna charta," and he recommended that it be allowed to display its "uselessness"—"let it, so to speak, exhaust itself."[3]

Although Dragan Tsankov had the reputation of being a man ready to compromise, he soon ran into problems of domestic politics that he could not handle, and was compelled to resign. His liberal government lasted only until the fall of 1880. Petko Karavelov formed the new ministry on October 28/November 9, 1880. He was forced to meet the first of the two great domestic problems of that year involving relations with Russia—the problem of the Bulgarian railroads.

THE BULGARIAN RAILROADS

The role assigned to the Bulgarian railroads in the Russian plans for the defense of the Straits has been discussed. The construction of the Bulgarian network was not, however, a matter to be settled exclusively by Russia and Bulgaria, since the other Balkan states and the great powers were directly involved. In the second half of the nineteenth century the Balkan Peninsula was looked upon as one of the most fertile areas for exploitation and development by the European railroad concerns. The move to tap the resources and markets of the Balkans and to unite Europe by rail with the vast Turkish Empire was a natural step in European economic expansion. The enthusiasm of Sultan Abdul Aziz and Sultan Abdul Hamid II facilitated the tasks of the entrepreneurs and contributed to the eventual political and economic domination of the Ottoman lands by foreign powers.

In the 'sixties British and French investors had obtained concessions to build railroads from the ports of Dedeagatch, Constantinople, and Varna extending inland into the Balkan Peninsula. These lines pene-

---

[2] Miliutin, III, 229–232.
[3] Skazkin, p. 266.

trated central Bulgaria, but they did not link up with the Austrian railroads. After the political and military defeats of the 'sixties and the economic crisis of the early 'seventies, Vienna was forced to look to her southern neighbors for new markets and raw materials. Through the efforts of the Austrian government, Baron Hirsch, an Austrian railroad magnate, obtained a concession from the Turks to build lines to the south, which ultimately were to join the railroads which commenced on the Aegean Sea and the Straits, but before the enterprise had really been launched, the crisis of 1875 forced the suspension of all plans.

As soon as the Russo-Turkish War was over, Austria-Hungary resumed her aggressive railroad policy. The Russian abandonment of Serbia to the Dual Monarchy in 1878 gave the latter a real opportunity. On June 26/July 8, 1878, during the meetings of the Berlin congress, Andrassy and Jovan Ristić, Serbian foreign minister, concluded a convention which stipulated that Austria was to join her rail network to that of Serbia at Belgrade within three years. Serbia in turn was to develop her system further and, with Austrian diplomatic aid, to unite her lines with those of Bulgaria and Turkey. In Article 38 of the Treaty of Berlin, Serbia formally assumed the sultan's responsibilities with regard to Austria and her companies for railroad construction in Serbian lands formerly under Turkish suzerainty. Article 10 similarly bound Bulgaria to undertake the obligations entered into by the Porte with Austria and her representatives, as well as with the British for the Varna-Ruschuk line. The Treaty of Berlin stated that immediately after the peace settlement the governments of Austria-Hungary, Turkey, Serbia, and Bulgaria were to meet to work out the details of the railroad settlement. This condition was not fulfilled for two years.[4]

Meanwhile Austria continued to press her plans in regard to Serbia. She was extremely anxious to see the completion of the lines Belgrade-Niš, Niš-Pirot, and Niš-Vranje, which would link Vienna with Constantinople and Salonika as soon as the Turkish and Bulgarian lines were completed. The main obstacle to the development of the Serbian railroads was the condition of the Serbian treasury. Serbia had emerged from the recent war with Turkey in no position to undertake an expensive construction program. The postponement of the building of the railroad beyond the three years envisaged in the Andrassy-Ristić agreement was thus of vital importance for the financial stability of the nation. Seeking a delay, Serbia proposed that the meeting of the four powers, Austria-Hungary, Turkey, Serbia, and Bulgaria, which had been agreed to in Berlin, be held at once to discuss the entire railroad

---

[4] *Ibid.*, pp. 256–260; Hertslet, *The Map of Europe by Treaty*, IV, 2788; Jovanović, *Milan*, II, 209–216.

problem on a quadripartite basis. In this manner the Serbian government hoped to remove the three-year limit on the completion of its lines. Since Bulgaria and Turkey were not so obligated, Serbia hoped to obtain an agreement in which all four powers were bound only to build their lines simultaneously, with no set date for completion. An extension of time would thus be gained.[5]

Although in principle Austria was not opposed to quadripartite negotiations, she insisted on the prior fulfillment of the Andrassy-Ristić agreement. Undoubtedly, Austrian interests would be served by the immediate completion of the Austrian-Serbian link in the international line. The Serbian position was just the opposite. Serbia could benefit from the railroad through her territory only if the Turkish and Bulgarian sections of the international line were completely open. Then she could find to the south alternate markets for her raw materials and could charge for the use of her railroads. If only the link to Vienna were built, and the Turkish and Bulgarian governments delayed the construction of their section, Serbia would continue to be bound firmly to the Habsburg monarchy because of the latter's overwhelming political and economic preponderance. The shaky condition of Serbian finances, burdened further by the necessity of building a railroad in three years, would increase Serbian subservience to Vienna. Although Austria was interested principally in the completion of the international line, which was of even greater importance to her than the connection with Serbia alone, she had no means of compelling Bulgaria or Turkey to complete their lines. In order to be assured of some immediate advantages from her railroad policy, the Habsburg government refused to accept the Serbian arguments for a four-power meeting, and put pressure on Belgrade to begin the line. Then, at least, Vienna would have been able to exploit more fully the Serbian resources.

Unable to gain a delay, the Serbian government next tried to obtain a postponement of the construction of the Niš-Pirot and Niš-Vranje extensions to the Belgrade-Niš line, which they had agreed to build. Vienna refused to consider a change. As a last resort Serbia reluctantly agreed to build the Belgrade-Niš-Vranje system, which would link eventually with Salonika, but not the other branch. When the Austrian minister continued to press for the full program, Ristić replied: "What can you do? You can occupy Serbia. That would be a political misfortune for us, but if we sign a clause which will effect our financial collapse, we will burden the land with a greater economic misfortune."[6]

[5] Jovanović, *Milan*, II, 255–257; Duchâtel to Saint-Hilaire, *DDF*, III, no. 289, Vienna, Nov. 1, 1880.

[6] Jovanović, *Milan*, II, 259.

Faced with the threat of Ristić that he would resign rather than agree to all the Austrian terms, the Austrian government finally yielded. On March 28/April 9, 1880, Serbia agreed to build within three years a railroad running from Belgrade to Niš to Vranje, but not a line from Niš to Pirot. When the Skupština (parliament) attacked the arrangement as furthering the economic exploitation of Serbia, Ristić could defend his position only by arguing that eventually the line would link Belgrade with Salonika, thus ending the dependence of Serbia on Austrian trade.[7]

Having assured the completion of the line through Serbia, Austria shifted her attention to Bulgaria and Turkey. She was now ready for quadripartite negotiations. Moreover, by the summer of 1880 Austria was convinced that the rights to railroad concessions in Bulgaria granted to her at Berlin were being threatened by a relative newcomer to the Balkan economic scene—Russia.

The economic importance of the Balkan Peninsula and the possibilities for investment in the area which attracted the Austrians and others did not escape the Russian entrepreneurs. These men, like the Russian government, believed that Bulgaria would show her gratitude to Russia for the sacrifices of the war of liberation by giving preference to the Russians in all matters where other powers were competing. They also believed that Russian rather than Austrian firms should be allowed to build the railroads in Bulgaria. The Russian company of Baron Giuntsburg and S. Poliakov thus ran into direct competition with the Austrian firm of Baron Hirsch.[8]

Giuntsburg and Poliakov represented one of the strongest Russian investment concerns. They wished to exploit especially the banks and railroads in Bulgaria. In 1879 a well-known publicist, E. I. Utin, had persuaded the Bulgarian government that Giuntsburg should be permitted to establish a national bank in Bulgaria. Utin was assisted in his endeavors by the Russian representatives in Bulgaria, who appeared eager to intercede in behalf of the Russian businessmen. In January, 1880, Shepelev informed Miliutin, who relayed the message to Giers, that the Bulgarian government, with the prince's consent, had approved Giuntsburg's request to establish a bank. This institution was to have the right to issue bank bonds, coin money, establish savings and municipal loan banks, and be exempt from various taxes and duties. S. A. Greig, Russian minister of finance, wrote a memorandum in opposition, claiming that Bulgaria would be dominated by such a bank. Moreover,

---

[7] *Ibid.*, pp. 259–263; Canclaux to Saint-Hilaire, *DDF*, III, no. 325, Belgrade, Jan. 3, 1881.

[8] Skazkin, p. 261.

since Giuntsburg had connections with Parisian banking firms, French influence in Bulgaria would increase. Greig urged that Bulgaria be advised to establish a state bank, not a private bank. The entire scheme collapsed when the Liberals took charge of the Bulgarian government. The negotiations for the bank had been carried on during the Conservative ministry and had been approved by it. Once out of power, however, the Conservatives were perfectly willing to use the issue to discredit their Liberal opponents.[9]

Although the Russian government showed no enthusiasm for the bank scheme, the activities of Russian financiers in regard to the railroads were bound to receive attention, since they involved Russian foreign policy. For both economic and strategic reasons, Russia wished to secure the construction of a railroad in Bulgaria which would commence along the Danube, probably at Ruschuk or Sistova, and proceed across the Balkan mountains down to the valley of the Maritsa River. This route would correspond in general to the avenue of advance followed by the Russian army in 1877, and could be used to bring Russian troops nearer the Straits in case of war with Turkey or Britain.

Certain important considerations stood in the way of the construction of such a line, however. In the first place, Bulgaria, like Serbia, was in no position to undertake a large program of railway building. She could not afford to construct both the Danube line and the international line running from Niš through Sofia to Constantinople, which she was obliged to complete according to the terms of the Treaty of Berlin. Moreover, the Russian line offered little of economic value to the Bulgars, especially in comparison with the international line, which could carry Bulgarian goods to the central European markets. Jomini was not surprised at the Bulgarian government's objections to the Russian line, since, he wrote, Russia had "nothing to buy or sell in Bulgaria."[10] The Russian line, though of benefit to Russia in time of war, would, as Jomini admitted, have turned Bulgaria into a future battlefield.[11] From the Russian point of view, the international line was disadvantageous in that it would result in the strengthening of economic ties between Bulgaria and central Europe.

The interest shown by the Habsburg government in the building of the Balkan railroads meant that if the Russian government were to push the construction of the Danube line, it would immediately be opposed by the Dual Monarchy. Since the Russian policy at this time was that of agreement with the German powers and maintenance of the *status*

---

[9] *Ibid.*, pp. 261–263.
[10] Jomini to Giers, *NKG*, St. P., Nov. 4, 1880.
[11] *Loc. cit.*

quo in the Near East, an active policy in regard to the Bulgarian rail-road problem could not be adopted. The position of the Dual Monarchy was legally correct; Russia could not openly challenge the Treaty of Berlin for the sake of the relatively small gains that could be won from a victory in the railroad controversy. The Russian government was unwilling to endanger its foreign policy by taking an open stand on the issue; but it was unwilling also to aid the Bulgarian government finan-cially, even though it might thereby have secured the construction of the Danube line.[12]

The negotiations for the formation of the Dreikaiserbund, which were under way at this time, were, of course, unknown to any but the actual participants. The Russian representatives in Bulgaria, the Rus-sian businessmen, and the pro-Russian Bulgars were not aware of, nor could they be expected to be sympathetic to, the policy of friendship and coöperation with the German powers. The Panslav zeal and crusad-ing spirit of the Russo-Turkish War had slackened, but it was not dead. The issue of German encroachment in the Balkan Peninsula to the detriment of the Slavs was vital to the Bulgars and the Russians on the scene. They wished not only to resist "German" or "western" domina-tion, but also to keep the profits of economic enterprise in Russian and Bulgarian hands. Two trends of opinion were thus in conflict in regard to the railroad: the desire of the Russian foreign office to come to an agreement with the German powers, and the natural desire of the Bulgarian and Russian interests in Bulgaria to keep the profits for themselves and to exclude the traditional opponent. To the basic conflict was added the struggle for power between the two major political parties in Bulgaria and between the rival concerns interested in rail-road construction. The tendency of the Russian representatives in Sofia to follow a personal policy of their own choosing played a part in this connection.

The confusion attending the railroad controversy, which remained a constant factor in Russo-Bulgarian relations, was largely the fault of the Russian government. In theory, the policy of the Dreikaiserbund should have taken precedence over other considerations of foreign policy. Since Bulgaria played a major role in the discussions with Germany and Austria-Hungary, Russia should have controlled the actions of her representatives in Sofia in a matter that was bound to have international repercussions. Instead, no serious attempt was made to guarantee that the Russians in Bulgaria would follow a policy con-

---

[12] Jomini to Giers, *NKG*, Aug. 25, Oct. 3, Oct. 28, 1880; Giers to Jomini, *NKG*, Livadia, Oct. 21, Oct. 28, 1880.

sistent with that of the Russian foreign office. Nor does it appear that
Russia abandoned the hope that the Danube line would be constructed,
even at the expense of the Austrian interests.[13] Affairs were allowed to
drift, and there was an unfortunate lack of liaison between Sofia and
St. Petersburg. Because of the failure of the Russian foreign office to
keep a firm hand on the actions of its agents in Bulgaria, the negotiations on the railroad issue were confusing and contradictory. The
eventual result was extremely disadvantageous to Russia.

Four principal groups were interested in railroad construction in
Bulgaria. The first two, that of Baron Hirsch, backed by Austria-
Hungary, and that of the Russians Giuntsburg and Poliakov, have been
mentioned. Two others were soon to appear. The Austro-French
Staatsbahn offered as an alternative to the Danube line a new scheme
which would nevertheless be favorable to Russia. The company proposed
to build a railway from Craiova in Wallachia to Alexandria, then by
way of Sistovo-Tyrnovo-Shipka to the Rumelian border. This line would
be of advantage in diverting traffic from the Belgrade-Sofia line, and
could be used by Russian interests as well as Austrian. Through Kumani
this group asked for a loan from the Russian government. St. Petersburg refused the request, but suggested that Russian entrepreneurs be
invited to participate in the company. Although Austrian interests were
represented in the company, it did not have the backing of the Habsburg
government in the manner enjoyed by Baron Hirsch and his concern.
Therefore the Staatsbahn commanded the support of Kumani and the
Bulgarian interests.[14]

To compete with the first three groups, another, of purely Bulgarian
character, soon appeared. In Sofia a group of businessmen, who were
active in the Conservative party, organized to try to gain some profit
from the Bulgarian railroads. The leaders of this group were the contractor Khadzhienov, mayor of Sofia, together with the Conservative
triumvirate of G. D. Nachevich, D. P. Grekov, and K. Stoilov. The
entrance of a purely Bulgarian firm was a great hindrance to the
Russian enterprise. Previously, when the issue had been that of granting concessions to Austrian or Russian firms, the Russian could expect
to triumph. Now Bulgarian national interest was to oppose both foreign
competitors.[15]

In the first phase of the controversy the leading role was played by
Kumani, who, irrespective of any instructions to the contrary from St.

---

[13] Skazkin, pp. 265–266; Miliutin, IV, 42; Giers to Jomini, *NKG*, Livadia, Oct.
30, 1880.
[14] Skazkin, p. 266.
[15] *Ibid.*, pp. 268–269.

Petersburg, pursued a personal policy of opposition to Austro-Hungarian interests and support for the Danube line.[16] In the summer of 1880 he had the sympathy and coöperation of the Liberal prime minister, Dragan Tsankov. When Austria requested that the quadripartite meeting be held to implement the provisions of the Treaty of Berlin, Tsankov immediately consulted Kumani. The Bulgarian government would delay its answer until advice had been received from St. Petersburg. Tsankov, at the same time, expressed the hope that the Russian government would support the desire of the Russian companies to build the Bulgarian railways. Otherwise Bulgarian interests would fall under Austrian control.[17]

Russia, in reply, advised the Bulgars to attend the quadripartite meeting. It was suggested, however, that they could plead that it was financially impossible for Bulgaria to undertake construction on the international line at once.[18] Russia did not, it should be noted, officially advise either that the Bulgars should try to avoid the obligations incurred under the Treaty of Berlin in regard to the international line, or that they should undertake the immediate construction of the Danube or "Russian" line. Kumani, nevertheless, continued to press the question. He supported the stand of the Staatsbahn group at first, but subsequently shifted to Giuntsburg and his interests.

Despite the fact that the Liberal party had thus shown itself sympathetic to Russian railroad interests, it began to change its position soon after the formation of the Karavelov government. Karavelov was extremely conservative and careful in regard to the handling of national finances. To him railways were in a sense a luxury which Bulgaria could ill afford so long as schools and roads needed attention.[19] Moreover, the Khadzhienov group, with Conservative party support, now joined the French-Austrian Staatsbahn faction to combat Kumani and the Giuntsburg concern. The Liberals, faced with a confused situation, had become reluctant to make concessions to any of the competitors. Kumani and the Russian interests in turn considered the Bulgarian government ungrateful and disloyal.

The recall of Kumani in March, 1881, was a serious blow to the Giuntsburg company. Ernrot, who now became concerned in the railroad controversy, had his own opinions and policies. Although, like Kumani, he believed that the Russian government should press for the construction of the Danube line, he thought it advisable that the rail-

[16] Miliutin, III, 276–277.
[17] Skazkin, pp. 265–266.
[18] Jomini to Giers, *NKG*, Aug. 25, Oct. 3, 1880; Giers to Jomini, *NKG*, Livadia, Oct. 25, Nov. 11, 1880; Miliutin, III, 276.
[19] Black, pp. 85–87, 261–264.

way be built by the Khadzhienov group in coöperation with the Staatsbahn. Thus Conservative party support could be obtained for an enterprise from which its members could hope to profit.[20]

The position of Prince Alexander in the struggle over the railroads was a difficult one. He was under pressure from the Austrian government, Baron Hirsch, the Russian representatives, and the Giuntsburg-Poliakov concern. He personally agreed with the official position of the Russian government that the international line was a "moral obligation." He also saw its advantages for Bulgaria, in particular the fact that it would tie Bulgaria closer to the culture and civilization of the west.[21]

The controversy over the railroads, however, was relegated to the background by the constitutional issue which now dominated the Bulgarian political picture. The conflict between the prince and the Liberal party had proceeded concurrently with the railroad discussions.

THE CHANGE IN THE CONSTITUTION

Once in control of the government in the spring of 1880, the Liberal party sought to exploit its position. Through the party newspaper *Nezavisimost* it advocated constitutional changes which, in effect, would have made the prince a constitutional monarch with ministers chosen by and responsible to the assembly. Although nothing came of these proposals, the Liberals did succeed in gaining for Karavelov additional powers when the assembly adjourned in the fall of 1880.[22]

These and other measures put through by the Liberals affected the prince's morale. He saw his power and prestige attacked, and feared that his popular support was waning. He understandably placed the blame squarely on the constitution and the Liberal party. The latter, he believed, did not represent the true interests of the Bulgarian people, but had gained power by grandiose promises beyond hope of immediate realization. The policy of the Liberals not only prevented the administration of the state in ways he approved, but also prevented his marriage. He could not believe, as he wrote his father, "that any father would give me his daughter so long as things were in such a state in the country."[23] Depressed and embittered, Alexander told the Austrian representative, Khevenhüller, that fate had pushed him into Slavic politics, but that his heart was not in it.[24]

[20] Skazkin, p. 271.
[21] *Ibid.*, p. 272.
[22] Black, pp. 187–190.
[23] Corti, *DTD*, p. 270.
[24] Khevenhüller to Haymerle, *HHS*, XV 18, no. 1A–J, vertraulich, Sofia, Jan. 15, 1881.

Alexander's solution to his dilemma was one he had frequently advocated in the past—a change in the constitution to give him the increased personal power he felt he needed. In January, 1881, he again wrote to the tsar of his difficulties and emphasized the patience he had exhibited in trying to administer the country under the "impossible" constitution.[25] In February he spoke to the British representative of the necessity of presenting to the Grand National Assembly the alternatives of a change in the constitution or his abdication.[26] His determination to solve the question at once is reflected in his letter of January 15/27, 1881, to his father. "Now that I have realized that a crisis is bound to come," he wrote, "my aim must be to bring it about as soon as possible."[27]

Meanwhile, events were occurring in Russia which were to strengthen his hand. On March 1/13, 1881, after numerous unsuccessful attempts, a group of Russian revolutionaries assassinated Alexander II, Bulgaria's "tsar-liberator." The atrocity was a terrible blow to Prince Alexander. He had frequently expressed his deep regard for his uncle, and had reserved his animosity for the tsar's close advisers.[28] Hitherto the prince had always had in the tsar a sympathetic adviser and a close friend. His relations with his cousin, the new tsar, had never been and were never to be so intimate and congenial. On the day after the assassination Alexander left for St. Petersburg to attend the funeral of the late tsar and to meet with Alexander III.

In the grave atmosphere of the Russian capital, the popular revulsion against the assassins was everywhere apparent. Wherever Alexander went, he heard talk of the need to suppress the radical agitators and those who sympathized with or supported the assassins. The brief revival of the reforming spirit in 1880 under M. T. Loris-Melikov, minister of the interior, was now abruptly ended. Alexander could see that those in power in Russia were determined to combat vigorously the expression of political sentiments which corresponded to those held by the Bulgarian Liberals. The impression that reaction had set in and that no type of liberalism would be tolerated by the new regime was the most important information that Alexander gained from his visit to Russia. He was able to exploit this fully only after his return to Bulgaria.[29]

---

[25] Miliutin, IV, 16.

[26] Lascelles to Granville, *FO*, 78/3308, no. 11, Sofia, Feb. 10, 1881.

[27] Corti, *DTD*, p. 270.

[28] *Loc. cit.*

[29] Matveev, "Bolgariia i Vostochnaia Rumeliia posle Berlinskago Kongressa," *Istoricheskii Viestnik*, XXIV (1886), 590.

Alexander again reminded the authorities in St. Petersburg of his feelings concerning the constitution and his difficulties in ruling with it. Although his views were more sympathetically received this time, the Russian government still would not alter the advice previously given that the prince rule within constitutional limits. And once more Alexander had to return home empty-handed.

In his absence a constitutional crisis had developed in Sofia which was to force the whole controversy into the open. Before leaving for the tsar's funeral the prince had been required to nominate a regent to act in his place. Instead of appointing the president of the council of ministers, Karavelov, the prince preferred to entrust the regency to the council of ministers as a collective body. Of this group he trusted only the Russian general, K. G. Ernrot, who was minister of war and who now became foreign minister as well.[30]

The role played by Ernrot in Bulgarian politics in 1880 had not been spectacular. Devoted to his work as war minister, he enforced order and efficiency, but he could not escape becoming involved in the domestic maneuverings and intrigues of Bulgaria. Whereas in the spring of 1880 he had given every indication that he would defend the constitution, by the end of that year his experiences convinced him that the Liberal party was seeking to use the constitution to destroy the power of the prince and to usurp his authority. Consequently, Ernrot turned against his fellow ministers and rallied to the support of the prince. For a time the situation was so delicate that he was not consulted, or invited to attend meetings of the ministerial council. By January, 1881, Ernrot was ready to resign, and it was feared that other Russian officers would follow his example.[31]

When Alexander was in St. Petersburg in March he had discussed the matter with Miliutin. Although opposed to Ernrot's resignation, Alexander hoped that if Ernrot did leave the ministry, he would be made the Russian diplomatic representative to replace Kumani, whose recall was being requested. As an alternative to this suggestion, Alexander wanted Ernrot to remain as an aide. Miliutin, apparently, made no positive decision on this occasion.[32]

During Alexander's absence from Sofia, Ernrot became convinced that the policy of the Liberal party would lead to chaos and anarchy in Bulgaria, and that Bulgaria's only hope lay in the adoption of the prince's suggestion that the constitution be amended or even tempo-

[30] Lascelles to Granville, *FO*, 78/3308, no. 19, Sofia, March 14, 1881; Black, p. 194.
[31] Miliutin, IV, 16.
[32] *Ibid.*, pp. 38–39.

rarily suspended in order to increase the royal power. When Alexander returned to Sofia, Ernrot presented him with an ultimatum: alter the constitution or he would resign.[33]

Ernrot's stand placed Alexander in a very difficult position. He had become attached to his minister of war and was ready to take almost any measures to induce him to remain in Sofia. In February he told the British representative, Frank C. Lascelles, that Ernrot had given him "most loyal" support and that without his assistance "he would not have been able to oppose the will of the chamber."[34] The prince had become isolated from his Liberal ministers and consequently more dependent on Ernrot. If Ernrot were forced to resign, the prince would find himself at the mercy of the Karavelovites, particularly if the constitution remained unaltered. Both Alexander and his war minister were convinced that the constitution was a hindrance to stable government, and both mistrusted the Liberals. Alexander believed that he had shown "patience" in permitting the Liberals to exhibit their administrative abilities under the "impossible constitution." The performance had been a manifest failure. His dislike for the Liberals was further increased when he heard a report that during his absence Karavelov had toasted the tsar's assassins.[35] Added to these considerations was the vivid impression that Alexander had gained in St. Petersburg that the new tsar and his immediate advisers had no sympathy for liberals or radicals.

Since 1879 Alexander had wanted to alter the constitution, but he realized that he could not do it alone. Now he could rely on the assistance of his minister of war, a Russian and the commander of the Bulgarian army. When Ernrot's predecessor Parensov held that position, Alexander had not dared to act against the constitution because he could not be certain of the army. Now he decided to adopt a positive course of action. A similar opportunity might not arise again. If he failed, he felt that he might as well abdicate at this time rather than be forced out later.

The decision to change the constitution involved not only Bulgarian domestic politics but relations with Europe as well. As a creation of the Congress of Berlin, Bulgaria was both a semiprotectorate of Russia and a ward of the other great powers. Their reaction to any tampering with the governmental structure of Bulgaria had to be taken into account. For several weeks before taking action, Alexander and Ernrot prepared the ground. On May 2 Alexander spoke to the British repre-

---

[33] Koch, p. 88; Corti, *Alexander*, pp. 99–100; Skazkin, pp. 238–239.
[34] Lascelles to Granville, *FO*, 78/3308, no. 11, Sofia, Feb. 10, 1881.
[35] Koch, pp. 47, 87.

sentative, Lascelles, of the difficulties in Bulgaria and of the arbitrary rule of the Liberals while he was abroad. Some solution to the problem was necessary. He assured Lascelles that "he would never make a *coup d'état* and that he would certainly not go beyond the limits of legality. He had sworn to observe the constitution and he would not break his oath." He would obtain the "necessary modifications in the constitution" by legal means. If he failed, he would abdicate. He promised to inform the great powers before taking definite measures, "in order that he might not be accused of taking Europe by surprise with a *'fait accompli.'* "[36] On May 4 Lascelles reported that Ernrot stated that the constitution had to be modified "in order to put an end to the present state of things which are intolerable."[37] On May 5, S. Burian, Austria's representative in Sofia, in a dispatch to Vienna, reviewed the Bulgarian situation in detail. He stated that the prince's respect for the constitution kept him from carrying out a *coup d'état*. Alexander and Ernrot wanted to form a new ministry, then call a constitutional assembly and have it suspend the constitution. The approval of the great powers would be requested for this action.[38]

The Austrian and British representatives thus knew that Alexander was contemplating changes in the immediate future, but they expected them to be carried out on a constitutional basis. The Bulgarian Liberals were not so confident of Alexander's devotion to legal means. On May 7 Dragan Tsankov came to the British representative to report and protest against the apparent threat of a *coup d'état*.[39] Two days later the blow fell.

On April 27/May 9, Alexander of Battenberg issued a proclamation to the Bulgarian nation. After referring to his endeavors during the past two years, he asserted that he had "sworn an oath to the constitution" and that this had been kept. The oath obligated him "at the same time to keep the happiness and well-being of the land before my eyes in all my actions." Conditions in the principality conflicted with the attainment of this ideal. Therefore, using his constitutional rights, he would convene the Grand National Assembly and submit to it the changes he deemed necessary, which would be announced later. If the assembly rejected his proposals, he would abdicate. Meanwhile, Ernrot was to form a new ministry of a provisional character "for the purpose of maintaining peace and order and of securing for the population the time necessary for them to comprehend and consider in all its

[36] Lascelles to Granville, *FO*, 78/3308, no. 25, Sofia, May 4, 1881.
[37] *Ibid.*, no. 26, Sofia, May 4, 1881.
[38] Burian to Haymerle, *HHS*, XV 18, no. 10A, réservé, Sofia, May 5, 1881.
[39] Lascelles to Granville, *FO*, 78/3308, no. 40, Sofia, May 7, 1881.

bearings the decisions they are about to make and also of assuring the complete freedom and impartiality of their choice."

On the same day the representatives of the great powers were invited to meet with Ernrot, who explained the reasons for the prince's action. Ernrot repeated the previous charges that the constitution had failed in its purpose, that the actions of the Liberals had discredited the country, and that, although the prince had worked honestly to fulfill his duties, he did not have sufficient authority. Ernrot outlined the main reforms desired, which were publicly announced two weeks later. First, Alexander must be given extraordinary power for seven years and the right to form a new executive body—the council of state. Second, the regular session of the national assembly was to be suspended for a year and the current budget was to remain in force. Third, within seven years Alexander would convene the Grand National Assembly to consider changes in the constitution on the basis of the experience gained in the interval.[40]

Although it was known that the prince was contemplating some action, the nature and suddenness of the announcement caught most people by surprise. The Liberals immediately protested. Tsankov considered Alexander's move "comical," and did not believe that the prince would abdicate. Where could he "find another principality with 600,000 francs a year"?[41] The great question, however, concerned the reaction of Russia. Because of Ernrot's open support of the prince, it was generally assumed that Russia had already given her approval. On May 5, Burian had even informed Vienna that no steps would be taken by the prince without preliminary agreement with St. Petersburg.[42]

Yet there is little doubt that the prince's proclamation came as a complete surprise to the Russian government. General Ernrot, writing in 1886 about the events, candidly stated his case. He asserted that he had informed St. Petersburg early in April, through K. N. Lishin, Kumani's temporary replacement, that a crisis was inevitable in Bulgaria. The Russian government seemed uninterested in this information. Ernrot stated that he did not have direct contact with the Russian foreign ministry on political matters, nor had he even been provided with a proper code. Because he wished to conceal his intentions until it was time to act, he did not deem it advisable to inform St. Petersburg through the Russian diplomatic agent in Sofia. "I had my own reasons

[40] Koch, pp. 90–93; Burian to Haymerle, *HHS,* XV 18, no. 11B, Sofia, May 12, 1881; London *Times,* May 10, 1881, p. 5.
[41] Burian to Haymerle, *HHS,* XV 18, no. 11B, Sofia, May 12, 1881.
[42] *Ibid.,* no. 10A, réservé, Sofia, May 5, 1881.

for this," concluded Ernrot.[43] Thus, while the British and Austrian representatives had been given some advance warning of the prince's plans, the Russian government learned of them only when they were made public to all of Europe.

Miliutin in his diary confirms the fact that the action was a total surprise. He would have expected something like this from Alexander, he confessed, but he could never have believed that such a suggestion would have come from a Russian general. Miliutin had indeed been deceived by Ernrot. When, in January, 1881, Ernrot threatened to resign, Miliutin had believed that the general wished to give up his post because of the current rumors of a *coup d'état*. Miliutin assumed that the latter action was being urged on Alexander by Count Khevenhüller, the Austrian diplomatic agent. Only now did Miliutin realize that his own general was responsible for the prince's decisive step.[44]

The Russian government was forced to take a firm public stand. Alexander's proclamation had many implications, all of which had to be considered carefully. Colonel A. A. Shepelev, who had played an important role in Bulgarian politics during Parensov's time, but who was now stationed in Vienna, wrote a long analysis of the problem on April 28/May 10, the day after the announcement of the intended change in government. Commenting on reports that Alexander wanted to form a ministry composed of foreigners and not Bulgarians, Shepelev said that he believed that this would result in the domination of the government by Austrians and Germans. This situation in turn could produce a popular reaction in Bulgaria which it might take the army to quell, an army which was trained and officered mostly by Russians. It would be sheer irony if these troops were used to subdue agitation against Russia's well-known Balkan adversaries.

Next, Shepelev considered what might happen if the national assembly refused to grant the prince's demands, a circumstance which he expected to arise. Alexander could then either abdicate, as he had threatened, or dissolve the assembly and proclaim a dictatorship. Both alternatives posed difficulties. If the prince abdicated, the Bulgarian problem would again become a European one, since the signators of the Treaty of Berlin would have to be consulted in the selection of a new

---

[43] Ernrot, "K Noveishei Istorii Bolgarii," *Russkaia Starina*, LII (1886), 477; for Sobolev's challenge to Ernrot's policy see pp. 480–483. Kalnoky to Haymerle, *HHS*, X 70, tel. no. 49, St. P., May 12, 1881.

[44] Miliutin, IV, 16, 66; Pokrovskii's claim that the Russian government knew and approved the plans for the *coup d'état* certainly cannot be substantiated by the evidence available. Pokrovskii, *Diplomatiia i Voinyi Tsarskoi Rossii v XIX Stoletii*, p. 346.

ruler. Russia would not be able to solve the problem unilaterally. The establishment of a dictatorship could be accomplished only by the use of the Bulgarian army. Again, since Russia in effect controlled the army, she would be labeled the defender of Bulgarian despotism. This would turn the Bulgarian people against the Russians, and repercussions would be felt in other Balkan lands. Shepelev's advice was that Ernrot should not be permitted to become the Bulgarian minister-president, or, as a stronger measure, should be recalled. Either way, the action would signify Russia's defense of the constitution and her disapproval of Alexander's proposals. Miliutin sent this analysis with his approval to Giers on April 29/May 11.[45]

The advice offered by Shepelev and agreed to by Miliutin appeared sound. The constitution, as Skazkin states, actually helped to preserve Russian influence in Bulgaria by preventing arbitrary action by the prince, by any Bulgarian faction, or by Russian officials in Bulgaria. The constitution was defended in Bulgaria by the Liberals, who commanded majority support from the electorate. Certainly, so far the Liberals had been more sympathetic toward Russia than the Conservatives.[46]

There was, however, one major weakness in this reasoning. If Russia disavowed the prince and Ernrot, a new problem would arise at once. Alexander would certainly not be able to muster enough support in the Grand National Assembly to have his measure approved. If, as seemed likely, the impulsive prince, who had already committed himself beforehand, should abdicate, the Bulgarian problem would then become a European one at precisely the time when it was most detrimental to Russia's general European policy. Since the last stages of the negotiations over the Dreikaiserbund were then in progress, Russia sought to avoid a Balkan crisis.

Opposing the Shepelev solution and revealing the duality of Russia's Bulgarian policy, as reflected in the views of Miliutin and Giers, was a report by Lishin, temporary Russian diplomatic representative in Sofia. On April 30/May 12 he sent his views on the Bulgarian developments to Giers. He insisted that Alexander had the right to ask the electorate to choose between their ruler and the demagogues who claimed to defend the people's rights. The latter, the basis of the Liberal party, came from the Bulgarian intelligentsia, educated in the west or in Russia, who had nothing in common with the average Bulgar. They had returned from abroad without resources but filled "with great hopes and even greater pretensions." Through able orators they had promised the

[45] Miliutin, IV, 72; Skazkin, pp. 243–244.
[46] *Ibid.*, p. 244.

people freedom and wealth. Not they, the Liberals, but the Conservative party truly defended Bulgarian national interests. Although few in number, the Conservatives, who came primarily from the prosperous class, were the real national party in Bulgaria. Lishin so argued in defense of Alexander's proposals. Giers sent Lishin's analysis to the tsar together with Shepelev's report. Alexander III was thus presented with alternative solutions.[47]

When the tsar read the reports, he wrote on Lishin's, "A very clear picture and I am convinced an absolutely correct one." On Shepelev's he wrote, "I never believed Shepelev and always considered him a harmful man and with very suspicious tendencies." The constitutional change was thus approved by the tsar. His decision did not come as a surprise to Giers, who, being aware of the tsar's conservative sentiments, had, according to Skazkin, purposely coupled the conflicting reports, knowing in advance their probable effect.[48]

The tsar's decision was not a hasty one, but the obvious result of Russia's internal and external difficulties. It is understandable that Alexander III should have been horrified at the circumstances of his father's death. The responsibility for the tragedy he assigned to the ideas which had been spread in Russia in the preceding decade by radical groups. His early training under K. P. Pobedonostsev, procurator-general of the Holy Synod, had been strongly conservative, and the revolutionary activities of the reforming groups merely tended to strengthen his previous views. His father's death was to him the clear proof of the danger inherent in all liberal doctrines for the future of Russia. He was prepared to combat revolutionary activity wherever he met it.[49]

In the months prior to his assassination the late tsar had entrusted to Count Loris-Melikov the task of trying to revive and salvage as many of the reforms of the 1860's as possible. Loris-Melikov's committee, the Supreme Directions Commission, had succeeded in working out new reforms which the tsar had approved on the very day of his death. Immediately the question arose whether the new tsar, who had participated in the Loris-Melikov commission and had approved its findings, would carry out his father's decision. Instead of issuing a proclamation to this effect, Alexander III decided to reconsider the entire problem. A week after the assassination he called together the leading minis-

---

[47] *Loc. cit.*

[48] *Loc. cit.*

[49] For a discussion of the reign of Alexander III see Gitermann, *Geschichte Russlands*, III, 272–341; Milioukov, *Histoire de Russie*, III, 979–1030; Lowe, *Alexander III of Russia*; Nechkina, ed., *Istoriia SSSR*, II, 666–693, 768–781; Stählin, *Geschichte Russlands von den Anfängen bis zur Gegenwart*, IV:1, 431–596; Firsov, "Aleksandr III," *Byloe*, XXIX (1929), 85–108.

ters. Miliutin, P. A. Valuev, president of the council of ministers, and A. A. Abaza, minister of finance, approved the report of Loris-Melikov and recommended its adoption. However, S. G. Stroganov, a member of the state council, argued that the reforms would lead ultimately to a constitution and to revolution. L. S. Makov, minister of post and telegraph and member of the state council, also spoke against the reforms, which, he argued, would place a limitation on the autocratic power of the tsar. It was left to Pobedonostsev to deliver the most determined attack on the reforms. He criticized not only Loris-Melikov's proposals but also the great reforms of the late tsar, labeling them a "criminal mistake." After considering these comments, Alexander III decided to postpone a decision. It was obvious that he was reconsidering his earlier acquiescence to the reforms.[50]

In the ensuing weeks Pobedonostsev cleverly and discreetly worked on his former pupil, seeking to turn him against reform. That he was making progress is evident from the comments the tsar wrote on a report from Saburov, dated April 3/15, 1881, in which the latter stated that Bismarck had advised Russia to adopt *"un régime de sévérité."* When the tsar read this, he noted, *"That is so true and right that God grant that every Russian, and especially our ministers* would understand our position as Prince Bismarck understands it and would not adopt for themselves unrealizable fantasies and nasty liberalism."[51] Alexander was not yet ready to make known his final decision. At another meeting of the committee on April 21/May 3 he advised the members to reconcile their differences and act in unison on all major issues.[52] For a while it appeared that some compromise might be reached which would prevent the total abandonment of the reforms, but such hopes were brought to an abrupt end a week later.

On the night of April 28/May 10 the ministers again met to discuss the reforms. The meeting lasted until 1 A.M. Just as the members were about to leave, D. Nabokov, minister of justice, announced that the next day a manifesto to the nation would appear, and he showed them a copy. It stated that Russia could not expect any diminution of the tsar's autocratic powers; the end of the Loris-Melikov reforms was thus signified. At once the members demanded to know who had formulated the manifesto. Pobedonostsev, admitting its authorship, "pale and confused, kept quiet standing as the accused before the judges." Miliutin referred to the episode as *un coup de théâtre,* since just the week before the tsar had ordered his advisers to reach an agreement. Now he pre-

---

[50] Miliutin, IV, 32–36. Pobedonostsev's influence on Alexander III is discussed in Shoob, "Konstantin Petrovich Pobedonostsev: A Study in Reaction."
[51] Skazkin, p. 244 n. 2.
[52] Miliutin, IV, 57–59.

sented them with a *fait accompli*. Loris-Melikov and Abaza immediately resigned and Miliutin said he would join them. The Conservatives had triumphed over the Liberals in Russia.[53]

The important point to note is that the tsar's announcement to his ministers followed by *one* day Alexander of Battenberg's declaration on the Bulgarian constitution. There is no evidence to indicate that this was anything but coincidence, but the prince could not have timed his action better. The news from Sofia reached St. Petersburg just when the tsar was making his decision to forego liberal reform and strengthen his autocratic powers. Now his cousin in Bulgaria was in effect trying to do the same thing. The two men seemed to be thinking similarly at the same time. It was, therefore, almost a certainty that the tsar would approve the prince's action. Alexander of Battenberg had in fact been aided by the actions of the terrorists in Russia.

Another important element must be considered in analyzing the tsar's decision. Whereas the emperor may have been motivated by personal dislike for the Liberals and Radicals, Giers, as acting foreign minister, had to think of the probable reaction of Russia's neighbors. Since the autumn of 1879 he had worked for the creation of the Dreikaiserbund. The months of tedious and at times frustrating negotiations seemed to be drawing to a successful conclusion. Now Alexander of Battenberg had created a dangerous situation. Much of the delay in the completion of the pact was due to Austrian and Russian disagreement over Balkan matters. Vienna was suspicious of the activities of Russia in the area, and questioned her reliability in keeping agreements. If Russia now forced the abdication of Alexander by failing to support his political plans in Bulgaria, Haymerle, who was sympathetic to the prince, might refuse to continue negotiations. Russo-Bulgarian relations belonged within the framework of the projected agreement and they could be understood only within that context. Russia could not afford to sacrifice her general European policy for the sake of a segment of that policy, even though it was an important one. Moreover, if Russia took steps which led to Alexander's abdication, not only might this end the Drei-kaiserbund, but the scope of the Bulgarian problem would be widened. It would be taken out of the hands of Russia, Germany, and Austria; in that event, the wishes of Great Britain, the great adversary of Russia in the east, would have to be considered. Russia, because of her internal and military weaknesses, might conceivably lose the advantages she had achieved in 1878. Prudence dictated that the Bulgarian problem be solved with the least amount of friction. Russian popularity was still so great in Bulgaria that, if Russia supported the prince, the Bulgarian

---

[53] *Ibid.*, pp. 61–63.

electorate would probably accept him. Thus, from the point of view of foreign policy also, Russia chose to endorse the prince of Bulgaria.[54]

Once having committed himself to a positive stand, the tsar gave Alexander his complete support. When, on April 29/May 11, Saburov reported from Berlin that Bismarck had said that if the prince could not rule with the constitution, then it was necessary to try to change it, the tsar wrote on the telegram, "I also have always held that this was the only solution for the disgusting situation in which the prince found himself."[55] On another report by Saburov the tsar wrote, "It is all the same to us how it happened and upon whose advice but *it is necessary for us and we are obligated* to support the prince."[56]

The tsar's feelings were not shared by all elements in Russian society. The first reactions in the press were hostile to the prince. The attacks were led by the liberal newspaper *Golos* with assistance from the conservative *Novoe Vremia* and *St. Peterburgskiia Viedomosti*. *Golos* called Alexander's action an *attentat* against the Bulgarian nation for whose creation thousands of Russians had sacrificed their lives. The conviction was still strong among many Russians that the only real success that Russian diplomacy had achieved in 1878 had been the establishment of a Bulgarian state friendly toward its liberator. Moreover, the constitution which Russia sponsored in Bulgaria appeared to them to be the instrument which kept the German prince from leading Bulgaria out of the Russian into the Austro-German orbit. Therefore, the constitution should be defended at all costs.[57]

In order to check this criticism the Russian government issued instructions to the censors not to permit the publication of attacks on the prince. Only favorable comments could "be freely indulged in."[58] Two very prominent publicists came to the defense of the tsar and the prince. Ivan S. Aksakov in *Rus'* and M. N. Katkov in *Moskovskiia Viedomosti* expressed their admiration for the prince and his "courageous" action. To them the Bulgarian constitution was dangerous and western; a radical change was necessary for the salvation of the Bulgarian nation in its present crisis.[59]

[54] Giers to M. de Fenton, *HHS*, X 70, St. P., June 11, 1881; Kalnoky to Haymerle, *HHS*, X 70, no. 34B, St. P., June 4/16, 1881; Wyndham to Granville, *FO*, 65/1113, no. 347, St. P., June 29, 1881; Trauttenberg to Haymerle, *HHS*, X 70, 39A, vertraulich, St. P., July 1/13, 1881.

[55] Skazkin, p. 245.

[56] *Ibid.*, p. 246.

[57] Kalnoky to Haymerle, *HHS*, X 70, no. 30, St. P., May 23/June 4, 1881; Schweinitz, II, 166–167.

[58] Wyndham to Granville, *FO*, 65/1112, no. 223, St. P., May 18, 1881.

[59] Aksakov, *Slavianskii Vopros'*, pp. 324–335; Radev, I, 276; Wyndham to Granville, *FO*, 65/1114, no. 4B, St. P., Aug. 8, 1881.

After taking measures to see that the proposed change in the constitution was presented to the public in a favorable light in Russia, the
tsar's government moved to secure support for the prince among the
Bulgarian people. A telegram was sent from the tsar to Alexander expressing the hope that his conservative goal would be achieved.[60] At the
same time the government expressed its complete trust in Ernrot, who,
along with the other Russian officers in Bulgaria, was told to aid and
support the prince in his plans.[61] These steps were necessary because the
Bulgarian Liberals were determined to thwart the prince's policy. They
informed the electorate that the action against the constitution had been
carried out against the wishes of Russia. They even appealed to the tsar
"to remind the prince of his oath to defend the constitution" and to
order the Russian officers not to interfere in Bulgarian internal affairs.
This appeal was significant, since the Liberals had the overwhelming
support of the electorate. Unless the tsar made it emphatic that he had
no confidence in them, they still had the power to block the prince. The
tsar, as could be expected, refused even to consider their request and
wrote on the petition, "I do not accept any telegrams from revolutionaries and these Liberals are not anything else but socialists. The Bulgarian people, I am convinced, will support the prince—for these are
only a band of rowdies and cowards."[62] The Liberals also appealed to
Miliutin to save Bulgaria from what they termed anarchy and a move
into the Austrian camp. The war minister, whose policy had been rejected and who knew his days in office were numbered, ruefully remarked, "What can I do in view of my own position?"[63]

These preliminary setbacks for the Liberals were not decisive. Their
real strength lay in the support they received from the Bulgarian electorate and, to a lesser extent, the sympathy of liberals abroad. In order
to defeat the majority party and its program, Russia and the prince
still had two principal hurdles to overcome. The first was to secure the
election of representatives to the Grand National Assembly who would
approve the prince's request; the second was to obtain the sanction of
the great powers for the changes advocated. The strength of the Liberals was formidable and only a concerted campaign could dislodge
them at the elections.

Alexander decided to test his popularity by making a personal tour
of his country to solicit support for the candidates who were ready to
endorse his changes. At this point the Russian government again inter-

---

[60] Kalnoky to Haymerle, *HHS*, X 70, tel. no. 51, St. P., May 13, 1881.
[61] Lascelles to Granville, *FO*, 78/3308, no. 47, Sofia, May 15, 1881.
[62] Skazkin, p. 249.
[63] Miliutin, IV, 66.

ceded. M. A. Khitrovo, Russia's recently arrived diplomatic agent, was ordered to accompany the prince on his tour. Ostensibly, Khitrovo was to serve as an adviser to the prince, but the real purpose was to demonstrate to the electorate that Russia continued to support the prince. This was open interference in the internal affairs of Bulgaria, but Russia was determined that Alexander's plan should be ratified. If there was still any doubt about the tsar's attitude, it was dispelled when the emperor placed his final seal of approval on the prince by presenting him with the order of Alexander Nevskii just before the Grand National Assembly convened.[64]

Now that St. Petersburg had come around to his point of view, Ernrot could work in harmony with his government. He immediately took measures against the Bulgarian opposition press. Through their leading journal, *Nezavisimost,* the Liberals bitterly denounced the prince and his supporters. The attacks became increasingly violent until, on May 23/June 4, Ernrot had the editor arrested. The next day the prince declared the freedom of the press suspended. When the Liberals challenged this ruling in court, the government, through a loophole in the constitution, was able to defend its action by reference to a Turkish press law of 1865. Ernrot was thus following the example set by the tsar in Russia. Meanwhile, the conservative newspapers in Bulgaria as well as in Russia could "freely indulge in" praise of the prince.[65]

Alexander's other principal support came from the Bulgarian church hierarchy. In the preceding year the Liberals had sought to usurp the power of the bishops by attempting to emancipate the village priests from the direct control of their superiors. The church officials, led by Exarch Iosif, wholeheartedly threw their support to the prince and the Conservatives, hoping thereby to influence the lower clergy.[66]

During the election campaign in Bulgaria, Russia sought to overcome the second hurdle and obtain the approval of the great powers for the prince's action. Bismarck was disturbed by Alexander's proclamation, which, he considered, was ill timed. The months-old Greek-Turkish controversy over a border settlement had reached an acute stage. Another serious Balkan problem could reopen the entire eastern question. Even

[64] Lascelles to Granville, *FO,* 78/3308, no. 63, Sofia, May 30, 1881; Burian to Haymerle, *HHS,* XV 18, no. 16A, Sofia, June 30, 1881; Schweinitz, *Denkwürdigkeiten,* II, 168.

[65] Matveev, *op. cit.,* XXV, 239–240; Stanev, *Istoriia na Nova Bulgariia, 1878–1928,* pp. 29–32; Radev, I, 284–285; Black, pp. 204–209; Parensov, "V Bolgarii," *Russkaia Starina,* CI (1900), 601.

[66] Burian to Haymerle, *HHS,* XV 18, no. 14D, Sofia, June 16, 1881; Arnaudov, *Eksarkh Iosif,* pp. 445–451; Matveev, *op. cit.,* p. 237.

more important, Bismarck believed that Alexander should not have acted without the approval of Russia. Once Russia gave her complete support to the prince, however, Bismarck withdrew his objections.[67] He too had worked determinedly for the Dreikaiserbund and feared any occurrence which threatened to jettison the months of painstaking deliberations. For him Bulgaria was basically of no importance. Khitrovo was thus able to report to Giers that Thielau, the German representative in Sofia, was supporting him and was urging the prince to carry out his plans.[68]

The Austrian government shared Bismarck's views that the action was not properly timed in view of the Greek-Turkish difficulties. Vienna was, nevertheless, ready to endorse the move; for months the Austrian representatives had sympathized with the prince's views concerning the constitution and the Liberals. In the weeks before the Bulgarian elections were held, Austria disagreed with Russia only on how best to aid the prince, but there was no quarrel concerning the step he had taken. Thus the three major conservative continental powers acted in harmony.[69]

Russia, however, met with a different reception in presenting her views to the British. The Russian government repeatedly emphasized to the British representatives that its sole aim was to ensure peace and order and prevent anarchy, which might spread to Eastern Rumelia and open the eastern question. To achieve this goal, unanimity was necessary among the great powers. Britain was therefore requested to join the other states in a collective endorsement of the prince which was to be announced just before the Bulgarian elections. The British tradition of sympathy for liberal and constitutional governments prompted the rejection of any such move. Granville stated that British public opinion was opposed to *coups d'état* against constitutions. The Bulgarian constitution might have deficiencies, but Alexander's remedy did not meet with British approval. This position was supported also by France and Italy.[70]

The failure to obtain British coöperation was disturbing, since the Bulgarian Liberals were thereby strengthened. Knowing the British fear of anarchy, A. B. Lobanov-Rostovskii argued further with Granville. Russia, he said, had not been informed in advance of the prince's

---

[67] Skazkin, p. 245.
[68] *Loc. cit.*
[69] Haymerle to Burian, *HHS*, XV 18, Vienna, May 19, 1881; Skazkin, pp. 242, 246; Saint-Hilaire to Challemel-Lacour, *DDF*, IV, no. 61, Paris, July 9, 1881.
[70] Granville to Wyndham, *FO*, 65/1109, no. 235, Foreign Office, June 14, 1881; Black, pp. 201–202.

action. If she had, she would have discouraged it. It was now a fact. If Alexander failed to gain the changes he desired and was forced to abdicate, it was very doubtful whether the powers could find another prince who would rule with the existing constitution. Turmoil would follow in Bulgaria and the entire Balkan problem would come into the open again.[71]

The Austrian government also endeavored to influence the British. Haymerle told the British ambassador in Vienna that Austria would regret it if the Liberals were aided by the British attitude. After all, the prince had not attacked the constitution, but in fact was acting legally, since he intended to present his proposals to a duly elected Grand National Assembly, as prescribed by law. If this body rejected his request, he would not resort to force but would abdicate. Haymerle emphasized that if the prince were given greater authority a more peaceful and permanent development would take place in the principality. The powers would then be able to negotiate with the prince and make him responsible for the conduct of his country. Hitherto the parties and their leaders, not the prince, had ruled the country.[72]

Despite his refusal to coöperate directly with the three conservative powers, Granville did say in the House of Lords "that it would be madness on the part of a population lately emancipated with little political experience—not to try to arrive at a friendly understanding with the prince." Granville subsequently wrote to Queen Victoria that Britain would accept modifications in the constitution only if they were made with the approval of the Grand National Assembly. He intended to urge moderation upon the prince. The Russian proposal was regarded as interference in the internal affairs of a nation.[73]

The Bulgarian elections resolved the entire problem in line with Russian wishes. When the ballots were counted, the Conservative supporters of the prince had an overwhelming majority. Giers now abandoned any thought of joint action by the great powers, since he felt assured of victory in the Grand National Assembly.[74] As expected, the assembly, meeting on July 1/13, almost two years to the day after Alexander entered Sofia as modern Bulgaria's first ruler, endorsed the prince's changes in a single day's session. Alexander of Battenberg and the Conservatives had defeated the Liberals and the constitution, just as two

---

[71] Granville to Wyndham, *FO*, 65/1109, no. 235, Foreign Office, June 14, 1881.
[72] Haymerle to Burian, *HHS*, XV 18, Vienna, May 19, 1881.
[73] Buckle, *Victoria*, III, 223.
[74] Wyndham to Granville, *FO*, 65/1113, no. 352, St. P., July 7, 1881; Trauttenberg to Haymerle, *HHS*, X 70, no. 39A, vertraulich, St. P., July 1/13, 1881; Saint-Vallier to Saint-Hilaire, *DDF*, IV, no. 68, Berlin, July 17, 1881.

months earlier Tsar Alexander and his conservative advisers had set aside the liberal reforms of Loris-Melikov. In the summer of 1881 both the tsar and the prince imposed a more conservative order on their respective domains.

The elections in Bulgaria had turned out favorably for Alexander chiefly because of Russian support, which was evident throughout the campaign. As a result of her contributions in the liberation of Bulgaria, Russia had built up a tremendous store of good will; so it was almost certain that the Bulgarian electorate would accept whatever the tsar recommended. It was therefore not exclusively the repressive actions of the government, such as the curbs put on the liberal press, that produced the election victory, but the outright endorsement of the prince by the Russian government.[75]

The preceding months of Russo-Bulgarian relations indicated certain trends in Russia's handling of the Bulgarian problem. Most striking was the lack of liaison between the home office and the representatives abroad. Certainly the best illustration of a foreign representative making his own policy is shown in Ernrot's handling of the constitutional problem. In theory, he was in Bulgaria as a Bulgarian minister responsible only to the Bulgarian government. In actual fact, he had been sent to Sofia to defend Russian interests. When he personally decided that this could best be done by sacrificing the constitution which Russia had initially sponsored, he went ahead with his own plans without consulting his government. Although no complications arose, his independent action might have had disastrous results if Austria, Germany, or Britain had wished to make an issue of the matter. Chaos and anarchy might have developed in Bulgaria, leading to the reopening of the eastern question at a time when Russia could ill afford foreign adventures. Yet Ernrot was not reprimanded for his behavior when he returned to Russia after the meeting of the Grand National Assembly.[76]

The incidents of this period illustrate the difficulty which the Bulgarian government had in dealing with Russia. It was almost impossible to know whether the Russian representatives spoke for their government or were merely expressing private views. Davydov, Parensov, Kumani, and Ernrot each had a different idea in regard to the manner in which Russian interests could best be served. The Bulgarian government thus had to deal not with the Russian government but with independent individuals.

---

[75] Skazkin, pp. 249–250; Lascelles to Granville, *FO*, 78/3310, no. 149, Sofia, Oct. 19, 1881.
[76] Skazkin, p. 253; Ernrot, *op. cit.*, p. 478.

Russia's solution of the problem presented to her by the precipitate actions of Alexander and Ernrot was the only one feasible at the time. It corresponded with Russia's emphasis on conservatism in internal politics and her desire to promote the Dreikaiserbund in foreign affairs. It was completely in harmony with the views of those who were now to guide Russia's future—Tsar Alexander III and Giers.

IV

TSAR ALEXANDER III SUPPORTS
BULGARIAN CONSERVATISM

In the summer of 1881 Russia and Bulgaria appeared to have settled their outstanding differences. With the change in the constitution and the defeat of the Liberals, Alexander had gained the type of government he desired. It remained to be seen whether he would demonstrate the capabilities of a real administrator and statesman, and whether he could make use of his additional powers. Also unknown were the feelings of the new tsar toward the prince and Bulgaria. The two rulers were closely related, however, and held similar views concerning the administration of a state.

Since Alexander III had reversed the policy of his father in internal affairs, he might alter the direction of foreign policy also. It was expected that the influence of his immediate advisers and his wife, the Danish princess Dagmar, could lead him away from the connection with Germany. On the contrary, not only did the tsar approve the conclusion of the Dreikaiserbund, but he maintained the policy of alliance with Germany until 1890, when it was dropped at the instigation of Germany, not of Russia. Russian policy under the new tsar thus followed the course set under Alexander II. Like his father, Alexander III ruled as an autocrat; he kept the reins of government in his hands and made the final decisions. Accordingly, he had to weigh and balance the claims of rival groups and individuals.

In this constellation the Russian foreign office was only one star. Because of his natural sympathies and personal feelings, Alexander III inclined toward the nationalist school. As the years passed, the advice of Katkov in particular had great weight; the tsar read his newspapers and received private reports from him. Although under the direction of Giers the foreign ministry remained conservative and "cosmopolitan" in tone, the danger always existed that the tsar would be swayed by the arguments of those who wished Russia to pursue a forward-looking policy. When foreign adventures were urged by such men as Nelidov and Saburov, there was little chance that their opinions would be heeded, but when support for active policies came from Pobedonostsev, Katkov, or others who were close to the tsar, the pressure on the foreign office was great.

Moreover, Pobedonostsev, as procurator of the Holy Synod, had con-

trol of all ecclesiastical affairs. In the Balkans the policy of the church
overlapped and supplemented Russian foreign policy. In the period
under discussion, despite the Dreikaiserbund the Russian church continued to sponsor the reconciliation of the rival Orthodox churches
and to foster their united stand against Moslem Turkey and Catholic
Austria-Hungary.[1]

Giers' position at the accession of Alexander III remained the same as
it had been under the previous reign. At first it was suspected that the
tsar intended to make Ignatiev minister of foreign affairs, but in 1882
Giers was given the post. In his attempts to block all foreign adventures,
Giers was aided by the temperament of the tsar. Although the latter
could become extremely emotional, as in his relations with Alexander of
Battenberg, and sometimes acted impulsively, Alexander III was
naturally cautious and deliberate. Having no desire to be a conqueror
or to make great extensions of Russian power and prestige, he usually
supported Giers against the competition of rival statesmen such as
Nelidov, A. Mohrenheim, and Saburov, and the more formidable opposition of Katkov and the Moscow nationalists. Despite the fact that the
tsar in the end remained loyal to his minister, the situation was often
delicate.[2]

When the tsar rejected the reforms of Loris-Melikov, Miliutin, who
under the late emperor had been responsible not only for the ministry
of war but also for influencing Russia's foreign policy, was forced to
resign. His successor, P. S. Vannovskii, adhered to the tsar's wishes.
However, Miliutin's views on the Bulgarian problem were shared by
his close collaborator General N. N. Obruchev, the new chief of staff;
but the general did not have the authority, the ability, or, more important, the opportunity to implement his ideas. The best he could
expect was to salvage as much as possible of the previous program and
hope that events might compel Russia to return to her earlier course.

The Russian government took strong measures to ensure public support of its Bulgarian policy. When Alexander's plans for the constitutional change were announced, *Golos*, which had led the attack, received
three official warnings. When these were not heeded, the minister of the
interior, on July 25/August 6, suspended the paper for six months. In
commenting on this action, the Austrian representative in St. Peters-

---

[1] Nolde, *L'alliance franco-russe*, pp. 272–278; Firsov, "Aleksandr III," *Byloe*,
XXIX (1929), 85–108; Skazkin, pp. 174–180; Arnaudov, *Eksarkh Iosif*, pp. 496–
501; Mousset, *La Serbie et son église, 1830–1904*, pp. 263–299; Wren, "Pobedonostsev and Russian Influence in the Balkans," *Journal of Modern History*, XIX: 2
(June, 1947), 130–141; Jomini to Giers, *NKG*, Aug. 24, Sept. 12, 1879.

[2] Jomini to Giers, *NKG*, July 4, 1888. See also Nolde, *op. cit.*, pp. 237 ff., 264–266,
279–295; Schweinitz, *Denkwürdigkeiten*, II, 166, 175, 187–188, 193.

burg wrote that the Aksakov-Katkov faction, which openly endorsed the new policy, had now lost its most troublesome opponent. It was obvious that Russia was determined that nothing should upset Russo-Bulgarian relations.[3]

In Bulgaria the prince did his share to see that sources of friction were eliminated. The liberal newspapers had been suppressed by the government, and pressure was exerted on the prominent Liberal leaders. Dragan Tsankov was compelled to leave Sofia for Ruschuk and Tyrnovo, where he continued his active opposition to the government. Subsequently he was imprisoned. Karavelov and P. R. Slaveikov fled to Eastern Rumelia. There, under the benevolent protectorship of Aleko Pasha, Karavelov started the Plovdiv edition of *Nezavisimost* in order to carry on the fight of the Liberals against the prince and the Russian policy.[4]

With Sofia clear of Liberal leaders, Alexander was free to organize the government as he wished. His first task was to form a new administration. Instead of a purely Conservative cabinet, as had been expected, he chose to appoint one which appeared to be nonpolitical, composed of Conservatives, independents, and two Russians, Colonel Remlingen and General Krylov. The two officers were to serve temporarily as minister of the interior and minister of war, respectively. The cabinet was not strong or impressive, but it could be expected to execute the prince's will in the same manner that the ministers in Russia followed the tsar's dictates.[5]

In foreign affairs Alexander's actions received the constant support of the Russian officials. Giers again told the British representative of his opposition to the Tyrnovo constitution, describing it as "impossible."[6] Alexander could not permit men like Tsankov to rule the state. When a report circulated that General M. A. Domontovich might be sent from Russia to serve as permanent minister of the interior in Bulgaria, the Austrian representative concluded that this was not true, since the general was a sponsor of the Tyrnovo constitution in 1878 and was believed to be hostile to its opponents.[7] Russia had succeeded in ousting Tsankov

---

[3] Trauttenberg to Haymerle, *HHS*, X 70, no. 41C, St. P., July 29/Aug. 10, 1881; Wyndham to Granville, *FO*, 65/1114, no. 413, St. P., Aug. 8, 1881; Schweinitz, *op. cit.*, II, 166–167.

[4] Matveev, "Bolgariia i Vostochnaia Rumeliia posle Berlinskago Kongressa," *Istoricheskii Viestnik*, XXV (1886), 239–240; Parensov, "V Bolgarii," *Russkaia Starina*, CI (1900), 601–602.

[5] Black, p. 211; Koch, pp. 97–98.

[6] Wyndham to Granville, *FO*, 65/1114, no. 436, St. P., Aug. 17, 1881; Skazkin, p. 250; Tatishchev, *Iz Prozhlago Russkoi Diplomatii*, pp. 372–374.

[7] Kalnoky to Haymerle, *HHS*, X 70, no. 42A, vertraulich, St. P., Aug. 12/24, 1881; Skazkin, pp. 254, 277.

and his adherents, and she did not want men in Bulgaria who might undermine the new conservative order. Recent developments had brought greater tranquillity to the Balkans, and this was to be preserved.

These direct and indirect signs of approval were heartily welcomed by the prince. Equally agreeable was the strong support given him by Ivan Aksakov. On July 30/August 11 the latter wrote a lengthy letter of advice and encouragement. In his opinion, only the Slavic races had truly democratic aspirations. In the west the intellectuals, using the "deceptive principle, the sovereignty of the people," were increasingly able to impose upon the people a government based on their passing fantasies and political passions. In contrast to western constitutional government, Aksakov offered the "Russian ideal," which he described as:

... a local self-government without political significance, sustained and crowned by a superior and central personal authority, perfectly free and unfettered in the sphere of government.... The people does not hanker after sovereignty nor seek to govern the state, but what it certainly does require is a government which inspires confidence by its energy, its strength, its *disinterestedness* and *national character*.

Aksakov next turned to the relationship of the ruler to popular assemblies. In Russia, he wrote, the tsar was "above all the first *man* in the land, and to the common people their own personification." Prior to Peter the Great, whom Aksakov disliked because of his western innovations, the tsars of Russia had summoned delegates from all classes when important questions arose or when they sought the wholehearted coöperation of the entire nation. Although autocratic, they did not consider themselves infallible and recognized the importance of knowing the thought of the country. However, continued Aksakov, "these assemblies were, naturally, only consultative, and influenced the course of events by an entirely moral force without prejudice to the dignity and authority of the tsar."[8]

The ideas expressed in the letter coincided in many respects with the prince's own convictions. By his past actions Alexander had demonstrated his belief in strong and centralized government. He opposed the binding nature of the assembly as it was embodied in the Tyrnovo constitution. Rejecting legislative action which prejudiced the "dignity and authority" of the ruler, he advocated a consultative legislature, which was, in essence, what he hoped to achieve through the constitutional changes. Aksakov's letter encouraged the prince to follow his chosen path, and assured him the open support of an important journalist.

[8] The text of Aksakov's letter is in Koch, pp. 79–82. Alexander's views on the constitution are recorded in Kennedy to Granville, *FO*, 78/3414, no. 57, Sofia, June 25, 1882.

Despite these favorable signs, grave doubts about the future of Bulgaria were expressed by one of the most influential Russians in Sofia. On July 31/August 12, a month after the Grand National Assembly had approved Alexander's constitutional changes, M. A. Khitrovo, Russian diplomatic representative, sent an analysis of Bulgarian developments to Giers. Acknowledging that his comments might make a disagreeable impression in St. Petersburg, Khitrovo nevertheless felt compelled to report that the prince's government was now in a more difficult position than it had been prior to the constitutional changes. Although he disliked the methods of the Liberals, he had to admit that their administration was superior to that of the Conservatives. Moreover, the Liberals had far greater support in the country.

Khitrovo personally was not against the constitutional changes, but he felt that neither Russia nor Bulgaria had been adequately prepared for them. Disappointment with the new system was felt by all groups. In the election campaign the Conservatives, in order to obtain the support of the peasantry, had promised a tax reduction, but this promise had not been fulfilled. The same old taxes were now being collected with the assistance of the Russian officers serving in Bulgaria. The Conservatives had been led to believe that, as a result of their success in the recent elections they would be asked to form a new government. Instead, the prince chose to maintain his personal authority through a coalition cabinet containing only two Conservative ministers.

Alexander's authority thus rested primarily on the support he received from the Russian officers, backed by the weight of Russian influence among the Bulgarian people. The Bulgars were now convinced, Khitrovo believed, that the prince's action against the constitution had been Russian-inspired and effected by the Russian military in the country. The electorate had ratified the prince's demands only because of its unlimited confidence in Russia; it had yielded to the Russian government and the tsar. "It is absolutely evident," concluded Khitrovo, "that Russia should escape as soon as possible from this abnormal and dangerous position ... because every development in Bulgaria which did not justify the necessity of the constitutional change would work against Russian influence and interests in Bulgaria."[9]

Khitrovo's analysis was not favorably received in Russia. Giers was unimpressed. The tsar, who saw only an extract of the report, noted that it might have some validity, but that Khitrovo was seeking to belittle the work of General Ernrot.[10] In the succeeding months Khitrovo himself

---

[9] Skazkin, pp. 251–252.
[10] *Ibid.*, p. 253.

was to forget his own observations and by his actions contribute to the very result he had cautioned against—the diminution of Russian influence in Bulgaria.

The strength of the Russo-Bulgarian friendship was quickly tested by the renewed negotiations over the construction of the strategic Danube-Sofia railroad which was favored by Russian interests. The Liberals, while in office, had refused to commit themselves on the matter, much to the disappointment of the Russian entrepreneurs. During the crisis over the constitution the discussions concerning the railroad had been suspended. With that matter settled, the Russian interests were ready to press their demands with new vigor. In view of the Russian support of the prince and the Conservatives in the recent crisis and attendant elections, the Russian railroad concerns expected that their requests would be received with favor by the new regime in Sofia. Colonel Remlingen, temporary minister of the interior, and Khitrovo were fully coöperative and pressed the Bulgars to build the "Russian" line. They had succeeded in convincing the prince that the permanent minister of the interior should be a Russian, and Remlingen now suggested that railroad matters be put within the jurisdiction of this same minister. Astute political maneuvering thus appeared to have secured Russian control over the allocation of railroad funds and the development of the entire project.[11]

Despite the coöperation between Russia and the Conservatives, the latter did not consider themselves under obligation to St. Petersburg. Led by the Khadzhienov railroad faction, they opened a strong attack through their newspapers on the Russians and their claims. The arguments were directed not against the proposed railroad itself but against the ways in which they feared the contracts for construction would be awarded. They did not want the profits to go to foreigners, even though the latter might be the liberating Russians. When they heard that Remlingen had used his position to promise G. E. Struve, representative of the Giuntsburg-Poliakov concern, a handsome sum to make a preliminary survey of the Ruschuk-Sofia route, the Conservatives were angry. The Bulgarian ministers in the cabinet promptly ordered that estimates be solicited from other firms, including the Khadzhienov group. Struve protested, but was informed that the other ministers could not be bound by Remlingen's promises. The concession was to be awarded to the lowest bidder.[12]

These unexpected developments disturbed Khitrovo. He decided to go directly to St. Petersburg for consultations on the railroad problem

---

[11] *Ibid.*, p. 273 n. 1, p. 274.

[12] *Ibid.*, pp. 274–275; Biegeleben to Kalnoky, *HHS*, XV 19, no. 1A–D, Sofia, Jan. 1, 1882.

and to seek the appointment of a Russian as permanent minister of the interior. The Russian government, however, was determined not to press the Russian line to the detriment of the other lines which had been settled by international treaty. Giers urged Khitrovo to move with caution. Khitrovo also failed to secure the appointment of a permanent minister of the interior. The tsar would send a Russian only if Alexander made a specific request. This had not been forthcoming.[13]

After two months in the Russian capital Khitrovo returned to Sofia without having obtained satisfaction, but, undaunted by the setback he had received, he pursued his objective with renewed energy. If the Russian government did not know its own interests and how to defend them, Khitrovo did.

At the end of the year Alexander dismissed Remlingen and replaced him, not by a Russian as Khitrovo wished, but by Nachevich, one of the most prominent Bulgars in the anti-Russian Conservative group. Alexander, however, informed Khitrovo that Nachevich had given his word to subordinate his own views on the Bulgarian railroad problem and to work for the success of the Russian interests. Unable to rely on Nachevich, as he had on Remlingen, Khitrovo decided to subscribe to a new plan for the railroads which he believed would appeal to Bulgarian national sentiment.[14]

On the basis of the Treaty of Berlin, Bulgaria owed Russia 28,000,000 francs for the occupation expenses. A note requesting payment was formulated by the Russian government at the end of September, but was not delivered to the Bulgars until December 19/31, 1881. Although the repayment of this sum would be a tremendous drain on the Bulgarian treasury, the Conservatives considered it a matter of honor that the debt be paid. Alexander now proposed that the Russians allow the Bulgars to use this amount for the construction of the Russian line. He was even ready to award the construction to Giuntsburg. The plan received the enthusiastic support of Khitrovo, who argued that this sum would ensure the construction of the line.

This solution of both the debt and the railroad problem seemed to be the most sensible and feasible yet advanced. Russia would gain the railroad which her strategic interests demanded; she would end the friction which had developed over the matter; and, by her charitable gesture, would regain much of the sympathy she had lost among the Bulgars. The Bulgars would have paid their debt, but would have a railroad to show for it. Despite the apparent advantages of the plan,

---

[13] Skazkin, pp. 276–277; Koch, pp. 99–100.
[14] Skazkin, pp. 279–280.

the Russian government refused to relinquish any part of the occupation debt. Instead, Khitrovo was informed that the tsar believed that the railroad problem had not been sufficiently studied. The Bulgars would have to decide about the railroad themselves on the basis of their own interests and resources.[15]

The position of the Russian government is difficult to understand. Certainly, the line would have been worth the 28,000,000 francs of the occupation debt, in view of the Russian strategy in regard to the Straits. The construction of the line was dependent on the good will of the Bulgars and their gratitude to Russia as their liberator. Every day the Bulgarian memory was growing dimmer. The use of the occupation debt for the improvement of Bulgaria would undoubtedly have created a resurgence of sympathy toward Russia. Yet the Russian government failed to seize this favorable opportunity. Its refusal was no doubt prompted by two important considerations: fear of jeopardizing relations with Austria-Hungary, and unwillingness to give financial aid to the Bulgarian railroads. The decision, once taken, would probably not have caused any serious problems if the Russian agents in Bulgaria had been required to follow the intent of the instructions issued by their government.

Despite the refusal of the Russian government to use influence or pressure to obtain the construction of the "Russian" line, Russian agents and individuals in Bulgaria, led by Khitrovo, continued to press their demands. The Bulgarians remained firm; the line, in their opinion, was of little economic value. If it were built, the construction contracts should go to Bulgarian, not Russian, firms. National pride, as well as profit, was involved here. After centuries of foreign domination and exploitation, it is not surprising that the Bulgars wished to develop their country independently.

Concurrent with the railroad dispute, another problem had arisen; this concerned the composition of the council of state. After the Grand National Assembly had granted Alexander the powers he demanded on July 1/13, 1881, the prince immediately set out to organize the council of state. This body had many important functions. It approved all bills before they were submitted to the assembly; it had jurisdiction over the administration as well as wide authority in financial matters. Its composition was thus of primary importance to all the political groups in Bulgaria. The Conservatives, now holding the dominant position in the state, wanted the council to be entirely appointive, since they expected to be able to influence the prince. With the Liberals temporarily out

---

[15] *Ibid.*, pp. 278–280; Koch, p. 59.

of the picture, opposition to the plan was led by the Russians. M. S. Drinov, a Bulgar who had formerly been a professor in Russia, proposed that the council be two-thirds elective, a plan which would prevent it from falling completely under the control of either the prince or the Conservatives. A modification of this system was finally adopted. The council was to be composed of twelve members, eight of whom were to be chosen on the basis of an indirect system of voting. The prince was to appoint the eight elective members from a list of the twenty who received the highest number of votes. On September 14/26 it was announced that the elections would be held on November 1/13. Despite the vigorous campaigning of Remlingen against the Conservatives, the latter party won an overwhelming victory.[16]

Because of his position as minister of the interior, Remlingen had control over the final tabulation and verification of the election returns. More than a month went by before the results were announced. In the meantime the colonel so altered the figures that the names of five of the nineteen victorious Conservative candidates disappeared from the list and were replaced by Liberals. Remlingen's action was immediately attacked by the Conservative newspaper *Bulgarski Glas*. The Russian colonel dealt with this opposition by suspending the paper for a month. It was soon obvious that his tenure in office would be brief. Alexander, nevertheless, did not dismiss him until the end of December, and only after Nachevich consented to replace him.[17]

Khitrovo, meanwhile, had returned from his two-month visit to St. Petersburg in time to witness the last stages of this episode. Even he had to admit that Remlingen had gone too far. Realizing that a new appointment would have to be made, he sought to influence the prince in his selection. As Khitrovo's relations with the Conservatives became increasingly strained because of their attitude in regard to the railroad, he began to look more and more to the Liberals for support against the Conservatives and the prince. Thus, when the question of a replacement for Remlingen came up, Khitrovo was able to gain the support of the Liberals. Khitrovo wanted Alexander to appoint a Russian who would favor Khitrovo's railroad plans. The Liberals were ready to endorse a Russian in order to weaken the power of the Conservatives. The appointment of Nachevich was thus made against strong opposition. In a gesture apparently designed to appease Khitrovo and the Liberals,

[16] Black, pp. 211–212; Skazkin, pp. 274–275; Matveev, *op. cit.*, XXV, 243–245; Trauttenberg to Kalnoky, *HHS*, X 70, no. 59A–B, St. P., Dec. 3/15, 1881.

[17] Biegeleben to Kalnoky, *HHS*, XV 18, no. 33A–B, conf., Sofia, Dec. 20, 1881; Lascelles to Granville, *FO*, 78/3310, no. 168, Sofia, Dec. 12, 1881; Skazkin, pp. 279–280; Black, pp. 213–214.

Alexander, in forming the council of state, awarded the Conservatives only half of the positions, the remainder being distributed to various groups including the Liberals. Despite this concession, the government remained definitely conservative in orientation.[18]

In January, 1882, the tsar sent a telegram approving the conservative course that the prince had adopted. The Austrian representative, in commenting on the message, noted that, although the tsar gave his approval, there was no *"applaudissement"* in his words. But, he added, dispatches from St. Petersburg usually had two possible interpretations and the question was which to follow.[19]

On January 17/29 Giers reaffirmed the position of the Russian government by communicating to Khitrovo the tsar's order that he refrain from interfering in Bulgarian politics and that he support the new ministry. He was also to avoid any action that might weaken the confidence of the nation in its ruler. Khitrovo's instructions from his government thus conflicted directly with his own policy and inclinations. With no hesitation, he made his decision. Instead of obeying Giers' directions, he swung completely to the Liberal side and joined in the agitation against the prince and the Conservatives.[20]

Since the Russian government refused to abandon the prince, Khitrovo continued to develop his own policy. He knew that the only real support the prince enjoyed was within the army, which was officered by Russians. "If this support were withdrawn," Khitrovo told the British representative, "His Highness would find himself in a helpless condition, and it would now become a question for the Russian government to consider whether they should render themselves unpopular in Bulgaria by supporting the prince in a line of action which was contrary to their [Russia's] interests.[21]

Khitrovo decided that he could best attack the prince through the Russian officers serving in the Bulgarian army. At first he was quite successful in causing a breach in their ranks. In a derogatory way he referred to the faction that supported the prince as the "Germans"; the "loyal" officers were those who followed Khitrovo. The struggle became so bitter that General Krylov, Alexander's minister of war, who had joined Khitrovo, submitted his resignation and left Sofia in April. Several days later he was ordered by the Russian government to return

[18] Black, p. 214; Biegeleben to Kalnoky, *HHS*, XV 19, no. 3B, réservé, Jan. 15, 1882.

[19] Skazkin, p. 280; Biegeleben to Kalnoky, *HHS*, XV 19, no. 7A–C, Feb. 12, 1882.

[20] Skazkin, p. 280; Biegeleben to Kalnoky, HHS, XV 19, no. 4B, réservé, Sofia, Jan. 29, 1882.

[21] Lascelles to Granville, *FO*, 78/3413, no. 8, Sofia, Jan. 15, 1882.

to his post. The other Russian officers were to maintain discipline and not resign from the Bulgarian army, as some had threatened to do.[22]

Through intrigues among the army officers Khitrovo had succeeded in deeply disturbing the prince. As Nachevich informed the British representative, "There is nothing that His Highness would be likely to resent more strongly than any interference in military matters, and it is evident that unless he is able to place implicit reliance in his army, in any emergency that may arise, his position which is at best a difficult one becomes very precarious."[23]

Alexander, who looked back with pride on his military training, demanded a strong army. Aware of his isolation and his unpopularity in Bulgaria, he had made every effort to strengthen his position by developing a personal loyalty to himself among his officers.[24] Now his strategy was blocked by Khitrovo, and all the progress he had made was in danger of destruction. Just as in the preceding years he had asked for the recall of Parensov and Kumani, he now felt he had to appeal to the tsar to remove Khitrovo.

Fortunately for the prince's plans, Khitrovo's actions were not unknown to the Russian government. On January 31/February 12 the tsar had written on a report from Khitrovo that the agent's position had become more untenable. On April 21/May 3, P. P. Ubri (Oubril), Russian ambassador to the Dual Monarchy, telegraphed Giers from Vienna concerning a conversation with Kalnoky, the Austrian foreign minister, about events in Bulgaria. The latter had commented on Khitrovo's behavior, his intrigues against the prince, and his attempts to undermine Alexander's "authority and the normal development of the country." When the tsar read this report, he wrote on it, "Even the Austrians have noticed this!"

When Alexander arrived in St. Petersburg, he found the tsar ready to agree to his request. Not only did Alexander III recall Khitrovo, but, to express further his displeasure with his representative and the Russian officers who had turned against the prince, he decorated General Lesovoi, who had supported and loyally obeyed Alexander, with the order of St. Vladimir, third class.[25]

Khitrovo's dismissal came approximately ten months after the "new

[22] Biegeleben to Kalnoky, *HHS*, XV 19, tel. no. 31, Sofia, April 26, 1882; *ibid.*, tel. no. 36, Sofia, May 2, 1882; Lascelles to Granville, *FO*, 78/3413, no. 41, Sofia, May 1, 1882; Koch, pp. 104–106.

[23] Lascelles to Granville, *FO*, 78/3414, no. 43, Sofia, May 5, 1882.

[24] Skazkin, p. 253.

[25] Skazkin, pp. 280–281; Kennedy to Lascelles, *FO*, 78/3413, no. 47, Sofia, May 20, 1882. Khitrovo had become deeply involved in the Bosnian revolt, which was taking place at this time. His activities caused the Russian government considerable embarrassment. See chap. viii.

era" in Russo-Bulgarian relations had begun. Russia certainly had not gained any concrete advantages during these months. Her influence had brought victory to the Conservatives during the constitutional crisis of 1881, but they had shown little inclination to heed Russian wishes. The behavior of the two Russian agents Remlingen and Khitrovo had alienated some of the most important political leaders in Bulgaria. The Austrian representative Biegeleben commented ironically that he could not think of a better agent than Khitrovo to counterbalance Russian influence in Bulgaria.[26] What is surprising is that the Russian government delayed so long in recalling representatives who were obviously working contrary to instructions, and whose policies were endangering the Russian position in Bulgaria. Both Remlingen and Khitrovo had been informed of the intent of Russian policy; both chose to ignore it. Neither was recalled until damage had been done to the interests of their country.

The conflicting actions of Russian agents since 1879 were now criticized even by the most enthusiastic followers of Russia among the Bulgars. Bishop Kliment of Tyronovo, who had received his ecclesiastical training in Kiev, was devoted to Russia. Repeatedly he had defended her policies in Bulgaria. Yet, at this moment, in a conversation with a Russian official, he questioned the vacillating Russian attitude. In the spring of 1879, when the Tyrnovo assembly, of which he was president, was in session drafting the constitution, the assembly was confused by contradictory advice from Russian officials concerning the meaning and importance of the various articles. Once the document was adopted, Davydov had openly proclaimed that it would hamper Bulgaria's development and would have to be changed. Davydov was replaced by Kumani, who held the opposite view. Kumani believed that Russia should defend the constitution. Next came Khitrovo, who had helped to secure the vote to suspend the constitution and who had even told Kliment personally that the tsar desired it. Afterward Khitrovo regretted his decision. Russia was evidently not providing through her agents the firm guidance that the new country needed.[27]

Despite Bulgaria's unfortunate experiences with previous Russian officials, Alexander, during his visit to St. Petersburg to seek the recall of Khitrovo, was determined at the same time to obtain Russians for the key posts in his cabinet. The prince had little choice in the matter because of his status in Bulgaria. Since he wished to maintain a strong

[26] Biegeleben to Kalnoky, *HHS*, XV 19, no. 3B, réservé, Sofia, Jan. 15, 1882.
[27] Shcheglov, "Russkoe Ministerstvo v Bolgarii," *Istoricheskii Viestnik*, CXXVI (1911), 556. Parensov had already expressed similar views. Parensov, *op. cit.*, CXXVI, 337–338; CXXXIV, 264.

personal position and reform the government in the direction indicated by the change in the constitution, he found it impossible to rely on either major political party. The Liberals refused to coöperate; the Conservatives wanted to control the ministry and dominate the prince. Alexander realized that he could rule independently and according to his own dictates only if he had foreign officials to organize the government and bring about the changes he desired. They would theoretically be bound primarily to himself and not tied to any political faction in Bulgaria. Because of her role as the liberating power, Russia was the only country which could supply such men. The electorate would see Russia behind the government if her representatives held important posts. Although the actions of previous agents had estranged some elements, the mass of the population was still pro-Russian. They expected Russia to send administrators and to back Bulgaria with military power and foreign diplomatic support. The quarrels and friction with previous agents thus did not deter Alexander from seeking to acquire new ones. He still needed Russia to maintain his authority as head of the state and to assure the sympathy of the Bulgars.

The selection of new ministers in Russia was not accomplished without difficulty. When Alexander made his request to the Russian government, he was told to find ministers from among his subjects. He explained that he wanted nonparty men who would have Russian aid and prestige behind them. His first choice for minister-president was General K. G. Ernrot, who had previously demonstrated his loyalty to the prince. Since Ernrot was not available at the time, Alexander was forced to look for other candidates.[28]

After a lengthy search Alexander finally selected two generals, L. N. Sobolev and A. V. Kaulbars,[29] although he did not know either of them personally. These two men were now to hold the highest appointive positions in the Bulgarian state: Sobolev as minister-president and minister of the interior, and Kaulbars as minister of war. In discussing his selections with the British representative, Alexander stated he hoped that with Sobolev as a *point d'appui* a ministry could be formed which would have "a fair chance of remaining a reasonable time in office, and that the constant change of ministers which up till now has contributed to make the government of this country so difficult

---

[28] Skazkin, pp. 282–283; Molchanov, "Prints Batenbergskii: Iz Nedavnikh Vospominanii," *Istoricheskii Viestnik*, XXV (1886), 101.

[29] Biegeleben to Kalnoky, *HHS*, XV 19, no. 25A–G, July 1, 1882. According to the prince's explanations to the Austrian representative, the two ministers were appointed on the recommendation of Ernrot and the Russian court. Other versions of the selection of the generals are in Skazkin, p. 283; Radev, I, 348–349; Black, p. 221; Koch, p. 107; Tatishchev, *op. cit.*, p. 377.

will be prevented."[30] Alexander believed that the lessons of the past had not been lost on the Russian government, and that the necessity of maintaining a proper attitude in Bulgarian matters would have been impressed upon the generals. This view was shared by Nachevich, who felt that the tsar's espousal of the conservative cause would prevent the generals from becoming a danger politically. Alexander thus considered that his power and authority in Bulgaria would be enhanced by the appointment of the two officers.[31]

While Alexander was in Russia, he again received encouragement from Aksakov. In an important article appearing in *Rus'* on May 15/27, 1882, Aksakov wrote that Moscow had the honor of entertaining within the historic walls of the Kremlin "the prince of Bulgaria." Only five or six years earlier, neither the Russians nor the Bulgars had thought of a ruler of Bulgaria. "The principality of Bulgaria, well, that signifies a hundred thousand Russian lives that were sacrificed, it signifies a tremendous accumulation of deeds of Russian bravery, valour, brotherly love and self-sacrifice." The prince of Bulgaria, Aksakov continued, was "the living symbol of Russian victory over five centuries of Bulgarian bondage."[32]

Aksakov went on to state that, although the prince was not a Bulgar by origin, he had become so through his ties with the Russian imperial family and his participation in the Russo-Turkish War. Moreover, Aksakov continued, the prince was honestly seeking to improve Russo-Bulgarian relations, attempts which distinguished him from the Russophobe Milan of Serbia. The great mistake that Russia had made, Aksakov believed, was to give the Bulgarian people a constitution modeled on western European ideals. As a result, national parties had appeared among a people just liberated from five centuries of Turkish domination who did not understand the true function of such political organizations. These parties were interested primarily in their own welfare and not that of the state. Aksakov condemned the Liberals and Conservatives alike for their "meetings, demonstrations, and deputations," which were alien to a people who were by nature quiet and hardworking. In conclusion, he appealed to the Bulgarian intelligentsia not to lead their fellow citizens down the road of constitutionalism, which he considered to be anti-Russian.[33]

The two generals dominated Bulgarian political life for the succeeding fifteen months. Sobolev, the new minister-president, a thirty-eight-year-old army officer, had been trained at the artillery school and the

[30] Kennedy to Granville, *FO*, 78/3414, no. 57, Sofia, June 25, 1882.
[31] Biegeleben to Kalnoky, *HHS*, XV 19, no. 24B, réservé, Sofia, June 17, 1882.
[32] Aksakov, *Slavianskii Vopros'*, pp. 447–448.
[33] *Ibid.*, pp. 447–459.

general staff academy. During the Russo-Turkish War he had participated in the assaults on Plevna and the Shipka Pass. He had also
assisted Prince Cherkaskii in the organization of the civil administration of Bulgaria.[34] Although Sobolev was not a total stranger to the
Bulgarian scene, one may question the wisdom of appointing a military
man to the delicate post of minister-president.[35] In view of the Bulgarian political developments, a person familiar with the workings of
constitutional government and party politics would certainly have been
a better choice.

Sobolev's associate, General Kaulbars, was also thirty-eight years old
and had graduated from the general staff academy. Most of his early
military service had been in central Asia and Siberia, where he made
valuable geographical explorations and was honored several times by
the Imperial Geographic Society. In 1877 he joined the Russian forces
in the war against the Turks and subsequently became a member of the
boundary commission to settle the Serbian, Bulgarian, and Albanian
frontiers. He was thus familiar with Balkan affairs, but his principal
work had been elsewhere.[36]

The first task facing Sobolev after his arrival in Sofia was the selection
of the remaining members of his cabinet. On June 23/July 5, 1882, the
new cabinet was formed; it included the prominent Conservative leaders
Grekov, Nachevich, and Volkovich. Next the prince and Sobolev had to
settle the questions arising from the elections to the national assembly,
which were to be held in the autumn. The existing electoral system was
considered too liberal, since it had resulted in Conservative losses in
previous elections. Alexander, through rights granted him in July,
1881, had the authority to formulate a new electoral law. It was decided that an indirect system of voting should be introduced and stricter
property and educational qualifications should be required of the voter.[37]

Alexander wished to initiate certain constitutional amendments which
would have completely reversed the principles upon which the Tyrnovo
constitution had been based. He told the British representative that he
wanted "a constitution such as he himself understood a constitution to
be." In it the ruler would "be vested with full executive power," and
the government would "not be dependent for its tenure of office on a

---

[34] "Leonid Nikolaevich Sobolev," *Brokgauz-Efron Entsiklopedicheskii Slovar'*,
XXX (1900), 645–646.

[35] Skazkin, p. 283, states that Sobolev "looked upon his new political role as
though he were commanding a division." See also Shcheglov, *op. cit.*, pp. 553–554;
Ernrot, "K Noveishei Istorii Bolgarii," *Russkaia Starina*, LII (1886), 482.

[36] "Baron Aleksandr Vasil'evich Kaul'bars," *Brokgauz-Efron Entsiklopedicheskii
Slovar'*, XXVIII (1895), 769. Biegeleben to Kalnoky, *HHS*, XV 19, no. 26A–H,
Sofia, July 15, 1882.

[37] Black, pp. 221–222; Radev, I, 355–356; Biegeleben to Kalnoky, *HHS*, XV 19,
no. 26A–H, Sofia, July 15, 1882; *ibid.*, no. 24B, Sofia, June 17, 1882.

hostile vote of the representatives of the people." Such a change, he admitted, would mean that he would have "far more power than was contemplated by the framers of the late constitution."[38]

Unfortunately for Alexander's plans, General Sobolev had his own conception of what he wanted to accomplish in Bulgaria. In no sense did he regard himself solely as a Bulgarian minister; he was a Russian representative in Bulgaria and as such he felt compelled to formulate and carry out policies which he believed would aid his country. There is no evidence that any of his plans were drawn up after consultation with the Russian foreign office or with representatives of any branch of the Russian government. In fact, in the succeeding months he received no support from the Russian government for his schemes. Nevertheless, he was extremely tenacious in pursuing what he felt were the interests of Russia.

Sobolev realized the necessity, for Russian strategy, of a friendly and sympathetic Bulgaria, but the "natural bonds" of race, religion, and culture were, in his opinion, not sufficient to ensure continued coöperation. Only "material ties" with Bulgaria would be real pledges for the future. Sobolev's plan was to use the occupation fund to further his purpose. He believed that Bulgaria and Eastern Rumelia would be united within a decade. The debt for each province he estimated at 25,000,000 francs. By spending 2,000,000 francs each year, first from Bulgaria and then, after the union, from Rumelia, Russia, he concluded, would have a "material force" in her hands for twenty-five years. Part of the sum could be used to establish better advanced schools in Sofia, where an entire generation could become imbued with a Russian or all-Slavic spirit. Another portion of the debt could be spent on a Russo-Bulgarian commercial fleet for the Danube, to counteract the influence of the Germans. The remainder could be used to defray the expenses of a Black Sea fleet for the defense of the Straits. Although nothing came of this plan, it was obvious that the general was determined to make Bulgaria a safe outpost for Russia.[39]

The appearance of Sobolev and Kaulbars in Bulgaria had not changed the railroad problem, since the new representatives were to champion Russian commercial interests. By this time the Bulgarian Conservatives had been won over to Khitrovo's plan to finance the construction of the Russian line by means of the occupation debt. Although, earlier, St.

[38] Kennedy to Granville, *FO*, 78/3414, no. 57, Sofia, June 25, 1882; Shcheglov, *op. cit.*, p. 559.

[39] Sobolev, "K Noveishei Istorii Bolgarii," *Russkaia Starina*, LI (1886), 736 n. 4; Biegeleben to Kalnoky, *HHS*, XV 19, no. 24B, réservé, Sofia, June 17, 1882; Skazkin, pp. 284–285; Shcheglov, *op. cit.*, pp. 554–555.

Petersburg had refused to yield one ruble, the Conservatives expected that Russian aid would eventually be given; hence they were not against the construction of the line under these conditions. Moreover, they hoped to gain the contract for themselves. In this manner both their country and they would benefit from Russian expenditure.[40]

Alexander shared the belief of the Conservatives that eventually Russia would give concrete assistance. In November, 1882, he informed the tsar that he wished to build the Sofia-Danube line but that Bulgaria could not afford it. The tsar's reply of November 21, drawn up by the foreign office, was short and to the point. Alexander III was pleased to hear that the prince wanted to build the line, but Bulgaria would have to finance it. Russia could only offer a loan for the necessary material.[41]

Ten days later Alexander sent another telegram which was more specific. The principal block to the construction of the Sofia-Danube line, stated the prince, was the fact that the Treaty of Berlin obligated the Bulgars to complete their share of the international line. The Bulgars were afraid to undertake the financial obligations which would be incurred by building both the international and the Russian lines. The problem could be resolved if the emperor would authorize Alexander to inform the Bulgarian assembly that Russian aid would be available to enable the Bulgarian government to maintain a balanced budget in spite of the tremendous expenses. Again the tsar refused to make concessions. He replied that he would like to help Bulgaria, but he could do no more than he had offered earlier. The Bulgars were the sole judges of their own interests.[42] From this exchange it was apparent that the Russian government had no intention of pressing for the construction of the Russian line. If the Bulgars could finance it in addition to their other obligations, Russia would be grateful. Otherwise it would have to be postponed indefinitely.

Not discouraged by this clear statement of the position of the Russian government, Sobolev on his own initiative continued to press the matter. According to the Treaty of Berlin, Bulgaria was obligated not only to build the international line, but also to purchase the British-owned Varna-Ruschuk line, which was already in operation. Since Bulgaria could not meet the costs of these two lines as well as of the Russian line without assistance, Sobolev and Kaulbars sent their own proposal to Giers on December 6/18, 1882. The generals suggested that

---

[40] Skazkin, pp. 282, 285. Nachevich, however, had told Biegeleben that he would not support plans for the Russian line. Biegeleben to Kalnoky, *HHS*, XV 19, no. 24B, réservé, Sofia, June 17, 1882.

[41] Skazkin, pp. 285–286.

[42] *Ibid.*, p. 286 n. 2.

they ask the assembly, which was to meet on December 8/20, to approve
the construction of the Sofia-Danube line at an estimated cost of
42,000,000 francs, which could be paid by the balance in the state
treasury together with the surplus revenue to be collected during the
next four years. The obstacle to the success of this plan was the cost of
purchasing the British line, which the generals estimated at 30,000,000
to 35,000,000 francs. The Bulgars would hesitate to incur the expense
of the Russian line without first having settled their British debt. Bulgarian reluctance might be overcome if the minister-president could
confidentially inform the influential members of the assembly that
Russia would, if necessary, come to the financial assistance of Bulgaria
in the purchase of the British line. This message was transmitted to
Giers by S. V. Arsen'ev, Russian diplomatic agent in Sofia, who in turn
endorsed the plan.[43]

There was little difference between the plans submitted by the prince
and by the generals. Alexander had previously asked that Russia finance
the construction of a new line; the generals wanted Russia to buy a line
that was already built. For either plan, Russia would be required to
contribute millions of francs. Although Giers' reply is not available, it
is safe to assume that this proposal too was rejected. The Russian government was not going to subsidize either the construction or the purchase of railroads in Bulgaria.

With great perseverence Sobolev and Kaulbars worked on a new
scheme in which all the railroads were to be financed exclusively by the
resources of the state without resorting to foreign loans. First, the
Russian line would be built at a cost of 42,000,000 francs. It was to be
financed by using the 15,000,000 francs in the treasury, and adding to
that amount 21,000,000 francs from the yearly revenue and the yearly
surplus of 5,000,000 to 6,000,000 francs which, according to the generals,
Bulgaria produced. Russia was to supply the rails and rolling stock.
Second, the Austrian international line was to be built piecemeal within
the resources of the state. Third, the British line was to be purchased at
the rate of 3,500,000 francs a year. Sobolev argued that all the lines
could be financed by Bulgaria without incurring a great debt.[44] The
other ministers were not enthusiastic over the prospects of these
enormous expenditures. They had, meanwhile, come into conflict with
the generals over another matter, closely allied to the building of railroads.

The demand had arisen that a new ministry, that of public works, be

---

[43] *Ibid.*, p. 286 n. 5; Hertslet, *The Map of Europe by Treaty*, IV, 3144; Koch, pp.
117–125.

[44] Sobolev, *op. cit.*, p. 726 n. 1.

established which would control and supervise the railroad development of Bulgaria. The point at issue was not the ministry itself but the minister who would run it. Sobolev's candidate was Prince Khilkov, an able and distinguished Russian who had demonstrated his capacity to deal with railroad problems in his native land. The choice had been made to secure a minister who would defend and advance the Danube line. The Bulgarian assembly, recognizing this, refused to approve the appointment, since Khilkov was considered an agent of Sobolev. Alexander also refused to accept his nomination. Sobolev sought to circumvent both the prince and the assembly by appointing his candidate, by means of a ministerial order, to be an assistant to the minister of public works at a good salary. This maneuver aroused bitter opposition from the Bulgarian ministers and the assembly. They considered it illegal because, first, such an important position should not have been filled by a simple ministerial decree, and second, the requirement that the council of state approved the appointment of foreigners to governmental positions had not been fulfilled. The assembly was determined to keep within its control the development of the railroads.[45]

The Khilkov episode finally led to an impasse which only the prince could break. Alexander yielded to the assembly and appointed G. D. Nachevich, the prominent Conservative, to the new post of minister of public works. The Conservatives had gained the initiative and were ready to push their advantage in dealing with the Russian generals. After the Khilkov affair they felt that coöperation was out of the question. Their outright attacks on the administration of the Russians drew unfavorable comments from both the Austrian and German representatives, who believed that prudence and moderation were more fitting simply because Bulgaria was materially in the power of the Russians. The Conservatives, nevertheless, having achieved one victory over the generals, now sought to challenge them on another issue—the control of the dragoon corps.[46]

After the proclamation of the change in the constitution in July, 1881, the Bulgarian gendarmerie had been converted into the so-called dragoon corps of armed mounted police, intended primarily for the suppression of local disturbances. Eventually these troops and the means they employed aroused much resentment. Most of the animosity was directed at the officers, who were Russians. The Conservatives thus had a concrete grievance on which to capitalize. In order to strengthen their

[45] Koch, p. 117; Biegeleben to Kalnoky, *HHS*, XV 20, no. 3A–E, réservé, Sofia, Jan. 9, 1883.

[46] Biegeleben to Kalnoky, *HHS*, XV 20, no. 3A–E, réservé, Jan. 9, 1883; *ibid.*, no. 4A–D, réservé, Jan. 26, 1883.

own position and to undermine Russian prestige, the Conservatives demanded that the dragoon corps be abolished. In reply Sobolev and Kaulbars suggested the transfer of the dragoons to the regular army, where they would form a cavalry unit without police power. Alexander endorsed the second solution because he wished to use every means possible to build up his army. The assembly, however, refused to provide funds in the budget to support the dragoons, and the council of state supported the assembly. These actions brought Alexander and the generals together in opposition to the assembly, whereas in the Khilkov episode the prince had sided with the assembly against the generals.[47]

Sobolev and Kaulbars urged Alexander to use the extraordinary powers which he had received in July, 1881.[48] Accordingly, the prince announced that he would refuse to approve the national budget unless it included funds for the dragoon corps. On February 23/March 7, 1883, he directed Sobolev to call the council of ministers into session the next day to inform them that the prince demanded that the funds be approved. Two of the Conservative leaders, Nachevich and Grekov, thereupon submitted their resignations, and the third, Stoilov, hesitated momentarily, uncertain of what to do.

Sobolev now had a unique opportunity opened to him. If the prince accepted the resignations and the ministry were abolished, Sobolev would be in complete command of the Bulgarian administration. However, even the general saw that such a situation would be dangerous: it would offend the national pride of the Bulgarian people. The Conservatives had done their best to disseminate the idea that the Russians were scornful of the Bulgarians and their abilities in government and politics. If a government were formed without the inclusion of some major figures in Bulgarian politics, the charges made by the Conservatives would indeed appear to be well founded. Under the circumstances no able Bulgar would have joined a new ministry. Alexander therefore refused to accept the resignations and persuaded the ministers to endorse the transfer of the dragoon corps.[49] Although the generals were successful, relations with the Conservative party had reached the breaking point. Another crisis would place Alexander in the difficult position of having to choose between the generals and the Bulgarian ministers—and such an incident was already in the making.

On February 23/March 7, 1883, a message arrived in Sofia from Exarch Iosif, whose headquarters were in Constantinople, for Stoilov,

---

[47] Sobolev, *op. cit.*, pp. 713–716; Shcheglov, *op. cit.*, pp. 569–570.

[48] Sobolev, *op. cit.*, p. 713; Shcheglov, *op. cit.*, p. 569.

[49] Sobolev, *op. cit.*, pp. 713–716; Lascelles to Granville, *FO*, 78/3528, no. 12, Sofia, March 5, 1883.

who held the triple positions of minister of foreign affairs, minister of religion, and director of post and telegraph. The exarch, with the concurrence of the Bulgarian Holy Synod, ordered Stoilov to remove Meletii, metropolitan of Sofia, from his post and to send him to Vratsa for six months. While in exile he was to be forbidden to conduct religious services.

This measure, intended as a punishment, was based upon an event that had occurred more than five years earlier. At the height of the Russo-Turkish War Meletii had succeeded in escaping from Constantinople, where he had been confined because of his pro-Bulgarian, pro-Russian, and anti-Turkish agitation, and had joined the Russian forces advancing against the Turks. His actions, which were considered patriotic by the Bulgarians, had been condemned by the church hierarchy, who feared Turkish reprisals against other church officials. On December 10/22, 1877, the Holy Synod decreed that Meletii should be deprived of his position, but the decision was not enforced at that time. After the Russian victory and the reëstablishment of peaceful conditions in Bulgaria, Meletii resumed his post as metropolitan of Sofia. The episode was forgotten until the exarch's order arrived demanding that the sentence of 1877 be carried out.[50]

Although Stoilov as minister of religion was required to execute the orders of the Holy Synod without question, on February 24/March 8 he consulted Alexander. The prince could not legally challenge the church's decision. Stoilov also called on Sobolev, who offered no opposition to the exarch's demand. Having spoken with his superiors, Stoilov ordered that Meletii should be removed that very night, February 24/25–March 8/9. The metropolitan, allowed only four hours to pack his personal belongings, was escorted out of Sofia by a sergeant major and five dragoons. Stoilov not only acted with unusual speed, but dealt with Meletii much as he would with a common criminal.[51]

As soon as Sobolev learned of the manner of Meletii's exile, he acted with equal precipitancy. Accompanied by Kaulbars, he went to the telegraph office and dispatched orders to have Meletii intercepted and returned to Sofia. When he was not successful, he sent his personal secretary, A. N. Shcheglov, to return the metropolitan.[52] By interfering with an order of the Holy Synod, Sobolev was unquestionably exceeding his powers as minister-president. Important political considerations were, however, involved.

[50] Radev, I, 368; Sobolev, *op. cit.*, p. 717.
[51] Sobolev, *op. cit.*, pp. 721–722; Shcheglov, *op. cit.*, pp. 570–572; Radev, I, 369–370; Biegeleben to Kalnoky, *HHS*, XV 20, no. 11A–D, Sofia, March 19, 1883; Lascelles to Granville, *FO*, 78/3528, no. 15, Sofia, March 17, 1883.
[52] Shcheglov, *op. cit.*, p. 571.

The abrupt execution of the exarch's order was considered by the generals to be a direct challenge to their authority and prestige. During the current governmental crisis the metropolitan had given unstinted support to the Russians. Like many of the religious leaders in Bulgaria, Meletii had received his ecclesiastical training in Russia and had returned to his native land with strong Russophil leanings which he repeatedly demonstrated. In 1877 he had joined the Russian army as it moved into Bulgaria; during the first years of the new state he had supported whatever policy Russia endorsed. Because of his influential position as metropolitan of Sofia, his espousal of the Russian cause and the generals was a source of embarrassment to the Conservatives. Meletii's removal would be of political advantage to them, particularly since the new metropolitan of Sofia was to be Grigorii of Ruschuk. The latter was in Sofia during the crisis and had agreed with Stoilov's decision to have Meletii sent away at once.[53]

Whereas Meletii had been sympathetic toward Russia, Grigorii had been just the opposite. In 1877, when Meletii fled to the Russian army, Grigorii had given what appeared to be real aid to the Turks. On June 11/23, 1877, in a pastoral letter to the clergy and members of his diocese, published in the Constantinople newspaper *La Turquie*, Grigorii praised the Ottoman Empire and called on all the sultan's subjects to rally around the throne and be ready to die for it. The Bulgars, he believed, had a sacred obligation to the sultan to pray for his health and long life. They should ask God to grant victory to the Ottoman forces over the attacking invader, the Russian army. The Orthodox should reject the ideas being disseminated by those who wished to turn Bulgar against Turk; all should work for peace and harmony with the Moslem overlord.

From Sobolev's point of view, Grigorii in this letter had committed the unpardonable sin of advocating the victory of the Turkish troops over the Russians, who were fighting for the liberation of the Orthodox Bulgars from the Moslem yoke. Now Grigorii was to be the replacement for Meletii, who had championed the cause of Russia. Certainly Grigorii, not Meletii, had acted as a traitor in 1877. Sobolev could not forget that in the past Grigorii had always sided with the Bulgarian Conservatives and had shared their anti-Russian feelings. If Grigorii were in Sofia, he would be able to use his office to assist the Conservatives against the generals.[54]

After Shcheglov had returned with Meletii to Sofia, Sobolev sent his secretary to Constantinople to explain the situation to the exarch. In the

---

[53] Sobolev, *op. cit.*, pp. 720–722.
[54] *Ibid.*, pp. 718–720; Parensov, *op. cit.*, CI, 123.

Turkish capital, Shcheglov consulted first with A. I. Nelidov, the Russian ambassador, who was following the affair closely. Nelidov said that he had been unable to make any arrangement with the exarch and that St. Petersburg was demanding information concerning the episode. He personally believed that Sobolev, since he had started the interference, should be the one to extricate himself. Shcheglov next went to see Exarch Iosif. Their first meeting was cold and unproductive. After a second conversation Iosif called the Holy Synod into session to review the case. This body now decided to soften the sentence in a few details. Meletii was to have ten days to straighten out his personal affairs in Sofia and could then go wherever he wished, outside the capital city. The incident thus ended in anything but a Russian victory. Although Meletii was given more time in which to leave Sofia, he was forced to go to Kustendil, where he could exert much less influence. The issue in the affair, that is, who should hold the office of metropolitan, resulted in a Conservative victory.[55]

The entire Meletii incident revealed how deeply the Bulgarian church was split on the issue of Russian influence in the principality. Previously it had been assumed that the closest bond between the Russians and the Bulgarians was that of religion. Now the head of the church hierarchy acted against Meletii and, indirectly, against Sobolev. What prompted the Holy Synod to take action and revive the old sentence against the metropolitan just at this time is a matter of conjecture. Sobolev claimed that indirect pressure was brought to bear on the exarch by the Conservative leaders, for Iosif was dependent on the Bulgarian government for a yearly subsidy of 300,000 francs for propaganda and educational activities in Macedonia, a program close to his heart. In previous political crises he had tried to mediate between the Russian agents and their opponents. When a decision was necessary, he had, however, always sided with the Bulgarians.[56] Although the Russian government had not officially interfered in the Meletii affair, it is significant that the Bulgarian church would not take dictation from an official simply because he was a Russian and therefore a representative of the greatest Orthodox power. Hereafter the church was to pursue the interests of Bulgaria first and to challenge Russia in the religious sphere.

The Meletii incident dealt the final blow to any hope of a reconciliation between the Conservatives and the Russian generals. Although Sobolev had not wished to break the government over the Khilkov episode, he now was ready to commit himself. On February 26/March 10, only three days after the controversy began, Sobolev informed the

---

[55] Shcheglov, *op. cit.*, pp. 574–577.
[56] Sobolev, *op. cit.*, pp. 717, 721.

prince that he and Kaulbars could no longer remain in the same government with Stoilov.[57] Alexander was forced to choose between his Conservative ministers, who were Bulgarian nationalists, and the generals,
who had the power and influence of the Russian government behind
them. The prince did not have a really free choice. The generals, whose
appointment had been made at his specific request, had been in office
only nine months. Their abrupt dismissal would have been an insult to
the Russians.[58] Since Alexander intended to go to the tsar's coronation
in May, that would give him the opportunity to discuss the problem
with the responsible Russian officials. Therefore, on February 28/March
12, Alexander accepted Stoilov's resignation. Despite Sobolev's request
that they remain in the government, Nachevich and Grekov resigned at
the same time. The Russian generals were now in complete control of
the Bulgarian ministry.

The fall of the cabinet of the Conservatives and the ascendancy of the
Russian generals underlined a development which had been going on
for months—the gradual alienation of large groups of the Bulgarian
people. The Meletii episode had shown that Russia could not depend
on the blind obedience of the Bulgarian clergy. The quarrels over the
building of the railroads had turned influential economic groups against
Russia. Although the Russian government had taken no official stand
in promoting the Danube line, and had refused to give any financial
assistance in its construction, individual Russian representatives had
tended to interfere in a manner calculated to bring profit to Russian
businessmen at the expense of their Bulgarian counterparts.

Most important, the Bulgarian people were beginning to feel the
presence of the Russians as a heavy burden. Sobolev was particularly to
blame. His position as a foreign adviser among a sensitive and proud
people was bound to be difficult, but he made the situation worse by his
arrogant, dictatorial attitude. When, for example, the Conservative
ministers submitted their resignations over the problem of the dragoon
corps, Sobolev confessed that he told them some "bitter truths." He informed them that he could take away their power and break them and
that they were in office at his pleasure.[59]

[57] *Ibid.*, p. 724 n. 1; Shcheglov, *op. cit.*, p. 573.

[58] Several sources indicate that Alexander had promised the tsar to retain the
generals for at least two years. Hence he could not dismiss them at this moment.
According to other versions, the prince decided to retain the officers in order to demonstrate the impossibility of ruling with them. Biegeleben to Kalnoky, *HHS*, XV 20,
no. 4A–D, Sofia, Jan. 26, 1883; *ibid.*, no. 11A–D, Sofia, March 19, 1883; Lascelles
to Granville, *FO*, 78/3528, no. 4, Sofia, Jan. 8, 1883; *ibid.*, no. 17, Sofia, March 17,
1883.

[59] Sobolev, *op. cit.*, pp. 715–716.

By February, 1883, Sobolev and Kaulbars had failed to gain their aims by coöperation with either political party. With the ministry solely in their hands, they would now have the opportunity to formulate a program according to their own desires. The working out of these policies would determine the fate of Russian influence in Bulgaria.

Four elements dominated Bulgarian political life: the prince, the generals, the Liberal party, and the Conservative party. Russia was directly involved in the success or failure of the generals either to control directly or to gain the coöperation of at least one of the other elements. Whether they followed the directives of their government or their own inclinations, Sobolev and Kaulbars would always be regarded as "Russian" by the Bulgarian population. The danger for Russia in Bulgarian political life was that the other three sections would unite against Sobolev if his policies proved too unpopular. The period of coöperation with the Conservatives, which had just ended, had not produced that result, although the Russian position had weakened. It remained to be seen whether the generals would be able to balance the other groups or whether they would destroy the position of the Russian government in the country for which so many sacrifices had been made.

V

THE RULE OF GENERAL SOBOLEV AND GENERAL KAULBARS

In the new cabinet, formed on March 3/15, 1883, General Sobolev retained his position as minister-president and minister of the interior, and Kaulbars remained as minister of war. The new government, described by Sobolev's secretary Shcheglov as a nonparty ministry, was distinguished by the fact that it contained three Russians, the third being Prince Khilkov, who became minister of public works. The ministers of finance and justice were T. Burmov and Teokharov, respectively, two Bulgars who had been educated in Russia and had lived there for many years. The other members were Kiriak Tsankov, minister of foreign affairs, and D. Agura, minister of education, "two second-rate Bulgarian officials completely devoted to Russia."[1]

The government thus consisted of three Russian nationals and four Bulgars who were loyal to Russia. The generals had what they had not had before, a ministry completely under their control. Now they had to demonstrate whether they could use the government to tighten Russian influence in Bulgaria, even though, as Shcheglov noted, "such a cabinet did not have deep roots in the country, and this was its weakness."[2]

The composition of the new government emphasized another point also. In the preceding nine months Sobolev had based his program upon the support he expected to receive from the Conservatives. As long as the assembly was in session Sobolev continued to work with them, though relations steadily grew worse. The general still considered the Liberals to be the real danger to the state. In February Sobolev informed Giers that with the assistance of the Conservatives he hoped to destroy the "odious Liberal intrigues."[3]

A few weeks later, however, when the break between the Conservatives and the minister-president became complete, Sobolev reversed himself and turned to the Liberals, the former "anarchists." Now the latter were designated the true representatives of the Bulgars and their interests, not the small Conservative clique whose sole purpose was to enhance

---

[1] Shcheglov, "Russkoe Ministerstvo v Bolgarii," *Istoricheskii Viestnik*, CXXVI (1911), 574.

[2] *Loc. cit.*; Radev, I, 373–374; Black, p. 233.

[3] Skazkin, p. 292; Shcheglov, *op. cit.*, p. 554.

its fortunes at the expense of the nation.[4] Without any prior assurance that the Liberals would coöperate, Sobolev placed his full support behind their policies, in the belief that the Liberals, who were out of office and anxious to return to power, would eagerly accept his endorsement. The Liberals, however, refused to commit themselves immediately: they had become highly critical of the methods employed by the generals, and did not trust them. Yet this was an excellent opportunity to exploit the estrangement of the generals and the Conservatives. Therefore the Liberals decided to await future developments before making definite commitments.

Caught between two antagonistic forces, Alexander found his position growing steadily more difficult. In the two-month interval before the coronation of the tsar it was hoped that some decisive event would demonstrate the incapacity of the generals to rule. Certainly, time seemed to be working in the prince's favor. Once in command of the ministry, Sobolev, who was described as a "vice-prince," assumed an overbearing attitude and used forceful means to attain his desires. The general's actions and methods of governing were always a point in favor of the prince and the Conservatives.[5]

The Conservatives, now in complete opposition to the generals, were not satisfied with Alexander's policy of noninterference with the administration. On March 22/April 3, Grekov, Nachevich, and Stoilov, the three leading Conservatives, sent a letter to the prince expressing their concern over recent developments and suggesting a course of action.[6] The triumvirate was deeply disturbed over the power held by the Russians, who controlled both the administration and the military forces. In 1881, they reminded him, extraordinary powers had been voted in order that he might rule. Instead, two foreign generals now exercised that authority. How could this be justified to the electorate, whose pride was injured by the necessity of using foreign rather than native administrators? Russo-Bulgarian relations were rapidly deteriorating; if continued, this trend would have serious consequences. If the Bulgarian people wished to attain their national ideal, the restoration of the San Stefano Bulgaria, they would need assistance from the great powers. This could be obtained only from Russia. Yet the achievement

---

[4] Skazkin, p. 292; Sobolev, "K Noveishei Istorii Bolgarii," *Russkaia Starina*, LI (1886), 728 n. 1.

[5] Skazkin, p. 289; Koch, p. 133; Biegeleben to Kalnoky, *HHS*, XV 20, no. 12A–C, geheim, Sofia, March 23, 1883; Lascelles to Granville, *FO*, 78/3528, no. 25, Sofia, April 6, 1883.

[6] The letter is printed in Sobolev, *op. cit.*, pp. 724–725. See also Lascelles to Granville, *FO*, 78/3528, no. 26, Sofia, April 6, 1883; Biegeleben to Kalnoky, *HHS*, XV 20, no. 13A–H, réservé, Sofia, April 7, 1883.

of the goal was being gravely endangered by internal political friction and the arrogance of the generals.

Every Bulgar who has dealt with the generals resents their scorn of all which the Bulgars hold great and sacred. The open preference for all that is Russian and all that comes from Russia, the appointment of Russians to such duties, which Bulgars could perform, the sending of our young officers to Russia, the flooding of the country with Russian officers who are brought in daily—these are the reasons for the increase of dissatisfaction with the Russians by the minute.[7]

The dismissal of the generals was the only way to prevent the further slackening of the ties with Russia, whose influence was being weakened by the tactlessness of her citizens. Once Sobolev and Kaulbars had left Bulgaria, the Conservative leaders maintained, Russo-Bulgarian friendship would be reaffirmed. They suggested that Alexander call the national assembly into session, preferably with the announcement that he desired to have the opinion of the nation on the current situation. By acting thus in a perfectly lawful manner, Alexander would not be open to censure by the Russian government. By such a move Alexander would place himself at the head of his people, and thereby gain the popular support he sorely needed. If the generals opposed convening the assembly, as was expected, they would in all probability tender their resignations, a practice which they had frequently employed. This time Alexander should accept the offer. He was advised also, to inform the tsar directly of his reasons for convening the assembly. The information should be transmitted to St. Petersburg by Metropolitan Grigorii—another sign of the confidence which the Conservatives placed in him.

Sobolev, who had managed to obtain a copy of this letter, subsequently refuted the charges against him: he was defending the real interests of Bulgaria, whereas the Conservatives were mere tools of the Austrians and Germans. If a break in Russo-Bulgarian relations occurred, the prince and the Conservatives, rather than the Russians and the Bulgarians, would be the chief sufferers. He agreed that the unification of the Bulgarian lands could be achieved only with Russian assistance.

Sobolev's most interesting observation concerned the proposal to reconvene the national assembly. He was not opposed to a session, but he wanted by-elections to be held, which he felt certain would produce a body favorable to him. If the Conservatives chanced to win, which was not expected, the general had a solution for that problem too. "I would use some measures in order to dissolve the assembly," he wrote. "I would not use any force, but would weaken the security [measures] about the

[7] Sobolev, *op. cit.*, pp. 740–741.

assembly." Sobolev meant that he would give the population of Sofia, which was anti-Conservative, the opportunity to exert pressure on the national representatives. Not only would 10,000 Sofians surge around the assembly hall, but crowds would appear from the provinces "without my summons or hint." In conclusion, he firmly stated that under no conditions would he resign.[8]

The prince's reaction to the suggestions of the Conservatives was favorable in principle. He too wished to end the rule of the generals, but his own position was not strong enough to allow him to adopt the tactics suggested. The recall of the generals was so important a matter that it could be settled only by a personal appeal to the tsar at the time of the coronation. In previous trips to Russia he had succeeded in obtaining the replacement of Russian representatives, and there was good reason to believe that this visit would be equally productive.

Instead of going directly to Moscow, Alexander left Sofia on April 15/27 and took a circuitous route through the Balkans. At Athens he received a message concerning the problem which had caused so much controversy in the past—that of the railroads. This time it was not the Russian but the international line that was in question. When representative of Austria-Hungary, Turkey, Serbia, and Bulgaria had met in Vienna in 1880 to consider the implementation of the provisions of the Treaty of Berlin, Russia had agreed that the Bulgars were morally obligated to build the international line. Since 1880 nothing positive had been done by the four powers. In the spring of 1883 Austria called the states together in order to settle the remaining details and to establish a terminal date for the completion of the lines. Once again Vienna was spurred to action by the agitation of the Russian railroad interests in Bulgaria. The Habsburg government did not object to the construction of the Russian line, nor was it particularly concerned over which company should have the contracts, but it wished to assure the prior completion of the international line.

In the meeting of May, 1883, in Vienna, the four powers finally agreed that each was to have completed by October 15, 1886, the lines designated in the Treaty of Berlin.[9] Just before the document was scheduled to be signed, the Bulgarian delegates received two conflicting sets of instructions, one from Sobolev and the other from Alexander. During the Austro-Bulgarian negotiations, the Bulgars had demanded the right to award the contract to the lowest bidder rather than to Hirsch, as had previously been agreed. Since the Austrian government was adamant

---

[8] *Ibid.*, p. 746 n. 3.
[9] Hertslet, *The Map of Europe by Treaty*, IV, 3127–3130; Koch, pp. 135–136.

only that the line be built, it promised to do its best to persuade Hirsch to surrender his contract. The Bulgarian delegates were ready to accept this proposal, but they first requested advice from both Sobolev and the prince. Sobolev replied that they should not sign until Hirsch withdrew. The prince, to whom the Austrians made a direct appeal, wired from Athens that the delegation should immediately sign the convention.

Confronted by conflicting directives, the Bulgarian delegation decided to ask the opinion of the Russian ambassador in Vienna, A. B. Lobanov-Rostovskii. He suggested that the convention be signed, but that the delegates should demand that Vienna obtain the withdrawal of Hirsch within six months. The Bulgarian representatives therefore signed the convention on April 27/May 9, with the provision that it be ratified by September 19/October 1, 1883.[10]

The final parting of the ways had now come for Alexander and his minister-president. In Sobolev's opinion, the prince had supported the Austrians against the Russians. The generals had thus succeeded not only in alienating the Conservative party but also in coming into open conflict with the prince. Since no arrangement had yet been made with the Liberals, Sobolev and Kaulbars were in effect trying to rule without popular backing. The basis for their power lay solely in the support given them by the Russian government. The struggle for the control of Bulgaria, as one observer remarked, shifted at this point from Sofia to Moscow, to which Alexander was journeying for the coronation.[11]

Understandably, the events of the past few months in Bulgaria had been followed with keen interest by the Russians. No one could deny that Russo-Bulgarian relations had reached a critical stage. The actions of the generals were widely commented upon. On March 31/April 12, Sobolev was directly blamed for the recent developments by the conservative newspaper *St. Peterburgskiia Viedomosti,* which considered it ominous that no Bulgar of prominence was included in the new ministry. The fact that Russian influence was being resisted in Bulgaria only five years after the Russo-Turkish War it attributed to the "ill-advised and peremptory measures" of the two generals. Sobolev was accused of adopting an "arrogant attitude" toward the political parties and of showing a lack of respect for "the assembly, the administration, and the state council." It was recognized that, although Sobolev's obstruction of the decisions of the Holy Synod had aroused antagonism,

[10] Skazkin, p. 290 n. 3; Black, p. 245. See also Karosseroff, *Zur Entwicklung der bulgarischen Eisenbahn;* Simeonoff, *Die Eisenbahnen und Eisenbahnpolitik in Bulgarien.*

[11] Biegeleben to Kalnoky, *HHS,* XV 20, no. 19A–F, Sofia, May 17, 1883; Schefer to Challemel-Lacour, *DDF,* V, no. 18, Sofia, April 5, 1883.

the railroad controversy had been the reason for the dispute. This question, the newspaper believed, should be settled on the basis of Bulgarian needs and interests alone. It was difficult to make the Bulgars believe that Sobolev's actions were not the direct result of his government's instructions. A more complete indictment could hardly have been made even by the Bulgarian press.[12]

Sobolev was well aware of the public criticism of his policy. In a report to Giers on April 13/25 he admitted that the "influence of Russia here is slowly diminishing" because he had been forced to take "some measures" to counteract the influence of Austria, the source of all the Russian difficulties. The general was referring to the obstructionist activities of Alexander and the Conservative party, who in his eyes were betraying Bulgaria in the interest of Russia's archrival in the Balkan Peninsula.[13] Austria was attempting to dominate the Bulgarian lands just as she was controlling Serbia and Bosnia-Hercegovina. Since the suspension of the constitution in 1881, Habsburg influence had steadily grown. Its further increase could be checked only "by energetic measures and by a definite program for the foreign and domestic policy of the principality." Hitherto, complained Sobolev, Russia had pursued no well-defined course of action.

The activities of the generals and the widespread criticism of their conduct caused deep concern to the Russian foreign office. Although admitting the partial responsibility of Alexander and the Conservatives for the strained relations, Giers and the foreign office officials in no sense exonerated the generals. In December, 1882, A. E. Vlangali, the immediate adviser to Giers, expressed fear for Russia's interests in Bulgaria, if, as he wrote, the Bulgars should begin "to hate" the generals.[14] In April Giers told Wolkenstein that it was in the interest of Russia to recall the generals, but that the time was not right.[15] Moreover, Bulgarian relations were to a large extent out of the hands of the foreign office in this matter. Sobolev's actions, wrote Skazkin, "took the form of a European scandal. The Russian government knew and saw all this, was indignant and even entered into a polemic with the general, but it could not do anything with him. . . . [The foreign office] was powerless. . . . In the episode with the generals its role was especially pitiful. It more than others opposed their nomination, it was compelled to tolerate their childish deeds [and] it, finally, was forced to cover up

---

[12] The article is found in Thornton to Granville, *FO*, 65/1155, no. 95, St. P., April 16, 1883.

[13] Skazkin, pp. 291–292; Sobolev, *op. cit.*, p. 728 n. 1.

[14] Vlangali to Giers, *NKG*, St. P., Nov. 23/Dec. 5, 1882.

[15] Wolkenstein to Kalnoky, *HHS*, X 72, no. 30B, St. P., April 8/20, 1883.

their activities with its authority."[16] Policy was being determined, not
by the normal agencies of the government, but by the personal opinions
of Alexander III.

By May, 1883, the tsar had come to regret his decision of July, 1881.
At that time he had supported the prince and the Conservative party
by strengthening the position of the executive branch and curtailing
the authority of the elected representatives. In 1881 Alexander had
acted without seeking prior Russian consent; the tsar had agreed to
the *fait accompli*. Now, in 1883, not the prince but the generals had
won the tsar's sympathy.[17] Again a policy was accepted which had been
undertaken without instructions from the Russian government. This
time the measures approved would limit the power of the prince and
would increase the coöperation with the Liberals, which was in direct
contrast to the decision of 1881. In both years the tsar acted from personal feelings. In 1881 he feared popular rule; in 1883 he accepted the
generals' denunciation of the prince and the Conservatives.

From the prince's point of view, the solution of the difficulties was
relatively easy. The generals should be recalled and be replaced by
Ernrot. But during his coronation visit Alexander was made to feel the
change of atmosphere in the Russian court. "Repeatedly and vainly" he
asked "for an audience with the tsar, until at length to the tsar's wrath
he forced his way unbidden to his presence."[18] The interview was a
failure. The prince's father, who was the uncle of Alexander III, was
given a similar reception. At a court ball Alexander of Hesse "was
introduced only to ladies of lesser degree, and he and his son were then
sent home, dripping with perspiration, while the immediate members
of the family went to supper with the empress. 'I'll be damned,' said
Prince Alexander of Hesse, 'if anyone ever sees me in Russia again on
any ceremonial occasion.' "[19]

The prince soon found that his hopes of securing the recall of the
generals were not to be realized. Sobolev and two special delegations of
Bulgars had come to the coronation also. Sobolev was anxious to defend
his past activities before the tsar, but above all to present a plan of
action for the future. In his opinion, the Russian government should
provide the leadership in the Bulgarian state, since both the prince and
the Conservatives had failed. Sobolev's policy called for a return to the
constitutional form of government which had been abandoned in 1881.

[16] Skazkin, pp. 284, 292–293.
[17] *Ibid.*, p. 284. Skazkin adheres to the view that Alexander III was his own
foreign minister. *Ibid.*, p. 183.
[18] Corti, *DTD*, p. 288.
[19] *Loc. cit.;* Skazkin, p. 293 n. 3; Shcheglov, *op. cit.*, pp. 583–584.

He wished the Bulgarian Grand National Assembly to be reconvened in order to consider amendments to the Tyrnovo constitution. The changes would be designed both to prevent the excesses of popular rule and to curb the power of the prince. Once the new plan was put into operation, the real power in Bulgaria would lie in the hands of the Russian ministers. Sobolev and the Liberals could then govern the country together. Sobolev's proposals were considered by the tsar and also by Giers and I. A. Zinoviev, head of the Asiatic department. After the tsar had approved this plan, Giers informed Alexander that he would have to accept a curtailment of his own power and Bulgaria would have to return to a constitutional form of government.[20]

Of the two Bulgarian delegations attending the coronation, the first was sent by Kaulbars, who was acting as regent while Prince Alexander and Sobolev were in St. Petersburg. The group, composed of Liberals, was led by N. Suknarov, whom Kaulbars had appointed mayor of Sofia. When Alexander of Battenberg learned that the delegation was on its way, he protested vigorously, particularly after he heard that the group was seeking his deposition and wished to have him replaced by Prince Waldemar of Denmark, the empress' brother. Despite Alexander's insistence that the tsar refuse to receive the group, Alexander III granted it an audience, but did not accede to its request.

The second delegation, composed of Bulgarian Conservatives favorable to the prince, was met in a correct but cool manner. The members of the delegation returned to Bulgaria almost immediately when they realized that there was no chance of recalling the generals. The way in which the two delegations were greeted was further proof to Alexander that he could no longer count on Russian favor.[21]

One of the prince's staunchest supporters in previous years, Katkov, now turned against him, asserting that he was responsible for the Russian failure to obtain economic concessions in Bulgaria. At the same time the prince learned that Arsen'ev, acting Russian diplomatic agent in Sofia, who did not conceal his criticism of the generals, had been recalled. Certainly, all signs indicated that Sobolev's role had not been *ausgespielt*, as was believed in early May; rather, it seemed that Alexander's prediction that Russia "wanted to break my neck and turn me out of Bulgaria" would come true.[22] The prince left Russia in despair.

---

[20] Shcheglov, *op. cit.*, pp. 578, 582–583; Nelidov to Giers, *NKG*, Pera, April 14/26, 1883.

[21] Skazkin, p. 293; Corti, *Alexander*, pp. 123–124; Wolkenstein to Kalnoky, *HHS*, X 73, geheim, St. P., June 7/19, 1883.

[22] Corti, *Alexander*, pp. 124–125; Biegeleben to Kalnoky, *HHS*, XV 20, no. 18C, Sofia, May 3, 1883; Wyndham to Granville, *FO*, 78/3509, no. 285, conf., Const., May 6, 1883.

The trip home was equally unpleasant. In Berlin, Bismarck made it clear that he had no sympathy for the prince. The German chancellor was concerned primarily with the maintenance of the Dreikaiserbund.[23] In Vienna, Franz Joseph received him in a friendly manner, but the news from Bulgaria reaching the Austrian capital was ominous. It was obvious that Kaulbars had assumed the role of a dictator. Reports indicated that he had dismissed numerous officers and more than one hundred thirty magistrates who supported Alexander. At the same time it was learned that the tsar had decided not to send Ernrot in any capacity to Bulgaria, although Alexander had received the impression that he would. This last news could be interpreted in only one way: Alexander had suffered absolute defeat in Russia, while the generals had won an equally decisive victory. On August 13/25 Alexander wrote to his father "not to take any more steps on his behalf with the tsar, whom he regarded as a 'poor specimen of a man of honor.' "[24]

Since Russia had officially adopted a plan calling for a return to the Bulgarian constitution and the limitation of the prince's authority, she had to send an agent to supervise its execution. The man chosen was A. S. Ionin, who had recently been in Montenegro. Compared to previous Russian representatives, Ionin appeared to be an admirable choice. In discussing the appointment with Wolkenstein, Giers stressed the fact that Ionin was considered one of the initiators of Russian policy. In contrast to the Panslav enthusiasm he had demonstrated in 1875–1878, Ionin was now considered prudent and well-balanced. In his report on the conversation, Wolkenstein concurred in Giers' analysis. The Austrian representative knew Ionin personally and described him as an intelligent and useful agent; although a warm patriot, he was not a Panslav agitator.[25] The only derogatory report came from W. Kirby Green, British agent in Scutari, who called Ionin "one of the cleverest of the Slavophil band."[26] Nevertheless, the choice for the post appeared a sound one for so difficult a mission.

Although Ionin was allowed considerable latitude in the means to be employed, his instructions were precise on what he should accomplish. First, he was to see that Russian prestige was upheld; second, the generals were to be kept in office for the present, but plans were to be made for their eventual recall; and third, the prince was to be deprived

---

[23] Skazkin, p. 294.

[24] Corti, *DTD*, p. 289; Skazkin, p. 294; Koch, p. 146; Corti, *Alexander*, p. 131.

[25] Wolkenstein to Kalnoky, *HHS*, X 73, vertraulich, St. P., July 20/Aug. 1, 1883. Skazkin, p. 297, described Ionin as "an intelligent man, an experienced diplomat, and politically talented—a very rare combination among Russia's agents in the Balkans."

[26] Green to Pauncefoote, *FO*, 102/23, pvt. letter, Scutari, Aug. 15, 1883.

of the powers he had won in 1881 and a return was to be made in the direction of the Tyrnovo constitution.[27] The influence of the tsar was apparent in these instructions. In complete sympathy with the generals, he wrote, on a report from Lobanov in Vienna concerning a conversation with the prince, "It is necessary for us to support Sobolev and Kaulbars . . . and I blame the prince *entirely* for all this."[28]

Before Ionin's arrival in Bulgaria, Alexander made one last attempt to rid himself of the generals. He informed the tsar that he was going to call into session the national assembly, which he expected would pass a vote of no confidence in the ministers. Alexander could then dismiss them. When the tsar heard of the intended action, he replied that he would not permit the national assembly to take such measures and that the prince would be held responsible for whatever happened. Alexander should do nothing, the tsar concluded, until Ionin arrived.[29]

On his way to Sofia, Ionin met Stoilov, the Conservative leader, in Vienna, and expressed the hope that they could coöperate. Ionin admitted that the generals were inexperienced and had committed mistakes, but others (he obviously meant the prince and the Conservatives) had erred, too. Consequently, it would be wise to forget the past and reconcile recent differences. When Ionin sent an account of the meeting to Giers, the foreign minister replied that the generals might have made mistakes, but that their intentions were correct. Ionin was thus provided with additional evidence that he was to maintain the authority of Sobolev and Kaulbars, "because such was the wish of the tsar."[30]

When Ionin arrived in Sofia, on August 10/22, he found that the national assembly was scheduled to meet in extraordinary session early in September in order to ratify two agreements. The first was the railroad convention, which had been signed in May and had to be approved by September 19/October 1. The second was the agreement setting the Russian occupation debt at 10,618,250 rubles, a figure which had been negotiated by Kiriak Tsankov, Bulgaria's foreign minister.[31] The danger for the Russian plans lay in the fact that, once the assembly was in

---

[27] Skazkin, pp. 295–296; Shcheglov, *op. cit.*, p. 587; Corti, *Alexander*, pp. 133–134. Giers made no attempt to conceal from Wolkenstein the fact that Russia's prestige was at stake; therefore the generals would have to be retained at least for the present. Wolkenstein to Kalnoky, *HHS*, X 73, no. 2, geheim, privatschreiben, St. P., Aug. 2/14, 1883; *ibid.*, X 72, tel. no. 84, St. P., Aug. 8, 1883; Lascelles to Granville, *FO*, 78/3529, no. 71, Sofia, Sept. 5, 1883.

[28] Skazkin, p. 294.

[29] Steinbach to Kalnoky, *HHS*, XV 20, tel. no. 53, Sofia, July 25, 1883; Lascelles to Granville, *FO*, 78/3528, no. 56, Sofia, Aug. 2, 1883; Welsersheimb to Kalnoky, *HHS*, X 72, no. 58A–C, St. P., Aug. 31/Sept. 12, 1883.

[30] Skazkin, pp. 298–299; Schefer to Challemel-Lacour, *DDF*, V, no. 69, Sofia, Aug. 9, 1883.

[31] Skazkin, p. 301; Hertslet, *op. cit.*, IV, 3131–3132.

session, other matters, such as a vote of no confidence in the generals, might be considered. Alexander himself had hopes that, during the debate on the railroad, opposition to the generals might become strong enough to force them to resign. Ionin had to use all the skill at his command to thwart any plan which might lead to the premature removal of the generals.[32]

On August 12/24 Ionin had a three-hour session with the prince, the first of a series of meetings characterized by acrimony, sarcasm, and outright insult. Ionin brought a letter from the tsar stating that the Russian representative was to survey the situation in Bulgaria and give advice on the policy to be followed.[33] Upon receiving this message, Alexander wished to dismiss Ionin, but the latter insisted that he had to explain his mission then and there. Thereupon Ionin, in his own words, delivered an "energetic protest" against the prince's attitude toward the generals. Then, in "the form of an ultimatum," he made the following demands. At the opening of the assembly in September, Alexander was to inform the delegates that they were convened "exclusively for the ratification of the Russian and Austrian conventions and for the adoption of a budget, and that no further debates of any kind would be allowed."[34] Sobolev and Kaulbars were to be retained, and a commission was to be established to study the changes needed in the Tyrnovo constitution. The Grand National Assembly was to be convened at a later date to study the recommendations. Since any constitutional change made under Russian sponsorship would deprive Alexander of the powers he had gained in 1881, it could not be expected that he would willingly consent to Ionin's proposal.

The two men then reviewed the history of Russo-Bulgarian relations, each presenting his own interpretation. Alexander complained that he was attacked for being a German; the generals were the first to shout this in the streets. He was proud of his German blood, but he had demonstrated his devotion to the tsar also, and his gratitude for all that Russia had done for Bulgaria. The country, however, could not endure Sobolev any longer. When Ionin replied that he had evidence to the contrary, Alexander answered that he would let the assembly decide. Ionin, countering that the assembly could not be allowed to consider the matter, accused Alexander of conspiring to use the assembly to make himself the supreme ruler. Ionin, as a Russian, believed in autocracy,

[32] Lascelles to Granville, *FO*, 78/3528, no. 53, Sofia, July 1, 1883; *ibid.*, no. 61, Sofia, Aug. 20, 1883; Wolkenstein to Kalnoky, *HHS*, X 73, geheim, St. P., June 7/19, 1883; Skazkin, pp. 294, 301–302.
[33] Corti, *Alexander*, pp. 133–134; Koch, p. 148; Skazkin, p. 302; Lascelles to Granville, *FO*, 78/3528, no. 62, Sofia, Aug. 20, 1883.
[34] Skazkin, p. 302.

but an autocracy based on the union of the nation and the ruler. In Bulgaria Alexander had the support of only a few individuals. Finally, Ionin demanded that the prince immediately and categorically accept his "ultimatum." Alexander asked if this was the tsar's wish. The answer was yes. When Alexander suggested a compromise, Ionin replied, "There will not nor can there be any concessions." At the end of the conference no decision had been reached, but both participants were well aware that they were embarked upon a struggle to the finish.[35]

Ionin now set out to gain the support of the Bulgarian political groups. He realized that Alexander would play a clever game, presenting himself to the Bulgarian people as an ultra-patriot who was defending the national interests from foreign domination. Alexander's position had great appeal for the Bulgarians, most of whom had seen enough of the generals. Ionin could combat the prince's policy only by joining hands with the Liberals, the strongest political faction in the nation. In a battle of the Russians and the Liberals against the prince and the Conservatives, it was almost a certainty that the former group would emerge victorious.

By this time, however, much had happened in Bulgarian party politics which made Ionin's task more difficult. When the generals took complete charge of the ministry in March, they had hoped to obtain the assistance of the Liberal party. Despite the failure of the Liberal leaders to grant them outright support, the generals had continued to work for the party and had backed its candidates in the municipal and general elections in the spring.[36] Notwithstanding the aid they had received, the Liberals were just as weary of the Russians as were the Conservatives. In March they were ready to consider joining with the Conservatives for the sole purpose of ousting Sobolev and Kaulbars.[37] Although nothing came of the negotiations, the two parties had finally found an issue on which they could agree. The Liberals also began to realize that in the struggle between the prince and the Conservatives, on the one hand, and the Russian interests, on the other hand, they held the balance of power. Above all, the Liberals wished to see the Tyrnovo constitution restored, because its principles would enable their party to dominate the assembly. The Liberal goal was thus to return to the constitutional regime prior to 1881. This was to be their price for cooperation with either of the rival groups.

The events connected with the coronation trip and Alexander's set-

[35] *Ibid.*, pp. 302–304; Koch, pp. 148–149; Corti, *Alexander*, pp. 134–135.
[36] Biegeleben to Kalnoky, *HHS*, X 20, no. 13A–H, Sofia, April 7, 1883; Skazkin, p. 299.
[37] Biegeleben to Kalnoky, *HHS*, XV 20, no. 12B, réservé, Sofia, March 23, 1883.

back in Russia hastened the negotiations between the Liberals and the Conservatives. The Conservatives, the minority party, had lost Russian support and knew that their position was precarious. To oppose both the Liberals and the Russians would be political suicide. Since the Liberals were certainly the lesser of the two evils, the Conservatives considered it better to make concessions to them than to perpetuate the Russians in power and indirectly to contribute to a Russian-Liberal alliance. In the negotiations with the Conservatives, the Liberals were now being led by Dragan Tsankov. He had been interned by Alexander in February, 1882, and had just been released. The two parties finally reached a tentative agreement, on August 8/20, to unite their efforts against the Russians; Alexander was to be asked to create a commission to consider amendments to the constitution which would be submitted to the Grand National Assembly.[38]

In agreeing to these terms Tsankov had been able to override the opposition of those in his own party who wanted no compromise with the Conservatives.[39] Everything, as Tsankov told the British representative, was now up to the prince. It was impossible to obtain the immediate dismissal of the generals: Russia was too powerful, and could not be challenged to an open fight with any hope of success. The Russian government controlled "the army, the gendarmerie and had agents in all corners of the state." The simplest and most effective way to get rid of the generals, Tsankov believed, would be to return to the Tyrnovo constitution; then there would be no need for Russian ministers. Tsankov proposed that the prince issue a manifesto, on August 30/ September 11, announcing that he would reëstablish a constitutional form of government.[40]

The Liberals, the Conservatives, and the Russian representatives were now in agreement that a return should be made to constitutional government. They differed only in regard to who should get the credit for the restoration, and the circumstances under which it would be accomplished.

Since the principal aim of the Liberals was to restore the constitution, they did not end negotiations with the Russians until their goal was achieved. Playing a dangerous and shifting game, they refused to come out completely and irrevocably against Ionin, but continued to use the Russian connection to obtain additional concessions from the Conservatives. Tsankov explained the policy by saying that the Liberals regarded

---

[38] Black, p. 238; Steinbach to Kalnoky, *HHS*, XV 20, no. 30C, Aug. 23, 1883.
[39] Black, p. 239; Skazkin, p. 300; Radev, I, 402–404.
[40] Lascelles to Granville, *FO*, 78/3528, no. 63, Sofia, Aug. 21, 1883; *ibid.*, no. 65, Sofia, Aug. 23, 1883.

the Russians as protectors against the prince. Until Bulgaria was again under the Tyrnovo constitution, the Liberals could not allow the defeat of the generals.[41]

Ionin knew of the agreement between the Liberal and Conservative parties, since it had been published. Despite the apparent union of the two parties, he still expected to obtain the support of the Liberals. Believing that the latter were on his side,[42] Ionin, on August 17/29, asked for an audience. Alexander, with illness as the excuse, refused. The next day, however, he received Ionin, and another spirited debate took place. Ionin pressed Alexander to agree to the demands presented earlier, but the prince refused to restrict the debates in the coming assembly, and "categorically protested" against keeping Sobolev in office until the assembly convened. When Ionin remarked that the dismissal of the generals would be an affront to the tsar, Alexander replied, "I also am the ruler in my own country and I ask you immediately to tell Sobolev that he submit his resignation." Since Ionin refused to carry out this order, the prince announced that he would telegraph the tsar. The answer would be in the negative, Ionin informed him. "In that case, I am not the prince here; if I cannot order my ministers I had better leave Sofia." "As it pleases you" (*Kak vam budet ugodno*) was Ionin's comment. Alexander gave warning of his intention to ask Grekov to form a new government without Sobolev. Ionin would not consent to this, either. Then, said Alexander, there would be two ministries. Ionin replied, "I know."

Ionin acknowledged to Giers that he had gone beyond his instructions in his threatening attitude and choice of words. But, in view of the conditions in Bulgaria and the importance which Russia attached to his mission, he could not rely exclusively on diplomatic measures.[43]

Ionin's tactics had indeed frightened Alexander. Well aware of the Russian representatives' attempt to enlist Liberal support, the prince felt that he was losing ground. Two days later, on August 20/September 1, he requested that Ionin visit him. This time Alexander expressed his concern that Russia was seeking to force him to leave Bulgaria. If this were true, he preferred to leave immediately rather than experience the humiliation of having his throne taken from him by the national

---

[41] *Ibid.*, 78/3529, no. 72, Sofia, Sept. 5, 1883; Steinbach to Kalnoky, *HHS*, XV, no. 30C, Sofia, Aug. 23, 1883.

[42] Skazkin, pp. 304–305.

[43] *Ibid.*, pp. 305–306. Both Giers and the tsar were greatly disturbed by this meeting. Giers believed that Ionin's action would compromise Russia before Europe, and Ionin was so informed. *Ibid.*, p. 306 n. 1. See also Schefer to Challemel-Lacour, *DDF*, V, no. 86, Sofia, Aug. 31, 1883.

assembly. Ionin assured him that Russia had no such plans.[44] Alexander nevertheless begged the Russian agent to use all his influence to prevent the assembly from publicly casting a vote against him. Ionin agreed, but only on the condition that Alexander acquiesce to all the Russian demands. The prince was forced to comply: the national assembly was to be limited in its activities to the ratification of the railroad convention and the occupation debt. In a public manifesto the prince was to proclaim his intention of creating a commission to prepare the draft of a constitution, which would be submitted in due time to the Grand National Assembly for ratification. Until this constitution was adopted, the present ministers were to remain in office. Although agreeing to the manifesto, which was issued on August 30/September 11, the prince telegraphed the tsar that he did so only because he had no other choice. He felt that the final result would be the destruction of his own personal authority and prestige.[45]

Ionin thus appeared to be on the verge of complete success. He believed that he had the support of the Liberal party; Alexander had submitted to Russian pressure and he was going to lose the powers he had gained in 1881. In discussing the crisis with the Austrian representative, Ionin defended his own actions energetically. Although agreeing with Biegeleben's remark that the prince's authority was compromised, since he did not have control over his ministers, Ionin expressed the view that the current developments would later serve to strengthen Alexander's position. When Biegeleben asked why Russian honor was involved more with Sobolev and Kaulbars than it had been with other Russian representatives who had been recalled, Ionin replied that it was "the last drop which always made the vase overflow."[46]

Before the convening of the national assembly on September 4/16, Alexander continued to look for some escape from his predicament.[47] On August 29/September 10 he sent a telegram to Alexander III in which he tried to capitalize on the tsar's strong conservatism by questioning the wisdom of the apparent Russian alliance with the Liberals, the outspoken opponents of autocracy and imperial rule. When the prince's message reached St. Petersburg, the tsar was in Copenhagen. Giers read the message, and sent it on with his own observations. Ionin, he wrote, was merely following his instructions in seeking to destroy the

---

[44] Giers, in fact, was emphatic on this point: the abdication of the prince would be a "calamity" because it would bring the other European powers into the Bulgarian problem. Kennedy to Granville, *FO*, 65/1157, no. 206, St. P., Sept. 10, 1883.

[45] Skazkin, p. 308 n. 2, p. 309 n. 1, p. 310; Koch, pp. 151–152.

[46] Biegeleben to Kalnoky, *HHS*, XV 20, tel. no. 33, Sofia, Sept. 7, 1883.

[47] Skazkin, p. 298; Lascelles to Granville, *FO*, 78/3528, no. 62, Sofia, Aug. 20, 1883; *ibid.*, no. 67, Sofia, Aug. 30, 1883; Steinbach to Kalnoky, *HHS*, XV 20, no. 29B, geheim, Sofia, Aug. 9, 1883.

influence of the small clique with whom the prince was associated. This group sought to remove the generals as an obstacle to their personal aspirations. The Grand National Assembly must put an end to these intrigues by restoring the constitution and giving the state a new legal basis. "I completely share your views," commented the tsar. Ionin's handling of the situation thus received a further imperial endorsement.[48]

The prince finally tried an appeal to the great powers, who as signatories of the Treaty of Berlin were concerned in Bulgarian developments. Bismarck's attitude, as could be expected, remained unchanged. The Dreikaiserbund and not Bulgaria was his interest. A similar reaction came from Vienna. Alexander, of course, did not know of the treaty relationship between the three conservative states. In March, Kalnoky had approved Sobolev's assumption of full command in Bulgaria, although he could not resist adding ironically that he thought "things could be worse."[49] Subsequently, he instructed Biegeleben not to become involved in Bulgaria's domestic affairs and to refrain from taking part in any protests against the Russian generals. Although Biegeleben did adhere to his instructions, he nevertheless let Ionin know that Austria-Hungary believed that the prince's authority should be maintained. It was the Habsburg view that the executive branch should rule the nation. Biegeleben did not conceal his personal sympathy for Alexander, but he never openly placed Austrian support behind the prince in opposition to the Russians.[50]

The only real encouragement to the prince came from Great Britain. On August 2, Lascelles told Alexander that he should act in a positive manner. He should announce either that the generals would be dismissed or that they would be retained; uncertainty was detrimental to the best interests of the nation. A month later Lascelles went one step farther and suggested that Alexander restore the constitution and reduce the size of the army. Neither measure met with Alexander's approval. A restoration of the constitution was, in his mind, a confession of his inability to rule. A reduction in the armed forces would be a reversal of the policy he had long supported. He expected the Russians to leave eventually, and he would then be in sole command of a large army. Although he did not wish to take the advice of the British, he welcomed their moral support in his battle for independence.[51]

As a last resort, Alexander and the Conservatives tried a new ap-

[48] Skazkin, p. 310 n. 1.
[49] *Ibid.*, pp. 290, 297.
[50] Biegeleben to Kalnoky, *HHS*, XV 20, tel. no. 23, Sofia, Sept. 7, 1883; Skazkin, p. 297 n. 2; Black, p. 242.
[51] Lascelles to Granville, *FO*, 78/3528, no. 56, Sofia, Aug. 2, 1883; *ibid.*, 78/3529, no. 69, Sofia, Sept. 2, 1883; *ibid.*, no. 70, Sofia, Sept. 3, 1883; Granville to Lascelles, *FO*, 78/3529, draft no. 2, Sept. 7, 1883.

proach. Through their newspapers the Conservatives charged that the
generals wanted to sell out Bulgaria "by insisting on the absolute
recognition of the Austro-Bulgarian railroad convention."[52] Until the
fall of 1883 the Conservatives had supported the position of the Russian
government, which had agreed, in 1880, that Austria's claims under the
Treaty of Berlin would have to be fulfilled. Now, for completely political
reasons, the Conservatives presented themselves to the public as patriots
who were defending Bulgarian national interests which Russia wished
to betray. In truth, they did not want to block the Austrian railroad, for
they expected to profit personally by its construction. Their sole aim
was to discredit the generals; if the latter remained in office, they
could prevent the Conservative interests from obtaining contracts. By
opposing the Austrian convention, the Conservatives were joining with
the Liberals, who feared a drain on the state treasury. It was hoped
that the association of the two parties on this question would bring a
vote of no confidence, which would lead to the removal of the generals.[53]

The Conservative maneuver, instead of strengthening the position of
its sponsors, played directly into Liberal hands. Recognizing the tactics
of the Conservatives, the Liberals felt that all three opposing groups—
the prince, the generals, and the Conservatives—could be forced to
accept the Liberal program. They therefore decided to try to gain the
complete and immediate restoration of the Tyrnovo constitution.
Previously, agreement had been reached only on the basis that a commission would be set up to study what amendments were necessary.
Now the full and final goal was to be achieved.

The Liberals first approached Ionin. Although the restoration of the
constitution would result in the dismissal of the generals, since the
ministers would be chosen from the majority party, Ionin did not object
to this eventuality. If they left as a result of Russian acquiescence in a
Bulgarian parliamentary shift, it would be entirely different from
being dismissed because of a public vote of no confidence by the
assembly. Ionin thus agreed to the Liberal demands.[54]

Although the Liberals desired the return of the Tyrnovo constitution,
they had a further aim—the removal of Russian influence from the
government. They could achieve their first objective by the agreement
with Ionin, but they would then be indebted to Russia for their victory.
Except for one extreme faction, the Liberals were even more hostile
to the Russians than were the Conservatives. Certainly, both the Con-

[52] Skazkin, p. 310.
[53] *Ibid.*, p. 311.
[54] *Ibid.*, p. 312.

servatives and the Russians agreed in principle that Bulgaria should have a strong conservative government. In contrast, the Liberals had little sympathy for Alexander III's autocratic regime. Therefore, as a second step, Tsankov went to Alexander, hoping to gain his approval for the restoration of the constitution, which would be done in such a manner that the generals would be forced out of the government. His proposal was accompanied by a clear warning: if the prince did not return to constitutional government immediately, the Liberals would coöperate with the Russians. Tsankov had already told Alexander, "Give us the Tyrnovo constitution again and on the same day the Russians in Bulgaria will be given a death blow." When Alexander sought to impose certain conditions, Tsankov replied, "Alles oder gar nichts."[55]

Alexander was trapped. It would certainly be less humiliating if he restored the constitution and remained as ruler of Bulgaria than if he were forced to abdicate or to become a Russian puppet. In returning to the constitution, he would sacrifice his personal power, but he would regain popular support and win respect for his bold action. Alexander accepted the Liberal demands because they were the lesser of two evils. His only condition was that the assembly should unanimously request him to reëstablish constitutional government.

By clever handling of the domestic situation, the Liberals had succeeded in obtaining support from all their opponents. On the night of September 3/15–4/16, the leaders of the two parties met to plan their strategy for ousting the generals.[56] As was expected, the prince opened the assembly on September 4/16 with a speech stating that the sole purpose of the meeting was to ratify the railroad convention and the Russian occupation debt. He alluded to the manifesto he had issued on August 30/September 11. To this point he had followed Ionin's instructions. The first suspicion the Russians had that they had been duped came two days later, on September 6/18. After endorsing the two conventions, the assembly asked the prince to restore immediately the Tyrnovo constitution.[57] When Tsankov indicated his enthusiastic endorsement, Sobolev and Kaulbars abruptly left the hall, followed by "shouts of triumph from the chamber." Although it was almost midnight, the

---

[55] Corti, *Alexander*, pp. 135–136. Prince Alexander reported another conversation. He claimed that Sobolev told Tsankov, who in turn relayed it to the prince, that Russia really wanted a ten-year protectorate over Bulgaria and the removal of Alexander by the assembly. It is extremely doubtful that even Sobolev would make such a statement, but Tsankov might have so informed the prince, as a means of exerting pressure on him. Koch, p. 153.

[56] Koch, p. 154.

[57] *Loc. cit.;* Radev, I, 410–412.

assembly adjourned to Alexander's residence to present the petition. The next day, September 7/19, the prince restored the constitution.[58]

The betrayal by the Liberal party came as a total surprise to the Russians, who had underestimated the harm done by Russian agents, and the suspicions aroused by their methods. The Russian government objected not to the return to the constitution but to the means by which it was accomplished. The assembly had openly expressed a lack of confidence in the ministers by reaching an agreement without their knowledge. In effect, the Bulgarian assembly had also delivered a rebuke to Alexander III.

Although the generals had previously been under orders not to resign, Giers on September 7/19 telegraphed Ionin that the tsar now agreed that Sobolev and Kaulbars should give up their positions. Thus, on the same day that Alexander restored the constitution, the generals submitted their resignations, which, needless to say, were eagerly accepted. Thus the era of Sobolev and Kaulbars came to an abrupt and unexpected end.[59]

The startling news from Sofia and its implications for Russian policy caused deep concern in St. Petersburg. Why had the Bulgars turned so violently against Russia? Certainly, the past two years had been a difficult period in Russo-Bulgarian relations. Twice Russia had been taken by surprise: the coup of 1881 and the restoration of the constitution in 1883. Russia could hardly claim that her influence prevailed in Sofia when she learned of major changes in the government only at the time they were announced to all the great powers simultaneously.

Moreover, the Bulgarians, not the tsar, had taken the initiative. Alexander III had been forced to shift his support from the Conservatives, whose political views most nearly corresponded with his own, to the Liberals, the former "nihilists and anarchists." Once they had received Russian endorsement, the Liberals had used it to bargain in domestic politics. In the end they had shown themselves far more concerned about their own position in the state and the welfare of their nation than they were with the interests of Russia. The gratitude for the Russian victory in 1878 had indeed been dissipated.[60]

The frequent admissions by Giers that the generals were not blameless in their conduct of affairs in Sofia, but that nothing could be done about it, are direct indications that the Russian foreign office did not wish to go all the way in defending their representatives. The inflexibility of Russian policy limited the possibilities open to the foreign office. The

---

[58] Koch, p. 155; Black, pp. 242–243.
[59] Skazkin, p. 318 n. 2.
[60] Welsersheimb to Kalnoky, *HHS*, X 72, no. 58A–C, St. P., Aug. 31/Sept. 12, 1883.

generals had to be kept in power temporarily because the tsar wished it. Ionin had little latitude in which to bargain. The Liberals, in contrast, were given an open field in which to maneuver.

Since Alexander III had concerned himself personally with Bulgarian affairs, the failure of Russian policy can be placed directly on his shoulders. In his handling of the Bulgarian problem the tsar was guided by personal feelings rather than by a detached study of the circumstances. Because of his strong dislike for Alexander of Battenberg, "the German," he blamed the prince almost exclusively for the Russian defeat. With little understanding of the workings of party politics or constitutional government, the tsar exaggerated the situation: the prince was trying to thwart the moves of the generals, who were acting from the purest of motives.

In supporting the generals, Sobolev in particular, the tsar was on weak ground. The minister-president had proved to be a poor administrator for a new state. A shallow thinker, Sobolev saw only the immediate problem and solved it without provision for future repercussions. He formulated bold plans and made rash statements. His use of frontal assaults to overwhelm his opponents reflected his military training. His methods and attitude reminded the Bulgars of the humiliations of the Turkish period, which they had hoped were gone forever. They suspected that Russia had plans for Bulgaria that went beyond those of protection and guidance. The British and Austrian newspapers and representatives, in carrying out the foreign policy aims of their governments, did what they could to implant doubt in the minds of the Bulgarians. Russia, they declared, treated Bulgaria as a province, and considered the Bulgarian people in the same class with the Asiatic nomads of the eastern provinces. The actions of Russian agents like Sobolev helped to support such charges.

The railroad issue had contributed to the intensification of Bulgarian national feeling. By allowing the Russian agents to champion individual undertakings which frequently were against the best interests of Russia as a nation, the Russian foreign office laid itself open to the charge of regarding Bulgaria as an open field for economic exploitation. Bulgarian nationalism throve on opposition to foreign control.

The importance of Bulgarian national pride was recognized by the Russians themselves in their explanations of the cause of the defeat. At first the tendency was to follow the tsar's reasoning, namely, that the prince was the sole cause of the disaster. After the first shock wore off, they realized that it would be an unfortunate commentary on Russian policy if one man, the prince of Bulgaria, could cause so much grief.

Shcheglov, Sobolev's secretary, who had been close to the scene, emphasized that the Bulgarian people disliked foreign control. He had to
admit that not only the generals but Ionin as well had shown an unfortunate lack of tact in the negotiations. The Russian policy of direct
interference in Bulgarian internal affairs was listed as the final cause
of the deterioration of Russo-Bulgarian relations.[61]

The conservative Russian paper *Novoe Vremia* argued to much the
same effect. According to an article published in December, the great
mistake had been Russia's direct participation in the administration of
the principality. Russia had become the target for all who wished to
attack the policies of the Bulgarian government, particularly since one
Russian citizen was minister of the interior and another was minister
of war. *Novoe Vremia* believed that Russia should withdraw completely
from the Bulgarian administration and gain her ends through diplomatic channels alone. The Bulgarians should be convinced that Russia
wished to help and not to threaten their country. So far, the newspaper
concluded, Russia had never let the Slavs know what she expected of
them, if she herself knew.[62]

The most interesting explanation of the events in Bulgaria came from
Ionin himself. In October, after he had time to consider the whole controversy, he wrote a fifty-page memorandum. The Russians, he concluded, were at fault for the decline in Russian prestige.

> Moreover, we ourselves could not define for ourselves the goal which we could and
> which we needed to pursue in Bulgaria. In connection with this we became confused
> in the selection of the means [to be used], so that each of our agents formulated his
> own special plan of action and destroyed the work of his predecessors.[63]

The Bulgars, Ionin continued, had looked to Russia to protect them
from the "possible political and economic" domination of other European powers and to assist them in reuniting all the Bulgarian lands.
Russia had failed to fulfill their expectations. Foreign sources had
spread falsehoods about Russian intentions and these had appeared to
be verified by the actions of the Russian agents. The generals in particular had compromised Russian interests. Bulgarian opposition was quite
understandable. Russian policy could be carried through only by mutual
understanding and the agreement of "two equal independent states,"
not by force and the use of Russians as administrators in Bulgaria.
Russian influence must be reëstablished through reliance on the Tyrnovo
constitution, whose return Ionin regarded as an element in Russia's

---

[61] Shcheglov, *op. cit.*, p. 589.
[62] Wolkenstein to Kalnoky, *HHS*, X 72, no. 81A–C, St. P., Dec. 7/19, 1883.
[63] Skazkin, p. 331.

favor. At least, he commented, "the Tyrnovo constitution would never bring us to the present, and especially for Russia, regrettable crisis. More important, with it we could never so strongly compromise our influence and prestige." Upon reading this report, the tsar, who had approved the suspension of the constitution in 1881, could only comment, "All of this is very detailed and clearly stated and just."[64]

Ionin's explanations are of special importance because he was one of the chief Russian agents. His rude and blunt language undoubtedly helped to precipitate the crisis, but his actions were limited by his instructions. He believed that only through strong words could he force the prince to submit to the tsar's demands. His methods might have succeeded if he could have obtained the loyal coöperation of the Liberal party. By the time he arrived in Sofia, the chance of reconciliation between the Liberals and the Russians was remote. Moreover, Ionin's method of handling the situation was adopted with the knowledge and approval of Alexander III. In September the tsar had written, "I am *very satisfied* with all the energetic actions of Ionin and I *especially* value his decisiveness, firmness and *his taking upon himself responsibility,* and not asking for instructions from Petersburg every time, by which he once more demonstrated his *ability* and his *resourcefulness."* Ionin was exonerated.[65]

Despite the unfortunate results of 1883, the Bulgarian episode had produced certain advantages for Russia as well as definite information about the prince. First, Russia had gained the restoration of the Tyrnovo constitution, which, it was believed, would be to her benefit in the future. Second, the crisis had remained local, mainly because of the Austrian adherence to the spirit of the Dreikaiserbund. Although the Dual Monarchy was delighted over the Russian difficulties in Bulgaria, no attempt was made to exploit the situation. Third, it was now clear to the majority of the Russians that Alexander of Battenburg could no longer be relied upon. Whatever policy Russia pursued in the succeeding years, it had to be based on the assumption that a hostile prince reigned in Sofia.

---

[64] *Ibid.,* pp. 330–333.
[65] *Ibid.,* p. 318.

VI

RUSSIA AGAINST THE PRINCE

THE UNION of the prince and the political parties for the purpose of forcing the resignation of the generals made a deep impression on the Russian foreign office. The defeat of the generals marked the end of the policy initiated by Russia in 1881, which had endorsed Alexander's suspension of the Tyrnovo constitution. The inability of the prince to govern the country, even with the increased powers which he had gained after the constitution was suspended, resulted in the appointment of Russian ministers. Subsequently, they, not the prince or the political parties, were made to carry the blame for all that went wrong in Bulgarian political life.

With the return of the Tyrnovo constitution the Russian government adopted a different plan, that of noninterference in the internal affairs of Bulgaria. Now, as Giers explained, Russia would divest herself of all responsibility and adopt a passive attitude. Her only interest would be to see that peace and order prevailed in the principality.[1] It is important to note, however, that a policy of noninterference meant only that Russia would not become involved in purely domestic issues. She did not in any sense renounce her general supervision of Bulgarian political development and her ultimate control over Bulgarian foreign policy and the army. Moreover, the shift of policy toward Bulgaria did not mark any change in the hostility between the prince and his cousin, which had so much significance in the relations of Russia and Bulgaria.

In June, 1877, before he had even been considered for the Bulgarian principality, Alexander of Battenberg had expressed his dislike for the tsarevich. From Russia, where he had gone to join the army, he wrote his father that "he did not care for the tsarevich. He disliked his long whiskers and his clumsy body; and thought his wife skinny and not particularly good-looking."[2] The tsarevich did not bear any strong animosity toward the prince, but neither did he have any feeling of close kinship or genuine friendship.[3] The relations between the two were polite and formal.

In 1881, when Alexander III became tsar, the situation changed. As emperor, he demanded the respect due his position. Prince Alexander,

---

[1] Welsersheimb to Kalnoky, *HHS*, X 72, tel. no. 92, St. P., Sept. 19, 1883; *ibid.*, no. 62A–C, vertraulich, St. P., Sept. 26, 1883; Kennedy to Granville, *FO*, 65/1157, no. 226, St. P., Sept. 27, 1883.

[2] Corti, *DTD*, p. 230.

[3] Corti, *Alexander*, pp. 10, 26–27.

evidently failing to comprehend that he was no longer dealing merely with a cousin who was heir to the imperial throne, neglected to employ the usual formalities when corresponding with the tsar. The latter would perhaps have forgiven these transgressions were it not that the prince seemed to be turning against Russia. The events of 1883 gave apparent confirmation to the Russian suspicions. In June, 1883, the tsar in his letter to Alexander employed the terms "Your Highness" and used "Sincere Greetings," whereas earlier he had used "Dear Cousin" and "Sincere and Cordial Greetings."[4]

Immediately after the restoration of the constitution, the prince sent the tsar a telegram explaining his actions and arguing that he was forced to abide by the wishes of his people.[5] Gloating over his success in the matter, Alexander subsequently informed his father, "I am supported so widely by the Bulgarians that Russia will have to come down a peg." When the tsar did not reply at once, Alexander sent another telegram to his father: "All the Bulgarians are on my side. Tsar will have to give way. Shall avoid open breach, but feel frightfully insulted."[6] Finally, on October 1/13, having still not received an answer, Alexander was forced to reconsider. He sent a fifteen-page report to the emperor on recent developments and concluded his message with an outright appeal.

> The present situation must not and cannot continue. Despite all that has happened, despite all the insults that your agents have inflicted upon us, I stretch out my hand to you, Sire. Bid your people to consider my views, to come to an agreement with me ... for no matter what anyone may say, I love Russia with my whole heart; and no matter what anyone may say to contradict it, I have a feeling of deep friendship for Your Majesty's august person and for the whole of the imperial family.[7]

Again, on October 3/15, Alexander wrote his father: "The tsar with his limited mentality believes that I do not know the country; and the reason why he is now so furious is that he is feeling guilty."[8]

When the tsar continued to ignore Alexander's communications, Alexander of Hesse decided to intervene on behalf of his son. He had received a medal from the emperor for his fifty years of service in the Russian army. In acknowledging its receipt, he wrote to the tsar, on October 7/19: "I implore you, Sasha, by the friendship which unites us and of which you have afforded me so many proofs, to hold out the hand

---

[4] Corti, *DTD*, p. 288.
[5] Biegeleben to Kalnoky, *HHS*, XV 20, tel. no. 83, Sofia, Sept. 19, 1883.
[6] Corti, *DTD*, p. 290.
[7] *Loc. cit.*
[8] *Ibid.*, p. 291.

of forgiveness to a young man who has had so many severe trials to
sustain. He will always be faithful to you and to Russia; I am as sure
of him as I am of myself."[9]

The expressions of loyalty and gratitude sent by the prince were
regarded in St. Petersburg as insincere and hypocritical—which they
undoubtedly were. The tsar no longer had any faith in his cousin's
words. The prince had been given ample opportunity to demonstrate
his professed devotion to Russia, but he had proved that he could not
be trusted.

On October 31/November 11, six weeks after Alexander had sent his
first telegram, Alexander III finally replied to the prince and his
father. The message, delivered by the tsar's aide-de-camp Colonel N. V.
Kaulbars, brother of the recent minister of war, read in part, "I note
your assurances of loyalty. Your Highness will doubtless not question
my good will. I am giving you a further proof thereof by sending you . . .
my personal aide-de-camp to settle the position of the Russian officers
in the Bulgarian service." This curt reply was preceded by a letter to
Alexander of Hesse in which the tsar frankly expressed his disappointment with his cousin.

The question of who was responsible for the break between the tsar
and the prince is irrelevant. Both had contributed to it. Alexander's
biographer, Corti, admitted that "the youthful impetuousness" of the
prince did a great deal of damage. The tsar of Russia could not be
expected to yield to the prince of Bulgaria on matters of propriety and
prestige, but that is what Alexander demanded. In the following months
he became even more intransigent. Even on points of common courtesy
he would not alter his position. In April, 1885, when discussing the
problem with the kaiser, Alexander said that he had always written to
the tsar as one cousin to another, but without being disrespectful.
"Cousin, cousin!" retorted the kaiser. "An emperor is an emperor. My
own son signs himself 'Your most obedient servant' when he writes to
me."[11]

Not only had the tsar turned against Alexander, but so had most of
official Russia. Giers, in a conversation with Welsersheimb, on October
5/17, 1883, blamed the prince. He did not exonerate the generals, but
he did not see how they could have remained calm. In his forty-five
years in the diplomatic service, he had never been associated with events
comparable to those in Bulgaria. The prince was nothing without

---

[9] *Ibid.*, pp. 291–292.
[10] *Ibid.*, p. 292.
[11] *Ibid.*, p. 296.

Russia; Russia had put him in Sofia. Giers' assistants Zinoviev and Vlangali shared his views.[12]

The Russian press assumed that as a result of Alexander's actions his country was falling under the domination of the Austrians and the Germans. As *Novosti* stated, Serbia and Rumania might be temporarily estranged from Russia, but "at all events Bulgaria must be retained under Russian control." *St. Peterburgskiia Viedomosti,* in its issue of October 25/November 6, wrote with particular passion on the loss of Russian influence in Sofia. After recounting the human and material sacrifices made by Russia for Bulgaria, the newspaper asked, "Shall we abandon the graves, still fresh, of our children? Shall we allow the German barbarians to pollute them?" No concessions, it was argued, should be made by Russia in the Balkans. "Concessions have never proved beneficial to any of the parties concerned. An enemy sees in the concessions of his opponent nothing but signs of weakness, and where weakness is discerned does not it excite arrogance?"[13]

Aksakov added his voice to the protests against the prince. In 1881, when Alexander III approved the suspension of the constitution, Aksakov had written to the prince advising him on the ideal type of rule for Bulgaria and the Slavic peoples. In the succeeding months Aksakov had steadfastly defended Alexander, but in 1883 he shifted his position. Perhaps because of his former support, he hesitated at first to come out openly against the prince. On October 1/13 in *Rus'* he wrote that until more facts were available it was impossible to draw positive conclusions from the recent events in Bulgaria. It did seem, however, that the whole affair was an Austrian intrigue. A month later, on November 1/13, there was no longer any doubt in Aksakov's mind that Alexander had committed the unpardonable sin of turning away from St. Petersburg and looking to Vienna and Berlin. Without excusing Alexander, Aksakov commented that the real responsibility for the developments in Bulgaria rested with "Russia herself or that false policy, which she employed in the last years of the late reign ... under the leadership of the falsely glorified Russian chancellor [Gorchakov]!"[14]

Russia now had to deal with a government in which the three principal elements, the prince, the Liberals, and the Conservatives, were united for the first time. Only one tie bound them—common hostility toward Russia. No one expected the coalition to last. Alexander ad-

---

[12] Welsersheimb to Kalnoky, *HHS,* X 73, vertraulich, St. P., Oct. 5/17, 1883; Kennedy to Granville, *FO,* 65/1157, no. 221, conf., St. P., Sept. 24, 1883; *ibid.,* 65/1158, no. 241, conf., St. P., Oct. 7, 1883.

[13] Kennedy to Granville, *FO,* 65/1157, no. 245, St. P., Oct. 10, 1883; Thornton to Granville, *FO,* 65/1158, no. 280, St. P., Nov. 7, 1883.

[14] Aksakov, *Slavianskii Vopros',* pp. 535, 544–552.

mitted that his only hope was that it would stay together until Bulgaria "was emancipated from foreign influence."[15] On the very day that the constitution was restored, the Liberals and Conservatives began to fight over control of the strategic ministry of the interior. Only when the prince exerted strong pressure did the Conservatives consent to relinquish the post to the Liberals.[16] Once this problem was settled, a government was readily formed, with D. Tsankov as minister-president and minister of the interior. The other Liberal ministers were M. D. Balabanov, foreign affairs, T. Ikonomov, public works, and D. Molov, education. Molov's inclusion in the cabinet was considered significant, since he was a known Russophil who had consented to work with the men who had ousted the generals. From the Conservative party Nachevich served as minister of finance and Stoilov as minister of justice; Grekov became president of the national assembly. The only position in the government which remained unfilled was that of minister of war, a post which had always been held by a Russian. The controversy over this appointment dominated Russo-Bulgarian relations for the next few months and was to test the alliance between the two political parties and the prince.[17]

From 1879 to 1883 the political scene in Bulgaria had been disturbed by issues that in themselves were too often of minor importance to Russia. Russian interest in the Balkans had centered in control of the Bulgarian army. From the beginning of the Russo-Turkish War, Russia had built up, equipped, and trained this army, which by 1883 had become a respectable force. The "Russian railroad line" was of importance to Russia only as a means of strengthening the military potential of the army. Russia wanted soldiers to help defend the Straits, and a railroad by which she could move these forces and send additional troops of her own toward Turkish territory.

In a very real sense the Bulgarian army owed its existence to Russia, since the principality was entitled only to a militia, according to the Treaty of Berlin. When, in 1879, it became obvious that the treaty was being violated, the British government demanded an explanation. The Russian government insisted that, because of the tremendous sacrifices Russia had made, the new state must be properly defended. Thereafter Russia continued to increase the number and improve the quality of the Bulgarian troops. To complete this task she retained in Bulgaria 250 to 300 officers, all of whom held the rank of captain or above. Hence,

---

[15] Biegeleben to Kalnoky, *HHS*, XV 20, tel. no. 83, Sofia, Sept. 19, 1883; Lascelles to Granville, *FO*, 78/3528, no. 56, Sofia, Aug. 2, 1883.

[16] Biegeleben to Kalnoky, *HHS*, XV 20, tel. no. 83, Sofia, Sept. 19, 1883.

[17] Black, p. 244; Koch, pp. 158–160.

although the Russian government was now abandoning interference in Bulgarian internal affairs, it was in no sense prepared to give up control of the army, which was a subsidiary but vital part of the Russian army itself.

Russian control of the Bulgarian army played a part in Bulgarian politics also. From the time of Parensov through Sobolev and Kaulbars, the representatives of Russia had been convinced that, because of the Russian officers in the army, they held the fate of the prince in their hands. They were certain that peace and order prevailed in the principality only because of the presence of the Russians. If the officers were removed, it was believed that anarchy would develop and that Alexander would not last twenty-four hours as Bulgaria's ruler. Giers and the officials in the Russian foreign office shared the belief that they could always force Alexander out of Bulgaria merely by recalling their officers.[18]

The prince, of course, was fully aware of the power which Russia could exert through the officers. For him Russian command of the army was both an insult and a menace. The situation reflected on his own military training and abilities, and was a constant threat to his position. As he wrote to his father in February, 1884, "From the Bulgarians I am threatened by no danger—danger threatens solely from the side of Russia, and that only so long as the army is in their hands."[19] The reëstablishment of the Tyrnovo constitution and the temporary union of all the political groups in Bulgaria gave the prince the opportunity to deal with the army problem. Exhilarated by his victory over the generals, he decided that the time had come to break another of the ties with Russia. In the past Alexander had very intelligently sought to develop a sense of personal loyalty in his army. Through strategic awards and promotions he had to a great extent succeeded. On August 21/September 2 Ionin wrote to Giers: "Unfortunately many of the Russian officers in Sofia have almost forgotten their fatherland and little by little are becoming not Bulgars (that at least would be something) and not servants of the prince but simply accomplices of the prince's clique."[20] Having at his disposal a group of "loyal" officers, Alexander sought to appoint one of these, General Lesovoi, to the vacant post of minister of war. He could not go to the extreme of appointing a Bulgarian citizen. When he consulted Ionin, the Russian

[18] Kennedy to Granville, *FO*, 65/1157, no. 247, conf., St. P., Oct. 10, 1883; Welsersheimb to Kalnoky, *HHS*, X 73, vertraulich, St. P., Oct. 5/17, 1883; Thornton to Granville, *FO*, 65/1158, no. 271, St. P., Nov. 2, 1883.

[19] Corti, *DTD*, p. 293.

[20] Skazkin, pp. 320–321; Jomini to Giers, *NKG*, Nov. 25, 1883.

representative refused to approve Lesovoi: "He is a friend of yours, and therefore an enemy of ours."[21] Ionin insisted that the tsar would have to endorse any candidate for the position. Unable to obtain the officer of his choice, Alexander was forced to appoint, on a temporary basis only, Colonel Rediger, a Russian officer whom Ionin was able to dominate completely.[22]

Still hoping to secure Lesovoi, the prince turned to the national assembly for support. On September 19/October 1 it passed a resolution requesting that Alexander put into effect Article 11 of the constitution, which stated: "The prince is commander-in-chief of all the military forces of the principality alike in time of peace and in time of war. He confers military rank and office in accordance with the law. Everyone who enters military service must take an oath of fidelity to the prince." Hitherto, in spite of the constitution, the minister of war had been in effect commander-in-chief. The intent of the resolution was to take out of Russian hands all military decisions save routine matters of administration. The prince was to assume the powers to which he was legally entitled.[23]

Ionin regarded this resolution as tantamount to "a declaration of war" on Russia with the purpose of ending her control over the Bulgarian army. To combat this possibility, Ionin forbade Rediger to execute Alexander's decree restraining the functions of the war minister. The situation was regarded as so serious that the tsar sent a telegram to Alexander directing him not to alter the *status quo* in the army organization until his aide-de-camp, N. V. Kaulbars, arrived in Sofia.[24] The prince consented, but he wrote to the tsar explaining in detail the reasons for the proposed change.

In his letter Alexander cited Article 11 of the constitution, which made him commander-in-chief, and Article 153, which stated that "ministers are responsible to the prince and to the national assembly collectively for the administration of the department entrusted to them." The constitution, the prince reminded the tsar, had been worked out by Prince Dondukov-Korsakov and later approved by the tsar. The army, continued the prince, was not popular among the Bulgars. He had repeatedly been forced to use his influence to secure the passage of the military budget, which the assembly always wished to cut. No one could accuse him of working against the army. However, difficulties had

---

[21] Lascelles to Granville, *FO*, 78/3529, no. 85, Sofia, Sept. 24, 1883.
[22] Koch, pp. 159–160.
[23] Lascelles to Granville, *FO*, 78/3529, no. 88, Sofia, Oct. 2, 1883; Koch, p. 160.
[24] Lascelles to Granville, *FO*, 78/3529, no. 88, Sofia, Oct. 2, 1883; Biegeleben to Kalnoky, *HHS*, XV 20, no. 37, Sofia, Oct. 11, 1883; Koch, pp. 160–161.

arisen because Russian officers had found it necessary to extend their activities beyond the military sphere and engage in politics. They were officers in the Bulgarian army, but their intervention in Bulgarian political life was in behalf of Russia. Alexander considered this dual allegiance a demoralizing factor in the army. To remedy the situation he wished to take the army completely out of politics "and by subjecting it exclusively to my influence I desire to define clearly the position of the officers, and render it possible for them to confine their attention entirely to military duties." Although he assured the tsar that the Bulgarian army under his command would "never do anything contrary to the interests of Russia," he could not permit officers to be in the army who were "not entirely subject" to himself. He would not appoint a Bulgarian as minister of war, as the assembly had requested, but the Russian citizen holding the post would have to be subordinate to the prince and the assembly, which by "its right of voting supplies has a check upon him."[25]

The prince's letter not only challenged Russian control of the army but also brought up the question that had never been settled: To whom was the Russian minister of war responsible, to the tsar or to the prince and the Bulgarian assembly? Precedents favored the latter view. In 1879 Miliutin had written Parensov that "he could not give official instructions to him *as the minister* of the Bulgarian prince, *responsible to the constitutional order.*" In June, 1882, the tsar himself had instructed the Russian officers to receive their orders from their superiors and the prince.[26] Although this directive could be interpreted as exempting the minister of war, it still recognized the prince's authority. Both of these statements had been made at a time when the Russian government was in sympathy with the prince. Now that the situation had changed, Russia could not, as Giers emphatically stated, suffer a defeat on the military issue.[27] Two important facts became apparent. First, the precise duties and obligations of the minister of war had never been satisfactorily defined. Second, in the past the minister of war had acted in violation of the constitution even when that document was in force, and no protest had been made.

Alexander's expressed preference for Lesovoi enraged Ionin. In his mind the officers loyal to the prince had betrayed Russia and her interests. His advice to the Russian government showed the violence of his reaction and the lengths to which he was prepared to go in securing

[25] Koch, pp. 166–170.
[26] Biegeleben to Kalnoky, *HHS*, XV 20, no. 37, Sofia, Oct. 11, 1883.
[27] Welsersheimb to Kalnoky, *HHS*, X 72, no. 69B, vertraulich, St. P., Oct. 21/ Nov. 2, 1883; *ibid.*, X 73, vertraulich, St. P., Oct. 12/24, 1883.

Russian control over the army. Ionin believed that Alexander desired Lesovoi as minister of war because then the prince would be in actual command of the Bulgarian army. He would be able to use it and the Russian officers who supported him to abrogate the constitution for the second time. Since Russia could not afford a repetition of 1881, Ionin suggested the immediate recall of Lesovoi and his followers. If Alexander persisted in the appointment, there were two possible courses of action: all Russian officers in Bulgaria could be recalled, which would lead to a rupture of relations with Bulgaria; or Alexander could be forced out of Bulgaria. The latter alternative, favored by Ionin, could be followed "by something in the form of a temporary occupation of Bulgaria" with the consent of the great powers. Russia could announce that she was taking steps "to save the country from chaos."

To initiate the action against the prince, Ionin advised that the Russian government send a general to take command of all the officers and troops. At the same time four battalions of Russian troops were to be sent from Odessa to Varna, not to undertake military action but "in order to make clear our wishes and goal and by this to lead the Bulgarian people from doubts concerning our intentions." "Our influence would be decisive," concluded Ionin.[28] The foregoing recommendations showed the Russian representative's complete lack of understanding of the European diplomatic scene. Austria-Hungary and Great Britain would never have given their voluntary consent to the occupation of Bulgaria in the manner proposed.

Recognizing these limitations, Giers and the Russian foreign office established a more moderate policy. It was agreed that Russia could not tolerate officers whose primary loyalty was to the prince. The Russian officers were in Bulgaria to serve Russian interests, and only incidentally Bulgarian. It would be "impractical and dangerous" to send Russian troops to Varna. The farthest that Russia could go would be to make a formal declaration to the prince that Russian officers were to be subordinate to the minister of war, who would be appointed by the tsar. If Alexander refused to abide by this decision, Russia could recall the officers and take measures against those who disobeyed the tsar's commands. The Russian government believed that the recall of the officers would result in the overthrow of Alexander, which Ionin advocated, but that the method would be preferable to violent measures such as a temporary occupation.

It was hoped that threats alone would be sufficient to gain Alexander's acquiescence. Russia had no desire to reopen the eastern question and thereby invite the intervention of the great powers in Bulgarian affairs.

---

[28] Skazkin, pp. 322–325.

She wanted only to block the influence of the Russian officers who had attached themselves to the prince and to gain the latter's acceptance of a Russian-named candidate as minister of war. Should Alexander refuse, all the Russian officers in the Bulgarian army would have to be withdrawn.[29]

On October 12/24 the Russian government took the first step. Colonel Rediger, acting minister of war, informed General Lesovoi and Lieutenant Polzikov, Alexander's adjutant general and aide-de-camp, respectively, that on the orders of the tsar they were to depart for Russia within forty-eight hours. By this action Russia expected to rid Bulgaria of the two officers who led the partisans of the prince. The news of their recall came to Alexander while he was vacationing in the country. Upon his return to the capital, he demanded an explanation from Rediger. In accordance with the agreement made with the tsar in 1882, the officers could in theory be dismissed only by the prince. Rediger replied that he was executing the tsar's order and that he considered the earlier arrangement null and void. Thereupon Alexander dismissed Rediger and replaced him by Colonel Kotel'nikov, who was also a Russian.[30]

The recall of the two officers deeply offended the prince. It appeared as if Alexander III wished to create a vacuum around the Bulgarian throne by depriving the prince of all the officers who were sympathetic to him. Alexander was particularly angered because the tsar had asked him not to alter the *status quo* until Kaulbars arrived to study the situation. Since the tsar had not adhered to his part of the agreement, Alexander telegraphed St. Petersburg that he considered himself no longer bound not to act. In retaliation for the Russian move, he called the ministerial council into session and persuaded it to support his dismissal of Rediger. At the same session the council agreed to the prince's demand that all the Russian officers in his suite be dismissed and that the Bulgarian officers studying in Russia, who numbered about forty, be recalled. The tsar, when referring to the happenings in Sofia, spoke of the "Don Quixote" actions of the prince; the latter wrote to his father about "the tsar's impossible and boorish conduct."[31]

The British government would have derived great satisfaction from the removal of the Russian officers from Bulgaria. Lascelles, strongly supporting Alexander's policy of resistance, urged the prince not to

[29] *Ibid.*, pp. 321–322, 325–326.
[30] Koch, pp. 171–173; Ternaux-Compans to Challemel-Lacour, *DDF*, V, no. 132, St. P., Nov. 7, 1883.
[31] Koch, pp. 172–173; Welsersheimb to Kalnoky, *HHS*, X 72, no. 69B, vertraulich, St. P., Oct. 21/Nov. 2, 1883; Lascelles to Granville, *FO*, 78/3529, no. 106, Sofia, Oct. 31, 1883; Corti, *DTD*, p. 292.

yield if the Russians threatened him with the mass resignation of the officers. He even suggested that the army could be disbanded completely to rid Bulgaria of the Russian influence in the military establishment. Either alternative would, of course, have improved the British position at the Straits. Apart from considerations of foreign policy and military strategy, British opinion favored the prince. Queen Victoria, in particular, was wholeheartedly on his side. Granville assumed that Russian policy was directed toward the removal of the prince, but the British government could give Alexander only moral support. Austria-Hungary, also, had to remain passive. Despite the repeatedly expressed suspicions of members of the Russian government and the press, there is no evidence to indicate that the Dual Monarchy ever tried to combat Russian influence by positive measures.[32]

Alexander could have achieved success in his fight on the army issue only if he had kept the full support of the two political parties. Although the Liberals had sided with Alexander initially, they were reluctant to endorse his plans when they saw how determined he was to gain control of the military forces. Unknown to Alexander, Tsankov called on Ionin and informed him that "the interests of Russia in the military question are absolutely identical with the interests of Bulgaria, that the nation and he [Tsankov] could not permit the unconditional power of the prince over the Russian officers and especially the absence of Russian control with regard to the nomination of the war minister."[33] The Liberals thus returned to the position which they had held before the restoration of the constitution: the presence of the Russians in the Bulgarian political scene guaranteed that the Liberals would not be forced out by a combination of the Conservatives and the prince. If necessary, Tsankov was ready to tell Alexander that, if he did not accept the Russian conditions, the Liberals in the ministry would resign. Much to Ionin's surprise the Conservatives took a similar stand. Both political parties feared that if Alexander controlled the army he would hold absolute authority in the state.

The ministers informed Alexander that he would have to reach agreement with Russia.[34] As a preliminary step, Tsankov insisted that Balabanov, the foreign minister, go to St. Petersburg to discuss the entire matter. Confronted with the united stand of the cabinet, Alexander was forced to agree, although he felt that Balabanov's visit would prove fruitless.[35]

---

[32] Lascelles to Granville, *FO*, 78/3529, no. 109, Sofia, Nov. 1, 1883; Buckle, *Victoria*, III, 444–446, 448, 454, 460–461; Corti, *DTD*, p. 292.

[33] Skazkin, p. 327.

[34] *Loc. cit.*

[35] Biegeleben to Kalnoky, *HHS*, XV 20, tel. no. 105, Sofia, Oct. 16, 1883.

In St. Petersburg, Balabanov saw both Giers and the tsar. Giers recited the Russian grievances against the prince, but the tsar was more encouraging. Balabanov frankly told him that Bulgarian hostility to Russia was of her own making because of the fluctuations in Russian policy. While admitting the truth of this statement, Alexander III expressed his extreme displeasure with the prince. However, he looked forward to a peaceful development in Bulgaria. The military question was the one great issue that still had to be settled.[36]

Balabanov's visit prepared the way for the final agreement, which was brought to a conclusion by Colonel Kaulbars, who arrived in Sofia on October 29/November 10. His first meeting with Alexander, on the following day, turned out satisfactorily. The next day Kaulbars presented the tsar's proposals for the regulations to control the activities of the Russian officers in Bulgaria. After considering the proposals for several days, the prince and ministerial council accepted them.

The essential points of the agreement were the following. Only Russian officers and officials who were approved by St. Petersburg could serve in the Bulgarian military forces and then only for three years. These men could serve only in the army or the navy, not in the gendarmerie, police, or other nonmilitary position. The Russian officers were to be subject to the Bulgarian military code and were accountable to the Bulgarian government in all matters pertaining to the service. They were not to be allowed "to intermeddle in any shape or form with the internal political affairs of the principality, or to join any political parties, open or secret societies." The tsar was to appoint the minister of war, and the Russian officers were to be under his direct control "in all questions affecting them in their position as Russian officers." The orders and regulations which Russia wished them to obey would be communicated through the minister. It was his duty to see that these were properly executed and, if they were disobeyed, to take action against the offenders.[37]

When these regulations were accepted in Bulgaria, the Russian government considered that it had scored a triumph over the prince. The tsar had retained the right to appoint the minister of war. Through his officers he still held the real command of the Bulgarian army and thus could always check the prince. Unfortunately, an ambiguity still existed. In admitting that the Russian officers were subject to Bulgarian military regulations and were accountable to the Bulgarian government

[36] Black, p. 248; Koch, p. 174.

[37] Koch, pp. 178–180; Vlangali to Giers, *NKG*, St. P., Nov. 13/25, 1883; Biegeleben to Kalnoky, *HHS*, XV 20, no. 45B, reserviert, Sofia, Nov. 15, 1883; Wolkenstein to Kalnoky, *HHS*, X 72, no. 79, St. P., Nov. 28/Dec. 10, 1883; Mountmarin to Ferry, *DDF*, V, no. 134, Vienna, Nov. 12, 1883.

for their actions, Russia paved the way for future conflicts. The old problem of how to deal with an officer who was violating Bulgarian regulations in executing Russian orders, and vice versa, had not been resolved. Nevertheless, the tension was relieved, and both the tsar and the prince could claim a victory.[38]

Perhaps the most important part of the agreement was the clear enunciation of a policy of noninterference by Russian officers in Bulgarian internal affairs. By forbidding political activity in the future, the Russian government was in effect admitting the errors of the past. Russian prestige and influence would have suffered much less damage if such an order had been enforced since 1879. Not only were the regulations specific in regard to military officers, but the Russian government flatly stated that it would no longer send men to occupy ministerial posts other than that of war. Russia was in Bulgaria to protect her military and strategic interests. Bulgarian local problems were to be settled by the Bulgars.[39]

In drawing up the agreement, both the Russian and the Bulgarian government chose to ignore an issue which would have been very difficult to resolve. In the past, serious friction had developed between Russian and Bulgarian officers in the Bulgarian army because all positions of captain and above were held by Russians, on the pretext that there were no Bulgarians capable of filling these posts. In practice this meant that not one Bulgar was yet qualified to be a captain in the army. In time, the Russians contended, the Bulgars would have received the necessary training, but at present they were not qualified. The first lieutenants, who could not be promoted, resented the implications strongly. The national pride which led the Bulgarian politician to detest Russian interference in Bulgarian domestic life was thus shared by his counterpart in the army.[40]

Additional grievances estranged the Bulgarian in the army from his Russian commanders. The Bulgarian officers complained that they were discriminated against on the basis of pay; and even their food was of an inferior quality. These conditions lowered the morale of the junior officers and increased their desire to throw off Russian tutelage.

Russian influence was thus becoming weak among the company-grade

---

[38] Ionin to Giers, _NKG_, Sofia, Nov. 4/16, 1883; Jomini to Giers, _NKG_, Jan. 3, 1884. Giers had also telegraphed Ionin on Nov. 24/Dec. 6 to inform Kaulbars that, should the prince attempt to use the army "to suppress agitation in Bulgaria or for any other forceful action against the people," the tsar forbade the Russian officers to take part. Skazkin, p. 328.

[39] _Ibid._, p. 329.

[40] Biegeleben to Kalnoky, _HHS_, XV 20, no. 51C, réservé, Sofia, Dec. 13, 1883.

officers, the most important ones in actual battle. Since the Russians did nothing to remedy the situation, Alexander of Battenberg had a fertile field in which to work. The officers reacted exactly as the prince had when Russia cast aspersions on his military training. Russia was thus indirectly and unintentionally contributing to a closer liaison between the prince and his Bulgarian officers.[41]

With the settling of the immediate issues concerning the army, Russo-Bulgarian relations again became amicable. The Russian government was fortunate in having at its service a really able administrator. In February, 1884, Prince M. Kantakuzin was nominated by the tsar as the new minister of war in Bulgaria. Kantakuzin stated that he would consider himself only as a member of Tsankov's cabinet. He would avoid domestic crises and discuss only military matters.[42] Concerning his tenure in office it has been said,

During the entire time of his ministry, Kantakuzin proved himself an extremely prudent, cultivated man of tact and a very able minister...He was always polite and obliging in his relations with the prince, and never infringed in the slightest degree any rule of polite society; he had received instructions from St. Petersburg to be polite, but reserved, and he acted accordingly...His chief merit was that he placed himself on a footing of fellowship with the Bulgarian officers.

This admission, coming from Koch, Alexander's court chaplain, who was violently anti-Russian, is the best indication that Kantakuzin followed a correct and conciliatory policy in obedience to instructions from St. Petersburg.[43]

When Alexander restored the Tyrnovo constitution in September, 1883, the assembly which was then in session was technically illegal. It had been elected under a law promulgated by the prince during his period of personal rule. Although a new election should have been held in accordance with the constitution, no one seemed concerned about the situation.[44]

On returning to constitutional rule, Alexander had been promised by both political parties that they would work for certain changes in the Tyrnovo constitution. The prince and the Conservatives favored an upper chamber with limited representation, a body naturally opposed by the Liberals. The change would require not only the approval of the

[41] *Loc. cit.*
[42] Wolkenstein to Kalnoky, *HHS*, X 74, no. 4C, vertraulich, St. P., Jan. 4/16, 1884.
[43] Koch, p. 195 n. 1. Russia's difficulties in finding a qualified person to take the post are discussed in Vlangali to Giers, *NKG*, St. P., Dec. 3/15, Dec. 15/27, 1883. See also Wolkenstein to Kalnoky, *HHS*, X 75, no. 26B, vertraulich, March 27/April 8, 1885.
[44] Biegeleben to Kalnoky, *HHS*, XV 20, no. 37D, Sofia, Oct. 11, 1883; Black, pp. 245–246.

assembly but also the convening of a newly elected Grand National Assembly. In attempting to introduce the matter into the assembly, Tsankov was opposed both by the left wing of his party and by Karavelov, who had recently returned from Rumelia. The latter took up defense of the constitution and tried to block the passage of the amendments. Tsankov and the Conservatives were able to gain support for their views only by promising that a Grand National Assembly would not be convened for three years.[45] When it finally met, on July 7/19, 1886, much had happened in the interval. The amendments were rejected, and the Tyrnovo constitution remained in force, with minor changes, for approximately fifty more years.

The return of Karavelov to Sofia altered the alignment of the political groups. He was the uncompromising defender of constitutional government and of economy in national finances, whereas Tsankov had been an opportunist, ready to bargain with anyone. Karavelov's resumption of active party leadership split the Liberal party into two groups. Karavelov was extremely popular throughout Bulgaria, and in many ways symbolized the national ideals of the Bulgars. When new elections were held in the summer of 1884, his candidates emerged triumphant. Tsankov was forced to resign, stating that he had fulfilled the mandate given him in 1883 to restore the constitution.[46]

The division of the Liberal party gave the Russians an added political opportunity should they care to exploit it. They could always exert pressure on the Tsankovites by threatening to coöperate with the Karavelovites. In January, 1884, Tsankov admitted that he had to follow a conciliatory policy toward Russia because he feared a Russian-Karavelov alliance.[47] The willingness to use the threat of coöperation with the left wing of the Liberal party did not mean that the Russian government had any sympathy for Karavelov. When the latter became minister-president, Giers described him as a radical who was close to being a nihilist, a fanatic who had learned "bad things in bad Russian schools." Giers had to admit that in money matters Karavelov was "absolutely correct." Because of his incorruptibility, he had the support of the Bulgarian people. Giers hoped that the great powers would unite to prevent him from disturbing the peace of the Balkans by seeking the union of Bulgaria and Eastern Rumelia.[48]

At this time, however, Karavelov was concerned primarily with

---

[45] Jomini to Giers, *NKG*, Dec. 14, 1883; Black, pp. 249–253. Tsankov himself had admitted in September that the amendments would never be approved. Lascelles to Granville, *FO*, 78/3529, no. 81, Sofia, Sept. 19, 1883.

[46] Kennedy to Granville, *FO*, 78/3638, no. 42, Sofia, June 19, 1884.

[47] Lascelles to Granville, *FO*, 78/3638, no. 8, Sofia, Jan. 9, 1884.

[48] Wolkenstein to Kalnoky, *HHS*, X 74, no. 46, geheim, St. P., July 3/15, 1884.

domestic policy. A tireless defender of the constitution, he sought to improve the conditions of the country and develop its economy. Since he was opposed to entrusting the financial credit of the state to foreign hands, he established a state bank to provide financial aid for Bulgarian business.

Karavelov's handling of the railroad problem followed the same pattern. In 1883 the assembly had provided that Bulgaria would build the international line, but it did not stipulate how or by whom. In December, 1884, Karavelov proposed to the assembly that the state build the line. He argued that private enterprise was interested in profit rather than in the welfare of the nation. If the government controlled the lines, national interest would be the prime consideration. His program appealed directly to the Bulgarian peasantry. In opposition, the Conservatives valiantly defended the principle of private enterprise, but fell before Karavelov's political machine. The Bulgarian government thus assumed full control of all railroad development. In June, 1885, a Bulgarian contractor was commissioned to start work on the international line.[49]

Karavelov's victory marked the end of the controversy with Russia over the railways. Russian strategic interests demanded the building of the Danube-Sofia line by means of which Russia could move her troops rapidly toward the Straits. Her refusal to contribute toward the construction of the line resulted in a major setback for Russian military plans. Karavelov could certainly not have been expected to agree to the building of the line at Bulgaria's expense when it was obviously of little economic value to the country. The presence of Russian officers in Bulgaria and the coöperation of the Bulgarian army with Russia in time of war were less significant for military strategy so long as no adequate means of transportation united the two countries.

After settling the problems connected with the army, the occupation debt, and the railroads, the Russian government remained outside Bulgarian domestic affairs in the sense that it did not take a decided stand on political issues, with the exception of the Macedonian question.[50] Because of this, the years 1884 and 1885 were not marked by as many conflicts as the previous period had been. Although a policy of noninterference was maintained, neither the tsar nor official Russia had become reconciled to Alexander of Battenberg. He was considered a danger to Russian interests and the champion of those who wished to eliminate Russian influence from the principality. Wherever possible,

---

[49] Black, pp. 261–264; Koch, p. 203.
[50] This question is discussed in chap. ix.

the Russian government sought to check the prince's plans and discredit him in the eyes of the world. A unique opportunity arose when Alexander finally found a princess whom he wished to marry.

Alexander had begun to think about a marriage almost immediately after he became the ruler of Bulgaria.[51] He naturally wanted to establish a dynasty which would strengthen his position in the state. His mother wished him to marry Princess Helen of Mecklenburg, daughter of Duke George of Mecklenburg-Strelitz and the Grand Duchess Catherine of Russia. Such an alliance would have brought the prince into closer relations with the Russian imperial family. Alexander, however, rejected her. Pressed by the Bulgarians to find a wife, the prince continued his search. The next candidate was the Archduchess Maria Antonia, daughter of the late Archduke Ferdinand of Tuscany. Although Alexander expressed an interest in her, he finally wrote his father on December 1/13, 1881, that an Austrian Catholic marriage would not be looked on favorably by the Bulgarian people. Since the Russian government also objected, the plans were dropped. In the ensuing months, when relations with Russia became worse, the prince realized that a Russian marriage would be impossible. Alexander then became attracted to Princess Victoria, who was described as "a slender and elegant, though not actually pretty, girl." She was the daughter of the German Crown Prince Frederick; thus her paternal grandfather was the kaiser and her maternal grandmother was Queen Victoria. The couple became secretly engaged in 1883, but by 1884 their attachment was common knowledge in court circles.[52]

From a political point of view, Alexander could not have made a worse choice. Russia could interpret such a marriage only as the strengthening of German influence in Bulgaria. Upon being informed of Russian opposition, Bismarck too became adamant. When Alexander arrived in Berlin, uninvited, in the spring of 1884, Bismarck categorically informed the prince, whom he described as a "hooligan," that as long as he was chancellor, no German princess would ever marry Alexander. Such a marriage could damage Germany's relations with Russia and "not all the Hesses and Battenbergs in the world were worth that." The chancellor's position was endorsed by both the emperor and the empress, and by Prince William, the future William II. The kaiser, in fact, forbade Alexander to see Victoria again. The British royal family and the parents of the princess alone supported the marriage. The interest of Queen Victoria was interpreted in Berlin as a

---

[51] The subject was discussed in July, 1879, when Alexander arrived in Bulgaria. Davydov to Giers, *NKG*, Sofia, July 11/23, 1879.

[52] Corti, *DTD*, pp. 266, 270, 281, 301; Corti, *Alexander*, pp. 157–162.

British attempt to bring about a Russo-German estrangement, and provided another reason for Bismarck's opposition.[53]

Alexander of Battenberg thus had ample evidence that the decisive obstacle to his marriage came from Russia. Negotiations for the marriage dragged on through 1884 and into the spring of 1885. Every new overture was met with stronger opposition from Bismarck and the tsar. Alexander became extremely bitter and disillusioned. He wrote his father that the Russians had spread the report among the Bulgars that he "was incapable of marrying" and "suffered from venereal disease."[54] "I *hate* the tsar and shall never be able to forget what he has done to me."[55]

Nevertheless, Alexander did not give up hope that, in spite of the tsar and Bismarck, he still might marry Victoria. However, in March, 1885, the kaiser intervened. He demanded that Alexander submit a written statement renouncing Victoria, and added a note advising the prince to effect a reconciliation with Russia. Alexander was thus faced with the alternative of abdication and a possible marriage with Victoria or a renunciation of the princess and the retention of the Bulgarian throne.

Confronted with the formidable opposition of the rulers of Russia and Germany and the German chancellor, Alexander decided to keep his throne. On April 14/26 he wrote the kaiser a letter yielding Victoria and expressing a desire for a reëstablishment of friendship with Russia. He informed the kaiser that he would follow the wishes of Russia in foreign policy and would defend her interests in domestic matters within the limits of the constitution.[56] The prince had thus been defeated by Russia. Although with the aid of the Bulgarian political parties he had been able to defend his position within the country, in foreign affairs the prince could not act with a free hand.

The documents relating to this period clearly indicate the extent of Russian hostility to Alexander. Giers considered him thoroughly reprehensible and referred to him in sarcastic phrases such as, "ein Komödiant, dieser Fürst," and "Ja, ja, der verleugnet seine *polnische* Mutter nicht."[57] His feelings were shared by the other Russian officials. However, the available evidence does not reveal whether the Russian government in 1884 actively embarked on a policy of forcing Alexander to leave Bulgaria or if it knowingly condoned actions directed toward

---

[53] See Langer, *European Alliances* ... , pp. 343–344; Ponsonby, ed., *Letters of the Empress Frederick*, pp. 199–206.
[54] Corti, *DTD*, p. 301.
[55] *Ibid.*, pp. 301–304.
[56] *Ibid.*, pp. 306–307.
[57] Wolkenstein to Kalnoky, *HHS*, X 74, no. 46, geheim, St. P., July 3/15, 1884.

this end. There are two separate statements relating to this subject. In May, 1884, Prince William went to St. Petersburg to assure the tsar that the kaiser and Bismarck were against Alexander's marriage to Princess Victoria. In their conversations Alexander III repeated his complaints against the prince, and added the cryptic comment, "He won't stay there much longer." To this William replied, "Perhaps that would not be such a terrible misfortune."[58] Four months later, in September, at the meeting of the three emperors in Skiernewice, Poland, Giers assured Germany and Austria-Hungary that Russia would not take measures against Alexander, although she was trying to prevent his marriage to the Prussian princess.[59]

The question whether Russia was seeking the abdication of the prince becomes even more difficult to answer in view of the domestic situation in Bulgaria. The two Russian agents Kantakuzin and A. I. Koiander, who replaced Ionin in March, 1884, had diametrically opposite careers in Bulgaria. As minister of war, Kantakuzin always maintained a correct attitude. He did not indulge in intrigues against the prince nor did he become involved in Bulgarian internal politics. Koiander, in contrast, followed the pattern set by previous Russian agents. He tried to induce the Liberal leaders to take measures to oust the prince.[60]

The British vice-consul in Ruschuk reported, in February, 1885, that one of Tsankov's friends had told him of a meeting between Tsankov and the Russian agent. When Koiander complained about the prince, Tsankov asked him frankly whether Russia desired his removal. The reply was that it would do no harm. Tsankov then asked if Russia had a replacement in mind. Koiander could not say, but he assumed that a regency would first have to be established.[61] The extent of Koiander's conspiratorial activities is indicated in three of his reports (analyzed in detail below) to his government. There is no record that he was ever reprimanded. However, Russian representatives had previously acted on their own account, against the established policy of the government, had reported their actions, and had been called to order only after they had done irretrievable damage to Russian prestige. Koiander's reports

---

[58] Corti, *DTD*, p. 299.

[59] Reuss to Bismarck, *GP*, III, no. 646, Vienna, Sept. 19, 1884.

[60] According to Radev, I, 457–459, Koiander immediately circulated the information that the tsar desired the removal of the prince. Tatishchev, *Iz Prozhlago Russkoi Diplomatii*, p. 396, concurs. Granville, British foreign secretary, stated that Russia was trying to discredit the prince. Granville to Paget, *FO*, 7/1075, no. 59, very conf., Foreign Office, Feb. 23, 1885.

[61] Dalziel to Lascelles, no. 6, conf., Roustchouk, Feb. 20, 1885, in Lascelles to Granville, *FO*, 78/3769, no. 17, Sofia, Feb. 23, 1885.

throw interesting sidelights on Bulgarian party politics, and reveal the methods that the Russian agent was willing to use.

In the first dispatch, sent to Zinoviev on January 18/30, 1885, Koiander described a meeting with the prince during the Christmas holidays. The main theme of his report, however, was the timing of Alexander's removal. Koiander thought it would be better to wait; when the final decision had been made, a new ruler selected, and the preparatory measures taken, the whole affair could be completed in two weeks. The Russian agent outlined the suggestions made by the prominent but ailing Liberal, Stefan Stambolov. The latter, according to Koiander, maintained that the prince could be removed only by force. He would have to be arrested and taken to the state boundaries under guard. During the interregnum the government would be in the hands of a "dictator" named by Russia. Koiander commented that the other Bulgarians had not yet reached the same conclusions as Stambolov, and seemed to believe that they could run their own affairs.[62]

In the next report, also to Zinoviev, on June 7/19, Koiander discussed a conference he had held with Karavelov and Tsankov in an effort to reconcile the two Liberal leaders. He told them that he was prepared to seek Russia's forgiveness for the prince if they believed that Alexander was necessary for Bulgaria and if they considered his rule satisfactory. But, he added significantly, he did not deem it prudent to conceal from them the fact that Russia would hardly desire the unification of Bulgaria under the aegis of an unfriendly prince—a clear appeal to their national sentiment. The meeting was apparently anything but a success from Koiander's point of view, since the remainder of his report contained little more than complaints about the Bulgarians, particularly the intelligentsia.

Koiander's description of Karavelov's duplicity is an excellent commentary on how the Bulgarian party leaders used the Russian representatives to improve their own position in the domestic political arena. Koiander, in an attempt to bring the two wings of the Liberal party together so that he could use them against the prince, tried to prevent Tsankov's newspapers from attacking Karavelov. The latter promised to influence his press in the same direction. Consequently, Tsankov, at Koiander's insistence, shifted his attacks to the prince. Thereupon Karavelov went back on his word and became the champion of Alex-

---

[62] Koiander to Zinoviev, *Avantiury*, no. 1, Jan. 18/30, 1885. This collection of documents was published by Soviet historians in an attempt to discredit tsarist diplomacy. Hence the documents are selective and emphasize the darkest aspects of Russian activity and diplomacy.

ander. The two Liberal groups thus ended by being farther apart than ever. These and other episodes convinced Koiander that there was not a single Bulgar who could be trusted. His reports indicated that he had failed to grasp the lessons to be learned from earlier Russo-Bulgarian relations.

In concluding his dispatch, Koiander admitted that the situation was serious. It was not for him to decide how the problem should be resolved, "but energetic measures are necessary, as palliatives would hardly help." By allowing Alexander to remain in power, he argued, Russia assumed responsibility for him. Since it was not possible to send a Russian governor-general, the Bulgars themselves must be forced to turn to Russia "for help and salvation." Koiander shared the opinion that only the presence of the Russian officers in Bulgaria saved the country from anarchy. The withdrawal of these troops, he believed, would lead the Bulgars to turn to Russia. Although this was a risky step, Russia would lose Bulgaria unless radical measures were undertaken.[63]

The third dispatch, written on August 4/16 to Vlangali, acting Russian foreign minister, discussed the other possibilities open to Russian diplomacy. By this time it was clear to Koiander that Russia could not expect the aid of any major political group in Bulgaria in expelling Alexander or in establishing direct Russian control over the government. The best solution, he thought, would be Russian occupation of Bulgaria, the appointment of a Russian governor-general, and the introduction of Russian laws into the principality. He did not know whether this would be feasible, but there had certainly been precedents for such an action in Egypt, Tunis, and Bosnia. Koiander's second choice was the removal of Alexander and his replacement by someone more favorable to Russia. Since the Bulgars would not coöperate in the replacement of the prince, the best method would be to invite him to St. Petersburg. There the tsar could inform him that he could not return to Bulgaria but would be given financial aid. The new prince would then be asked to suppress the freedom of the press and assembly and the other constitutional liberties which Bulgaria possessed. He would have to be given strong Russian support because he would receive no assistance from the Bulgarian people. A third possibility was a reconciliation with Alexander and the formation of a ministry headed by Kantakuzin. This, of course, would introduce the danger of reviving the era of Sobolev. Koiander proposed that if Kantakuzin did become

    [63] Koiander to Zinoviev, *Avantiury*, no. 2, June 7/19, 1885; Vlangali to Giers, *NKG*, St. P., July 27, 1885. See also Goriainov, "Razryv," pp. 176–177; Lascelles to Granville, *FO*, 78/3769, no. 17, Sofia, Feb. 23, 1885.

head of the government, Alexander should be controlled by bribing him with funds from the occupation debt. He advised that Russia either effect a reconciliation with the prince or remove him from Bulgaria, as it was impossible to continue long under the present conditions. The fourth and last choice was for Russia to recall her officers. Their withdrawal was expected to lead to anarchy and eventually to foreign occupation "by Austria, Rumania, Turkey, or Russia." Of the four measures proposed, Koiander considered that a reconciliation with the prince would be easiest, but also that which carried the greatest risk.[64]

Although it is difficult to judge how far the Russian government would have been willing to go in order to remove the prince, the extent of the change in the official Russian attitude toward Bulgaria was witnessed in the negotiations for the renewal of the Dreikaiserbund. In 1883–1884, when the entire question came up for discussion, it was apparent that Russia's situation in regard to the other great powers had shifted significantly. First, although the struggle with Britain continued in the Middle East, Russia was not so concerned over the immediate seizure of the Straits as she had been in 1879–1881. Second, the Russian fear that Turkish troops might enter Eastern Rumelia and thereby provoke a second Russo-Turkish war had been allayed. The Dreikaiserbund had done its work; Russia had been given a period in which to recover and had been saved from the dangers of a hostile coalition. Although the Dreikaiserbund had functioned well for the negative purposes for which it was designed, Russia had been unable to exploit the one positive aspect of the treaty—the union of the Bulgarias. Instead, by 1883 it was considered that such an event would be detrimental to Russian policy. The independence and resistance to Russian influence shown by the prince and the Bulgarian political parties had clearly indicated to the Russian government that a united Bulgaria might be a hostile Bulgaria. It was therefore better that she remain weak and divided. Moreover, by 1883 Austria-Hungary had replaced Britain as the chief Russian adversary, despite the fact that the Dual Monarchy was an ally. The principal field of competition was, of course, the Balkan Peninsula. If Russo-Bulgarian relations continued in their present course, not only would Bulgaria not be a Russian asset, but she might join Russia's enemy in combating Russian interests.[65]

The official Russian attitude toward both Austria-Hungary and Bul-

[64] Koiander to Vlangali, *Avantiury*, no. 3, Aug. 4/16, 1885; Vlangali to Giers, *NKG*, St. P., Aug. 8/20, 1885.

[65] The negotiations for and an analysis of the renewal of the Dreikaiserbund are discussed in Skazkin, pp. 331–355. Saburov's views are discussed in Vlangali to Giers, *NKG*, St. P., Dec. 15/27, 1883; Dec. 21, 1883/Jan. 2, 1884; Dec. 27, 1883; Jan. 3, 1884.

garia was succinctly stated in the circular that was sent to A. P. Mohrenheim, Russia's ambassador to Great Britain, on August 6, 1883, stating the program that had been approved by Alexander III.

The separation of the two parts of the Bulgarian nation by the Treaty of Berlin weighs heavily on both parts. They cannot be united without the risk of leading to conflicts as dangerous for them as for us, and it is very difficult to develop them separately, so as to prepare for their future. . . . We are therefore obliged to follow our thankless task with perseverance while containing as much as possible the premature aspirations which push the Bulgars toward fusion.

These delicate questions react inevitably on our relations with Austria. They are able to conserve an ostensibly friendly character only if each of the two governments, while following the path of [their own] interests, avoid hurting those of the other. The *status quo* of the Treaty of Berlin remains the sole ground on which the two cabinets are able to take a position in order to avert conflicts. We will continue on it as long as Austria does not diverge.[66]

With these considerations in mind, and despite the pressure of both Saburov and Nelidov to negotiate a more ambitious agreement, the Russian government renewed the Dreikaiserbund in March, 1884, with only two minor changes which in no way altered the spirit of the alliance.

The Russian determination to prevent the extension of Bulgarian power and the disturbance of the *status quo* in the Balkan Peninsula were further evidenced in a conversation between Giers and Prince Alexander at Franzensbad in August, 1885. Giers stated that Russia desired a reconciliation with Alexander and not his abdication. At the same time he warned that Russia and the great powers would insist that the *status quo* in the Balkans be maintained. Alexander agreed, adding that, from the information which he had received, the unification movement had not yet attained serious proportions.[67]

How little control Russia had over Bulgaria and Alexander and, in turn, Alexander had over the forces of Bulgarian nationalism, became clear in September, 1885, when the union of Bulgaria and Eastern Rumelia took place. At the moment that Alexander was meeting with Giers, preparations for the reunification of the two Bulgarian provinces were in their final stages in Eastern Rumelia. From 1883 to 1885 Russia had worked energetically to strengthen her hold over the Bulgarian army and to discredit the prince before his subjects and Europe. On the surface it appeared that she had succeeded in both objectives. Russia still seemed to maintain the dominant position in Bulgaria which

---

[66] *Staal*, I, 19–20.

[67] Corti, *Alexander*, pp. 225–226; Flesch to Freycinet, *DDF*, VI, no. 63, Sofia, Sept. 10, 1885; Langer, *op. cit.*, pp. 345–346.

she had acquired in 1878, but in the fall of 1885 she was given a severe setback. Although Russia had come to appreciate fully the potential force of Bulgarian nationalism and its harmful effects on Russian policy, she was not able to control it. The union of the two provinces drew other powers into the Bulgarian sphere, in particular Austria-Hungary and her protégé, Serbia. Consequently, Russia's entire European and Near Eastern policy was placed in jeopardy, and the Balkans again became the center of European diplomacy.

VII

AUSTRIA AND RUSSIA IN SERBIAN POLITICS

PARALLEL to the decline of the Russian position in Bulgaria was the growth in Serbia of a situation that was potentially dangerous for Russia. The reëstablishment of the Bulgaria of San Stefano and the control of the policy of that state remained Russia's long-range goal. The first step toward the achievement of that objective would be the union of Bulgaria and Eastern Rumelia, in accordance with the Drei-kaiserbund agreement. Once union was achieved, Bulgaria would seek to acquire the Macedonian lands.

In 1881, however, Russia was still too weak to face the reopening of the eastern question; by 1884 it was extremely doubtful whether a union of the Bulgarias would be to Russia's benefit. She there-fore wanted to maintain the *status quo,* including the separation of the Bulgarias and the Turkish control of Macedonia. Despite these considerations, the Russian government was powerless to halt the agi-tation in Bulgaria for union, or, more important for her relations with Serbia, to deal with the struggle of the nationalities in Macedonia. It was in the latter area that the Russian policy of the *status quo* and alliance with the German powers faced its most severe test.

Russia's attitude toward Macedonia had been determined in the 'sev-enties, when, under Russian sponsorship, the Bulgarian exarchate was created. After the Congress of Berlin, Russian policy, working through the Orthodox church, called for the unification under the exarch of all the San Stefano Macedonian lands, thus re-creating the Greater Bul-garia through a religious if not a political union. To this end the exarchate in Constantinople, backed by funds from the Bulgarian government and with Russian support, waged a strong campaign in Macedonia to extend Bulgarian control and gain new Bulgarian dio-ceses. Under the slogan "Orthodox Unity" the Russian government endeavored to bring as many Orthodox as possible into the fold of the exarchate and also to reconcile the exarchate and the patriarchate for the benefit of the former.[1] In Macedonia proper many people of Serbian nationality were being proselyted for the Bulgarian church.

The Russian sponsorship of Bulgarian religious interests in Mace-donia naturally was opposed by the Greek and the Serbian churches.

---

[1] Grim, "K Istorii Russko-Bolgarskikh Otnoshenii," *Novyi Vostok,* V (1924), 69–70; Koz'menko, "Proekty," pp. 241–243; Greig to Giers, *NKG,* Aug. 21, 1878; Mousset, *La Serbie et son église,* pp. 263–299.

The struggle of the nationalities over the Macedonian area, once commenced, could not easily be halted. Although official Russian policy after Berlin no longer called for the immediate political union of the Bulgars, the agents of Bulgaria, Greece, and Serbia carried on the battle already begun. Even the Russian representatives in the area continued to be involved. In fact, after 1878 the Macedonian question became one of the main issues in Serbian politics, a development which proved highly detrimental to Russian interests in the Balkans.

The Russian attitude toward Serbia after the Congress of Berlin contributed to the intensification of the Macedonian problem. When Russia abandoned Serbia to Austria-Hungary, a difficult situation was created within the principality. The position of the Dual Monarchy in regard to Serbia was fundamentally different from that of Russia in regard to Bulgaria. Despite the events of 1877 and 1878, the Serbian people still looked to Russia as a kindred nation whose people were of the same race and religion. In contrast, Austria-Hungary occupied a position somewhere between Russia and the Ottoman Empire, but closer to the latter. The Habsburg empire with its multitude of Slavic subjects was regarded as the natural enemy of Slavic nationalism. The policy forced upon Serbia of collaboration with Vienna was thus destined to be very unpopular with the Serbian people.

The Serbian ruler Milan, a weak man under the best of circumstances, was in an unenviable position. His people never really understood or accepted the necessities of international politics. His only hope of securing support for the pro-Austrian orientation forced upon him by Russia lay in the use he could make of Serbian nationalism. Outside the Serbian state remained the South Slav areas of Bosnia, Hercegovina, Croatia, Slovenia, and Dalmatia. These lands were within the Dual Monarchy and could not be reclaimed under the existing circumstances; Montenegro was an independent state backed by Russia. Macedonia thus remained the single area where Serbian agitation would not conflict with Milan's pro-Austrian foreign policy.

A struggle between Bulgaria and Serbia over the Macedonian lands was detrimental to Russian interests in all respects. Russia had no desire to see a conflict between states which were both Orthodox and Slavic; in the future Serbia too might fall into the Russian orbit. Moreover, there was always a danger that the quarrel might lead to open conflict with Austria-Hungary and the reopening of the eastern question at a time when Russia was ill prepared to defend her interests. Yet the developments within Serbia, occasioned primarily by her position after the Congress of Berlin, made such an outcome inevitable.

From 1879 to 1885 Serbian foreign policy was dominated by the necessity of accepting a large measure of control from Vienna. During this period, few direct conversations were held between the Russian and Serbian governments. Russian policy in Serbia followed with remarkable consistency the lines established by the Treaty of Berlin and the Dreikaiserbund. Serbia was regarded as being within the Austrian sphere, just as Bulgaria was within the Russian. The strength of Russian influence in Serbia rested primarily on negative factors and not on the activities of the Russian agents in Belgrade or on the decisions of the Russian government. The principal disturbing factor in the foreign policy of Serbia was the conflict between the government, which was collaborating with Austria-Hungary, and the overwhelming majority of the Serbian people, who were Panslav and pro-Russian in sentiment. Through this three-way struggle of the Habsburg government, the Serbian ruler, and the Serbian political parties, the problem was eventually resolved to the advantage of Russia. Therefore, it is to events in Belgrade and Vienna rather than in St. Petersburg that attention must be directed.

At the head of the Serbian state, Prince Milan occupied a controversial position. His adherents considered him a very able man, gifted with unusual insight. Undoubtedly he had an alert and retentive mind. He was an excellent speaker and knew how to judge men and make use of their capabilities. He preferred to deal with practical rather than theoretical problems. Despite the positive aspects of his character, the negative qualities in perspective dominated his reign. His pettiness and the intensity with which he would pursue a personal grievance were perhaps his chief vices. He was tactless, avoided work when possible, and took every occasion to enjoy himself. Self-discipline was foreign to his nature. His opponents accused him also of corruption and the placing of personal ambition above the interests of his country. In domestic politics he was strongly conservative and fought any challenge to his position as ruler.[2]

In the decade prior to 1878 Milan had been "blindly devoted to Russia."

He looked upon the Russian tsar as his national defender, he allowed himself to come into close intimacy with Russian diplomats and officers; he danced to their tune. His young wife, who was half Russian, also advised him to follow Russia. Russophilism in foreign policy was for him as much an article of faith as was conservatism in domestic [policy]; these two things mutually supplemented and supported one another.[3]

---

[2] Jovanović, *Milan*, III, 496–511; Mijatovich, *The Memoirs of a Balkan Diplomatist*, pp. 103–123.
[3] Jovanović, *Milan*, II, 207–208.

The Treaty of San Stefano, with its provision for a Greater Bulgaria whose borders embraced lands in Macedonia coveted by Serbia, caused a complete revolution in the political ideas of the Serbian prince. From a strong Russophil he became a violent Russophobe and an equally ardent Austrophil. Almost overnight, Russian influence in the Serbian court disappeared.[4]

In the past, Serbia had relied upon Russia for support abroad, but at the critical moment she was abandoned. At the Congress of Berlin the Serbian national territories of Bosnia and Hercegovina were assigned to Austria-Hungary, and Serbia was told to look to her northern neighbor for support. The prince was now forced to reconsider the Serbian diplomatic position. The problem before Milan and his government was that of achieving a satisfactory relationship with the Habsburg monarchy in which all the advantages would not be on the side of the more powerful state. The one major gain which Serbia could hope to secure from an agreement with Austria-Hungary was the promise of Habsburg support for Serbian expansion into Macedonia. When this price was agreed upon, Serbia embarked on a new course, turning away from St. Petersburg to Vienna.

The negotiations regulating the relations of Austria-Hungary and Serbia extended over two years. During the first year the realignment of Serbian policy proceeded under the direction of the Liberal party and the prime minister, Jovan Ristić. Although the Liberal party had previously been regarded as the Russian party in Serbia, Ristić, as its leader, recognized the realities of the situation. An able and experienced diplomat, he correctly appraised the relative helplessness of Serbia before Russia and Austria-Hungary. Nevertheless, his goal, even after the Treaty of Berlin, was to remain on friendly terms with both powers and to try to keep Serbia from becoming a vassal of any state. He realized that Serbia would have to come to a formal agreement with Austria-Hungary, since Russia had abandoned the protection of Serbian interests. He did not, however, wish to see his country completely subservient to the Dual Monarchy.[5]

The first step taken by Ristić toward agreement with Austria was his compliance with the Habsburg demand that Serbia proceed with her section of the Belgrade-Sofia line. Serbia had hoped to postpone construction until Turkey and Bulgaria agreed to complete their part of the international line. The convention caused great discontent, particularly since Serbian finances were already overburdened as a result

---

[4] *Ibid.*, p. 208.
[5] Gould to Granville, *FO*, 105/13, no. 100, Belgrade, Nov. 1, 1880; Jovanović, *Milan*, II, 209.

of the recent war. Although Ristić was willing to defend the sacrifices imposed upon Serbia, he soon rebelled against the unequal terms which the Dual Monarchy wished to incorporate in a commercial treaty.

Whereas Austria had pressed for the conclusion of the railroad convention, Serbia was interested primarily in the negotiation of a commercial agreement. In this matter the chief point at issue between the two states was the interpretation of Article 37 of the Treaty of Berlin: "Until the conclusion of fresh arrangements no change shall be made in Serbia in the actual conditions of commercial intercourse of the Principality with foreign countries." The Austrian government considered that its treaty of 1862 with the Ottoman Empire was still valid for the regulation of Austro-Serbian trade. Under the terms of this agreement Serbia could impose only a 3 per cent tariff on Austrian imports, whereas no comparable restriction applied to Serbian exports to the Dual Monarchy. In effect, Austria was free to place a tariff of 5, 10, or even 20 per cent on Serbian items. The Serbian economy was thus at the mercy of Habsburg tariff policy. More than 75 per cent of Serbian exports, chiefly cattle and pigs, went to Austria-Hungary, but this sum represented only 1½ per cent of the total Austrian imports. Changes in the Austrian tariff schedule or the cessation of trade would have a drastic effect on Serbian life but little or none on the Austrian economy. The Habsburg monarchy wished to retain this provision in the new agreement, and also to receive most-favored-nation rights from Serbia without granting her the same privilege within the Dual Monarchy. The Serbs wanted and needed a commercial agreement, but this lack of reciprocity would signify that Serbia had fallen completely under the domination of her northern neighbor.[6]

Supported by his party, Ristić rejected the Austrian terms. He was against any arrangement in which Serbia would not receive most-favored-nation rights in Austria-Hungary. The Austrian government was in no hurry to negotiate, since, until a new treaty was signed, Serbia was bound by the agreement of 1862, which was so favorable to Habsburg interests. Ristić was now faced with a major policy decision: whether to accept the Austrian terms or to embark upon a tariff war with Vienna. Ristić himself was willing to engage in such a struggle. All his life he had fought for Serbian independence, which had not been fully achieved until 1878. Subservience to another great power did not appeal to him. Moreover, since he belonged to the protectionist school, which advocated high tariffs to guard Serbian crafts and infant indus-

[6] Jovanović, *Milan*, II, 263–280; Živanović, *Politička Istorija Srbije u Drugoj Polovini Devetnaestog Veka*, II, 102–103; Duchâtel to Saint-Hilaire, *DDF*, III, no. 289, Vienna, Nov. 1, 1880.

tries, he considered an economic war with Austria as of real advantage to Serbian industry. Finally, he judged that the nationalistic temper of the Serbian people would support the government's opposition to any attempt by a foreign power to impose controls on the Serbian economy. He therefore opposed the conclusion of any commercial convention which was not based upon negotiations between two equal, sovereign states with reciprocal commercial rights for each.[7]

Ristić recognized that in a struggle with a great power he would need foreign assistance. Despite the developments in 1878, Ristić turned to the Russian government, which was then engaged in negotiations for the Dreikaiserbund. Haymerle, however, requested Russia to use her good offices to advise Serbia to come to an agreement with Austria. Thus Ristić found that pressure rather than support was forthcoming from St. Petersburg.[8]

Within Serbia the chief resistance to Ristić's policy came from the peasantry and merchants. Industry, which would have benefited, was a minor factor in the total economic picture, but for merchants and peasants a tariff war with Austria-Hungary, without the prior acquisition of new markets for Serbian livestock and grain, would have meant economic suicide. Taxes were already excessive; a further burden could not be undertaken.

Ristić was disturbed by this unexpected reaction. When he had urged the completion of the Serbian portion of the international line, he had been attacked as the promoter of Austrian interests. Now, when he wished to defy Austria on a far more important issue, he did not have national support. The popular opposition to his policy became so strong that by the fall of 1880 Ristić found his government fighting for its very existence.[9]

The decisive blow to Ristić's program came from Prince Milan, who, after two visits to Vienna in the summer of 1880, felt sure that Austria would undertake an economic war rather than grant equal treatment to Serbia. In urging Ristić to yield, Milan argued that the Austrian demand was nothing more than "the recognition in principle of a right it already possessed in practice."[10] Ristić replied that it "would gravely compromise the political and commercial position of the principality, since it would virtually deprive it of one of the most valuable privileges

---

[7] Jovanović, *Milan*, II, 263–280.
[8] Jomini to Giers, *NKG*, n.d. [1880?]. See also Simpson, *The Saburov Memoirs*, p. 150; Jovanović, *Milan*, II, 279. The assertion by the British minister in Belgrade that Russia was against the commercial treaty is inaccurate. Gould to Granville, *FO*, 105/13, no. 108, Belgrade, Nov. 17, 1880.
[9] Jovanović, *Milan*, II, 277–278.
[10] Gould to Granville, *FO*, 105/13, no. 96, Belgrade, Oct. 23, 1880.

of an independent state—that of making treaties with foreign powers and irrevocably hand over its material interests to the mercy of Austria-Hungary."[11] When Milan refused to be convinced, Ristić resigned in October, 1880.

As long as Ristić remained in power, the policy of the government had been to try to keep on good terms with St. Petersburg. With the departure of the foreign minister, Milan proceeded to break what ties remained with Russia. He needed, first, to form a new government. With the Liberal party out of favor, Milan had to choose between the Progressive party, which was pro-western, or the Radical party, which followed the socialistic program of Svetozar Marković but was not yet fully organized. The Progressive party, because of its aims and its greater popular strength, was the logical successor to the Liberal government.

When Milan approached the Progressives, he placed two conditions on their assumption of power: they must sign the commercial treaty with Austria; and Milan's trusted friend, Čedomil Mijatović, must be given the ministry of both finance and foreign affairs. Anxious to take over the leadership of the state, the Progressives accepted and Milan Piročanac became prime minister. The Progressives were joined by the Radicals in the Skupština (parliament) elections for the sole purpose of defeating the Liberals. Together the Progressives and Radicals captured 121 seats, whereas the Liberals secured only 7.[12]

The Progressive party, in power for the first time, reflected the western orientation of the prince. Its leaders were mostly young Serbs who had attended European universities and who wished Serbia to follow in the path of western rather than eastern Europe. In politics they adhered to the beliefs of the nineteenth century liberal, campaigning on the platform of an independent judiciary, a free press, freedom of assembly and association, and local autonomy. In their everyday life they sought to copy the standards of the western middle class, whose material comforts they fully appreciated. Many of them preferred to converse in French, which they associated with a higher civilization. The Progressive party became in a sense anti-Russian, since its members saw little to attract them in autocratic, Orthodox, and backward Russia.

Mijatović held opinions typical of the members of his government. He had lived abroad for many years and was proud of his ties with the west. He once said that he knew England better than his native Serbia. With his western outlook it is understandable that he should have con-

---

[11] *Ibid.*, no. 95, Belgrade, Oct. 23, 1880.
[12] Živanović, *op. cit.*, II, 108–110; Jovanović, *Milan*, II, 307–310.

sidered Russia a "huge, half-barbarian state." He distrusted Russia's Balkan policy, wisely noting that Russia wished to use the Balkan states only to gain the security she needed at the Straits. If Serbia had to ally with another state, he preferred her destiny to be tied to that of the western Habsburg empire rather than to Russia. Prince Milan and his new government were thus basically in agreement. The path was now clear for the resumption of negotiations with Austria-Hungary.[13]

The first problem confronting the Progressive government was the implementation of the railroad agreement. The Ristić government had agreed that the railroad would be built in three years, that is, by 1883, but who was to build it and how it was to be financed had not been settled. It was finally decided that the state would pay the costs and the railroad would remain national property, but construction and operation would be let to a foreign concern. A loan had to be raised and a company chosen to run the railroad. Since the credit of the Serbian state had not been established on the international market, the government expected to have difficulty in obtaining the necessary funds.

The hope of making a quick and easy profit attracted many bids, but the Parisian firm of E. Bontoux held the advantage from the beginning.[14] Bontoux had been director of the Südbahn firm in Vienna when he was called to Paris to assume the directorship of the Union Générale, which was organized in 1878. Under his leadership the company prospered and won universal respect. Bontoux now approached the Serbian government with an offer both to secure the loan and to construct the railroad. The essential feature of his complicated plan was that Serbia was to pay 198,000 francs per kilometer of rail line. Realizing the political significance of the Balkan railroads, Bontoux sought to secure the support of the Habsburg government for his scheme. In Serbia he faced competition from the Russian firm of Poliakov, which enjoyed the support of the Radicals, and a Russo-Belgian firm. Mijatović in his memoirs states that he first advised Milan to grant the concession to the latter firm, but, when it could not make the necessary loan, gave his approval to the project of the Union Générale. The competition between the firms was so intense that Mijatović claims one company offered him a bribe of 2,000,000 francs.[15]

The Bontoux concession was subsequently criticized severely by the

---

[13] Prodanović, *Istorija Politički Stranaka i Struja u Srbiji*, I, 438, 442–443; Jovanović, *Milan*, II, 306–311, 340–341.

[14] Mijatovich, *op. cit.*, pp. 254–255.

[15] *Ibid.*, pp. 255–257; Jovanović, *Milan*, II, 387–392. See also Meyer, "German Economic Relations with Southeastern Europe, 1870–1914," *American Historical Review*, LVII:1 (Oct., 1951), 77–90.

Radicals in the Skupština, who objected to the cost, the method by which
the agreement was made, and the possible Austrian connections of the
company. They protested because all the negotiations were conducted in
secret and the contract was awarded without open bidding. The price
of 198,000 francs per kilometer appeared excessive, since it would allow
a profit of 40,000 francs per kilometer, or a total of 30,000,000 francs
for the entire railroad.[16] The Austrian aspect of the affair caused difficulty too. Although the Progressive party turned to the west and preferred an agreement with the Dual Monarchy to one with tsarist Russia,
most of its members wished to limit Austrian control where possible,
a feeling which was shared by the other parties and the majority of the
population. Mijatović was forced to state publicly that if there were
even a suspicion that Bontoux was under Austrian influence, Serbia
would break off relations with the company. Later, however, he admitted
that he knew that "intimate ties" linked Bontoux with Vienna; "he considered it probable that by this agreement Bontoux had bound himself
to the Austro-Hungarian government, and that he would, if he gained
the right to exploit the Serbian railroad, keep in consideration the
Austro-Hungarian interest." In spite of numerous protests voiced in
the Skupština, that body, in March, 1881, approved the Bontoux contract 97 to 57.[17]

After the settlement of the railroad question, the Progressive government turned to a consideration of the commercial treaty, which proved
a less difficult problem to solve, since the policy of agreement with
Austria had already been decided upon. The Progressives justified their
surrender to Austria on the ground that Serbia had little choice.
Mijatović argued that Serbia was too weak to defend both her agricultural and her commercial interests; therefore she had to concentrate on
one. Agriculture, being dominant, was the logical choice. The Serbian
peasant needed the markets of Austria-Hungary; hence it was the duty
of the state to obtain the best terms possible. The convention, embody-
ing the controversial terms wherein Austria received most-favored-
nation treatment without reciprocal rights for Serbia, was signed in
April and ratified in June, 1881.[18]

Prince Milan had now bound Serbia to Austria-Hungary through the

---

[16] Jovanović, *Milan*, II, 391; Canclaux to Saint-Hilaire, *DDF*, III, no. 325, Belgrade, Jan. 3, 1881; *ibid.*, no. 365, Feb. 6, 1881.

[17] Mijatovich, *op. cit.*, pp. 254–258; Živanović, *op. cit.*, II, 171–179; Jovanović,
Milan, II, 399 n. 1, 400–403. Mijatović further revealed that Milan was "involved"
in this entire affair. The prince's adjutant and uncle, General Catargiu, told
Mijatović that Bontoux was ready to liquidate Milan's personal debt of 3,000,000
francs. Jovanović, *Milan*, II, 437–453. Milan's personal financial history is discussed in Jakšić, *Iz Novije Srpske Istorije*, pp. 206–236.

[18] Jovanović, *Milan*, II, 321–333.

railroad plan and the commercial agreement. It was, however, the highly controversial political agreement which formed the heart of his program. Close collaboration with Austria-Hungary, now espoused enthusiastically by Milan,[19] had been virtually forced on the prince by the Russian policy of backing Bulgarian interests exclusively, and by the surrender of Bosnia-Hercegovina to Austrian control.

Macedonia was now the sole area where Milan could hope to obtain territorial gains. Since this land too had been assigned to Bulgaria in the Treaty of San Stefano, Serbia could expect only opposition from Russia. Thus, in seeking a treaty with the Dual Monarchy, Milan was motivated not only by his intense hatred for Russia but also by the fact that Serbia could not expand without great power assistance. Ignorant of the terms of the Dreikaiserbund, Milan was confident that in time war would break out between Russia and Austria-Hungary. In the belief that the latter power would be victorious, he expected to use the opportunity to gain Macedonia.

Certainly, Milan's position in Serbia was not strong enough to maintain the *status quo,* particularly in view of the recent tremendous gains of the rival Bulgarian nation. The majority of the Serbian people in the elections soon demonstrated their lack of faith in their ruler. Outside Serbia the rival Karadjordjević family was ready to seize every opportunity to regain power. Only by advocating a strongly nationalistic program, with the acquisition of Macedonian lands as its goal, could Milan hope to stay on the throne. Moreover, even if he had wished to pursue an independent policy, or to seek closer ties with Russia, the pattern of international diplomacy would have prevented him from doing so. Russia had abandoned Serbia not only at the Congress of Berlin but also in the discussions on the Dreikaiserbund agreement. Assured of the support of Russia and Germany, the Dual Monarchy had no qualms about putting pressure on Belgrade. During the negotiations Benjamin Kallay stated frankly that, if events in Serbia took an unfavorable turn, Austria might have to "occupy" the country.[20] Milan's personal inclinations, the Russian support of Bulgaria, and Austrian pressure all contributed to assure the completion of an agreement which would bind Serbia close to the German states.

The final terms of the political treaty were signed on June 16/28, 1881, just ten days after the completion of the Dreikaiserbund.[21] In the

---

[19] Milan's overtures to Austria are discussed in Herbert to Haymerle, *HHS*, XIX 15, réservé, May 29, 1881.

[20] Jovanović, *Milan*, II, 348.

[21] The complete terms of the treaty are in Pribram, *The Secret Treaties of Austria-Hungary*, I, 50–55. For a detailed study of this treaty see Jakšić, *op. cit.*, pp. 70–

agreement Milan made two positive gains. In the first place, Austria agreed that if Milan should decide to raise his title from prince to king, she would recognize the change and use her influence to obtain the approval of the powers. In the second place, Austria agreed to support Serbian expansion into Macedonia, but not into Novi Pazar, if future circumstances should permit such a development. Milan thus strengthened his own position and paved the way for the enlargement of his state.

However, in return for these concessions, Milan in effect converted his state into a vassal of the Dual Monarchy. He agreed, first, that he would not tolerate any "political, religious, or other intrigues" directed against the Dual Monarchy, including Bosnia-Hercegovina and the Sanjak of Novi Pazar. In other words, Serbian nationalism would be directed away from Bosnia-Hercegovina or union with Montenegro. Second, if either power found itself threatened or at war, it was agreed that the other would follow a policy of friendly neutrality. If the two powers joined in a war, a military convention would be concluded regulating the command and the passage of troops. Third, in Article IV, the crucial section of the treaty, it was agreed that "without a previous understanding with Austria-Hungary, Serbia will neither negotiate nor conclude any political treaty with another government, and will not admit to her territory a foreign armed force, regular or irregular, even as volunteers." It was this provision which aroused the greatest controversy within the Serbian government.

In Serbia, only four men knew about the terms of the treaty: the prince, Mijatović, Piročanac, and M. Garašanin, minister of the interior. The last two were not consulted during the negotiations, but were informed of the terms only after they had been agreed upon. After reading the stipulations, both submitted their resignations. They were particularly incensed over Article IV, which they regarded as detrimental to the sovereignty of the Serbian state. Their strong reaction caught Milan by surprise. He was afraid that their resignation would lead to the disclosure of the terms of the agreement. As one authority stated, the prince "was much more afraid of his ministers than of the Austrian diplomats."[22] Milan and Mijatović, in an attempt to hold the government together, made every effort to pacify the two ministers.

161. See Jakšić (Jacktschitch), "Le traité secret austro-serbe du 28 juin 1881 et du 9 février 1889," *Revue d'histoire diplomatique*, LI–LII (1937–1938), 429–466, 65–105. See also Živanović, *op. cit.*, II, 179–183; Jovanović, *Milan*, II, 333–350; Ueber-sperger, "Zur Vorkriegsgeschichte Serbiens," *Berliner Monatshefte*, XI (1933), 15–54; Pribram, "Milan IV von Serbien und die Geheimverträge Oesterreich-Ungarns mit Serbien, 1881–1889," *Historische Blätter*, I (1921–1922), 464–494.

[22] Jovanović, *Milan*, II, 340.

Finally, a solution was reached in which Mijatović surrendered his post of minister of foreign affairs to Piročanac, but remained minister of commerce.

Piročanac then went to Vienna to try to obtain a new interpretation of Article IV. In face of the Serbian protests, the Habsburg government agreed, on October 18/30, to a declaration which stated that the article in question could not "impair the right of Serbia to negotiate and conclude treaties, even of a political nature with another government." The article was interpreted to mean that Serbia would not enter into any treaty which was contrary to the spirit and tenor of the secret treaty with Austria.[23] Piročanac now felt that he could continue in office and that Serbian sovereignty had not been surrendered to the Dual Monarchy. What he did not know, however, was that Milan had meanwhile nullified this interpretation.

One week earlier, on October 12/24, Milan had sent a personal declaration to Kallay, acting foreign minister, that it was a "question of honor" with him "to develop relations of cordial understanding" with the Dual Monarchy. Expressing his "profound respect" and "unchanging affection" for Franz Joseph, he stated that Piročanac "was not invested by me with any official mission, and that, far from approving, I condemn his scruples." Milan hoped that the Austrian government would "make a sacrifice in form and not at all in substance." He thanked Kallay for his willingness to come to an understanding with Piročanac, but reassured him that *"of my own free will ... I hereby ... assume the formal engagement on my honor and in my quality as prince of Serbia, not to enter into any negotiations whatsoever relative to any kind of a political treaty without communication with and the previous consent of Austria-Hungary."*[24]

The political treaty together with the railroad and commercial conventions brought Serbia decisively into the Austrian sphere. By the treaty the Dual Monarchy not only assured its control over Serbia but also protected its interests in Bosnia-Hercegovina. Whereas the advantages in the agreement for Austria were immediate and apparent, Serbia's reward depended upon future developments. The elevation of the principality to a kingdom probably would not cause difficulties, but the disposal of Macedonia was an integral part of the eastern question and was not dependent solely upon the good will of Austria-Hungary. Since it was an international problem, it would be settled on that basis. Milan had thus yielded Serbian freedom of action in foreign affairs for an uncertain future reward.

[23] Pribram, *The Secret Treaties of Austria-Hungary*, I, 61.
[24] *Ibid.*, p. 59.

The reaction of the Russian government to the developments in Serbia was conditioned solely by her concern over the maintenance of the Dreikaiserbund. The secret treaty between Serbia and the Dual Monarchy was, of course, unknown to the Russian government. The provisions concerning Macedonia were certainly to the detriment of Russian interests. The purpose of the Dreikaiserbund had been to assure the maintenance of the *status quo* in the Balkans, except for the eventual annexation of Bosnia-Hercegovina and the union of the Bulgarias. Austria's promise of aid to Serbia in Macedonia was a violation of the spirit of the Dreikaiserbund, and could only lead to a disturbance of peace in the area; yet future Macedonian gains were the sole justification of the treaty for Serbia. There was little hope that the Serbian government or people would remain passive in the matter. Moreover, after 1883, when her position in Bulgaria began to deteriorate, Russia was anxious to avoid the revival of the Macedonian issue: on the one hand, she had no desire to strengthen the position of Alexander of Battenberg, nor was she sure that a united Bulgaria would be pro-Russian; on the other hand, she could not favor the claims of Austria's protégé, Serbia.

Milan and the Progressive ministers had thus completed the reorientation of Serbian foreign policy. The basic weakness of the shift, however, soon became apparent. Although events had in a sense forced Serbia along the path she now followed, Prince Milan was not the man to lead his nation in a direction that was basically unpopular. Without the necessary strength either within himself or in his country, he soon ran into opposition which he could not handle.

To the Serbian people the most important unredeemed Serbian national lands lay within Austria-Hungary. The shock of the loss of Bosnia-Hercegovina had not worn off; the Dual Monarchy remained the chief "oppressor" of the Serbian nationals outside the principality. Alliance with the northern state under such conditions appeared unnatural and objectionable. The assimilation of Macedonian lands and the struggle over religion and education in the area aroused the emotions of the people, but not to the same degree. Despite the Russian attitude after Berlin, the Serbs in general were convinced that it was Russia, not Austria-Hungary, to whom they should turn for aid in the unification of their national territories. Under these circumstances any conflict between the interests of Austria-Hungary and those of Russia was bound to arouse a storm of patriotic feeling.

Russia's strongest influence in the Balkans was exercised through the Orthodox church. In this sphere Russia could sway not only the Balkan governments but also the individual citizen. Although in Macedonia the Russian government supported the Bulgarian exarchate against both the Greek and the Serbian ecclesiastical organizations, in the large conflict of Catholic and Orthodox the Russian church did not hesitate to join the Serbian church in its fight against Austrian control. In an issue involving the struggle of Orthodox against Catholic, Russian opinion would force the intervention of the Russian government, no matter what its diplomatic policy. In the same manner the Serbian population would react strongly even though the foreign policy of Serbia were affected. It was into this hornet's nest that Milan stepped when, in his efforts to reduce Russian influence in Serbia, he dismissed the exceedingly popular metropolitan of the Serbian church, Mihailo.

The immediate cause of the prince's action was the desire of the Serbian government to impose additional taxes on the church. Mihailo objected to these taxes in principle, and also to the method by which they were to be levied. They had been decided upon without the knowledge and consent of the Holy Synod and some of them were believed to be contrary to the church canons. When Mihailo would not give in to the government's demand, he was summarily dismissed from his post in October, 1881.

The real reason for Mihailo's removal, however, was far more significant. From the time that he became the Serbian metropolitan in 1859, he had been the leader of the pro-Russian faction in Serbia. Educated in Russia, Mihailo was devoted to the Orthodox state and had done all he could to further her interests. After 1869 he became "for Russia, for the Russian church, and for the great Russian nation the most significant person among the non-Russian Slavs, in the Orthodox circles and in the east in general."[25] In Russia he was widely known and respected. Ivan Aksakov wrote of him:

This man—Metropolitan Mihailo—untiringly and without selfish motives ... devoted himself to the service of the Orthodox church and his people. A student and holder of a degree from the Kiev Ecclesiastical Academy, one of the most educated men in Serbia, he loved Russia, he had a great respect for her charm, he understood her historical role in the Slavic world and invariably believed in her destiny and future.[26]

---

[25] Mousset, *op. cit.*, p. 243, citing St. M. Dimitrijević, *Mihailo 'Arhiepiskob Beogradski i Mitropolit Srbije* (Belgrade, 1933), p. 25.

[26] Aksakov, *Slavianskii Vopros'*, p. 359. The noted Serbian historian Živanović, *op. cit.*, IV, 32, wrote: "Metropolitan Mihailo was important in Serbia as a prominent political personality and at home and abroad as a great Russophil. As a Russian student he possessed complete love and devotion for the great Orthodox Tsardom, just as, conversely, in Russia, Mihailo enjoyed the general respect of all classes and even the tsar's court ... His church ideal was Orthodox Russia, in which he had received his higher theological-philosophical training at the Kiev Ecclesiastical Academy ..."

Since Serbian policy was now directed toward Vienna, it was understandable that the Russophobe prince should seek to place in the highly influential position of metropolitan a candidate whose views corresponded more closely with his own. Mihailo had been dismissed with the backing of Austria-Hungary, who, with her considerable Slavic population, was ever alert to the dangers of Orthodox agitation. On October 31/November 12, 1881, the Austrian foreign minister informed his representatives in Constantinople and Athens:

[Mihailo was] the center of Panslavic agitation not only in Serbia but for the whole Balkans, that the Serbian government had to throw him out in the interest of peace in the Balkans, and that Austria could not permit his restoration, because in the first place his agitation would spread in Bosnia and after that in the Jugoslav parts of the Monarchy.[27]

Besides the desire to remove a Russian sympathizer from the leadership of the Serbian church, Milan had another reason. Mihailo was a supporter of the Liberal party which had dominated Serbian politics for the preceding twelve years. When in office, the party had placed its followers in the most important civil and administrative posts. Once in power, the rival Progressive party, after the manner of the spoils system, decided on a systematic house cleaning so that it could fill the lucrative governmental offices with its own adherents. Mihailo supported the ousted officials and protested strongly against the government's actions. Milan thus saw Mihailo as an active opponent of the only party that was willing to carry through his pro-Austrian policy.[28]

Milan was acting against the dominant opinion in his nation when he dismissed Mihailo. Moreover, the means by which the dismissal was accomplished was unfortunate. The synod as a whole had adopted the position that the matter of taxation might be reconciled with the church canons. Mihailo, in discussing the problem with the minister of religion, had stated that the synod would not accept the tax measures, but he failed to mention the qualifying decision. When the government learned of the omission, it had a tactical advantage. Although Mihailo was popular, friction and jealousy existed within the hierarchy which a wise prince could have exploited. Instead of using his natural advantages, Milan committed two errors: first, Mihailo was dismissed without the approval of the synod, an act which was contrary to the canons; and second, the metropolitan was deprived of his pension. Both of these

---

[27] Cited in Jovanović, *Milan*, II, 416–417. See also Pinter to Haymerle, *HHS*, XIX 15, no. 68A–B, Belgrade, June 20, 1881; Herbert to Kallay, *HHS*, XIX 15, no. 103, Belgrade, Nov. 4, 1881.

[28] Mousset, *op. cit.*, pp. 314–315, 316–319; Jovanović, *Milan*, II, 407; Pinter to Haymerle, *HHS*, XIX 15, no. 38A, Belgrade, June 20, 1881.

actions closed the ranks of the hierarchy and united all factions behind Mihailo.[29]

The government policy now aimed at dominating both secular and ecclesiastical phases of national life. Although this was not contrary to tradition in the Orthodox states, Milan did not have the necessary power or popularity to carry out such a policy. Even though he succeeded in persuading the bishops not to resign, he lost the support of the Serbian clergy, who feared for their ecclesiastical prerogatives and their livelihood. Milan had thus divided his country on an issue which was not to his advantage. He and his government were faced with the opposition of the Liberals, who were in turn supported by the clergy. The Radical party remained neutral for a time, since Mihailo was regarded as a Liberal, and the Radicals did not want to have the clerical label attached to themselves.[30]

By joining the foreign policy issue with the question of the rights of the Serbian church, both Austria-Hungary and Milan's government found themselves at a great disadvantage. The Serbian public recognized the issue for what it was: Milan, with the support of the Habsburg government, had dismissed Mihailo because of his strong Panslav sympathies, which were shared by the majority of the electorate. The method by which this was accomplished drew attention to the entire problem of the independence of the church and the economic position of the clergy. Through his action against Mihailo, Milan had hoped to destroy the center of the opposition to his western orientation; instead, he had created an issue on which all his opponents could unite and which enjoyed popular support.

When Alexander II was assassinated, Milan forbade Mihailo to deliver a funeral oration in honor of the tsar, nor did the Serbian government forward to Alexander III the expressions of sympathy of the Skupština.[31] The Russian press naturally regarded Milan's anti-Russian attitude and his closer relations with Austria-Hungary as betrayals of the Slavic world. The climax of the increasing hostility of the Russian press came with Milan's dismissal of the metropolitan. Here was a clear issue which appealed to the emotions of the Russian public: Catholic Austria-Hungary appeared to have triumphed over Orthodox Russia. Katkov's *Moskovskiia Viedomosti*, on October 27/November 8, 1881, made the following statement.

[29] Jovanović, *Milan*, II, 410–411. See also Herbert to Kallay, *HHS*, XIX 15, no. 104, Belgrade, Nov. 7, 1881; Khevenhüller to Kalnoky, *HHS*, XIX 16, no. 5B, Belgrade, Jan. 20, 1882; *ibid.*, no. 16B, Belgrade, Feb. 13, 1882.

[30] Mousset, *op. cit.*, pp. 344–347; Jovanović, *Milan*, II, 411.

[31] Gould to Granville, *FO*, 105/19, no. 32, Belgrade, March 21, 1881.

An act of outrageous injustice has recently been committed in Serbia. To whom in Russia is the name of the Metropolitan Mihailo not known? Who does not recollect his heart-stirring appeals to the Russian people on behalf of Serbia at the time of the greatest need and distress? And now Metropolitan Mihailo, the zealous patriot and faithful friend of Russia, the healer of wounds inflicted on Orthodoxy in Serbian lands under the yoke of Turkey and Austria, is with the aid of a *cudgel* driven from his sacred post by an obscure government, which, born yesterday, may well disappear tomorrow. Does not this show that since the Berlin congress the authority of Russia in the East has declined and that the designs of her opponents, the foes of Orthodoxy and Slavdom, are being successfully carried out?

He encouraged the hopes of the Serbian people; he always reminded his flock of that great northern Slav empire which had been the benefactress of the Serbian people, ever since the connection between Russia and Serbia began. Every Russian found in him refuge, aid, and kind encouraging speech. The Russian people believed in Serbia only in the person of the Metropolitan, and aid to Serbia from Russia proceeded mainly through him.[32]

These opinions were shared by Ignatiev, who for a decade had been one of the chief architects of Russia's Near Eastern policy. In a letter to Pobedonostsev he lamented:

The removal of Father Mihailo—our most trustworthy ally, a student of our ecclesiastical academy and a resolute and enterprising man—is a disastrous blow inflicted on our influence by the Hungarians and the Germans. I continuously supported him for fifteen years against various enemies and intrigues. At one stroke they were able to shatter this firm foundation. We are now tasting the fruits of the Berlin agreement and of our humiliation.[33]

Pobedonostsev in turn wrote to Alexander III, on November 11/23, 1881:

Other detachments of this same army [of Catholic priests] are undermining our strength, nationality, and church—in alliance with Austria—in Bosnia and Hercegovina, in Bulgaria, in Hungary, and, finally, in Serbia. It is impossible to deceive oneself in [finding] the clue to the latter's [Austria's] history with the Serbian metropolitan. Austria, together with Rome, understands very well that it is possible to undermine Russia and her influence in the East only by undermining the Orthodox church. Prince Milan is a man without a heart, without patriotism, and without noble ideas; his ministry is made up of Liberals and unpopular cosmopolitans who do not believe in anything. They have contrived to introduce into Serbia a *Kulturkampf* which has no significance in an Orthodox state. It is apparent that in all this they are only the soulless tools of Austrian policy.[34]

Bound by the Dreikaiserbund, the Russian foreign office remained cautious. Milan was informed that the expulsion of the metropolitan

[32] Thornton to Granville, *FO*, 65/1115, no. 547, St. P., Nov. 15, 1881. These views were shared by most Russian newspapers. Kalnoky to Kallay, *HHS*, X 70, no. 54B, St. P., Nov. 4/16, 1881.

[33] Pobedonostsev, *K. P. Pobedonostsev i Ego Korrespondenty*, I, Ignatiev to Pobedonostsev, no. 80, Oct. 22, 1881. Hereafter cited as *Korrespondenty*.

[34] Pobedonostsev, *Pis'ma Pobedonostseva k Aleksandru III*, I, Pobedonostsev to Alexander III, no. 283, Nov. 11/23, 1881.

had made a "bad impression" on the tsar and that "Orthodoxy could not remain indifferent to such violations of the canons." The prince was advised that Russo-Serbian relations could not be "tolerable" until the metropolitan was restored to his post.[35] Although the Russian government took no further official action, it had an issue that could be used to advantage when necessary. As one writer has stated, Russia "considered the question open, and whenever she had the opportunity she sought the restoration of Mihailo. This restoration had to be a sign that Milan repentantly was returning to Orthodoxy, and through Orthodoxy to the great Slavic idea, whose bearer was Russia."[36]

Despite the fact that the issue was not exploited directly, the Mihailo episode was of great advantage to Russian policy. Without violating the terms of the agreement with her German neighbors, Russia now enjoyed the significant shift of opinion which had taken place in Serbia.

Austrian policy was bound up with Prince Milan and the Progressive government. Should they fall, Vienna would in all probability lose control of the Serbian state. Although the Austrian diplomats threatened to occupy the country, they knew that such an act would be difficult to carry out without endangering the peace of the Balkan area. Like Russia, the Habsburg monarchy sought to consolidate her power in her vassal areas without a direct display of force.

The importance of the Mihailo controversy to Austrian and Russian relations was apparent in the Serbian opposition press, which made the dismissal and the relations with Austria the issue of the day. Austria, it was repeatedly pointed out, had taken control of Serbian commerce and communications; now she sought to dominate the Serbian church, the last stronghold of Serbian independence. As these arguments gained in currency, the popularity of Russia as the protector of the Slavic peoples grew. Reporting on the situation, the British minister in Belgrade commented that Milan now even feared for his personal safety. The army was disaffected and the population ripe for rebellion. Russia was "now looked to as the natural protector of the country against all those at home and abroad who are supposed to harbor designs against its newly acquired independence."[37]

Milan's dependence on Habsburg support was underlined by sub-

---

[35] Jovanović, *Milan*, II, 412; Mousset, *op. cit.*, pp. 335–336. See also Herbert to Kallay, *HHS*, XIX 15, no. 105, reserviert, Belgrade, Nov. 9, 1881; *ibid.*, tel. no. 885, Belgrade, Nov. 10, 1881; *ibid.*, no. 106, Belgrade, Nov. 12, 1881; Khevenhüller to Kalnoky, *HHS*, XIX 16, no. 10, Belgrade, Feb. 1, 1882; *ibid.*, XIX 17, no. 20A–B, vertraulich, Belgrade, March 20, 1883.

[36] Jovanović, *Milan*, II, 413.

[37] Gould to Granville, *FO*, 105/19, no. 27, conf., Belgrade, March 12, 1881; *ibid.*, no. 46; secret and conf., Belgrade, April 12, 1881; Herbert to Haymerle, *HHS*, XIX 15, no. 94, Belgrade, Oct. 2, 1881; Khevenhüller to Kallay, *HHS*, XIX 15, no. 109A–B, Belgrade, Dec. 2, 1881.

sequent developments in the Mihailo issue. To carry on the metropolitan's duties, Milan appointed Bishop Mojsej, but only on a temporary basis. In order to make his victory over Mihailo complete, Milan
had to secure the election of a new metropolitan, which was not an easy
task. According to the canons of the church, unless Mihailo were dismissed by the synod, he remained the metropolitan even if he did not
administer the office. Since Milan could not control the synod, he
altered its composition through a new law, introduced in December,
1882, which allowed the government to appoint enough representatives,
including the minister-president, to form a majority in the synod. The
Serbian bishops immediately condemned the law as being against the
canons and as permitting secular officials to participate in the election
of the metropolitan. They further declared that Mihailo was still the
metropolitan and that no decision could be taken without his participation in the discussion. At this point even Mojsej deserted the government, for it was seeking to dominate the church hierarchy. The
government simply ignored the opposition. Although the bishops boy-
cotted the reformed synod, it met in March, 1883, to elect a new
metropolitan. The government's candidate was a retired professor of
theology, Archimandrite Teodosije Mraović. The election took place,
but Teodosije could be confirmed only by another bishop. Since none in
Serbia could perform the ceremony, Milan was forced to seek the assistance of the Austrian government.[38]

Milan's request placed the Austrian government in a difficult position. The Dual Monarchy was interested in the dismissal of Mihailo,
but it had no desire to become involved in the religious controversy,
because of the probable effect on Austrian influence in the principality.
At the same time the Habsburg government could not abandon Milan
or take the chance that he might be overthrown on the religious issue.
Consequently, the Austrian government reluctantly consented; in
March, 1883, Teodosije journeyed to Karlovac, where he was confirmed
in office by German Angelić, the Orthodox patriarch in Austria-Hungary, who resided in Sremski Karlovci.[39] When the Serbian bishops still
refused to recognize the election, they were dismissed without a pension
and the government appointed its own bishops. Thus Milan had ostensibly triumphed over the opposition. With Austrian support he had
gained a completely subservient church hierarchy.[40]

---

[38] Khevenhüller to Kalnoky, *HHS*, XIX 17, no. 21A–B, Belgrade, March 24, 1883;
Mousset, *op. cit.*, pp. 319–333; Jovanović, *Milan*, II, 410–417.

[39] Khevenhüller to Kalnoky, *HHS*, XIX 17, no. 24, vertraulich, Belgrade, April
19, 1883.

[40] Jovanović, *Milan*, II, 415–420; Khevenhüller to Kalnoky, *HHS*, XIX 17, tel.,
Belgrade, Feb. 23, 1883; Kalnoky to Khevenhüller, *HHS*, XIX 17, Vienna, April 8,
1883.

In Serbia the popular reaction to this deed was just what the Austrian government had feared. Mihailo emerged as a national hero who was fighting for Serbian independence against Austria and Milan. Moreover, the selection of Teodosije was considered an insult, since "women, song, and wine and, in addition, cards" were regarded as his principal interests in life. Mihailo had now become the symbol of Serbian independence; only his restoration would signify that Serbia was again free.[41]

The Russian press was concerned over the method by which Teodosije had been appointed. It appeared as conclusive proof that Russia was losing ground in the Balkans before the Catholic Habsburg empire. Since these events took place in 1883, when Alexander of Battenberg was showing signs of independence, it looked as if Vienna were behind a concerted plot to drive out Russian influence from both Sofia and Belgrade.

The Russian Holy Synod shared in the concern of the public. It refused to recognize Teodosije and continued to regard Mihailo as the head of the Serbian church. In Moscow the Serbian priest who conducted services for the Serbs in that city was informed that he could not mention Teodosije's name in the church ceremonies. When he refused to obey, the church was closed by the Russian authorities.[42]

The Russian Synod went one step farther and sought to persuade the Orthodox churches not to recognize the appointment. In this campaign the position of the patriarchate of Constantinople was of the highest importance. In spite of the interchurch quarrels on the Balkan Peninsula, the Greek patriarch enjoyed the greatest prestige. His refusal to recognize Teodosije would serve as a precedent for the other Balkan churches.

Milan, supported by Austria, sought the patriarch's recognition for the same reason. At the time of his dismissal in 1881, Mihailo had asked for the aid of the patriarch against Milan. However, because the patriarchate had been at odds with Russia since the founding of the Bulgarian exarchate in 1870, it had no wish to defend a protégé of that nation. Therefore the patriarch let it be known, in December, 1883, that he would recognize Milan's action "provided the change were officially announced to him by the Serbian government."

At first Milan refused to comply, for he cherished the independence of the Serbian church. Throughout the nineteenth century the Serbian church had sought to regain the status it had lost in 1766, when the

---

[41] Mousset, *op. cit.*, pp. 383–386; Jovanović, *Milan*, II, 417–418.

[42] Wolkenstein to Kalnoky, *HHS*, X 72, no. 51C, St. P., July 20/Aug. 1, 1883; Locock to Granville, *FO*, 105/39, no. 26, Belgrade, Aug. 9, 1883; see also Schiessl to Kalnoky, *HHS*, XIX 17, no. 32, June 6, 1883.

Serbian patriarchate of Peć was abolished and incorporated into the Greek patriarchate. However, as the Mihailo episode became more confused, and threatened Milan's position, Milan was ready to seek external support wherever possible, just as he had used the aid of German Angelić of Karlovac. In 1883 and 1884 both the Serbian government and the Russian Synod sought to influence the patriarch. Not until November, 1884, was the decision finally made. When a new patriarch was chosen in that year, Teodosije sent him a telegram of congratulations. Thereupon the new patriarch recognized Teodosije and his hierarchy. Milan had thus triumphed over the Russian opposition.[43]

The failure of Russian attempts to influence the patriarch had an added significance. The Russian goal after the establishment of the exarchate had been to heal the breach between the Balkan Orthodox churches. So far little success had been achieved. The struggle had further embittered the participating nationalities. Now, in the recognition of Teodosije, the patriarch of Constantinople had supported the Serbian government against Russia. In 1885 the Greek and Rumanian synods also recognized Teodosije.[44] It thus appeared that, as a result of Russia's Bulgarian policy, the Orthodox hierarchies in the Balkans had united with the metropolitanate at Belgrade to oppose Russian interests.

Despite this setback, Russia had gained great advantages in Serbia from the Mihailo episode. The entire issue of Austrian domination was now before the Serbian public. Although the Russian government never overstepped the limits imposed by the Dreikaiserbund, it naturally rejoiced in any embarrassments or setbacks suffered by Austria-Hungary. The Mihailo dismissal had forced the Habsburg monarchy openly to throw its support behind the weak, unpopular prince, and it had been drawn into a religious controversy from which it could hope to extract no political advantages. Russia was now able to exert influence within the Austrian sphere without endangering its position as an ally of the German powers.

---

[43] Khevenhüller to Kalnoky, *HHS*, XIX 18, no. 90A–C, Belgrade, Dec. 9, 1884; *ibid.*, XIX 17, no. 54, Belgrade, Aug. 18, 1883; *ibid.*, XIX 18, no. 96B, Belgrade, Dec. 21, 1884; Jovanović, *Milan*, II, 417.

[44] Schiessl to Kalnoky, *HHS*, XIX 19, no. 18, Belgrade, March 1, 1885; Khevenhüller to Kalnoky, *HHS*, XIX 19, no. 59, Belgrade, Aug. 5, 1885.

VIII

THE GROWTH OF KING MILAN'S RUSSOPHOBIA

AT THE same time that Milan became involved in the dispute over Mihailo, he found himself in equally serious difficulties in other fields of foreign and domestic politics. Within Serbia he had to face the active opposition of a political party that was gaining strength rapidly. By the beginning of 1882 the newly formed Radical party was ready to challenge the rule of the Progressives, and it had become openly hostile to Milan. In the next few years this group formed the core of opposition to the prince and attracted into its ranks those who favored close ties with Russia and an end to the agreement with the Dual Monarchy. Simultaneously, in foreign relations a series of incidents occurred which were damaging to Milan's prestige. These setbacks, internal and external, had one element in common. Milan could interpret all of them, rightly or wrongly, as arising from Russian hostility. His growing obsession with the fear of Russian intrigue forced him to seek even closer ties with Austria-Hungary, which in turn increased the opposition to his rule among his own people. This situation was exploited to the maximum by the Radical party. Although its platform contained many of the ideas of the great Serbian Socialist, Svetozar Marković, the party was not in fact socialistic. In its formative years its members were young enthusiasts, inspired by many of the ideals associated with the Paris Commune. Although this program appealed to the intellectuals, it evoked little response from the conservative, property-owning Serbian peasants. The Radicals stood primarily for the sovereignty of the national Skupština and for local community autonomy. Their immediate aim was to break the power of the police, whose interference, they argued, had enabled the government in power to perpetuate itself in the elections. Only in this way would the Skupština be free of the control of the prince.[1]

Two members of the Radical group, Nikola Pašić and Pera Todorović, eventually were able to give the party a program more acceptable to the peasants. Previously, the peasant had been taught to feel that the government was not his affair. The Radicals now sought to develop a critical, fighting attitude in the peasants and to overcome their fear of the

---

[1] Živanović, *Politička Istorija Srbije*, II, 112–149; Prodanović, *Istorija Političkih Stranaka i Struja u Srbiji*, pp. 438, 446; Jovanović, *Milan*, III, 1–13; Jovanović, "Svetozar Marković," *Političke i Pravne Rasprave*, I, 59–289; Skerlić, *Svetozar Marković: Njegov Život, Rad i Ideje*.

police. By means of cells organized throughout the country, the Radicals achieved a large measure of success, and were the first party ever to organize the Serbian peasantry. The leader of the movement, Todorović, believed that victory depended more on the methods employed than on the slogans and ideas of the party. While Todorović devoted himself to the task of organizing the countryside, Pašić led the debates in the Skupština.[2]

In foreign relations the Radicals understood that, because of the principality's geographic position, an openly hostile policy toward Vienna could not be pursued. However, they did not wish to see Serbian independence abandoned to Austria nor did they support the policy of hostility to Russia. In domestic matters they advocated a review of the entire tax program before new taxes were imposed. Opposing the government in both domestic and foreign policy, the Radical party opened its campaign in January, 1882, by refusing to consent to the Progressive party's reply to the address from the throne, and by directly attacking the program of the government and the prince. Milan was convinced that the Radicals were a revolutionary party bent on the overthrow of the dynasty, but before he could take active measures to crush them, another problem arose.[3]

On January 18/30, 1882, the day of the open break between the Radicals and the Progressives, word arrived from Paris that the Union Générale, the French firm which was to build the Serbian railroads, had collapsed as a result of numerous irregularities in its administration. An investigation followed, and its president, Bontoux, drew a five-year prison sentence. The news was a tremendous blow to Milan and the Progressives.[4] The opposition to the original concession to Bontoux now appeared justified; Serbia had apparently lost the 34,500,000 dinars which she had invested in the firm—a significant sum in view of the fact that the Serbian national budget for one year was only 26,000,000 dinars. Such a loss could not be borne by the weak and unstable economy of the nation. Milan, who had speculated in the firm on his own account, faced the possible loss of 230,000 francs.[5] Mijatović, minister of finance, immediately left for Paris to see what could be recovered.[6]

The Bontoux scandal provided excellent political ammunition for the

---

[2] Jovanović, *Milan*, III, 1–5.

[3] Živanović, *op. cit.*, p. 194.

[4] Khevenhüller to Kalnoky, *HHS*, XIX 16, no. 9A, vertraulich, Belgrade, Jan. 30, 1882.

[5] *Ibid.*, no. 25B, geheim, Belgrade, Feb. 28, 1882; Jovanović, *Milan*, III, 30–31.

[6] Mijatovich, *The Memoirs of a Balkan Diplomatist*, pp. 258–260; Živanović, *op. cit.*, pp. 195–198; Jovanović, *Milan*, III, 30–31, 38; Jakšić, *Iz Novije Sprske Istorije*, pp. 208–212; Khevenhüller to Kalnoky, *HHS*, XIX 16, no. 25B, geheim, Belgrade, Feb. 28, 1882.

Radicals. As reports from Paris brought increasing evidence of the type of operation carried on by the concern, the Radicals, seeking the fall of the government, became more vociferous in their denunciations.[7] The two Progressive leaders, Piročanac and Garašanin, were ready to resign, believing that their position had become untenable, but Milan would not surrender. The Progressive Club supported the prince and demanded that its leaders remain. Simultaneously, Vienna added her voice to persuade the ministers to stay.[8] Piročanac and Garašanin finally agreed, but only on the stipulation that some popular measure would be introduced which would command the support of Progressives, Radicals, and Liberals alike. The one possible step was the elevation of Serbia from a principality to a kingdom.[9]

In Article III of the secret treaty, Austria had promised her support for this eventuality. When Milan proposed the move, Austria, followed by the other great powers, recognized the action. The announcement of the change undoubtedly accomplished what the Progressives desired, and was acclaimed throughout Serbia as another step toward the restoration of the nation's past glory. Even the Radicals joined in the celebration, but would not permit themselves to be diverted from their attack on the government.[10] They demanded a full explanation of the railroad fiasco. When the government refused to be drawn into debate, fifty-one Radicals and twenty-one Liberals withdrew from the Skupština. The body was thereby deprived of the quorum demanded by the constitution, and no legislation could be enacted.[11]

The purpose behind this move was to force Milan to dissolve the parliament and call for new elections. Considering the popular feeling in Serbia, it was almost certain that if elections were held the Radicals would gain a majority in the Skupština. No one realized this better than Milan. The government therefore announced that the Skupština would not be dissolved, but that elections would be held only for the posts vacated by the abstaining representatives. Although this action was illegal, Milan was ready to violate the constitution in order to remain in control of the government. The Progressives hoped to capture twelve of the vacated seats, which would give them a quorum. Every effort was to be exerted toward this goal.[12]

---

[7] Khevenhüller to Kalnoky, *HHS*, XIX 16, no. 24A–B, geheim, Belgrade, Feb. 25, 1882.

[8] Kalnoky to Khevenhüller, *HHS*, XIX 16, tel., Vienna, Feb. 22, 1882.

[9] Jovanović, *Milan*, III, 39–40.

[10] Živanović, *op. cit.*, II, 198–200; Jovanović, *Milan*, III, 41–42; Thornton to Granville, *FO*, 65/1135, no. 81, St. P., March 9, 1882; Canclaux to Freycinet, *DDF*, IV, no. 272, Vienna, March 7, 1882; Sala to Freycinet, *DDF*, IV, no. 273, Belgrade, March 8, 1882.

[11] Jovanović, *Milan*, III, 43.

[12] *Ibid.*, pp. 43–44; Živanović, *op. cit.*, II, 202–203.

At this opportune moment, Mijatović returned from Paris with the announcement that a national financial catastrophe had been averted. A newly established firm had assumed most of the obligations of the Union Générale. Serbia, instead of losing 34,500,000 dinars, had only 12,800,000 dinars outstanding, and even this sum might be recovered. Despite the welcome news, the government felt that it would still need police assistance to ensure victory in the coming election. Pressure was put on the electorate, and local officials who were known to sympathize with the opposition were removed or transferred.

Instead of adopting the neutral attitude which was constitutionally correct, Milan openly supported the Progressive candidates and denounced the opposition mercilessly. From April 8/20 to May 9/21, he traveled throughout Serbia waging a vigorous campaign in behalf of the Progressives. The election became in effect a battle between the prince and the Radical party. By the end of the campaign Milan was convinced that the odds against him were overwhelming. He still trusted the peasantry, but regarded them as misled by the Radical leaders, particularly the priests and the teachers.[13]

On May 15/27 the results of the elections were tabulated. The Progressives received only five seats, seven short of the necessary quorum. Piročanac, who felt that the nation had expressed itself, saw no alternative but resignation. Again Milan and the Progressive Club exerted pressure and he remained in office. Another scheme was then adopted to deal with the situation. If the Radical representatives persisted in refusing to attend the Skupština, new elections would be held for their positions, and they would be disqualified as candidates. Should the electorate reëlect a Radical to the vacated position, the government would disregard the candidate and designate the man with the second highest number of votes as duly elected. When the new election was held, on May 31/June 12, the results were again unfavorable to the government. This time the Progressives received not five representatives, but only two. Nevertheless, the government proceeded with its plan to seat only non-Radical representatives, even though some of them had received only two votes. Again Piročanac sought to resign, but again Milan refused.[14]

---

[13] Živanović, *op. cit.*, II, 203–205; Jovanović, *Milan*, III, 37, 44–49; Khevenhüller to Kalnoky, *HHS*, XIX 16, no. 49, Belgrade, May 1, 1882; Locock to Granville, *FO*, 105/32, no. 27, conf., Belgrade, Feb. 27, 1882.

[14] Locock to Granville, *FO*, 105/32, no. 93, Belgrade, May 29, 1882; *ibid.*, 105/33, no. 107, Belgrade, June 13, 1882; Kalnoky to Schiessl, *HHS* XIX 16, confidentielle, Vienna, May 31, 1882; Schiessl to Kalnoky, HHS, XIX 16, no. 65, geheim, Belgrade, June 4, 1882; Khevenhüller to Kalnoky, *HHS*, XIX 16, no. 70, Belgrade, June 16, 1882; Jovanović, *Milan*, III, 53–60; Živanović, *op. cit.*, II, 205–209.

Despite the repeated expression of the electorate's disapproval of the Progressive government and of Milan's policy, the king felt that he occupied a strong position because of the backing of the Dual Monarchy.[15] The Austrian government knew that it could not hope to win the sympathies of the South Slav peoples either within or without Serbia, nor was any serious attempt made to do so. In dealing with Bulgaria, Russia had two advantages: she had liberated the country from Ottoman rule; and she shared with the people a common race and religion. Austria-Hungary in Serbia was dealing with a people who were alien in almost all respects. Even the Serbs who favored a western orientation turned to Paris or even to London rather than to Vienna. Only through force could the Habsburg monarchy control the territories acquired through the Treaty of Berlin and the Dreikaiserbund. The threat of occupation was used repeatedly in Austrian relations with Serbia.[16] However, Austrian policy aims in Serbia coincided with Milan's own views.

The Austrian representative in Belgrade charged with the duty of keeping Serbia in line was Count Khevenhüller, who guarded Milan's position in every way possible. The king turned to him frequently for advice and sought his support in times of difficulty. Khevenhüller's influence was described by the British minister in Belgrade as follows:

It is noticed that since the Austrian legation was raised in rank and increased in number, and since Baron Herbert was replaced by Count Khevenhüller, the attitude of the [Serbian] ministers has become overbearing and their course of action more determined. It is noticed that the present representative of Austria-Hungary is a man of greater energy and stronger will than his predecessor, and that his relations with the king and his ministers are more confidential.

My own belief is that Count Khevenhüller has been frequently consulted, and judging from his character and from the opinions to which he gives expression when talking with his colleagues on the subject, I can hardly doubt that if consulted his advice would be for heroic remedies. He thinks (as he himself has told me since I have begun to write this despatch) that the only way to treat with the opposition is with the "baton."[17]

In another dispatch Locock continued: "Large sums are expended on the secret service of the [Austrian] legation, which has its agents spread widely throughout the country. Count Khevenhüller himself told me that he was better informed as to what was going on in the country than the Serbian government itself."[18]

---

[15] Kalnoky to Schiessl, *HHS*, XIX 16, confidentielle, Vienna, May 31, 1882; Schiessl to Kalnoky, *HHS*, XIX 16, no. 65, geheim, Belgrade, June 4, 1882; see also Khevenhüller to Kalnoky, *HHS*, XIX 16, Belgrade, Nov. 29, 1882.

[16] Jovanović, *Milan*, III, 57.

[17] Locock to Granville, *FO*, 105/33, no. 110, conf., Belgrade, June 14, 1882.

[18] *Ibid.*, 105/32, no. 28, conf., Belgrade, Feb. 28, 1882.

Although Khevenhüller realized that it would be difficult for the Progressive government to remain in office in face of the overwhelming opposition of the electorate, he warned Piročanac of the dangers in store for Serbia should he and his ministers resign: if "internal disorder" within Serbia became uncontrolled, Austria could not "remain a passive spectator," but would send troops into the kingdom. Evidence indicates that the threat was made on the suggestion of or at least with the connivance of Milan, who sought to use every means possible to ensure the continuance in office of the only government that would support him.[19]

Khevenhüller had one great advantage in dealing with Milan—the king's Russophobia. Milan was convinced that Russian intrigue was behind all the difficulties he had faced since 1878. In particular, he associated the rise of the Radical party with Russian interference in Serbian politics. Khevenhüller did what he could to strengthen this conviction.[20] Certainly, after 1881 Milan was a frightened man who felt that he was surrounded by enemies. The electorate had repeatedly demonstrated its lack of faith in his Progressive government; the clergy had been alienated by the dismissal of Mihailo. Only the power of the Habsburg government appeared to ensure Milan's continuance in office. From 1881 to 1885 Milan saw the hand of Russia wherever opposition arose.[21] In that period four major episodes occurred: the revolt in Bosnia-Hercegovina, the marriage of Peter Karadjordjević, the Timok revolt, and the Bregovo incident. Each of these, Milan felt, was either instigated or used by Russia in order to hasten the downfall of his dynasty.

The revolt in Bosnia-Hercegovina commenced in the fall of 1881. The immediate cause of the uprising in the Austrian-occupied province was the attempt of the Habsburg monarchy to impose military conscription in areas which had previously been exempt from service. The underlying reason for the rebellion was, however, discontent with Habsburg rule and the disillusionment of the province, which had hoped to be incorporated in the Serbian state after the Russo-Turkish War.

The forceful methods used by the Dual Monarchy in dealing with the revolt produced a tremendous reaction throughout the Orthodox world. The people of Serbia and Montenegro were overwhelmingly sympathetic to the rebels. In Bulgaria, volunteers and contributions were solicited in behalf of the rebels. Although the people of the three coun-

---

[19] *Ibid.*, 105/33, no. 115, Belgrade, June 16, 1882; *ibid.*, no. 116, Belgrade, June 16, 1882; *ibid.*, no. 120, conf., Belgrade, June 22, 1882; Jovanović, *Milan*, III, 57.
[20] See, for example, Khevenhüller to Kalnoky, *HHS*, XIX 17, no. 24, vertraulich, Belgrade, April 19, 1883; *ibid.*, no. 25A–C, vertraulich, April 28, 1883.
[21] See, for example, Khevenhüller to Kalnoky, *HHS*, XIX 16, no. 3A–C, vertraulich, Belgrade, Jan. 10, 1883; *ibid.*, no. 18, confidentielle, Belgrade, March 18, 1883.

tries were openly partisan, their governments did not wish to become involved because of the strength of the Dual Monarchy and the indifference of official Russia. Prince Nikola of Montenegro made every effort to maintain a correct policy, although one of his ministers did render aid to the rebels. Prince Alexander of Bulgaria likewise remained neutral. Milan, however, publicly endorsed the policy of the Dual Monarchy, in open opposition to his subjects.[22]

In his espousal of the Habsburg cause, Milan was concerned primarily over the implications of the revolt for his own policy. He had received numerous reports that men and supplies were being smuggled from Bulgaria through Serbia to the disaffected provinces. The movement of guns and munitions worried the king, not so much because of the effect on his Austrian policy but because he feared that the weapons were destined for the rebels and that they would be made available to the Radicals for use in the Serbian elections.

Milan thus took extraordinary precautions. On May 17/29, at the village of Čačak in central Serbia, government officials seized two wagonloads of guns, apparently destined for Hercegovina, convoyed by sixty armed Montenegrins. The important fact was that the Montenegrins had used Russian passports to enter Serbia. Here indeed seemed clear proof of Russian intrigue directed against both Milan's regime and the Habsburg monarchy. When the Radicals condemned Milan's seizure of the guns, the king believed that this was added proof of a Russian-Radical plot directed against his throne.[23]

In the Dual Monarchy the press viewed the Čačak incident in the same light as did the Serbian king—as fresh evidence of Russian machinations. In February the Vienna and Budapest newspapers had been aroused when the controversial Russian general M. D. Skobelev praised the insurgents and stated that, if necessary, Russia should once again fight "shoulder to shoulder against the common enemy"—the Germans. In Russia the highly influential publicist Aksakov voiced open sympathy for the rebels and condemned their domination by a German power. Although some of the more sober Russian newspapers regretted the stand taken by Skobelev and Aksakov, their restrained sentiments were disregarded in Vienna, Budapest, and Belgrade.[24]

---

[22] The Bosnian crisis is discussed by the author in "The Revolt in Bosnia-Hercegovina, 1881–1882," *Slavonic and East European Review* (London), XXXI (1953), 420–436.

[23] Jovanović, *Milan*, III, 52–53.

[24] O. K. (Olga Novikova-Kireieva), *Skobeleff and the Slavonic Cause*, pp. 253–262; E. Tarle, "Rech' Gen. Skobeleva v Parizhe v 1882 g.," *Krasnyi Arkhiv*, XXVII (1928), 219–220; Aksakov, *Slavianskii Vopros'*, p. 390; *Neue Freie Presse* (Vienna), Feb. 5, 1882, p. 2; Feb. 21, 1882, p. 1.

Notwithstanding the suspicions of Milan and the Habsburg press, Russian intervention would have been contrary to the basic principles of Russian foreign policy at that time. Giers and the Russian foreign office had one major goal in mind—the preservation of the Dreikaiserbund. For official Russia the Straits and Bulgaria were of far greater importance than Bosnia-Hercegovina, regardless of the sympathy of individual Russians for the Slavic inhabitants of these territories. Moreover, Russia had agreed to permit the Dual Monarchy to annex these provinces when it was deemed opportune.

Although the influential press of Austria-Hungary condemned Russia, Kalnoky did not support its position. During the parliamentary debates in January and February, Kalnoky publicly stated that Russia was not involved in the uprising. Nevertheless, he asked the Austrian ambassador to St. Petersburg, Wolkenstein, to make representations to Giers concerning the activities of certain Russian subjects. When Wolkenstein questioned Giers about the reports that Russian officers were en route to Hercegovina, Giers denied that any military personnel were involved, but admitted that some retired servicemen might be implicated. Despite this admission, Wolkenstein reported to Kalnoky that he was convinced that neither Giers nor the Russian government had given any official support to the rebels. On the contrary, they were deeply concerned by the turn of events in the Balkans. Similar observations were made by the Austrian and British representatives in Bulgaria.[25]

Giers and the Russian foreign office did what they could to prevent the revolt from developing into a European crisis, but Khitrovo, the Russian consul in Sofia, organized aid for the rebels, solicited and distributed funds to the volunteers, and arranged for issuance of Russian passports to the volunteers who crossed Serbia into Hercegovina. The best illustration of his lack of discretion and the steps he was willing to take is the fact that he requested funds from the Bulgarian prince himself. Alexander of Battenberg, needless to say, refused to coöperate. In May, 1882, Khitrovo was recalled, not because of his role in the rebellion, which was unknown to the Russian government until after his return, but because of his constant interference in the internal affairs of Bulgaria. With his departure all Russian intervention in the revolt ceased.[26] Thus, although the trend of events in Bosnia and Hercegovina

[25] Trauttenberg to Kalnoky, *HHS*, XL 209, no. 16E, vertraulich, St. P., Feb. 17/ March 1, 1882; To Wolkenstein, *HHS*, XL 209, Vienna, May 1, 1882; Wolkenstein to Kalnoky, *HHS*, XL 209, no. 32D, vertraulich, St. P., May 12/24, 1882; Biegeleben to Kalnoky, *HHS*, XV 19, no. 10, Sofia, March 4, 1882; Lascelles to Granville, *FO*, 78/3413, no. 34, Sofia, March 24, 1882.
[26] Skazkin, pp. 209–210; Black, pp. 195–219.

closely paralleled that of the period 1875–1876, the Russian government did not allow itself to be pushed into a policy which did not conform to its national interests.

Milan, however, was convinced that the Russians were prodding the South Slavs to rebellion in the Dual Monarchy, and that Russian rubles had enabled the Radical party to win the elections.[27] Khevenhüller, playing on the king's fears, repeatedly asserted that Russia was behind the Serbian opposition. Nothing could have been farther from the truth. The rapid rise of the Radical party and the tremendous popular support which it enjoyed found many Conservatives, in an attempt to discredit the Radicals, indiscriminately labeling them as communists, socialists, or anarchists. Eventually this view was adopted by the Russian government also.

Russia's policy both at home and in Bulgaria at this time was extreme conservatism in domestic politics. In Bulgaria the tsar supported the strengthening of the powers of Alexander of Battenberg. Therefore, instead of supporting the Serbian Radical party, as Milan firmly believed, the Russian government had become greatly concerned over the growing unrest and the strength of the opposition in Serbia. In Giers' opinion, Milan was a man without character or principle, but if he were overthrown, anarchy would develop in Serbia. This view was shared by the tsar. Since Russia wished to avoid disturbances in the Balkan Peninsula, Milan's fears of Russian agitation had no basis in fact. The Russian government supported Milan's regime because it coincided with the Russian policy of the Dreikaiserbund and the abandonment of Serbia to Austrian control.[28]

Milan's fears, however, continued to grow. In the fall of 1882 an attempt was made on his life by Jelena Ilka Markovićka, widow of Colonel Jevrem Marković, who had been executed on Milan's orders for participating in an uprising. Despite the fact that it was obviously a matter of personal vengeance, Milan preferred to regard it as a Radical plot.[29]

In January, 1883, Milan's concern was increased by the report that Peter Karadjordjević had gone to Montenegro to arrange for his marriage to Princess Zorka, eldest daughter of the Montenegrin ruler. It could scarcely be said that Peter was attracted by her beauty. The British consul commented that she looked far too much like her father to

---

[27] Speculation concerning the coöperation of suspected persons with the Russians is found in Khevenhüller to Kalnoky, *HHS*, XIX 16, no. 4B/IB, geheim, Belgrade, Jan. 19, 1882; Jovanović, *Milan*, III, 58.
[28] Wolkenstein to Kalnoky, *HHS*, X 72, no. 19, geheim, St. P., March 5/17, 1883.
[29] Živanović, *op. cit.*, II, 217–219; Jovanović, *Milan*, III, 73–75.

be called pretty: "His Highness' features are so masculine and his complexion so dark that they can hardly be reproduced to advantage under a feminine form."[30] Milan immediately sensed a plot in the marriage alliance. The recent attempt on his life appeared to him to have been part of a scheme developed by the Radicals and the Russians to restore the Karadjordjević dynasty to the Serbian throne. The marriage of Peter to Zorka would strengthen the Karadjordjević position immeasurably. The pretender to the Serbian throne would thus become son-in-law to the Montenegrin ruler, who had close ties with Russia. Milan's apprehensions were shared by the Austrian government, which at once took steps to investigate the proposed alliance.[31]

When Wolkenstein discussed the subject with Giers, the latter replied that he had advised Nikola to be cautious and moderate. In the summer of 1883, when Nikola came to St. Petersburg, Giers urged the Montenegrin ruler to discourage the marriage. Although the tsar apparently did not object to the marriage, neither did he enthusiastically support it. Moreover, the Russian foreign office was determined to prevent any Karadjordjević plot against the Obrenović dynasty. This view was communicated to Jovan Marinović, Serbia's representative in St. Petersburg, but Milan remained suspicious.[32] In truth, the marriage plan had been developed by Peter and Nikola for the purpose of discrediting and embarrassing Milan, but only for personal reasons. Nikola was incensed by the fact that Milan had elevated Serbia to a kingdom while Montenegro remained a principality and its ruler a prince. To add insult to injury, Nikola, when he met Mijatović in Vienna, not only denied that the marriage was aimed at Milan, but also suggested that the Serbian king stand as godfather, or *kum*, an almost sacred position in a Serbian marriage, for Zorka. By this means, he argued, the Petrović, Karadjordjević, and Obrenović dynasties would be firmly united. Milan not only scorned the proposal, but severely criticized Mijatović for considering it seriously.[33]

[30] Green to Pauncefoote, *FO*, 103/22, pvt. letter, Scutari, April 19, 1883.

[31] Khevenhüller to Kalnoky, *HHS*, XIX 17, no. 11, vertraulich, Belgrade, Feb. 8, 1883; *ibid.*, no. 14, vertraulich, Belgrade, Feb. 23, 1883; *ibid.*, no. 16, vertraulich, Belgrade, March 3, 1883; *ibid.*, no. 23, vertraulich, Belgrade, March 31, 1883; Schiessl to Kalnoky, *HHS*, XIX 17, no. 31, vertraulich, Belgrade, June 2, 1883; Kalnoky to Khevenhüller, *HHS*, XIX 17, Vienna, Feb. 5, 1883; *ibid.*, March 5, 1883; *ibid.*, tel., geheim, Vienna, March 7, 1883; *ibid.*, XIX 17, Vienna, Aug. 11, 1883.

[32] Wolkenstein to Kalnoky, *HHS*, X 72, no. 14B, St. P., Feb. 16/28, 1883; *ibid.*, X 73, St. P., June 7/19, 1883; *ibid.*, geheim, St. P., June 9/21, 1883; *ibid.*, vertraulich, St. P., July 20/Aug. 1, 1883; Khevenhüller to Kalnoky, *HHS*, XIX 17, no. 38B, Belgrade, July 4, 1883; Kalnoky to Khevenhüller, *HHS*, XIX 17, Vienna, July 12, 1883.

[33] Mijatovich, *op. cit.*, p. 158; Jovanović, *Milan*, III, 86–91; see also Khevenhüller to Kalnoky, *HHS*, XIX 17, no. 36, vertraulich, Belgrade, June 30, 1886.

The marriage of Peter and Zorka, on July 30/August 11, coincided with the arrival of Ionin in Bulgaria. His mission was to resolve the differences of the Russian generals Sobolev and Kaulbars with the prince and the Bulgarian parties. In Belgrade the two events were interpreted as signs that Russia was preparing for a major move in the Balkans. These suspicions were strengthened by the frequent and vigorous attacks on Milan in the Russian press.

Finally, in October, 1883, a rebellion broke out in Timok, in eastern Serbia, which brought to the fore the entire question of Russian and Radical intrigue in Serbia. The immediate cause of the revolt was the attempt of the Serbian government to force the peasants to surrender their weapons to the government. Serbia possessed two military forces, the regular army and the home guard or militia; both were armed by the state. In 1883 the government replaced obsolete rifles with those of a more modern design. Since the new weapons were expensive and required greater care, it was decided that the home guard would not be allowed to keep their guns at home; instead, they would be stored in regular arsenals. Although the arguments of the government appeared to be reasonable, the Radicals feared that the new regulations were designed to strengthen Milan's position in the face of a constitutional crisis which had meanwhile arisen.[34]

For several years there had been agitation, especially in the king's own Progressive party, that a constitutional convention be held to examine and amend the constitution. This had been one of the campaign promises of the Progressives, and they felt obliged to put it into effect. Milan was opposed to the entire scheme because a new election would have to be held for representatives to the convention. If the resultant body were dominated by Radicals, as could be expected, they would so alter the constitution that the king would become little more than a figurehead. Milan would therefore approve new elections only for a general assembly called to ratify the railroad convention of 1883. Although this body would be allowed to study constitutional questions, it was not to act on them.[35]

Once the elections had been set for September, the government launched an intensive campaign to intimidate possible Radical party sympathizers. Police pressure was used, unreliable officials were dismissed, and suspected teachers were transferred or removed from their posts. In reprisal, the Radicals spread malicious rumors to discredit

[34] Jovanović, *Milan*, III, 118; Milošević, *Timočka Buna, 1883 godine*. I obtained the use of the two volumes of documents edited by Nikolić, *Timočka Buna, 1883* (1954–1955), after I had completed and submitted the manuscript.
[35] Jovanović, *Milan*, III, 97; Živanović, *op. cit.*, II, 223–233.

the government. The campaign on both sides was waged with little regard for fairness or honesty. In the elections held on September 7/19,
the largest number of votes yet cast in Serbia showed the extent of the
unpopularity of the government: the Radicals held a two-to-one
majority.

Milan nevertheless remained undiscouraged. He accepted the prof-
fered resignation of the Progressive government, but refused to allow
the Radicals to take office. Instead, he turned to Nikola Hristić, an old
Conservative, who had seen much service in the government. The first
act of Hristić, when the Skupština assembled, was to read a decree from
the king opening the parliament. Then, without allowing any business to be transacted, he presented another decree declaring the
Skupština adjourned. As for the ratification of the railroad convention,
Milan took care of this without the approval of the assembly.[36]

The Radicals were momentarily stunned by Milan's action, and their
alarm was intensified when Hristić issued a decree enforcing the collection of arms. Although the original decision, made in July/August,
had not been put into effect, the government now, two months later,
decided to carry it out. In view of the means by which the assembly had
just been disbanded, the Radicals were convinced that Milan's goal was
the abolition of the constitution. In neighboring Bulgaria they had seen
how Alexander of Battenberg, with whom Milan had only recently con-
ferred, had abrogated the Bulgarian constitution. If Milan succeeded
in disarming the peasantry, who were solidly behind the Radicals, his
task would be much easier. The Radical leaders, in secret meeting, decided that the constitution should be defended at all costs, even if a
resort to arms were necessary.[37]

In spite of this decision, no specific plans were made for a revolt
against Milan. The conclusion reached in the closed meeting became
known, however, to the Radical leaders throughout the country. They
had already received an intimation of how they should act from their
party newspaper *Samouprava*. Although its cleverly worded article
carried no signature, Pašić was obviously the author, for the tactics
recommended were characteristic of those used by Pašić throughout
his political career. He wrote that every Serb knew that without a rifle
there is no freedom. He advised the Serbs to surrender their arms if
ordered to do so, but at the same time not to leave their homes unarmed.
Obviously, the two proposals were incompatible. When in October the

---

[36] Locock to Granville, *FO*, 105/39, no. 38, Belgrade, Sept. 20, 1883; *ibid.*, no. 58,
conf., Belgrade, Oct. 6, 1883; *ibid.*, no. 60, conf., Belgrade, Oct. 7, 1883; Jovanović,
Milan, III, 105–115; Živanović, *op. cit.*, II, 239–244.

[37] Jovanović, *Milan*, III, 116.

government began to collect the arms, many adopted Pašić's first suggestion.[38]

The greatest opposition to the government came from eastern Serbia, especially from Pašić's electoral district. Initially it was not realized how serious the peasant resistance was, but by October 21/November 2 the government was forced to proclaim an emergency in eastern Serbia, the first public admission of the true state of affairs. In Belgrade Pašić and several other Radical leaders immediately met to consider the developments. They decided that, since the revolt had started, they should not desert the peasants but should assume leadership of the movement. No definite strategy was decided upon; each man was to return to his electoral district and act as he deemed necessary. Pašić at once crossed over into Austrian territory. From there he planned to proceed to Bulgaria and then reënter Serbia. The others hesitated, however, and, before they were able to leave Belgrade, the government seized them.[39]

Meanwhile, in the eastern districts, the peasants were in arms. At their head stood the local Radical party functionaries, among whom a priest, Marinko, was the most prominent. The crucial question was whether the regular army would obey orders and fire upon the peasantry. When the command was given, the troops responded, loyal to their monarch. Within a week the army was able to crush the rebellion, mainly because their modern rifles had a much greater range than those of the rebels. The government forces also were able to use artillery. The peasants finally surrendered, and by November 1/13 the revolt was over. The government quickly rounded up the leaders; ninety-four were condemned to death, but only twenty of these sentences were carried out.[40]

Milan was certain that the revolt had been instigated by Russian intrigue. He believed that Russian bribes accounted for the unfavorable results of the election and that, subsequently, Russian officers had directed the operations in eastern Serbia. When the Bulgarian government refused, after the rebellion had been suppressed, to surrender the refugees who had fled into the neighboring state, Milan was convinced that Prince Alexander was acting under Russian orders.[41]

Even the Dual Monarchy was concerned over possible Russian participation in the events. In March, when Wolkenstein had discussed

[38] *Ibid.*, pp. 118–119.
[39] *Ibid.*, pp. 120–121.
[40] Mousset, *La Serbie et son église*, pp. 391–395; Živanović, *op. cit.*, II, 248–262; Jovanović, *Milan*, III, 126–129.
[41] Locock to Granville, *FO*, 105/40, no. 88, Belgrade, Nov. 13, 1883; Jovanović, *Milan*, III, 112.

with Giers the growth of radicalism and socialism in Serbia, he had
warned that if unrest developed and if Serbia became a breeding place
(*Brutstätte*) for socialism, Austria would be forced to take steps.[42] In
August, immediately after the marriage of Peter and Zorka, Wolkenstein, on orders from Kalnoky, again spoke to Giers: if a revolt in Serbia
resulted in the overthrow of the regime, Austria might find it necessary
to intervene to restore peace and order.[43]

After the Timok revolt, the Habsburg government became greatly
concerned over the Serbian refugees in Bulgaria, who had concentrated
in Vidin, a town directly across the Serbian border. Most of them were
women and children, but Nikola Pašić was among them. He had been
condemned to death *in absentia* as the principal instigator of the revolt.
The Austrian government believed that until the refugees, Pašić in
particular, were removed from Vidin, the state of unrest would continue in eastern Serbia. Hence it pressed Russia to use her influence
with the Bulgarian government. Russia instructed Ionin to request the
Bulgarian government to remove Pašić and the other refugees from the
border zone. When the Bulgarians agreed, the immediate problem was
solved.[44]

As had been true of the revolt in Bosnia-Hercegovina, the Russian
press and public sympathized deeply with the uprising against Milan.
The ouster of Mihailo and the Serbian pro-Austrian orientation were
both attacked anew. *Novoe Vremia* praised Peter Karadjordjević and
hailed his possible assumption of the throne. Katkov, in the *Moskovskiia
Viedomosti*, observed that Milan would in time disappear, but that the
Serbian people would always remain a bulwark of Orthodoxy and
Slavdom. Any action against them would only unite them more firmly
with Russia. Because of the current difficulties in Bulgaria, the Russian
press felt more concerned than ever about Serbia, and it was feared that
Russia would find herself without influence in either Slavic, Orthodox
state. While the press thus lamented the course of events, the Panslav
elements sent aid to the rebels, particularly to the refugees in Bulgaria.[45]

In spite of the partisanship of the Russian public, the Russian government pursued in the Timok revolt the same policy which it had

[42] Wolkenstein to Giers, *HHS*, X 72, no. 19, geheim, St. P., March 5/17, 1883.
[43] *Ibid.*, tel. no. 86, geheim, St. P., Aug. 14, 1883; Khevenhüller to Kalnoky, *HHS*,
XIX 17, tel. no. 31, Nov. 3, 1883; *ibid.*, tel. no. 32, Nov. 4, 1883; *ibid.*, tel. no. 37,
urgent, Nov. 9, 1883; *ibid.*, no. 75, vertraulich, Belgrade, Nov. 17, 1883.
[44] Wolkenstein to Kalnoky, *HHS*, X 72, tel. no. 97, St. P., Dec. 12, 1883; *ibid.*,
no. 81C, St. P., Dec. 7/19, 1883; Biegeleben to Kalnoky, *HHS*, XV 20, tel. no. 132,
Sofia, Dec. 16, 1883; *ibid.*, tel. no. 134, Sofia, Dec. 17, 1883; Kalnoky to Khevenhüller, *HHS*, XIX 17, no. 32, Dec. 18, 1883.
[45] Kennedy to Granville, *FO*, 65/1157, no. 240, St. P., Oct. 5, 1883; Wolkenstein
to Kalnoky, *HHS*, X 74, no. 11A–C, vertraulich, St. P., Feb. 29/March 12, 1884.

adopted with respect to the Bosnian revolt, radicalism in Serbia, and the marriage of Peter and Zorka. Russia did not want any crisis to develop to the point of reopening the entire eastern question. Russia undoubtedly benefited from Milan's setback and the increasing resentment of the Serbian electorate at Austrian domination. The more unpopular the Serbian king became, the more hope Russia had of future influence in the state, but she was unwilling to initiate or support active measures against Milan.

The government's victory in the Timok rebellion was particularly pleasing to Milan, who believed he had again triumphed over those who conspired against his life and throne. The army had proved loyal; the Radical party leaders were jailed, executed, or exiled. The party as a whole, for whom the revolt had been a disaster, had been rendered impotent. When the refugees in Vidin had appeared to be a danger, Austria had induced Russia to intervene in Bulgaria to halt their activities. Further proof of Milan's success was yet to come. In January/February new elections were held. Once again measures were employed to intimidate the electorate, and this time they succeeded. The Progressive party now gained a ten-to-one majority. In 1884 Milan appeared to have secured control of his kingdom.[46]

A temperamental and emotional ruler, Milan was susceptible to moods. Certainly, the situation in 1884 did not justify excessive optimism.[47] Although the Radical party as an effective force was for the time being immobilized, its strength rested on real foundations and its return as an active body could be predicted. The Dual Monarchy had given staunch support to Milan's regime, but that state controlled only Serbia's northern and northwestern frontiers. The real danger to the Obrenović dynasty was on Serbia's other borders. Serbia was separated from Montenegro by the Sanjak of Novi Pazar. Nikola and his son-in-law Peter Karadjordjević were, however, a constant threat. Nikola was at heart an adventurer whose actions were difficult to predict. Moreover, Peter Karadjordjević had a valid claim to the throne and could count on support inside Serbia.

The situation in Bulgaria was potentially dangerous to Milan. Russian influence, although shaken, was still strong, and the Bulgarian army remained under Russian control. The Serbian refugees had been moved inland, but their more ambitious leaders would soon try to return to the border areas to foment disorder in Serbia. Nikola Pašić

---

[46] Locock to Granville, *FO*, 105/45, no. 8, Belgrade, Feb. 7, 1884; *ibid.*, no. 10, Belgrade, Feb. 16, 1884.

[47] After analyzing various aspects of the revolt, Locock concluded, "In plain words—for it comes to this—the king himself has been the cause of the insurrection." Locock to Granville, *FO*, 105/40, no. 99, Belgrade, November 18, 1883.

and Metropolitan Mihailo were active in their own interests inside Bulgaria; both sought to create conditions whereby they could return to Serbia.

The major source of contention between Serbia and Bulgaria, however, was not the conduct of these men but the ownership of the Macedonian territories. Milan's ambition was to be remembered in Serbian history as the man who reunited old Serbia and Macedonia to Serbia proper. Although he had received Austrian approval in the treaty of 1881, the problem of Macedonia, which was an integral part of the Ottoman Empire, could be solved only on an international basis. Bulgaria, because of the Treaty of San Stefano, considered that her prior claims to the disputed lands had already been established. Behind Bulgaria stood Russia, who, despite the Dreikaiserbund and the ideas of some of her statesmen, had no desire to proceed with the partition of the Balkan Peninsula. Before Milan could attain his desires in Macedonia, he would have to deal with both Bulgaria and Russia.

Milan's attitude toward neighboring Bulgaria was ambiguous. He detested the Bulgarian government, which he regarded as a tool of Russian interests, but, in contrast, he did have much in common with Alexander of Battenberg. Both had recently suffered extremely disagreeable experiences in their relations with Russia; both had been educated in the west and believed that they were representatives of a higher civilization than that of the countries which they ruled. Milan, for example, wrote to Alexander:

> We must support each other, for the *peoples of this peninsula have a tendency to change rulers like their shirts*. If you ever have to pack your trunks, you can pass through Belgrade and I will give you a part of my luggage, and vice versa. We can say the same to King Karl of Rumania ... Do not rely on your Bulgarians; do not believe that they are good and naïve, as you say. They are Slavs and that explains everything. My Serbs are worth no more, and it is *in spite* of them and *against* their will that one must do one's duty and then come what may as the old proverb states.[48]

Since both rulers were westerners, they distrusted the historic attachment of their peoples to Russia. Both wished to rule as autocrats and not as constitutional monarchs. Despite their common interests, relations between them remained formal. Being extremely ambitious, each sought precedence over the other. This rivalry was brought into the open by a series of incidents which followed the Timok revolt and the arrival of the refugees in Bulgaria.

Although the Bulgarian government had moved the Serbian refugees inland, they soon made excursions across the border and spread the

---

[48] Corti, *Alexander*, pp. 206, 208–209.

impression within Serbia that another uprising was at hand. They could be checked only if the Bulgarian government kept them under surveillance and at some distance from the frontier. As the activities of the refugees became more widespread, Serbia demanded that Bulgaria halt the operations which were directed from inside the principality. The plight of the refugees had aroused the sympathy of the Bulgarian people, however, and the government was both unwilling and unable to intervene.

In order to distract the Serbs, the Bulgars produced a grievance of their own concerning the administration of the Bregovo area.[49] Bregovo was a piece of land lying along the Timok River which in the early part of the nineteenth century had been on the western, Serbian side of the river. The Timok changed its course slightly until, by 1884, it veered a little into Bulgaria, then turned and made a semicircle into Serbia before rejoining the original flow.[50] Since the Timok was considered the boundary between the two states, it meant that Serbia lost a piece of land which had formerly belonged to her, but that Bulgaria also yielded a strip of approximately the same size. Nature could hardly have provided a more equitable solution; but the Serbian government had other ideas.

On the land which the Serbs were to lose, they had maintained a military outpost garrisoned by several soldiers. When the river changed its course, the outpost was still held. At the same time, Serbia took over the strip of land which had formerly been Bulgarian. The Bulgars thus lost in both instances. Although the arrangement had existed for years, the Bulgarian government chose the moment when Serbia brought up the matter of the refugees to ask for the removal of the outpost and the soldiers. When the Serbs refused, the Bulgarians ousted the garrison by force. All signs indicated that a major Balkan crisis was at hand.[51]

Milan immediately replied to the Bulgarian action by drafting an ultimatum demanding that Bulgarian troops be withdrawn from Bregovo, that the refugees be removed from the frontier, and that Mihailo, who was at that moment in Sofia, be expelled from the Bulgarian capital. The Bulgarian government was given three days in which to comply with the terms, or the Serbian minister was to be recalled from Sofia. When the deadline passed without any action being taken, Serbia severed relations with her neighbor. The Serbian action was considered abrupt and untimely: first, the ultimatum had been

[49] Jovanović, *Milan*, III, 193–194.
[50] A map of the disputed area is in Hertslet, *The Map of Europe by Treaty*, IV, 3202.
[51] Radev, I, 443.

made public in Belgrade before it was delivered to Sofia, an offense to the Bulgarians; and second, although Serbia might have been justified in delivering an ultimatum on the Bregovo affair, the refugee problem was not in the same category, since it was still in the discussion stage. The introduction of the Mihailo affair seemed completely unjustified. As a result, Serbia lost much of the sympathy she had enjoyed with the western states, which considered that her position in regard to the refugees was valid. Serbia's action left Bulgaria no choice but resistance.[52]

In Sofia Prince Alexander faced a dilemma. He was willing to satisfy the Serbian demands, since they involved primarily Radical party members, for whom he had no sympathy. Moreover, he wished to keep on good terms with Milan. However, whereas Milan dominated the Progressive party, Alexander did not exert the same influence over the Liberal government of Dragan Tsankov. The latter was trying to strengthen his position within his party in face of the opposition from Karavelov. A firm stand on the Bregovo affair was an excellent issue on which to win popular support. Tsankov was seeking Russian approval at this time; so he turned to the Russian minister for advice. Koiander urged him not to yield one piece of Bulgarian territory, which had been liberated by Russian blood and arms. With the apparent backing of Russia, Tsankov declared to his cabinet that in case of extreme necessity he was willing to go to war against Serbia.[53]

The Russian attitude toward the Bregovo incident and the ultimatum was determined by her position in Bulgaria. She supported the Bulgarian government in order to regain some of her lost prestige. Although Giers did not spare his criticism of Milan for the attack on Mihailo, the Russian government did not wish the Serbo-Bulgarian dispute to lead to war. Therefore Austria-Hungary and Germany were consulted. In the ensuing discussions, Austria championed the Serbian position; Russia backed Bulgaria. Bismarck, forced to act as arbiter, believed that Serbia was justified in her complaints on the refugee problem, but that the issues in the Bregovo dispute were not clear. Bulgaria, he advised, should pay Serbia an indemnity for the attack on the outpost.

Before the three powers could announce their decision, Alexander and Milan produced their own solution.[54] The two rulers agreed that

---

[52] Jovanović, *Milan*, III, 195–198; Persan to Ferry, *DDF*, V, no. 295, Belgrade, June 7, 1884.

[53] Radev, I, 443–444.

[54] Jovanović, *Milan*, III, 199; Granville to Kennedy, *FO*, 78/3637, no. 23, Foreign Office, June 16, 1884; Schiessl to Kalnoky, *HHS*, XIX 18, tel. no. 42, Nish, June 17, 1884; Welsersheimb to Kalnoky, *HHS*, X 74, streng vertraulich, St. P., Dec.

Bulgaria should immediately return the outpost to Serbia and that discussions should be opened on an equitable exchange of territory. The
refugees should be prohibited from living within fifty kilometers of the
Serbian border. When Alexander submitted these reasonable terms to
the Bulgarian government, it refused absolutely to accept them.
Karavelov had by now taken control from Tsankov, but he supported
his predecessor's stand. With the advice and backing of Koiander, the
Bulgarian government remained adamant. Since neither Milan nor
Alexander was able to accept any compromise because of the firm
attitude of their peoples, the Bregovo problem was to remain unsettled
until 1888, and the emigrant problem was resolved only after Milan
abdicated in 1889.[55]

The domestic situation in Serbia continued to deteriorate. The question of Russian influence and the Austrian alliance, which divided Milan
from his people, caused a split in his own family as well. While Milan
had become a fanatical Austrophil, his wife Natalija, the daughter of a
Russian colonel of Rumanian extraction, was an equally ardent Russophil. She had become very popular with her subjects, and was known
for her charitable works. A devoted and loyal wife, she was extremely
upset when she learned that the king was having an affair with one of
her closest friends. Although Natalija took a great interest in national
issues, she could not refrain from expressing her sympathy for Russia
and her distrust of Austria-Hungary. She particularly objected to
Milan's plan to have their son Alexander educated in Austria. Milan, as
could be expected, reacted violently to his wife's pro-Russian bias, and
became convinced that she was actually an agent of St. Petersburg
seeking to undermine his support among the Serbs. The relations of the
king and queen became a public scandal, since they did not hesitate to
quarrel openly in the cafés of Belgrade. One became the leader of the
Austrophil, the other of the Russophil, faction in Serbia.[56]

Milan now believed that Russia was trying to effect his removal by
soliciting the support of the queen and other prominent persons. In the
spring of 1885 Jovan Ristić, Liberal party leader and former minister-
president, was invited to St. Petersburg. Ristić was known for his sympathies for Russia, although he was not considered completely anti-

15/27, 1884; Kalnoky to Schiessl, *HHS*, XIX 18, *privatschreiben*, Vienna, Aug. 14,
1884; Busch to Bray, *HHS*, XIX 18, no. 7, Berlin, June 5, 1884; Promemoria by
Bucher, *GP*, III, no. 644, Berlin, Sept. 5, 1884.

[55] Corti, *Alexander*, pp. 205–211; Radev, I, 461–462; Jovanović, *Milan*, III, 200;
Locock to Granville, *FO*, 105/46, no. 93, conf., Belgrade, Dec. 26, 1884; Hertslet,
op. cit., IV, 3202–3203.

[56] Jovanović, *Milan*, III, 207–208; Khevenhüller to Kalnoky, *HHS*, XIX 19, no.
39A–B, vertraulich, Belgrade, May 15, 1885.

Austrian. In Russia he was received by the tsar, Grand Duke Vladimir, and many of the Panslav leaders. The Russian press devoted much space to his visit. It was natural that Milan, in his state of mind, should assume that Ristić had been called to Russia to discuss plans for his removal.[57]

The problem of Mihailo, nevertheless, remained the chief issue in Russo-Serbian relations. His influence had reached to the tsar himself through Pobedonostsev and the Orthodox officials. Alexander III was sympathetic, but took no active steps in Mihailo's aid. Giers, in particular, was well aware of the dangers inherent in the situation. When he heard, in 1883, that Mihailo planned to come to Russia, he feared that the metropolitan would be used by the Panslav elements to incite Russian public opinion against the policy of agreement with Germany and Austria-Hungary. In 1884, when Serbian politics became more unsettled, he decided that it would be better if Mihailo were in Russia, where he could be prevented from joining in the conspiracies against Milan.[58]

Milan, of course, did not know the attitude of the Russian foreign office. Mihailo's presence in St. Petersburg, where he was honored as a champion of Orthodoxy and Slavdom against the encroachments of the Catholic Habsburgs, only proved to Milan that Russia was determined to remove him. In February/March, 1885, he made attempts to counteract the metropolitan's influence. On Milan's instructions, Colonel Horvatović, Serbia's representative in St. Petersburg, mentioned to Wolkenstein that, since the patriarch at Constantinople had recognized Teodosije, Russia should do the same. If Austria and Germany interceded in Serbia's behalf, Giers' approval might be forthcoming. Wolkenstein replied that such a suggestion should be presented to his government in writing, but that he did not expect much success. Although he did not know what Giers' reaction would be, it was probable that Katkov, Pobedonostsev, and the nationalists would determine the Russian reply. Horvatović later complained to Wolkenstein about the Russian treatment of the Mihailo affair. Whenever he talked with Giers or other officials in the foreign office about Serbo-Russian relations, they spoke to him of only one question—"the restoration of ex-Metropolitan Mihailo." If Mihailo were restored to office, relations between the two countries would return to normal.[59]

[57] Wolkenstein to Kalnoky, *HHS*, X 75, no. 37B, geheim, St. P., April 13/25, 1885; *ibid.*, no. 54E, vertraulich, St. P., May 27/June 8, 1885; *ibid.*, no. 59, St. P., June 19, 1885.
[58] *Ibid.*, X 74, no. 43C, vertraulich, St. P., June 28/July 10, 1884.
[59] *Ibid.*, X 75, vertraulich, privatbrief, St. P., Feb. 27/March 11, 1885; Kalnoky to Wolkenstein, *HHS*, vertraulich, privatbrief, Vienna, March 15, 1885.

The apparent Russian intrigues in the Bosnia-Hercegovina revolt, the Timok rebellion, and the Bregovo incident, together with the visit of Ristić to Russia and the quarrels with the queen, drew Milan closer to the one source of strength on which he felt he could still rely— Austria-Hungary.[60] The meeting of the three emperors at Skiernewice in September, 1884, aroused his suspicions that Austria and Russia would not go to war, as he had hoped, but would agree to the annexation of Bosnia-Hercegovina and the union of the two Bulgarias. Serbia would then be left in a weaker position relative to Bulgaria and would suffer a great loss in prestige. Actually, at this meeting Giers assured Kalnoky that Serbia was in Austria's sphere and that, even though he had no sympathy for Milan, Russia would not support the Karadjordjević dynasty against him.[61]

Despite his fears, Milan still felt that the Dual Monarchy alone could save him from his internal enemies and the Russian conspiracies.[62] In June, 1885, he proposed that five new articles be added to the earlier treaty of 1881. The first stipulated that Milan would maintain the secret treaty until his son became of age. The second provided that Milan would not abdicate before his son became of age, unless the Dual Monarchy should so desire. In return, the Austrian government was to guarantee the social and financial security of the Obrenović dynasty. The third article stated that the Dual Monarchy would not tolerate any member of the Karadjordjević family on its soil. The fourth provided that, if Milan desired it, his son, Prince Alexander, would be educated in Austria. The last article stipulated that should Milan die when Alexander was in Austria-Hungary, the Habsburg government would recognize the latter as king, but not permit his return to Serbia until he reached his majority. If Milan should be deposed when Alexander was not in Austria, the Habsburg army was to occupy Serbia. These five points were designed solely to protect the Obrenović dynasty even at the cost of Serbian independence.[63]

When these far-reaching proposals were shown to Khevenhüller, he immediately expressed the opinion that his government would reject any addition to the treaty. In June, when Milan met Kalnoky in Vienna,

---

[60] Schiessl to Kalnoky, *HHS*, XIX 19, no. 54, Belgrade, July 10, 1885.
[61] Reuss to Bismarck, *GP*, III, no. 646, Vienna, Sept. 19, 1884.
[62] See, for example, Khevenhüller to Kalnoky, *HHS*, XIX 17, no. 25A–C, vertraulich, Belgrade, April 28, 1883.
[63] Jakšić, *op. cit.*, pp. 105–110; Jovanović, *Milan*, III, 210–211. In April, 1883, Khevenhüller reported his belief that Milan was ready to regard Serbia as an enclave of the Dual Monarchy. Khevenhüller to Kalnoky, *HHS*, XIX 17, no. 25A–C, vertraulich, Belgrade, April 28, 1883.

the Austrian foreign minister emphatically asserted that the annexation
of Serbia was not Austria's goal. Kalnoky believed that Milan's aim was
to secure funds from Vienna to meet his personal debts.[64]

When Milan was unable to strengthen his ties with Austria-Hungary,
he again turned hopefully to the possibility of an Austro-Russian war.
Russo-British tension mounted in the Middle East in 1884, and by 1885
it seemed possible that war might be near. The settlement of the crisis
without war was a real disappointment to the Serbian king, who had
hoped that the conflict would have Balkan repercussions.[65]

By 1885, therefore, Russia had both gained and lost in Serbia. Milan
had lost the support of the majority of his people and had alienated the
leaders of both the Liberal and the Radical parties. The policy of alliance with Austria-Hungary, which would have been unpopular under
any circumstances, was rendered doubly so when it came to be regarded
as Milan's personal policy. The Serbs, who sought to release their nation
from the ties with the Dual Monarchy, naturally looked to Russia for
assistance. Russian influence in Serbia thus became much stronger in
the period from 1878 to 1885. Russia, however, had no interest in exploiting her improved position at this time. Following the policy of the
Dreikaiserbund, the Russian foreign office wished Serbia, at least for
the present, to remain within the Austrian orbit. Internal tranquillity
and orderly government in Serbia were in Russia's interest. There is no
indication that the Russian government realized that Milan was willing,
by 1885, to seize any opportunity which might lead to an Austro-Russian
war in order to strengthen his own position. The danger to Russian
policy in the Balkans was that a crisis might arise which would give
Milan an opportunity to act. In 1885 the union of the Bulgarias and
the Macedonian problem provided such a situation. In addition, the
Russian policy of alliance with the German powers was to meet its most
severe test.

---

[64] Jakšić, *op. cit.*, pp. 110–118; Jovanović, *Milan*, III, 214–215.
[65] Jovanović, *Milan*, III, 91–92, 215–218; Khevenhüller to Kalnoky, *HHS*, XIX
19, no. 34A–C, vertraulich, Nish, May 3, 1885.

IX

THE TRIUMPH OF BULGARIAN NATIONALISM

ON SEPTEMBER 6/18, 1885, the union of Bulgaria and Rumelia gave rise to the most serious European crisis since the outbreak of the Russo-Turkish War. The unification itself caused little surprise in Europe, although the timing of the event was unexpected. Even in 1878 few considered that the artificial separation of the Bulgarian people would endure. By 1881, Russia, Austria-Hungary and Germany had already agreed to the union in principle. From 1878 to 1885, agitation for it was continuous both in Bulgaria and in Eastern Rumelia. To the Bulgars, union was only the rectification of a grave injustice inflicted upon their nation by the great powers; it was the one issue on which opinion was unanimous throughout the country. Both Europe and the Bulgarian people felt that union was inevitable, but the general assumption was that it could be accomplished only under the patronage and direction of Russia.

Although Russia at the Congress of Berlin had been tacitly recognized as the dominant power in Bulgaria, she was not given such a position in Eastern Rumelia. Here the powers established a joint commission which was instructed to formulate an organic statute for the administration of the province and to supervise its introduction.[1] The governor-general of the territory was to be a Christian appointed by the sultan with the consent of the great powers. Only through unification, therefore, could Russia hope to be dominant in the entire territory and, until it was apparent that Alexander of Battenberg would not become a Russian puppet, Russian policy aimed at this goal. Wherever possible, Russia worked for the advancement of the interests of the Bulgarians in Eastern Rumelia as well as those of Bulgaria proper.

The first problem which arose concerned the prescribed evacuation of Russian troops from Rumelia within nine months. According to the Treaty of Berlin, Ottoman troops had the right to reënter the province and to garrison the frontiers. The recent war had generated such bitterness between the Turks and the Bulgars that the return of Turkish troops would almost certainly result in armed conflict. The Russian government feared that, if Christian blood were shed, public opinion in Russia would force its intervention. Russia was not in a position to risk another war or to submit to the decisions of a second international congress. Every means possible was thus sought to delay the evacuation

[1] Hertslet, *The Map of Europe by Treaty*, IV, 2774–2778.

of the Russian troops. Russia favored a solution that would keep Turkish troops out of Rumelia and would leave the policing of the province
to native militia and gendarmerie. Not only would the threat of a new
Turko-Bulgar conflict thereby be removed, but a local military force
would be available to provide help in securing unification at the proper
time, and to render assistance, even if limited, to Russia at the Straits.[2]

Great Britain and Austria, on the contrary, pressed for evacuation of
the Russians within the prescribed limit of nine months, irrespective
of Russian fears over a renewal of the conflict. The British concern
over the continued presence of Russian troops was so great that in
October, 1878, Salisbury stated that he did not see how peace could be
preserved if they were not withdrawn within the time limit.[3] To meet
the Russian objections, the Austrian and British governments proposed
a joint military occupation of the province by the great powers, including the Ottoman Empire. Although Miliutin and Shuvalov were
willing to accept this suggestion, Gorchakov and Giers preferred a guaranty that Turkish troops would not enter the province; thereafter the
Russian evacuation could proceed. Curiously enough, the Turks showed
the greatest opposition to the proposal for a joint occupation; apparently they were more concerned over the threat from Vienna than from
St. Petersburg. The Austrian occupation of Bosnia-Hercegovina had
caused great hostility to the Dual Monarchy in the Ottoman Empire.
It was feared that a joint occupation, requiring the passage of Austrian
troops through Macedonia, would lead to the loss of this territory, for
it was well known that Austria had designs on Salonika.[4]

During the first year of Eastern Rumelia's existence, the suspicions
of the great powers were repeatedly aroused over the activities of
Russian agents in the Balkans. Despite the assurances of the Russian
government that it intended to abide strictly by the provisions of the
Berlin agreement, events in the area seemed to belie these declarations.
The partition of the San Stefano Bulgaria had naturally evoked violent
protests throughout the Bulgarian lands. Agitation reached a fever
pitch in October, 1878, when the joint European commission began to
work out the details of Rumelian administration. Demonstrations were
held throughout Rumelia and, at the same time, armed bands of Bulgars
were reported crossing on raids into Macedonia. Behind all these disturbances the representatives of the powers could find evidence of

---

[2] Russia's concern over the possible return of Turkish troops to Rumelia is evident
throughout the negotiations for the Dreikaiserbund. The extensive correspondence of E. P. Novikov, Russian ambassador to Constantinople, with Giers, which is
in the *NKG* collection, deals mainly with this problem. See also Miliutin, III, 115,
131; Medlicott, *Berlin*, p. 189; Jomini to Giers, *NKG*, St. P., May 23, 1879.

[3] Medlicott, *Berlin*, p. 180.

[4] *Ibid.*, pp. 198–202, 234, 253; Miliutin, III, 124, 131.

Russian encouragement and participation. It thus appeared that while the Russian government professed to support the international agreements, it was unable to control the actions of its agents, who were acting in a contrary sense.[5]

That Russian officials were encouraging the Rumelian activities is evidenced in the diary of D. A. Miliutin. The Russian minister at first discounted the reports of Russian intrigue as propaganda of the Porte, but, as information continued to come in, he acknowledged that Russian agents were implicated. He blamed, in particular, Dondukov-Korsakov, the highest Russian official, who, he felt, must have known that Russian officers were connected with the bands operating in Macedonia. He was even prepared to believe that they were acting under Dondukov's orders. The entire course of events reminded him of the actions of the Slavic Societies in 1875 and 1876.[6] He, like the Russian foreign office, feared a recurrence of the events of 1877. Miliutin's comments throw an interesting sidelight on the inability of the minister of war to control those under his jurisdiction. Although Alexander II was alarmed by the reports on Dondukov-Korsakov, he only rebuked the general mildly when he came to St. Petersburg in November, 1878.[7]

Despite the fact that both Miliutin and Giers were aware that their agents in the Balkans were acting contrary to instructions, they were powerless to halt such activities. In January, 1879, Miliutin again noted in his diary that Russian officers were making declarations to the effect that Russia would not abide by the Treaty of Berlin. They assured the Bulgars that Russian troops would not be withdrawn within the time limit. Circulars were distributed, stating that the Bulgarian assembly should not elect a prince until the San Stefano Bulgaria was restored. In the face of these reports, the tsar was forced to instruct his representatives that Russia did indeed intend to evacuate her troops as stipulated in the treaty.[8] In February he once more cautioned his agents strictly to observe their instructions.[9]

The unfortunate repercussions of the activities of Dondukov and his colleagues are well illustrated in the following account. On October 2/14, 1878, S. A. Greig, the tsar's minister of finance, wrote to Giers concerning his travels in Europe:

... everyone is convinced that we are about to hatch something. No one wishes to admit that with finances so strongly shaken by the last war, we are not able with

---

[5] Miliutin, III, 97, 99; Jomini to Giers, *NKG*, April 25, 1879; Medlicott, *Berlin*, p. 195.
[6] Miliutin, III, 99, 101, 132–133; Medlicott, *Berlin*, pp. 78, 180, 190.
[7] Miliutin, III, 101–102.
[8] *Ibid.*, pp. 114–115.
[9] *Ibid.*, p. 119.

gaiety of heart to continue to spend immense sums for the maintenance of our army in Turkey without having a goal which was in relation to the magnitude of the sacrifices imposed on the country. Waddington [the French foreign minister], among others, who asked for a meeting with me, spoke in this sense. When, in the course of the conversation, I reproached him in a friendly manner of rowing in England's waters, he said that I was wrong, that France had for us the most friendly sentiments and that while following a policy of abstention, she could not, as a great power, completely efface herself; that she could not do otherwise than to remain strictly on the terrain of the Treaty of Berlin, that she had signed. Strengthened by the reassuring words contained in your letter, I believed myself correct in affirming that the emperor's policy had no other purpose. Yes, he said, officially you are very correct and I can only praise all the assurances that you transmit through diplomatic channels. I do not wish to put in doubt the sincerity of the Russian government, but your agents in Bulgaria and in Eastern Rumelia, great and small, hold continually to an interpretation diametrically opposed to these assurances and to the clauses of the Treaty of Berlin. Everyone is thus put in the difficult dilemma of doubting the intentions and the sincerity of the Russian government or of doubting its power. We have not, he added, the pretension of passing for a strong government, but I assure you that we would not tolerate for one instant an agent, no matter how highly placed, who would have dared to make policy that was not strictly in accord with that which was indicated to him.... The diplomatic dossier that I went through upon my arrival in St. Petersburg proved to me, alas, that Waddington was right. I will not hide from you, dear Nikolai Karlovich, that I blushed alone in my chamber, in reading about the stupid and tall tales of that humorist Dondukov and his naïve admissions on the tacit protection that he accords to the troubles of Macedonia. Yes, I thought, a government cannot for an instant tolerate that kind of a person, without bringing into question its sincerity or its power. It was a consolation to me to see by another dossier the firm and correct direction that the emperor gave to this affair.[10]

Although both Giers and Miliutin as well as the majority of the responsible Russian officials avoided actions which conflicted with Russia's international obligations, Miliutin in particular sought to gain all the advantages he could from the situation in Rumelia. In Bulgaria proper the Russian army had directed the organization of the Bulgarian forces; but according to the Treaty of Berlin, Eastern Rumelia could have only a militia, and these troops were to be kept strictly separated from those of Bulgaria.

Undeterred by the lack of control over the Rumelian forces, Miliutin, in March/April, 1879, instructed Dondukov to introduce "gymnastic societies," whose members were to be armed, trained, and prepared to supplement the militia.[11] The Russian officers in Rumelia responded with alacrity; one general is reported to have informed the Rumelians

[10] Greig to Giers, *NKG*, St. P., Oct. 2, 1878. See also Miliutin, III, 132; Medlicott, *Berlin*, pp. 182, 197.

[11] Miliutin, III, 45, 90, 109, 132, 293 n. 52; Jomini to Giers, *NKG*, Oct. 24, 1879; Dufferin to Granville, *FO*, 78/3392, no. 977, Constantinople, Oct. 14, 1882; Arnaudov, *Eksarkh Iosif*, pp. 315–319.

that "the Congress of Berlin separated you from the Bulgars. As compensation for that Russia is sending you 10,000 rifles. Train yourselves, in order that you can fight for unification and freedom when the moment arrives! And the tsar sends you greetings and the belief that you will attain that moment within three or four years."[12] The gymnastic societies proved very successful. Despite the fact that Giers, in April, 1879, informed the British ambassador that he had ordered the disbanding of the organization, these groups eventually became the principal agencies by which unification was accomplished.[13]

Meanwhile, the international commission, under great handicaps, had completed the Organic Statute for Eastern Rumelia. Beginning early in 1879, its members by April 14/26 had completed a massive document of fifteen chapters and 495 articles.[14] Since the commission as a whole was not allowed sufficient time to study Rumelian administration, the work was parceled out among the nations. One observer described the results in the following terms:

... the English delegates taking charge of the electoral Law, the Austrians the organization of the Tribunate, the French copied the Administrative Laws of France for the benefit of the Roumeliotes, the Italians introduced the financial system of Italy. Colonel Shevetoff and Commandant de Forcy elaborated the Chapters on the militia and the gendarmerie. Articles involving political questions were often warmly discussed in the general Sittings of the Commission which had not sufficient time however to enquire how far Regulations—crudely borrowed from foreign Sources, and which had hardly been brought into harmony with the Spirit of the Statute—were applicable to the Turkish province just emancipated. Hence the Statute labours under the disadvantages of being not only too voluminous, hastily composed and ill-digested, but also of containing many contradictions and discrepancies.[15]

The confusion wrought in Rumelia by the introduction of foreign systems was especially evident in local administration.

Before the war of 1877, the present Province of Eastern Rumelia was divided into two Sandjaks [Departments] and fourteen Cazas [Cantons]. The two Prefects with the fourteen Baillis who then governed the Province were found more than sufficient. Now, then to the System with which the French delegate has endowed it, there are six Departments and twenty-eight Cantons, and consequently, six Préfets, six "Conseils généraux," six "Commissions permanentes" twenty-eight "Baillis," twenty-eight "Commandants de Gendarmerie," twenty-eight "Commissaires de Police" and so forth ... Obscure Hamlets which before the War never saw an Offi-

---

[12] Jovanović, "Srpsko-Bugarski Rat," *Političke i Pravne Rasprave*, III, 9–10. Hereafter cited as Jovanović, *SBR.*

[13] Medlicott, *Berlin*, p. 248.

[14] Hertslet, *op. cit.*, IV, 2860–2863.

[15] "Report on the Working of the Organic Statute in Eastern Rumelia," Jones to Dufferin, no. 5, Philippopolis, April 10, 1884, in Differin to Granville, *FO*, 78/3623, no. 132, Constantinople, April 22, 1884.

cial—except the tax collector—have now been erected into "Chef lieux de Cantons" with each of them a "Bailli" "Commandant de Gendarmerie" "Commissaire de Police" a "Juge de Canton" a "Percepteur de Finance" a "Caissier" a "Chef des Contributions indirectes" and a Brigade of Gendarmerie consisting of six or eight gendarmes ... A province which contains at the utmost 800,000 inhabitants—the population of a City of the second rank—has been endowed with an Executive worthy of a Kingdom. Besides the Governor General, there is the Secretary General or Director of the Interior, Directors of Justice, Public Works, Education, and a Commander in Chief of Militia and Gendarmerie.[16]

At the head of this unwieldy apparatus was the governor-general, Aleko Pasha, a Russian candidate whom the British ambassador in Constantinople described as "a weak, silly fellow, very disloyal to the sultan and a mere tool in the hands of the Russians and the Bulgarians."[17] The highly conservative provincial assembly was composed of fifty-six members, of whom twenty were nominated and thirty-six elected on the basis of a property or educational franchise. Since the Rumelian people lacked experienced administrators, officials of foreign nationality held the chief posts. Thus a German became director of finance, the chief of the gendarmes was English, and the head of the militia and the chief of staff were French. Most of the officers in the army were Russian or Russian-trained Bulgars. With this conglomeration of personnel, it is remarkable that the administration of the country worked at all. Moreover, every issue in Rumelian internal politics immediately became the subject of international debate. Unfortunately, the statute, whose weaknesses were soon apparent, could be changed only through the action of the powers. The initiative had to come from the provincial assembly, which hesitated to act: first, the unionists did not wish to show any interest in or sympathy with the statute, which they considered a barrier to unification; and second, the Rumelians feared that the Turks would demand an increase in Rumelian contributions to Constantinople.[18]

The most important position in Rumelia was, of course, that of the governor-general, who was appointed by the sultan with the approval of the powers and served as the link between the sultan and his subjects. Aleko Pasha soon found himself in a position analogous to that of Alexander of Battenberg. The demands of the Russian representatives for favors and concessions turned Aleko into a Russophobe. As in Bulgaria, one of the chief points of friction was the relationship of the Russian officers in the Rumelian militia to their subordinates. Here again the Russians were determined to maintain control over the junior

[16] *Loc. cit.*
[17] Sumner, *Russia and the Balkans*, p. 566 n. 1; Radev, I, 485–486.
[18] Tatishchev, *Iz Prozhlago Russkoi Diplomatii*, pp. 399–400.

officers and soldiers, who repeatedly demanded promotions and greater responsibilities. The reluctance of the Russian officers to yield to these requests was resented as a reflection on the capabilities of the Rumelians. Aleko Pasha sided firmly with the Rumelians, thus choosing precisely the same issue as had Alexander of Battenberg on which to challenge the Russian position.[19]

The political as well as the military situation in Rumelia was very similar to that in Bulgaria. Two parties emerged: the National Conservatives and the Liberals, one pro-Russian and the other anti-Russian Their divergent policies became clearly defined after Alexander of Battenberg's coup of 1881. Agitation for unification had subsided somewhat in Eastern Rumelia, which finally realized that Russia would not support the movement. Events in Bulgaria were, nevertheless, followed with the closest attention. When Alexander suspended the constitution, he at the same time determined the line of political cleavage in the southern province. The Conservatives, who momentarily expressed disappointment, quickly sided with their northern colleagues in support of Alexander. The Liberals, in contrast, condemned the attack on the constitution. When the tsar indicated his support of the prince, the Conservatives in Rumelia became the pro-Russian faction and the Liberals became anti-Russian.[20]

The leader of the Russophobes was Karavelov, the Bulgarian Liberal who had been forced to flee Sofia after the *coup d'état*. Once in Rumelia he began to work for the restoration of the constitution in Bulgaria. Since the tsar had approved of Alexander's actions. Karavelov believed that Russian influence would have to be destroyed before a liberal government could rule in Sofia. He therefore launched a vigorous campaign through his newspaper, *Nezavisimost*, against Russia, her policy, and her interference in Bulgarian and Rumelian affairs. Russia, he wrote, should not be considered the liberator of Bulgaria; the Bulgars would eventually have thrown off Turkish rule themselves. Bulgaria would never be really free until Russian control, also, was removed.

In the fall elections for the Rumelian assembly, the Liberals, led by Karavelov, easily defeated the Conservative party, which supported the Russian position. The valuable assistance given by Aleko Pasha to the victorious party was balanced by the vigorous campaigning conducted by the Russian agents in behalf of the candidates opposed to Karavelov.[21]

[19] Radev, I, 486; Jones to Granville, *FO*, 78/3311, no. 45, Philippopolis, Sept. 21, 1881; Dufferin to Granville, *FO*, 78/3392, no. 977, Constantinople, Oct. 14, 1882.
[20] Radev, I, 485–490; Tatishchev, *op. cit.*, p. 402; Madzharov, *Istochna Rumeliia*, pp. 235–247; Stephen to Granville, *FO*, 78/3311, no. 5, Philippopolis, Jan. 28, 1881.
[21] Tatishchev, *op. cit.*, p. 402; Stanev, *Istoriia na Nova Bulgariia*, p. 53; Jones to Granville, *FO*, 78/3311, Oct. 29, 1881; *ibid.*, no. 48, Philippopolis, Nov. 16, 1881.

In 1882, after the elections had been held, the command of the Rumelian military forces again became a major issue. The Russian consul in Plovdiv, Brebel, now sought the dismissal of Colonel de Tourtain, who held the position of chief of staff of the militia and the gendarmerie. The consul pointed out that the three important military posts in Rumelia were held by a German, an Englishman, and a Frenchman, none of whom spoke Bulgarian. The chief of the general staff, at least, should be a Russian. If Aleko Pasha would retire Tourtain on leave, Russia would pay the salary of his Russian substitute.[22] The tsar himself, Brebel emphasized, was interested in the outcome of this proposal. Aleko refused to replace the French officer; nor would he agree to a Russian plan whereby Rumelia would be obligated to buy 25,000 Russian rifles and the necessary ammunition. Russian pressure in the military field led Aleko subsequently to adopt an anti-Russian attitude in other matters. He dismissed several prefects who were known for their Russian sympathies. He supported the Liberals, and he gave the important commands in the Bulgarian forces to Bulgarians or to foreign officers whom he felt he could trust. His final break with Russia, however, came as a result of the controversy over the Shipka Pass memorial.[23]

At the Congress of Berlin, Russia had announced her intention of erecting a memorial to commemorate one of the great Russian victories of the recent war.[24] No objections had been made, since it was believed that the building would have no military or political significance. But when the plans were disclosed, in 1882, Aleko Pasha refused to sanction them. The memorial, a church, had "walls of Great Thickness, cellars in which vast quantities of arms might be stored, and cells for monks which constituted a series of Block Houses, the cost of which edifice, it was estimated would amount to about three milion francs."[25] The Russian press thereupon demanded the removal of Aleko. His action was declared to be the greatest insult which could be offered to the victims of the war and a betrayal of all that Russia had done for the Bulgarian people. Although Russia could do nothing against Alexander of Battenberg, who had fallen from favor, action could be taken against Aleko. His original appointment as governor-general in 1879 had been for

---

[22] Madzharov, *op. cit.*, pp. 277–278; Vlangali to Giers, *NKG*, St. P., Nov. 23/Dec. 5, 1882.

[23] Lamb to Dufferin, Philippopolis, Sept. 30, 1882, in Dufferin to Granville, *FO*, 78/3392, no. 977, conf., Constantinople, Oct. 14, 1882; Wyndham to Granville, *FO*, 78/3393, no. 1030, conf., Constantinople, Nov. 11, 1882.

[24] Hertslet, *op. cit.*, IV, 2754.

[25] Wyndham to Granville, *FO*, 78/3393, no. 1030, conf., Constantinople, Nov. 11, 1882; Madzharov, *op. cit.*, pp. 274–277.

only five years. In 1884, when he would again have to be approved by the great powers, an opportunity would arise to secure his removal.[26]

In the summer of 1883 the Russian government made clear to the Rumelian delegation which attended the tsar's coronation that it was opposed to the reappointment of Aleko.[27] Early in 1884 these views were communicated to the powers, who were unwilling to make an issue of the matter.[28] In presenting her case against Aleko, Russia emphasized Aleko's anti-Russian activities and his championship of the unification movement. The latter point was of real importance to the Russian government. When the Dreikaiserbund agreement was studied, before its renewal in 1884, Russia decided that the union of the Bulgarias was not in her interest. She was therefore concerned when, at the end of March, 1884, demonstrations were held throughout Rumelia demanding union with Bulgaria. Many Rumelians were under the impression that Russia's declarations of disinterestedness were designed merely to disguise her true intentions, and that, when the moment came, she would stand behind the union. Realizing the danger in the situation, the Russian foreign office naturally sought a candidate who would discourage unionist agitation.[29]

Whereas Russia had turned against the Bulgarian national movement, the Habsburg monarchy now looked upon it more favorably. Kalnoky commented to Dufferin, the British ambassador, in September, 1884, that he "would not be invincibly opposed to the union of Rumelia with Bulgaria"; he believed that "in time independence would turn these states against Russia."[30] For the present, however, he supported the wishes of his Russian ally on the dismissal of Aleko. To replace the latter, another Russian candidate, Gavril Effendi Krustevich, was appointed. Although the British consul considered him "old and feeble and destitute of prestige," he proved to be an honest and patriotic governor.[31]

[26] Wyndham to Granville, *FO*, 78/3393, no. 1038, conf., Constantinople, Nov. 13, 1882; *ibid.*, 78/3394, no. 1096, conf., Constantinople, Dec. 4, 1882.

[27] *Ibid.*, 78/3511, no. 462, conf., Therapia, July 11, 1883.

[28] Kalnoky to Wolkenstein, *HHS*, X 74, vertraulich, privatbrief, Vienna, Feb. 9, 1884; Wolkenstein to Kalnoky, *HHS*, X 74, no. 8B, vertraulich, St. Petersburg, Feb. 14/26, 1884; Dufferin to Granville, *FO*, 78/3623, no. 103, Constantinople, March 31, 1884.

[29] Thornton to Granville, *FO*, 65/1181, no. 92, St. P., April 9, 1884; Lascelles to Granville, *FO*, 78/3638, no. 33, conf., Sofia, April 16, 1884. Throughout 1882 and 1883 Russia's representatives were unofficially encouraging the union. Radev, I, 491–492. However, the assertion of Corti (*Alexander*, p. 228) that "Die russische Regierung schürte wohl die Bewegung" in 1884 and 1885 is incorrect.

[30] Dufferin to Granville, *FO*, 78/3626, conf., London, Sept. 24, 1884.

[31] *Ibid.*, 78/3624, no. 158, secret and conf., Constantinople, May 8, 1884; Wolkenstein to Kalnoky, *HHS*, X 74, tel. no. 38, geheim, St. P., April 26, 1884.

The great upsurge of the unionist movement in Rumelia in 1884 led the populace to believe that the moment for action was at hand. Before his removal, Aleko Pasha had been active in organizing demonstrations, apparently in the hope that he could thereby gain support for himself and discredit the Russians. In the regular elections held in 1884 the anti-Russian Liberal party again emerged victorious. The new governor-general, Krustevich, was powerless to stop the course of events. His only contribution to the Russian cause was to remove some of the supporters of Aleko Pasha. To make matters worse, the Liberal party in Bulgaria, led by Karavelov, who had meanwhile returned from Rumelia, won the elections in that state. Bulgaria and Eastern Rumelia now had administrations with similar aims.[32]

Despite the popular feeling, the unionist movement in both sections of the divided nation lacked a strong uniting force. The Rumelian revolutionary committee, headed by Z. Stoianov, D. Rizov, N. Genadiev, and A. Liapchev, could direct the overthrow of the Rumelian government, but the leadership of Alexander of Battenberg was needed to secure a unified Bulgaria. The position of the prince had by 1884 become very difficult. He knew that union was the one issue on which he could unite his subjects and win their support. His attitude was similar to Milan's in regard to Macedonia. Both rulers recognized that their chances of remaining in power depended on the extent to which they could identify themselves with the national aspirations of their peoples. Since Alexander, unlike Milan, now had the backing of no great power, he had to act with extreme caution. On March 19/31, 1884, a public meeting was held in Sofia to promote the unification movement. It was decided to appeal to the prince for support. When the latter learned of this, he is reported to have said:

> On the one hand it would be impossible for him to refuse to receive the deputation, for if he did so he would lose all his popularity, and lay himself open to the charge of want of sympathy with Bulgarian aspirations. On the other hand he believed that the time had not arrived for bringing about the union, and that any action at present with that object would lead to disaster. He would therefore be very prudent in the answer he should return to the deputation, and, while assuring them of his sympathy with their desire for the union, he intended to express the opinion that it would be inopportune to take any action for the present.[33]

In Rumelia, the Russian consul Sorokin did his best to aid the pro-Russian National party. In Bulgaria, Koiander faced a similar thankless task. After the public meeting in Sofia, he sent two protests to

[32] Tatishchev, *op. cit.*, p. 404; Wyndham to Granville, *FO*, 78/3624, no. 187, Constantinople, May 30, 1884; Jones to Wyndham, no. 18, Philippopolis, Dec. 8, 1884, in Wyndham to Granville, *FO*, 78/3628, no. 475, Constantinople, Dec. 6, 1884.
[33] Lascelles to Granville, *FO*, 78/3628, no. 28, conf., Sofia, April 2, 1884.

Alexander, the first on instructions from the Russian foreign office, the second on the personal order of the tsar.[34]

Although the Russian attitude toward union had thus been made exceedingly clear, every opportunity was used to emphasize the official policy. In March, 1885, Nelidov sent a telegram, which was published, to the acting Russian consul in Plovdiv, declaring that the Russian government did not approve of the agitation or of the meetings held in behalf of the union.[35] In September, General Kantakuzin, Russian minister of war in Bulgaria, held a lengthy conversation with Alexander on Russo-Bulgarian relations and the unionist problem. Alexander pleaded that in Bulgaria there were only two powers—Russia and himself—and that they must act in unison. Men like Karavelov, Tsankov, Stoilov, and the others were not important. Neither Russia nor he could rely on any of the Bulgar parties, which hated both Russia and their ruler and sought to exploit the misunderstanding between the two. This, continued Alexander, could not go on much longer; either he must be accepted in St. Peterbsurg or he would be forced to leave Bulgaria.[36]

Alexander thus found himself between two camps. He knew that plans for union were being formulated and that they involved revolutionary action, but he warned that the time was ill chosen. When he met Giers in Franzensbad in August, 1885, he did not realize the imminence of the situation. His assurances to Giers were therefore undoubtedly given in good faith. It was while the prince was abroad that final plans for the revolt were drawn up without his knowledge or participation.[37]

When Alexander returned to Bulgaria in September, he was met at Varna by two members of the secret committee from Plovdiv, who informed him that the revolt would take place at the end of September or the beginning of October. Alexander was expected to take command. According to Koch, Alexander's court chaplain, the prince was surprised at the news but did not take it seriously.[38] He tried to persuade the delegates that the moment was not propitious, and apparently a postponement was agreed upon. However, before the two delegates could return to Plovdiv, the revolt commenced. The event was precipitated by the fear of the revolutionaries that the Turkish authorities had

---

[34] *Ibid.*, 78/3638, no. 33, conf., Sofia, April 16, 1884; Giers to Kapnist, *DDF*, V, no. 228, St. P., March 20/April 1, 1884; Ferry to Flesch, *DDF*, V, no. 232, Paris, April 10, 1884; Courcel to Ferry, *DDF*, V, no. 240, Berlin, April 18, 1884.

[35] The text of the telegram is found in Wyndham to Granville, *FO*, 78/3749, no. 137, Constantinople, March 15, 1885.

[36] Koiander to Vlangali, *Avantiury*, no. 3, Aug. 4/16, 1885.

[37] Radev, I, 499–531; Corti, *Alexander*, pp. 225–227; Lascelles to Salisbury, *FO*, 78/3770, no. 77, Philippopolis, Oct. 5, 1885.

[38] Koch, p. 232; Radev, I, 520; Lascelles to Salisbury, *FO*, 78/3770, no. 77, Philippopolis, Oct. 5, 1885.

learned of the plan and would act. Therefore, on the night of September 5/17–6/18, 1885, Rumelian troops marched on Plovdiv and proclaimed the unification of Eastern Rumelia and Bulgaria.[39]

The union placed the Russian officials in Bulgaria and Eastern Rumelia in a difficult position. On September 4/16, one of the leaders of the revolt, Ivan St. Geshov, and two other delegates went to the Russian consulate in Plovdiv and asked G. V. Igel'strom, secretary of the consulate, who was in charge of the office during Sorokin's absence, if Russia would support the union. Igel'strom replied that Russia condemned such a move: revolution at that moment would be a catastrophe for the Bulgarian people. When the revolt began the next day, Igel'strom was without instructions. Lieutenant Colonel Chichagov, Russian military attaché in Plovdiv, begged Igel'strom to give him authority to use troops to stop the revolt. Igel'strom hesitated and then replied that he would try to solve the matter by arbitration. Nevertheless, Chichagov on his own initiative proceeded to the residence of the governor-general and told the milling crowd that the tsar had not been informed of the revolt in advance, and that Russia would not support the action taken.[40]

The revolutionaries had no difficulty in securing the removal of the governor-general, Krustevich, who had been a Russian candidate. Chichagov had apparently warned Krustevich of the plan to force his resignation, but the governor-general replied, "I have heard nothing." He asked the Russian officer not to tell anyone that he knew of the plot. Being a patriotic Bulgar, Krustevich was undoubtedly sympathetic to the union; he willingly left his post when the crowd broke into his residence. After his resignation the people marched through the streets shouting, "Long live Prince Alexander! Long live United Bulgaria!" A telegram was immediately dispatched to Alexander.[41]

When the news reached the prince, he was alone in Varna without immediate counsel. Karavelov, the minister-president, was in Tyrnovo and his fellow ministers were in Sofia—an indication that the Bulgarian government did not expect the developments in Plovdiv. Although Alexander felt that he should abide by his recent promises to Giers, his ministers, once they could be consulted, swept aside his objections and urged that he take the leadership of the movement. Stambolov presented the issue with the utmost candor: "Sire, the union is made—the revolt is an accomplished fact, past recall, and the time for hesitation

[39] Radev, I, 533–535; Koch, p. 232; Corti, *Alexander*, pp. 229–231.

[40] Radev, I, 533–536; Tatishchev, *op. cit.*, p. 410.

[41] Radev, I, 536–537. Graves to Salisbury, *FO*, 78/3770, no. 68, Sofia, Sept. 29, 1885, gives a somewhat different version of the event.

is gone by. Two roads lie before Your Highness: the one to Philippopolis and as much farther as God may lead; the other to Sistoff [Sistova], the Danube, and Darmstadt. I counsel you to take the crown the nation offers you."[42] Indeed, such was the choice before the prince. If he accepted the leadership of the united Bulgaria, he would gain the unanimous support of the Bulgarians and become a national hero, but he would incur the wrath of Russia. If he refused to support the revolution, his subjects would undoubtedly turn against him and he had little hope of gaining Russian support after the events of the past years. He therefore accepted the offer and turned to the task of defending the union before foreign opposition.

Returning to Sofia, Alexander immediately made a series of crucial decisions. Fearing possible military action by the Turks, he ordered the army mobilized, and simultaneously convened the national assembly in order that it might ratify the mobilization act and provide for the necessary expenditures. He then sent a telegram to the tsar asking for Russian approval of the union. Finally, he made hasty preparations for departure to Plovdiv to assume command of the revolt. By these actions the prince irretrievably committed himself to the union.[43]

The Russian government was now presented with a *fait accompli* for which it was obviously unprepared. Despite the fact that Russian policy demanded that, under the circumstances, the *status quo* in the Balkans be maintained, public opinion in Russia strongly favored the union of the Bulgarias, a step toward the reëstablishment of the goal of San Stefano. In the years after the Treaty of Berlin, the Russian government had been unable to restrain the enthusiastic activities of her officials in Rumelia, who supported the extension of Bulgarian influence in Macedonia. Even in 1885 it was obvious that Russian representatives on the scene were personally sympathetic to Bulgarian national aspirations. Their actions often gave a false impression of official Russian intentions. For instance, it was reported that the Russian consul and the military attaché in Plovdiv were present at the meeting, in June, 1885, which set a time for the revolt.[44] Whether the Russian agents were in attendance as active sympathizers or merely as observers, their actions were compromising to Russian policy. Even Igel'strom, who had warned the representatives of the revolutionary committee against precipitating a revolt, was confused and uncertain. Once the union had

[42] Beaman, *M. Stambuloff*, p. 59; Corti, *Alexander*, pp. 231–233. Alexander's father wired the prince on September 19: "Am utterly appalled. Cannot think that this is the right moment. God keep you." Corti, *DTD*, p. 309.
[43] Radev, I, 560–569; Graves to Salisbury, *FO*, 78/3770, no. 76, conf., Sofia, Oct. 5, 1885.
[44] Koch, p. 235.

been proclaimed, Chichagov, who initially had wanted to use force to suppress it, went with Igel'strom to meet and congratulate Alexander when he arrived near Plovdiv.[45] Other Russian officers were openly partisan and became neutral only after strict orders arrived from St. Petersburg. It was reported that after the revolt, certain of the participants went to the Russian consulate and there drank toasts in honor of the union.[46]

In Bulgaria, Koiander was in a similar position. Without instructions he could do nothing but caution the Bulgarian government not to march troops into Rumelia, since a war with the Ottoman Empire might result. Kantakuzin had an even more difficult problem to solve. As minister of war his signature was needed on the mobilization decree. He did not know whether he should act as a Bulgarian minister and obey the prince, or, in his capacity of a Russian officer, await instructions from St. Petersburg. Adopting the line of least resistance, he signed the decree.[47]

The Russian press could not conceal its delight at the extension of Slavic power in the Balkans. Aksakov wrote, "The Treaty of Berlin is broken!" *Novoe Vremia* stated that the whole Slavic world rejoiced; *Russkiia Viedomosti* extended congratulations to the Bulgars. Even Katkov, who had developed a deep distrust of the prince as a result of the Sobolev-Kaulbars incident, supported the union.[48]

The unification of the Bulgarias was thus endorsed by the Bulgarian people, the Russian public, and even the Russian agents in the Balkans. The Russian foreign office had already provided for such an eventuality in the Dreikaiserbund. The Russian military called for a strong Bulgarian base to support Russian strategy in regard to the Straits. Salisbury, who had just formed a new conservative cabinet, believed that Russia would endorse Bulgarian union,[49] since it would be greatly to her advantage. It was Alexander III, however, who made the final decision, and his immediate reaction was highly unfavorable.

On September 9/21, three days after the revolt, when the prince had already left for Plovdiv, Alexander III, who was in Copenhagen, made his position clear. Expressing extreme disapproval, the tsar ordered Kantakuzin to resign as Bulgarian minister of war, and announced that all Russian officers serving in the Bulgarian army were to be recalled.

---

[45] Corti, *Alexander*, pp. 233–234; Radev, I, 563. An interesting account of the personal feuds among the Russian agents in Bulgaria and Rumelia is given by Tatishchev, *op. cit.*, pp. 416–417.

[46] Radev, I, 551.

[47] *Ibid.*, p. 560.

[48] *Ibid.*, pp. 569–574; Wolkenstein to Kalnoky, *HHS*, XV 80, tel. no. 109, St. P., Sept. 21, 1885.

[49] Buckle, *Victoria*, III, 690–693.

Koiander was instructed to avoid conversations with the prince.[50] The tsar's reaction came as a profound shock to the Bulgarian people. Prince Alexander immediately replied by telegram that if the tsar had recalled the officers because he, the prince, had placed himself at the head of the union, he was willing to abdicate for the welfare of the nation. His only wish was to gain Russian approval of the events, which had taken place without his knowledge and in spite of his expressed opposition. Alexander's action had the immediate effect of gaining the sympathy of his subjects and underlining the negative nature of the Russian stand.[51]

Meanwhile, the Bulgarian assembly, which had voted the necessary funds for mobilization, decided to appeal to the tsar to reverse his decision. When the delegation requested Koiander to transmit its message to the tsar, the Russian agent replied that he could not do so, in view of the tsar's attitude. The refusal to transmit a message from the duly constituted Bulgarian assembly only added to the mounting bitterness of the Bulgars toward their former patron. No alternative existed but for the assembly to send a special delegation to plead its cause in person.[52]

The Bulgars were particularly desirous of obtaining Russian support because of their fear of the reaction of the Ottoman Empire. Rumelia was, after all, technically a province of the empire under the direct authority of the sultan. The union, if allowed, would further weaken Turkish power. When reports reached Sofia that Turkish reinforcements were approaching the Rumelian border, Alexander immediately sent a note to the great powers pleading that the two provinces had been united without unfriendly intent toward the sultan, whose suzerainty the Bulgars still recognized. The prince promised to maintain law and order in both Bulgaria and Eastern Rumelia, and to protect all citizens regardless of religion or nationality.[53]

It was this fear of a war with Turkey that made the recall of the Russian officers appear at first to be the death blow to the united Bulgaria. Since the liberation, Russian officers had managed to hold all military ranks above the grade of first lieutenant; the removal of field grade officers and general officers left the Bulgarian forces without experienced leaders. The Russians were under the impression that peace and stability prevailed in Bulgaria solely because of the presence of

[50] Vlangali to Giers, *NKG*, St. P., Sept. 14/26, 1885; Wolkenstein to Kalnoky, *HHS*, XV 80, tel. no. 110, St. P., Sept. 21, 1885.

[51] Radev, I, 566.

[52] *Ibid.*, pp. 567–568; Tatishchev, *op. cit.*, p. 419; Graves to Salisbury, *FO*, 78/3770, no. 67, Sofia, Sept. 26, 1885.

[53] Radev, I, 584; Grand Vizir to Ambassadors, *BD*, no. 105, Sept. 9, 1885.

Russian officers, and that they could be held as a permanent weapon over the heads of the Bulgarian people. If a crisis occurred, and the officers were recalled, it was expected that chaos and anarchy would ensue. The Bulgars would then be forced to plead for the return of the officers and to accept whatever terms Russia imposed.

The recall of the officers in September, 1885, was designed for this end, but, to Russia's dismay, the reaction was entirely contrary to that expected. Instead of leading to the overthrow of the prince, the Russian action underscored Alexander's role as the leader of the united Bulgaria and aroused extreme hostility toward Russia. As one observer commented, "Having paid the Russian officers like Princes during six years, they [the Bulgars] are now abandoned by them in their hour of need."[54] The Bulgars could not understand how Russia, who had created a united Bulgaria in the Treaty of San Stefano, could now oppose its reconstitution. It was, moreover, Russia who had originally designated Alexander of Battenberg as prince and had supported his coup in 1881 against the wishes of the majority of the nation.[55]

One element in the country greeted Russia's recall of her officers with great satisfaction—the rank and file of the Bulgarian army. The presence of Russian officers had meant that all opportunity for advancement had been denied the Bulgars for six years. Young and ambitious, the Bulgarian soldiers and officers could now look forward to positions of responsibility and command. As one prominent official remarked, the unification had accomplished at least the great service of securing the withdrawal of the Russian military.[56]

Alexander of Battenberg shared the views of the army. His six-year struggle to gain control of the armed forces of Bulgaria had unexpectedly been carried to victory. He alone now held the supreme command and, like the Bulgarian officers, had the opportunity to demonstrate his own military abilities. It is reported that Alexander, upon receiving the news of the tsar's order, exclaimed that this was the happiest day of his life; now the Bulgarian army would be completely staffed by loyal Bulgars.[57]

Few, however, believed that the Bulgarian union could be preserved without Russian sponsorship. The act of unification, a direct violation of the Treaty of Berlin, had upset the balance in the Balkan Peninsula. The final decision would depend upon the judgment of the powers.

On September 18/30, 1885, the delegation appointed by the Bulgarian

[54] White to Salisbury, *FO*, 78/3753, no. 409, Therapia, Sept. 29, 1885.
[55] Goriainov, "Razryv," pp. 174–177; Lascelles to Salisbury, *FO*, 78/3770, no. 71, Sofia, Oct. 3, 1885; Dalziel to White, *FO*, 364/2, no. 26, Ruschuk, Oct. 16, 1885.
[56] Radev, I, 566–567.
[57] Goriainov, "Razryv," pp. 177–178; Tatishchev, *op. cit.*, p. 422.

assembly reached Copenhagen, where both the tsar and Giers were staying. The group was headed by the Russophil Metropolitan Kliment and included I. S. Geshov, I. Gerdshikov, D. Papazoglu, and D. Tonchev, the last three from Eastern Rumelia. On September 20/October 2, they held their first meetings with Giers, who informed them that the whole affair had been "thoughtless" and "rash," but that the union could not now be dissolved, for the late tsar had desired it. The Russian foreign minister recited his grievances against the Bulgarian government, but assured the delegates that Russia would do all she could to solve the problem created by the Rumelian revolution.[58]

On the next day the delegates spoke with the tsar, who repeated his assurances of sympathy for the Bulgarian cause, but complained that the action had placed him in a very difficult position. The union could not be dissolved, but its exact form had still to be determined. The Bulgarians, he continued, had no pressing need for union, since the administration of both provinces was in Bulgarian hands. On the real issue, that of Russian aid in obtaining great power approval, the tsar stated that Russia could not assist the Bulgarians so long as the present government of Bulgaria was in power.[59] The implication of this statement was plain: Russia was not against the union, but she was against Alexander of Battenberg. According to the report of Tonchev, Kliment omitted this statement from his official report to Sofia because he did not wish to cause alarm in Bulgaria.[60]

The Russian position in the Bulgarian crisis was settled at Copenhagen, where Giers had joined the tsar. The tsar's personal animosity toward Prince Alexander doubtless played a part in the final decision, but the course was dictated by Russia's national interests at the time. Russia could afford no major upset in the Balkan balance. Although the Dreikaiserbund was in effect, the Russian foreign office could not be certain that it would withstand a Balkan crisis. Commenting on the necessity of avoiding "a general collapse in the east," Jomini wrote to Giers: "The Dreikaiserbund will be able to perform this task if it is maintained. But will it withstand this test which obliges it to pass from negation to action? That is the question."[61]

Moreover, if the Bulgarian union were approved, other powers would

---

[58] Geshov, *Spomeni i Studii*, pp. 142–143; Flesch to Freycinet, *DDF*, VI, no. 86, Sofia, Oct. 5, 1885.

[59] Geshov, *op. cit.*, pp. 144–146; Radev, I, 576–580; Trifonov, *V. Drumev-Kliment: Branitski i Turnovski: Zhivot, Deinost i Kharakter*, pp. 123–124.

[60] Radev, I, 577–578.

[61] Jomini to Giers, *NKG*, Sept. 11, 1885; Morier to Salisbury, *FO*, 65/1219, no. 400, secret, St. P., Nov. 22, 1885. The British ambassador, Morier, reported that he was convinced that as long as Giers remained in office "the main object of Russian policy will be to prevent the Eastern Question from being reopened, in order that a European war may be avoided."

immediately demand compensation. This could take the form of an Austro-Hungarian demand for the annexation of Bosnia-Hercegovina or agitation by Greece and Serbia for additional territory. If these claims were met, potential Russian enemies would make concrete gains, whereas Russia would have suffered what was in effect a loss. For, although Russia in the past had worked for a united Bulgaria, it was now obvious that such a Bulgaria would be hostile to St. Petersburg. Giers frankly admitted that the tsar was going against all of Russia's traditions in opposing the union, but practical politics and prestige necessitated this.[62] It was feared that if the union were recognized, the Bulgarians would turn to Macedonia to complete the re-formation of the San Stefano Bulgaria. The dangers of a war between Greece, Bulgaria, and Serbia would then arise. Russia had no desire to see Slavic or Orthodox states pitted against each other, for some day these states, united, could be used for the furtherance of Russian aims.

Russian policy was thus devoted to the attainment of two ends: the prevention of war among the small states and the maintenance of a solid front by the great powers. At Copenhagen it was decided that the *status quo ante*, in relation to the Rumelian revolution, should be restored. This, however, did not mean that Russia desired a complete restoration of the conditions prior to the union. Giers suggested to Bismarck that the Dreikaiserbund should seek to provide for the economic and administrative union of the provinces "without withdrawing in form from the *status quo ante*." The tsar believed that "eine Art Realunion" would thus come about, but under no condition would he agree to a personal union through Alexander of Battenberg.[63] During the subsequent negotiations Russia made minor modifications in her position, but never departed from her basic aim of securing the expulsion of the prince by means of a return to the *status quo ante*. She now sought to implement this policy by direct negotiations with the great powers and a series of ambassadorial conferences in Constantinople.

The solution agreed upon was thus designed to meet the dangers which the unification movement had created for Russia. First, the fears of the great powers in regard to Russian intentions would be quieted.

---

[62] Wolkenstein to Kalnoky, *HHS*, X 75, geheim, privatbrief, St. P., Oct. 14/26, 1885; Morier to Salisbury, *FO*, 65/1219, no. 415, secret, St. P., Dec. 2, 1885.

[63] Bismarck to Wilhelm I, *GP*, V, no. 959, Friedrichsruh, Oct. 9, 1885; Giers to Bouteneff, *Staal*, no. 155, St. P., Sept. 24/Oct. 6, 1885; Medlicott, "The Powers and the Unification of the Two Bulgarias, 1885," *English Historical Review*, LIV (1939), 70–71. Hereafter cited as Medlicott, "Unification." The most novel solution was proposed by the Russian consul in Rumelia, Sorokin, who suggested that the union be considered as Bulgaria joining Rumelia. Thereby the Rumelian ruler and not Alexander would become the head of the new state. Jomini to Giers, *NKG*, Sept. 11, 1885; Zinoviev to Giers, *NKG*, Sept. 14, 1885.

Second, Bulgaria, now hostile to Russia, would be seriously weakened by her second loss of Eastern Rumelia. Third, the prevention of real union would gravely compromise the position of Alexander of Battenberg. The Bulgarian people would be shown that they would have to sacrifice their prince if they wished to unite. Fourth, the return to the *status quo ante* would quiet the demands of the little states. If Bulgaria received no appreciable gains, Greece, Serbia, and Montenegro would have no basis for their claims. Russia at this time had no desire to weaken the power of the Ottoman Empire, at whose expense the small states would gain; if Bulgaria continued to prove intractable, the Porte was always a possible ally.[64]

The Rumelian revolution had taken the great powers as well as Russia by surprise. Of primary concern to Russia was the reaction of her allies, Germany and Austria-Hungary. Bismarck, like Giers, was concerned that no step should be taken which would jeopardize the Dreikaiserbund. He supported the *status quo ante:* it was the Russian position, and its adoption would prevent the reopening of the eastern question under unfavorable circumstances. He even suggested that the British fleet be used to intimidate Greece, and that Russia intervene to prevent a Macedonian uprising.[65]

The Habsburg government, whose interests were more closely involved than those of Germany, had watched the recent political evolution of Bulgaria with satisfaction. A united Bulgaria under Alexander of Battenberg would, under the circumstances, not be a menace to Austria-Hungary. Kalnoky's first reactions were thus not unfavorable to the union. He, however, deplored the fact that the unification had taken place on the eve of the meeting of the Habsburg delegations; he feared the reaction of the Magyar nationalists, who were anti-Russian

---

[64] A Russo-Turkish alliance was apparently given serious consideration by the Russian government. More than a dozen secret dispatches in the British foreign office archives for 1885 deal with this subject. By bribing responsible Turkish officials, the British regularly were informed on Russian moves. In one dispatch, Wyndham wrote that "by chance" he had secured a copy of a telegram—he could not vouch for its authenticity—from the Turkish ambassador in St. Petersburg concerning a conversation with Giers. The telegram read in part that Giers "held out most tempting baits to Chakir Pasha pointing out that the Turkish government will through an alliance with Russia obtain the faculty of governing Eastern Roumelia in accordance with its own ideas, that it will make sure of retaining Bulgaria as a dependency, that Russia would give proof of her generosity by restoring to the Sultan Kars and Ardahan, and by modifying some of the clauses of treaties which bear hardly upon Turkey, and that Monsieur de Nelidoff will be charged to make further communications to the Sublime Porte on this subject on his return to Constantinople." Wyndham to Granville, *FO*, 78/2748, no. 61, secret, Constantinople, Feb. 4, 1885. See also *ibid.*, 78/3749, no. 91, secret, Constantinople, Feb. 20, 1885; *ibid.*, 78/3758, tel. no. 31, Constantinople, March 11, 1885. This subject is referred to also in Miliutin, IV, 7; Vlangali to Giers, *NKG*, Sept. 21, 1885.

[65] Medlicott, "Unification," p. 75.

and sympathetic to the Bulgars. These considerations led him to drop any suggestion that Austria-Hungary should now be free to annex Bosnia-Hercegovina, an idea which had occurred to him immediately after the announcement of the union. In his conversations with G. Kantakuzin, first secretary of the Russian embassy in Vienna, who was in charge in the absence of Lobanov, Kalnoky expressed his fears of the effect of the crisis on the Dreikaiserbund, complaining that the revolution threatened to reduce "to nothing all the fruits so painfully acquired of the rapprochement between us."[66] Kalnoky's principal concern, however, was the reaction of the other Balkan powers, in particular that of Austria's protégé, Serbia. The suddenness of the revolution had prevented the powers from arranging compensation for the other states, and Kalnoky feared a general conflagration. Lobanov, on his return to Vienna, commented that Kalnoky had no concrete suggestions and appeared to look to Russia for direction.[67]

The Austrian apprehension over the conduct of the small states was indeed justified. Immediately after the union, King Milan went to Vienna, where he expressed his intentions in no uncertain fashion. On September 8/20 he told Kantakuzin that he was ready for war to back the Serbian claim for compensation. The Russian agent commented that "the means appeared to me the worst and that it would be an imitation of the game of Prince Alexander, who placed all his future on one card." Three days later, Milan told Kantakuzin that if Alexander profited from his coup, he, Milan, would have to imitate him or lose his throne. Kantakuzin replied that Milan would risk more by such an action than he would gain, for Europe would declare him an outlaw.[68]

Serbia, however, was the client not of Russia but of Austria-Hungary. Kalnoky could not risk Milan's losing prestige within his own kingdom. If the king did not obtain compensation to offset any Bulgarian advance, his position, which was now precarious, might become untenable. Since his overthrow could lead to the return of the anti-Austrian Karadjordjević dynasty, Milan's interests had to be taken into account. Nevertheless, Kalnoky repeatedly warned Milan that he must be prudent and avoid precipitating any action.[69]

Despite the advantages to Austrian policy of a united Bulgaria under

---

[66] Cantacuzene to Giers, *NKG*, Sept. 8/20 and Sept. 11/23, 1885; Careil to Freycinet, *DDF*, VI, no. 110, Vienna, Nov. 1, 1885.

[67] Lobanov to Giers, *NKG*, Vienna, Sept. 14/26, 1885; Vlangali to Giers, *NKG*, Sept. 14/26, 1885; Paget to Salisbury, *FO*, 364/2, no. 353, conf., Vienna, Oct. 21, 1885; Medlicott, "Unification," pp. 71, 76–77; Giers to Staal, *Staal*, no. 158, Oct. 19/31, 1885.

[68] Cantacuzene to Giers, *NKG*, Sept. 8/20, Sept. 11/23, 1885.

[69] Medlicott, "Unification," pp. 71, 76–77, 265, 271; Jovanović, *Milan*, III, 227, 234, 242–253.

the aegis of a Russophobe prince, the Austrian government joined in the support of the *status quo ante*. The three powers of the Dreikaiserbund had thus reached accord; all feared that a general conflict would arise, at least among the small states, if the union were not dissolved. Great Britain now came to the defense of Alexander of Battenberg. When the news of the union reached London, Salisbury suspected that the developments in Rumelia were the result of Russian intrigue and that a united Bulgaria was as dangerous for Britain in 1885 as it had been in 1878. In contrast, Queen Victoria argued that the unionist movement was popular, that the prince had no choice but to lead it, and that a united Bulgaria would be anti-Russian. Like Alexander III, Queen Victoria was much influenced by her personal affections. The Battenberg family and Prince Alexander were close to her. When the Russian stand confirmed the correctness of the queen's judgment, Salisbury shifted his position to conform to hers.[70] A complete reversal had thus been accomplished. In 1878 Russia had sponsored a united Bulgaria; in 1885 she opposed it. In 1878 Britain had secured the destruction of the San Stefano Bulgaria; in 1885, seven years later, she supported its partial restoration. The policy thereafter adopted by Salisbury called for a personal union of the two Bulgarias; the institutions of the two provinces were, however, not to be amalgamated. Britain was particularly careful to protect the position of Prince Alexander, whose downfall could pave the way for a complete Russification of Bulgaria. Bulgaria under the prince had become for Britain a bulwark against Russian influence at the Straits rather than an outpost for their seizure.[71]

Meanwhile, the Russian government continued to discredit the prince. On November 5/17 the tsar, in an order of the day, struck Alexander's name from the Russian army list. The public expulsion of a prominent individual from the army was carried out only under extreme circumstances and was considered the greatest insult. The tsar himself fully recognized the significance of his act. In a letter to Alexander of Hesse he explained:

> I have been obliged to resort to a measure with regard to Sandro that has cost me a good deal. I have done my best for him for the sake of the memory of my dead parents. I have been grieved to see the forces that have estranged him from us, and to see him succumb to the hostile influences that have led him to behave as the avowed enemy of Russia.[72]

---

[70] Buckle, *Victoria*, III, 690–693; Staal to Giers, *Staal*, no. 156, Oct. 16/28, 1885.
[71] Medlicott, "Unification," pp. 73–75; Giers to Staal, *Staal*, no. 162, St. P., Oct. 24/Nov. 5, 1885.
[72] Corti, *DTD*, pp. 311–312, 374; Appert to Freycinet, *DDF*, VI, no. 112, St. P., Nov. 5, 1885; Giers to Staal, *Staal*, no. 157, Oct. 19/31, 1885.

The tsar criticized the union which could "set the East ablaze" and endanger Bulgaria's existence.

The prince's father replied in a forthright manner. He deplored the measures that Russia had taken against his son, who had been treated like a common criminal when he was dismissed from the army. The tsar had not even sought an explanation from the prince, nor had he allowed the latter to present one. In particular, Alexander of Hesse objected to the assertion that the prince was alone responsible for the Russian position in Bulgaria and her loss of prestige. Alexander had not brought about the union, continued his father, but once it had been accomplished he had no choice but to lead it: *"I should have done the same in his place."*[73]

In the weeks following the union, numerous attempts were made to resolve the differences between the British position and that of the Dreikaiserbund. Neither Britain nor Russia would modify her basic stand: the one in support of the prince and personal union, the other for the *status quo ante.* Despite the fact that Austria-Hungary officially backed the Russian stand, Kalnoky made the obvious objections to the Russian proposals. How, he asked, could the *status quo ante* be restored when none of the powers were willing to use force and none wished to see the provinces occupied by Turkish troops? When Giers suggested that moral pressure should be exerted on Alexander, Kalnoky pointed out that the position of the three empires would be even more difficult if this did not succeed. It would be better to do nothing at all if they could not agree upon the measures to be taken.[74]

Salisbury, in effect, asked the same questions. British public opinion, he emphasized, would never condone the use of Turkish troops to force Alexander out of Rumelia and to reoccupy the province. When it appeared that the sultan might order his army to march, the British government informed the Turks that an attack on Bulgaria would immediately open the way for a Serbian and Greek war against the Ottoman Empire.[75] In regard to the Russian policy of the *status quo ante,* the British position has been summarized as follows:

The British government could put forth plausible, but not particularly logical, arguments against the Russian policy. Salisbury had been quite willing for Austria to use threats of force in order to restrain the Serbians, and he could not deny that a reversal of the unification would have the welcome effect of depriving Serbia and Greece of all excuse for intervention. Nor could the actual fact that the Berlin treaty

[73] Corti, *DTD*, pp. 375–376.

[74] Lobanov to Giers, *NKG*, Sept. 14/26, 1885; Medlicott, "Unification," pp. 263, 269.

[75] Medlicott, "Unification," p. 276; Staal to Giers, *Staal*, no. 168, Nov. 15/27, 1885; *ibid.*, no. 169, Nov. 15/27, 1885.

had been violated be denied. His real objective was stated in a private letter to Lord Lyon on the 16th [of October]. "This proposal is obviously intended to upset Prince Alexander, and, if we acquiesce, we may find ourselves with a big Bulgaria under a Russian Prince."[76]

When the great powers reached a deadlock, King Milan decided to take matters into his own hands. The developments in Bulgaria had come as a great shock to him. In his opinion the union would be a threat to Serbian independence. He could not forget the developments of the past fifteen years, beginning with the establishment of the Bulgarian exarchate. Russian sponsorship of Bulgarian claims in this period had been highly detrimental to the interests of Serbia and to her position as a power in the Balkan Peninsula. Milan was certain that Bulgaria would never rest satisfied until the boundaries of San Stefano were again realized. The Russian government was perfectly willing to support this goal, given the proper time and favorable conditions, but Serbia could not tolerate such an extension of Bulgarian influence under any circumstance. When Serbia lost the possibility of expansion westward after Austria-Hungary occupied Bosnia-Hercegovina, only the path to the south remained open. The secret treaty of 1881 prepared for a move in this direction. The re-creation of the San Stefano Bulgaria would prevent Serbian expansion southward; moreover, the shift in relative power would relegate Serbia to a position much inferior to that of Bulgaria and she would be hopelessly landlocked. Thereafter, Serbia would face the danger of being partitioned between Bulgaria and the Dual Monarchy. Milan saw it as his duty to keep the avenue of expansion to the south open; otherwise, he believed, Serbia was doomed.[77] Hence he strongly supported the Russian demands for the restoration of the *status quo ante* and the defense of the Treaty of Berlin. Should Bulgaria remain united, he would go to war to obtain compensation. To back up his threat, he ordered the army mobilized, with the concurrence of the Skupština.[78]

Serbian historians have praised Milan for his understanding of the importance of Macedonia to the Serbian state, but they have severely criticized his failure to make his views clear to his subjects in 1885. His bellicose attitude on Bulgarian unification made him extremely unpopular. The Progressive ministry followed his orders, but without

---

[76] Medlicott, "Unification," p. 268; Staal to Giers, *Staal*, no. 160, Oct. 23/Nov. 4, 1885.

[77] In May, 1885, Milan told Khevenhüller that he would be prepared to enlarge Serbia's boundaries in a southerly direction either if a general Balkan war broke out or if Bulgaria and Rumelia were united. Khevenhüller to Kalnoky, *HHS*, XIX 19, no. 34A–C, vertraulich, Nish, May 3, 1885.

[78] Jovanović, *Milan*, III, 219–238; Jovanović, *SBR*, pp. 63–75.

enthusiasm or conviction. The Radicals expressed open opposition to Milan because of their sympathy for the Liberal party in Bulgaria, which had given political asylum to the Serbian refugees and whose political views were much the same as their own.

The Radicals were interested also in promoting Balkan union and Slavic solidarity; a war between Serbia and Bulgaria was deeply antipathetic to them. Their attitude was shared by the Serbian Liberals, who, although they recognized the need for compensation, felt that it should be taken at the expense of the Ottoman Empire and not of Bulgaria. Throughout 1885 many meetings were held in Serbia by various groups in preparation for the acquisition of Macedonia. Even the Skupština secretly appropriated funds for agitation in Macedonia. The Serbs wanted this land and not a war against the union of the Bulgars, which they saw as natural and legitimate.[79] They welcomed the triumph of Bulgarian national aspirations as a step forward of the Slavic, Orthodox peoples.[80]

Although Milan was well aware of his subjects' sympathies and would himself have preferred to receive compensation in Old Serbia and Macedonia, he realized the consequences of an attack on the Ottoman Empire. Moreover, Britain, Austria-Hungary, and Germany had already agreed that if Serbia received land it would have to be from Bulgaria and not from the Turkish territories of Macedonia.[81] The war with Bulgaria was designed not only to gain additional areas, but also to weaken the neighboring state so that it would not be in a position to effect its claims in Macedonia to the detriment of those of Serbia. Milan's goal remained the acquisition of Macedonian territories, not Bulgarian, but he could not proceed at once toward his real objective. He therefore acted to protect Serbia's future interests.[82]

Milan believed that he had secured Austrian support in the treaty of 1881, but Vienna was not ready to give him unqualified assistance. The political changes in Bulgaria had been all to the advantage of Austria. Kalnoky had no interest in endangering the Dreikaiserbund or in defeating the anti-Russian Prince Alexander. Consequently, even though Kalnoky recognized the justice of the Serbian claim to compensation if the *status quo ante* were not restored, he nevertheless repeatedly

[79] Schiessl to Kalnoky, *HHS*, XIX 19, no. 19, Belgrade, March 6, 1885; *ibid.*, no. 22A–B, Belgrade, March 13, 1885; Khevenhüller to Kalnoky, *HHS*, XIX 19, no. 25A–B, vertraulich, Belgrade, March 20, 1885; *ibid.*, no. 35C, Belgrade, May 10, 1885.

[80] Jovanović, *Milan*, III, 225, 239, 253–258.

[81] Medlicott, "Unification," pp. 77–78, 282, 284.

[82] Milan, of course, hoped that his action would precipitate an Austro-Russian war. Jovanović, *Milan*, III, 223, 301.

urged Milan to let Austria-Hungary handle the Serbian demands, and to withdraw Serbian troops from the frontier until the great powers had reached a solution.[83] He did not, however, tell Milan that if Serbia went to war the Dual Monarchy would abandon him.

Although Milan listened to this advice, he had little confidence in Kalnoky. He preferred to heed the words of the Austrian war party and the Magyar extremists, just as the Serbian government, in 1876, had accepted the opinions of the Panslavs rather than those of the tsar and the Russian foreign office.[84] The man who was closest to Milan and who had the greatest influence on him was Khevenhüller, the Austrian minister in Belgrade.[85] Although there is no evidence that Khevenhüller failed to convey to the king the exact views of his government, it appears that during his term of duty in Belgrade he was never averse to expressing his personal views. In numerous talks with Milan during the crisis, Khevenhüller urged the adoption of an aggressive policy. He agreed that the union must be prevented in order to forestall the loss of Macedonia, for the sake of both Serbia and the Dual Monarchy. The creation of a strong Serbia, he was convinced, was Austria's best protection against Russian influence in the Balkans. In his support of the Serbian claims, he went so far as to tell the British minister in Belgrade that, since Serbia could not expand westward, her "only outlet therefore was toward Macedonia and Old Serbia, through Sofia [!] which town with its surrounding districts ought, in his opinion, to have been assigned to Serbia in 1878."[86] It was the advice of Khevenhüller, not of Kalnoky, which Milan finally accepted.

The possibility of a Balkan war had been a matter of concern to the Russian government from the beginning of the crisis. When the Bulgarian delegation visited the tsar in Copenhagen, he had warned of possible trouble with Serbia. Giers feared that Milan would commit some rash act to restore his prestige among the Serbs. Action against the Moslem Turks was one matter, but conflict between Serbia and Bulgaria was distinctly against the interests of Russia. An open struggle over Macedonia would jeopardize the Russian attempt to effect a reconciliation among the Balkan Orthodox churches and, at the same time,

[83] Medlicott, "Unification," pp. 76–77, 265, 271–272; Jovanović, *Milan*, III, 227–229, 234, 240; Nelidov to Giers, *NKG*, Pera, Nov. 21, 1885.

[84] Jovanović, *Milan*, III, 243–244, 249–253. The pressure against Kalnoky from Crown Prince Rudolf and the Magyars was so great that only the support of Franz Joseph kept him in office.

[85] Khevenhüller himself wrote: "Der König ist gewohnt sehr mit mir zu reden, vielleicht zu offen! Seine Wünsche, Pläne, ja ich möchte sagen, seine fixen Ideen sind mir vollkommen geläusig." Khevenhüller to Kalnoky, *HHS*, XIX 19, no. 39A–B, vertraulich, Belgrade, May 15, 1885.

[86] Wyndham to Salisbury, *FO*, 105/55, no. 10, Belgrade, Jan. 5, 1886.

to strengthen the power of the exarch in the region. The Russian government thus supported the Habsburg government with counsels of restraint to Serbia.[87]

Before launching the attack, Milan sought an understanding with the Porte. The sultan agreed to remain neutral if the war were solely for the restoration of the *status quo ante* and not for the acquisition of territorial compensation. On October 27/November 8, Kalnoky, recognizing the hopelessness of the situation, told Bismarck emphatically that a Serbo-Bulgarian war should not be allowed to affect the Dreikaiser-bund; Giers, speaking without the authorization of the tsar, concurred. On November 2/14 the Serbian attack commenced.[88]

In declaring war on Bulgaria, Milan, instead of basing his action on the preservation of the Berlin treaty, preferred to follow the advice of Khevenhüller that a minor border violation by Bulgarian troops be used as the immediate pretext. Milan repeated the charges he had previously made against Bulgaria because of her position on the Bregovo incident and the problem of Serbian refugees in Bulgaria.[89] The latter issue was still a vital one in Serbian politics. Milan's officials had only recently seized a circular signed by Nikola Pašić and Peka Pavlović, whom Milan considered in the pay of Russia. The pamphlet was addressed to the Serbian people and declared in part, "The moment has come for us to rise and throw off the yoke which has endeavored to separate Serbia from the other Slavic people; overthrow the officials who have been imposed upon you and replace them with those of your own choice."[90]

This call for revolution, together with a letter purportedly written by Pašić to a friend in Russia, which stated that it was necessary to place one of the grand princes of Russia on the Serbian throne, was enough to convince the king that Russia was planning to depose him.[91]

The general impression in Europe and in the Balkans was that a Serbian victory was inevitable: first, because the Serbian military forces were considered superior; and second, because Russia's recall of her officers was believed to have been a disaster for the Bulgarian army. This analysis appeared to be confirmed by the first engagement of the campaign. Hostilities began on November 2/14, 1885, and by November 6/18 the fall of Sofia seemed imminent. Metropolitan Kliment was even

---

[87] Giers to Staal, *Staal*, no. 166, Nov. 11/23, 1885; Geshov, *op. cit.*, p. 143; Medlicott, "Unification," pp. 270–272; Radev, I, 579–580.
[88] Jovanović, *Milan*, III, 239–240; Medlicott, "Unification," pp. 282–284.
[89] Jovanović, *Milan*, III, 268.
[90] *Ibid.*, p. 268.
[91] Jovanović, *Vlada Aleksandra Obrenovića*, I, 137; Jovanović, *Milan*, III, 545–551; Radev, I, 605–606.

ready to meet the Serbian army in order to declare Sofia an open city.[92] On the morning of November 6/18 General Kantakuzin informed the Bulgars that "everything is finished; by evening the Serbs will be here [Sofia]."[93] On the same day Koiander expressed similar sentiments. When the latter was asked what the Bulgars should do, he replied that only one course was open—to appeal to the tsar as Milan had done in 1876.[94]

The Russian representatives, like the leaders of the great powers, were convinced that Bulgaria was doomed to defeat. It was hoped that the catastrophe would prove to the Bulgars the futility of their independent, anti-Russian policy and would lead to the overthrow of the prince. The Russian agents, however, failed to consider what would happen if Serbia, not Bulgaria, were the defeated nation.

On November 7/19 the news reached Sofia that the Bulgarian army had routed the Serbs at Slivnica. At first the information was discounted, since preparations had been made to receive the Serbian troops in Sofia. Subsequent reports confirmed the unexpected developments. Alexander of Battenberg, displaying real talent in the field, had been able to bring some of his troops from Rumelia. The young Bulgarians who had assumed the positions vacated by the Russian officers had filled their posts with distinction and honor. The tide of battle had been abruptly turned, and the Serbian troops were in full retreat. With each hour the prestige of Alexander of Battenberg and the Bulgarian army rose. As the Bulgarian forces marched into Serbia and approached Niš, there was even speculation that they might be able to accomplish what the Serbs had failed to do, namely, occupy the enemy capital.[95]

The sudden reversal of Serbian fortunes found the Habsburg government totally unprepared. If Milan had triumphed, his position in Serbia would have been strongly reinforced, but his dismal failure as a war lord meant that his overthrow and the establishment of the Karadjordjević dynasty in Belgrade were again dangerously imminent. Austria-Hungary was faced with the necessity of direct intervention. Milan, panic-stricken, had already demanded Austrian action.[96] Kalnoky requested the Ottoman Empire to try to arrange an armistice. When this failed, he telegraphed on November 12/24 to Biegeleben, the Austrian minister in Sofia, to urge Alexander not to pursue Milan into Serbia: "This might force us to take up a position which would have disastrous

---

[92] Trifonov, *op. cit.*, p. 127.
[93] Radev, I, 667.
[94] *Ibid.*, p. 668; Jovanović, *Milan*, III, 270.
[95] The military details of the war are found in Jovanović, *SBR*, pp. 134–153; Jovanović, *Milan*, III, 260–297; Radev, I, 629–723.
[96] Jovanović, *Milan*, III, 290–293.

consequences for the situation as a whole and also for him personally."[97]
This message failed to reach the prince, since he had forbidden the dispatch of all cipher telegrams once hostilities began. Austria-Hungary,
Russia, and Germany then sent identical notes to Sofia and Belgrade
demanding the cessation of hostilities. Naturally, Serbia agreed, but
Bulgaria, flushed with victory, continued to march, and on November
15/27 Pirot was occupied. Milan, now desperate, was ready to abdicate.
In this crisis, Kalnoky abandoned the policy of joint action with his
two allies and sought unilaterally to stem the Bulgarian advance.[98]

On November 16/28 he ordered his representative in Serbia to go personally to Alexander's headquarters to deliver Austria's "friendly advice." Khevenhüller's instructions were:

> ... make most serious representations to him [Alexander] concerning the immediate
> cessation of hostilities and the acceptance of an armistice, as it would be unscrupu-
> lous to allow the war to expand to unforeseen dimensions. I leave it to Your Excel-
> lency to employ the necessary arguments and beg of you not to adopt a threatening
> but rather a friendly tone, for the purpose of your mission is a peaceful one and
> we have certainly no interest in estranging the Prince of Bulgaria. If circumstances
> render it necessary, will Your Excellency firmly explain to the Prince that he would
> come into conflict with Austria-Hungary if he does not follow our present friendly
> advice.[99]

Armed with this information, Khevenhüller arrived at Alexander's
headquarters on November 16/28, after passing through the military
outposts. The Austrian minister informed the prince that his mission
should not be considered as a threat or an ultimatum, but, nevertheless,
the advice of Austria should be heeded. When Alexander refused to
agree to the Austrian proposal, Khevenhüller, on his own initiative,
delivered what was in effect an ultimatum: any further advance of the
Bulgarian armies would bring Austrian troops to the defense of Serbia.
Simultaneously, Russia would occupy Bulgaria.

Prior to this, Alexander had received messages from his father urging
him to sign an armistice. Even Great Britain, who had opposed the
stand of the Dreikaiserbund, urged him to end hostilities, but, at the
same time, to press for recognition of the union. The advice of his
friends, as well as the threats of Khevenhüller, induced the prince to
yield. Moreover, his troops were suffering from the winter cold, and
supplies were low. In view of this unpromising situation, Alexander
gave up the campaign and consented to make peace. The war had lasted
two weeks.[100]

---

[97] Corti, *Alexander*, p. 263.
[98] Langer, *European Alliances* ... , pp. 354–356.
[99] Corti, *Alexander*, p. 267.
[100] *Ibid.*, pp. 267–270; Jovanović, *Milan*, III, 297–300, 551–552; Radev, I, 729–
730; Lascelles to Salisbury, *FO*, 78/3771, no. 213, Sofia, Dec. 28, 1885.

Although Khevenhüller's mission had been successful in stopping the war, he had gone far beyond his instructions. His warning of a possible Russian occupation of Bulgaria drew vigorous protests from the tsar, Giers, and the Russian press. The unilateral nature of the Austrian action, together with its expressed threat of a military occupation of Serbia, was not in harmony with the Dreikaiserbund agreement. Although Russia was as deeply concerned in ending the war as was Austria, Khevenhüller's remarks on possible Russian action were injurious to her relations with Bulgaria. It appeared that Russia was indeed willing to use force to impose her will on the Bulgarian people. Giers, who had been informed of the general purpose of Khevenhüller's mission and had approved it, now termed the threat "completely inadmissible."[101]

Bismarck, even more critical of the Austrian action, considered that the Dreikaiserbund had been seriously endangered by Kalnoky and Khevenhüller. When Kalnoky sought to justify his intention of sending Austrian troops into Serbia by saying that it would be only a temporary occupation, Bismarck replied with the obvious query: Would Austria under similar circumstances be ready to permit a temporary occupation of Rumania, Bulgaria, or Constantinople by Russia?[102] Later, Kalnoky publicly repudiated Khevenhüller's remarks and informed Russia that they were "regrettable" and went beyond his instructions. Kalnoky was obliged to give assurances to both Russia and Germany that Austria would not march into Serbia without first informing her allies. The tension between Vienna and St. Petersburg over the incident gradually subsided, much to the relief of Giers. He deplored the Austrian move, but, like Bismarck, he did not wish to disrupt the alliance which was the cornerstone of Russian policy at the time.[103]

The great powers next concentrated on the settlement of the conflict. Milan, in an attempt to exonerate himself, blamed the defeat on everyone, including his wife. At one point he even talked of renewing hostilities. Finally he was forced to accept the decision of the armistice commission for a joint, simultaneous withdrawal of Serbian and Bulgarian troops, with Serbia making the start. Milan had hoped to force Alexander to withdraw first, thus saving some of his prestige out of the fiasco. The final peace was signed on February 19/March 3, 1886, and consisted of one article: "Peace is restored between Serbia and Bulgaria."[104]

[101] Corti, *Alexander*, p. 269; Langer, *op. cit.*, p. 356; Morier to Salisbury, *FO*, 65/1219, no. 411, most conf., St. P., Dec. 2, 1885; Schweinitz to Auswärtige Amt, *GP*, V, no. 967, St. P., Nov. 30, 1885.
[102] Bismarck to Reuss, *GP*, V, no. 969, Berlin, Dec. 6, 1885; *ibid.*, no. 972, Berlin, Dec. 13, 1885.
[103] Nolde, *L'alliance franco-russe*, pp. 333–367.
[104] Jovanović, *Milan*, III, 301–310.

In Serbia, Milan was now forced to bear the full responsibility for the defeat in what was termed "Milan's war." Certainly, his policy had ended in failure. Unity had been maintained between St. Petersburg and Vienna despite the king's desire to see the outbreak of a Russo-Austrian war. Nor had Milan been able to achieve compensation in any direction. The great powers had prevented his acquisition of Turkish lands, the area to which his subjects preferred to turn their attention. Bulgarian arms had proved too strong when he tried to seize the territories which the powers would have allowed him if he had won the war. The defeat, together with his unpopularity within Serbia, forced the king to rely now almost entirely on the Dual Monarchy. The opposition parties, in turn, looked with increasing favor on Russia. In this split, Milan's separation from Natalija played a major role. The queen more than ever became the center of the Russophil circle; the king led those who supported the ties with Austria-Hungary.[105]

Whereas the war had gravely weakened Milan, it gained for Prince Alexander a strong bargaining position which he exploited to the full. His personal position was for the moment unassailable. He had defied the Russians and led the movement for union; Russia had sought to break the new nation by forcing a return to the *status quo ante*. Alexander had then taken to arms to defend the united Bulgaria. His prestige as a national hero reached a peak after the battle of Slivnica. The mistakes of the past, the skepticism and even hostility of his subjects, were forgotten before his display of diplomatic skill and military courage.[106]

The Bulgarian victory signified that the results of the Rumelian revolution could not be reversed. Without the use of force neither Russia nor the suzerain Ottoman Empire could restore the *status quo ante*. Nothing so well confirmed the Bulgarian success as Kalnoky's judgment that the ambassadors' conference at Constantinople, which had been organized by Russia, had failed and should no longer meet. Soon thereafter, Giers acknowledged that the union could not be dissolved. Alexander of Battenberg had thus defied Russia with success; throughout Europe the unification was regarded as a distinct victory of the prince over the tsar.[107]

The adverse result of the Balkan crisis was difficult for the Russians to accept. They had suffered two defeats: both the union and the war had taken place against their wishes. The extremist element among the

---

[105] *Loc. cit.*

[106] Marinov, *Stefan Stambolov*, p. 263.

[107] Morier to Salisbury, *FO*, 65/1219, no. 435, secret, St. P., Dec. 21, 1885; *ibid.*, 65/1220, tel. no. 77, conf., St. P., Dec. 23, 1885.

Panslavs was willing to wage a war against the German power and the "German prince." The tsar, in fact, had to issue a warning to the newspaper *Rus'* to temper its bellicose language.[108] Alexander III was, however, primarily responsible for the results of Russian policy, since he had made all the final decisions in the critical days after the union had been proclaimed. Giers, who had worked steadfastly to preserve the Dreikaiserbund and prevent a complete breakdown of the Balkan situation, described the recent events in a conversation with Morier. In order to understand the difficulties in Bulgaria, he explained, one had to consider the past.

> The internal administration of Bulgaria was from the beginning thoroughly badly composed. The employees sent from Russia . . . were worse than ill-chosen, many of them representing the scum of their respective professions—but this was not the worst; as very many were so tainted with ultrarevolutionary and even nihilistic doctrines—On the other hand the Bulgarians of sufficient education and knowledge to be appointed to civil posts had to a man been educated in the Russian universities where they had been poisoned with the anarchic views which unfortunately had so entirely prevailed there.[109]

All this, continued Giers, signified that a "Russian anti-Russian" administration had been formed in Bulgaria. Once these men got into power, they declared "war on all that Russia held most sacred." They attacked the church and recruited their teachers from among the Russian emigrants in Geneva. Finally, they produced the Plovdiv revolution. Consequently, said Giers, Russia had a different perspective on Bulgarian developments from that of the west. It was particularly important to understand the reaction of the tsar.

> [He] still lived as it were in the shadow of his father's assassination. How was such a movement to affect him in which the brother disciples of his father's murderers had a hand? Hence, unless the burning sense of ingratitude manifested by the Bulgarians, or rather by the leaders they blindly followed, such as it was felt by the Russian people, was realized, the altogether different ground in reference to Bulgarian affairs which Russia occupied as compared with all other countries could not be understood.[110]

---

[108] Grosvenor to Salisbury, *FO*, 65/1218, no. 352, St. P., Oct. 16, 1885.

[109] Giers' conservative outlook was shared by his assistant and confidant, Vlangali. Writing immediately after the union, Vlangali lamented the events in Bulgaria which had become "the center of nihilism." Serbia also had her problems. However, in Serbia the king was a conservative. The actions of the king, he continued, vacillated first in one direction and then in another. The Liberals—whom he considered to be radicals, revolutionaries, nihilists—carried their activities to an extreme, in one direction only. Consequently, Vlangali was able to justify Austria's dominant role in Serbia because, after all, the Dual Monarchy was "still a conservative state." Vlangali to Giers, *NKG*, Sept. 21, Sept. 24/Oct. 6, 1885.

[110] Morier to Salisbury, *FO*, 65/1219, no. 384C, secret and conf., Nov. 11, 1885. See also Brief an Graf Welsersheimb, *HHS*, X 76, vertraulich, Vienna, April 19, 1886.

Giers stated that he knew that Prince Alexander did not have any sympathy with the revolution or revolutionaries and that his tendencies were autocratic. Nevertheless, he had seized upon the revolution in order to present the tsar with a *fait accompli.*

He committed the immense blunder of not seeing that, in touching the revolutionary note, he struck that which, on every ground, was certain to estrange the tsar from him. From this capital error all else flowed. From leading he became the tail of the revolutionary party, and, allowing his temper to get the better of him, he indulged in language deeply wounding to the tsar and to the honor of Russia.[111]

In concluding the conversation, Giers reiterated "several times and in a voice and with a tone which proved the depth of his conviction— 'we have had a lesson we can never forget and which is most wholesome for us—Never again to go forth making moral conquests with our blood and money but to think of ourselves and our own interests only.' "[112]

Giers' statement that Russia would now pursue only nationalistic aims received an even stronger confirmation from the tsar. On September 12/24, 1885, Alexander III wrote to Obruchev, Russian chief of staff, concerning the problem of the Straits and the possibility of a Russian occupation of Constantinople: "Everything else that takes place in the Balkan Peninsula is secondary for us. There has been enough propaganda to the detriment of the true interests of Russia. The Slavs must now serve us and not we them."[113]

---

[111] Morier to Salisbury, *FO*, 65/1219, no. 384C, secret and conf., Nov. 11, 1885.
[112] *Ibid.*
[113] "Zapiska A. I. Nelidova v 1882 g. o Zaniatii Prolivov," *Krasnyi Arkhiv*, XLVI (1931), 180 n. 1.

X

THE COLLAPSE OF RUSSIA'S BULGARIAN
POLICY

THE UNION of the Bulgarias, a great personal triumph for the prince and a humiliation for the tsar, as well as a defeat "for all of Russia,"[1] resulted in a further shift in Russian policy toward Bulgaria. When the powers failed to reëstablish the *status quo ante,* the Russian government realized that further efforts in this direction would not be to its advantage. The Bulgarian people were interested primarily in national unity, and Alexander had become the symbol of Bulgarian nationalism. If Russia could prove to the Bulgars that Alexander was in fact a hindrance to their advancement, Russian influence might again be dominant in Sofia. Russian policy therefore changed to that of supporting the union but of expelling the prince. In the pursuance of this aim, the Russian government abandoned all attempts to deal directly with the prince, and turned to the opposition groups and those who were actively conspiring against Alexander.

The Russian attitude toward Alexander was reflected in the opinion of Zinoviev, who as director of the Asiatic department was in charge of Bulgarian affairs. Eight days after the union had taken place, he wrote to Giers that Russia's difficulties in Bulgaria were due "exclusively" to the Bulgarian government, and that a change was absolutely essential. Bulgaria had to be cleansed of the "ulcer which had been grafted on her." Zinoviev discounted the enthusiasm of the Bulgarians for union; they were, after all, "still children" who needed a firm and stern leadership, which Russia could and should provide. Even if a suitable new candidate could be found for the Bulgarian throne, he would need the guidance of an adviser sent by the tsar.[2] Whereas a few weeks earlier, at Franzensbad, Giers had been ready to reach a *modus vivendi* with the prince, Zinoviev was now ready to work for his removal.

Alexander well knew how bitter his successes had been to the tsar. Alexander of Hesse urged his son to appeal to the tsar, to soothe his feelings, and to seek his blessing for the union. Although Alexander was not enthusiastic about this advice, he recognized its wisdom. He therefore approached the Russian representative on the military commission of the great powers, General (Baron) Kaulbars, brother of the

---

[1] Wolkenstein to Kalnoky, *HHS,* X 75, geheim, privatbrief, St. P., Oct. 14/26, 1885.
[2] Zinoviev to Giers, *NKG,* Sept. 14, 1885.

former minister of war, and asked him to intercede with the tsar on behalf of Bulgaria.

Kaulbars agreed to act as intermediary, and suggested that the prince issue an order of the day expressing Bulgaria's gratitude to the Russian instructors who had trained the Bulgarian army and made possible the victory over Serbia. Kaulbars hoped that this would detract from Alexander's prestige as a military leader and nullify the effect of the prince's condemnation of the Russian officers when the latter were recalled during the unification crisis. Alexander recognized that this gesture of appeasement would harm his relations with his Bulgarian officers, but, nevertheless, he issued an order which attributed "the victory of the Bulgarian army to some extent to their Russian instructors."[3]

On Kaulbars' suggestion the prince also sent a message to the tsar in which he expressed his gratitude to the Russian army and requested the tsar's permission to come to St. Petersburg to discuss the future relations of the two countries. On December 12/24, 1885, Alexander III replied that, although he still regarded the Bulgarian people with affection, he would not allow the prince to visit him.[4] His intention was clearly to break the unity between the prince and his subjects. The personal feelings of the tsar had now become so intense that there was little chance of reconciliation. He told the grand duke of Hesse that the prince was an anti-Russian revolutionary, that he was responsible for the revolt at Plovdiv, and that he had "told lies to Giers at Franzensbad."[5]

After this rebuff, Alexander decided to negotiate with his sovereign, the sultan. Although the union was an accomplished fact, Bulgaria and Rumelia were still in theory two separate units under the Ottoman Empire. The problems of the exact form of the union, the position of the governor-general, and the fate of the organic statute had yet to be solved. Prince Alexander naturally favored a complete union under his leadership. However, such a thoroughgoing revision of the provisions of the Treaty of Berlin could be done only through great power participation, and it was unlikely that Russia would agree.

With the support and assistance of Great Britain, who hoped that an accord between Bulgaria and the Ottoman Empire would strengthen the opposition to Russia, the prince and the sultan in February, 1886, drew up an agreement comprised of three principal points. The first

---

[3] Corti, *DTD*, p. 276; Corti, *Alexander*, p. 199; Radev, I, 759–760; Flesch to Freycinet, *DDF*, VI, no. 155, Sofia, Dec. 29, 1885. Subsequently Kaulbars denied that he had ever advised Alexander to thank the tsar for Russia's military instructors. Lascelles to Rosebery, *FO*, 78/3893, no. 19, conf., Sofia, April 15, 1886.

[4] Corti, *DTD*, p. 316.

[5] *Ibid.*, p. 319.

stated that "Prince Alexander of Bulgaria was to be the governor-general of Rumelia as long as he faithfully executed his duties," and was to be reappointed every five years in accordance with the provisions of the Treaty of Berlin. Second, if the Ottoman Empire were threatened by foreign aggression, Bulgarian and Rumelian troops would render aid; in like manner, a threat to the two provinces would bring Turkish assistance. Third, a commission was to be established to study the organic statute and to propose any changes that might be necessary. A personal union was thus approved. The two provinces were to have similar, but not the same, administrations. Bulgarian security was fortified also by the assurance of Turkish aid in the event of war.[6]

Salisbury agreed not only to support these terms but also to seek their acceptance by the other powers. The French were willing to comply, but they pointed out that the reappointment of Alexander every five years would cause periodic disturbances. Austria-Hungary took the same position, and proposed that Alexander be invested with the office for life. It was suggested that no distinction be drawn between Bulgarian and Rumelian troops. However, even without these modifications, the Habsburg government was ready to give its assent. Bismarck, although not against the treaty as such, would not accept the arrangement until Russia had consented, since he judged Russian interests in Bulgaria superior to those of Austria-Hungary and Turkey.[7]

Since the Turko-Bulgarian agreement was obviously designed to forestall any Russian move against Bulgaria and the prince, it could not be expected that the Russian government would agree to the terms. Legally, the Russian position was entirely correct, since the agreement was in violation of the Treaty of Berlin. Russia particularly objected to the article calling for mutual assistance. Russia, stated Giers, could not condone terms which might oblige Christian Bulgars to support the infidel Turks against Christians in areas such as Macedonia and Montenegro.[8] Undoubtedly the Russian government realized that these same troops could be used against Russia. Despite the Turkish arguments that these troops, after all, were from territories under Ottoman sovereignty, the Russians refused to consent.[9]

[6] Corti, *Alexander*, pp. 290–291; Said Pasha to Rustem Pasha, *AP*, LXXV:2, no. 124, Constantinople, Feb. 2, 1886; White to Salisbury, *AP*, LXXV:2, no. 87, Constantinople, Jan. 20, 1886.

[7] Salisbury to White, *AP*, LXXV:2, no. 132, Foreign Office, Feb. 4, 1886; Scott to Salisbury, *AP*, LXXV:2, no. 148, Berlin, Feb. 6, 1886; Lascelles to Rosebery, *AP*, LXXV:2, no. 155, Sofia, Feb. 9, 1886; Lyons to Rosebery, *AP*, LXXV:2, no. 156, Paris, Feb. 9, 1886.

[8] Morier to Rosebery, *AP*, LXXV:2, no. 190, St. P., Feb. 10, 1886; *ibid.*, no. 278, St. P., Feb. 17, 1886; Süreya to Grand Vizir, *BD*, no. 120, Feb. 8, 1886.

[9] Morier to Rosebery, *AP*, LXXV:2, no. 190, St. P., Feb. 10, 1886; Süreya to Grand Vizir, *BD*, no. 127, Feb. 19, 1886.

Hitherto both the prince and the sultan had relied on British support. When Gladstone replaced Salisbury in February, the British attitude shifted, leaving Bulgaria and Turkey to face Russia alone.[10] Austria-Hungary, while favoring the agreement, had no desire to stir up a fresh quarrel with Russia. The two states therefore decided that the Russian objections on the military clause would have to be met, although Alexander remarked that "the whole arrangement" was based on this provision.[11] In yielding to Russia on this vital point, both the Bulgarian and Turkish governments expected to ensure Russian approval for the other clauses. Instead, the Russian government objected to the first article of the treaty, which mentioned Alexander by name as the governor of Eastern Rumelia. The omission of his name would make it possible for Russia to secure his removal either as prince of Bulgaria or as governor of Eastern Rumelia, and thereby break the union. Russia also demanded that any changes in the organic statute should be submitted to the great powers for "an *ex post facto* sanction."[12] Lacking great power support, first the Ottoman Empire and then Bulgaria were forced to accept these modifications.

Alexander had not been enthusiastic about the original agreement. He especially disliked the provision which called for his reappointment every five years, which, he claimed, "would encourage every description of intrigue, would allow of his position, not only in Eastern Rumelia, but also as prince of Bulgaria, to be called in question every five years."[13] He claimed that I. Tsanov, his foreign minister, had made a mistake in agreeing to this condition and that he, the prince, would not accept it.[14] For two weeks after the conclusion of the negotiations, he maintained his defiant attitude. When he saw that the powers were going to approve the terms despite his views, he finally submitted, in April, 1886. Alexander thereby became governor-general of Eastern Rumelia for five years and the Bulgarias were united only in his person.[15]

[10] White to Rosebery, *FO*, 78/3869, no. 73, secret, Pera, Feb. 15, 1886; White to Rosebery, *AP*, LXXV:2, no. 204, Constantinople, Feb. 12, 1886; Corti, *Alexander*, p. 291.

[11] Lascelles to Rosebery, *FO*, 78/3892, no. 58, Sofia, Feb. 14, 1886; Süreya to Grand Vizir, *BD*, no. 129, March 7, 1886.

[12] Morier to Rosebery, *AP*, LXXV:2, no. 190, St. P., Feb. 10, 1886; *ibid.*, no. 233, St. P., Feb. 21, 1886.

[13] Said Pasha to Rustem Pasha, *AP*, LXXV:2, no. 321, March 4, 1886; Lascelles to Rosebery, *AP*, LXXV:2, no. 350, Sofia, March 12, 1886; Thornton to Rosebery, *FO*, 78/3869, no. 130, Constantinople, March 20, 1886.

[14] Lascelles to Rosebery, *AP*, LXXV:2, no. 350, Sofia, March 12, 1886; *ibid.*, no. 428, Sofia, April 1, 1886.

[15] *Ibid.*, no. 450, Sofia, April 12, 1886; Süreya to Grand Vizir, *BD*, no. 132, March 8, 1886; Zinoviev to Giers, *NKG*, April 15, 1886. See also Giers to Staal, *Staal*, no. 13, March 9/21, 1886; *ibid.*, no. 14, March 11/23, 1886; *ibid.*, no. 15, March 13/25. 1886.

The form of the union finally agreed upon was a victory for Russia, which clearly demonstrated that she was still recognized as the power with primary interest in Bulgaria. Alexander himself fully realized the significance of what had happened. Later he wrote to Queen Victoria that the failure of the original Turko-Bulgarian treaty and the subsequent signing of the protocol in the form desired by Russia was "my political death warrant."[16] The prince had assumed the leadership of the movement for unification, and he had protected it from the Serbs, but he had failed to persuade the great powers to establish a uniform administration for the two provinces. The relation between the two Bulgarias remained ambiguous; the prince was the only bond between them. The *status quo ante* had not been reëstablished, but neither had full union been achieved.

The April treaty disillusioned many Bulgars. It was obvious that the prince was *persona non grata* with the one power which had the greatest control over Bulgaria's destiny. Whereas formerly the majority of Bulgarians had been willing to credit the prince for the success of the Plovdiv revolt, they now saw him as the obstacle to real union. Alexander was increasingly a victim of intrigue and betrayal.[17]

On his return to St. Petersburg after the Serbo-Bulgarian war, General Kaulbars stated in the presence of the tsar that the unification and the victorious war had made Alexander so popular that within two years he would become king of Bulgaria. Alexander III replied that, on the contrary, within six months the Bulgars would be trying to get rid of the prince.[18] Both the tsar and the general were in error; plans for the prince's removal were already being formulated.

In the first years of its autonomous existence the young Bulgarian state was administered by men of varying degrees of capability, many of whom were outright opportunists. A typical example of the latter was Dragan Tsankov. Like many young Bulgars, he had studied in Russia but returned home a Russophobe. He even became one of the leaders of the Uniate movement in the 'sixties, although he subsequently abandoned it to work for the liberation of Bulgaria. After 1878 he occupied a prominent position in the Liberal party, and in 1880 became the first prime minister chosen from that party. In 1882 he was interned, but soon released, by the government. When the constitution was restored in 1883, he again served as prime minister, a post which he relinquished to

---

[16] Buckle, *Victoria*, 3d ser., I, 208.

[17] Lascelles to Rosebery, *FO*, 78/3892, no. 84, Sofia, March 19, 1886; Corti, *DTD*, p. 319.

[18] Kartsov, *Sem Liet na Blizhnem Vostoke, 1879–1886*, pp. 276–277; Radev, I, 760–761.

Karavelov in the summer of 1884. During these years, despite his affiliation with the Liberals, he retained much of his earlier dislike of Russia.

Gradually Tsankov began to question the wisdom of the policy of defying Russia, and, after his defeat in 1884, he advocated closer coöperation with the tsar. During the next decade he became the unofficial spokesman for Russia in Bulgaria. He maintained liaison with the Russian representatives in the Balkans, and also met with Giers and the tsar. Ultimately, he was convinced that Russian support had to be gained even at the price of an occupation or the appointment of a Russian as ruler of Bulgaria.

During most of 1885 Tsankov remained in close touch with Koiander, and they often discussed plans for Alexander's removal. Their activities were interrupted by the unification crisis, but were resumed in December. On December 17/29 Koiander wrote to I. A. Zinoviev, director of the Asiatic department, that Tsankov, prior to his departure from St. Petersburg, had confided to him that:

... his material position was extremely difficult and that for the last year and a half [i.e., since he was replaced as prime minister] he lived exclusively on money which was loaned to him by his friends and followers. At the present time this source is completely exhausted and he does not have any means for further existence. In view of these needs he is compelled to turn to the imperial government with a plea to render him monetary assistance.[19]

Koiander described the important role which Tsankov had hitherto played in Bulgarian politics. Although he had lost some of his influence recently through his own errors and the intrigues of others, Koiander expected him to regain his prestige. Formerly, Tsankov had worked against Russia, mainly because she supported the prince, but now he recognized that Bulgaria could not survive under present conditions. He was therefore willing to accept Russian interference in Bulgarian internal affairs and even a temporary Russian administration as the only means of salvation for the principality. In concluding his report, Koiander urged that Tsankov be used to discredit the prince and his government and hasten the day of their removal from office. He recommended that Tsankov be given 12,000 francs from the occupation fund.

Tsankov's plans and Koiander's views indicate the nature of the relationship between the Bulgarian politician and the Russian representative. Tsankov also approached Koiander's successor, P. M. Bogdanov, former secretary in the consulate. A week after Koiander wrote his letter, Bogdanov telegraphed Giers that Tsankov, M. Balabanov, and T. Burmov were planning to publish a newspaper in order to show

[19] Koiander to Zinoviev, *Avantiury*, no. 4, St. P., Dec. 17/29, 1885. See also Lascelles to Salisbury, *FO*, 78/3892, no. 36, Sofia, Jan. 25, 1886.

that the present anti-Russian policy of the government was contrary to the true interests of Bulgaria. Burmov wished to go to Russia to raise a public subscription for the paper. Since it was desirable to start publication immediately, on January 1/13, 1886, Tsankov asked for a Russian subsidy of 6,000 francs. When this telegram was shown to the tsar, he wrote on the margin, "He has already been given 12,000 francs."[20]

Through the expenditure of money from the occupation fund, the Russian government thus obtained the services of the former prime minister of Bulgaria and a newspaper through which its views could be disseminated. The name first proposed for the newspaper was *Sredets* (The Moderator). Tsankov suggested *San Stefanskaia Bulgariia* (San Stefano Bulgaria). When Zinoviev decided that the latter title was unwise, *Svetlina* (Light) was chosen. Bogdanov told the opposition leaders that the newspaper was not to be exclusively for party matters; its purpose was to explain to the Bulgars "their true interest."

In order to assist the paper further, Giers instructed Bogdanov, on March 21/April 2, to give Tsankov, Burmov, and Balabanov an additional 40,000 francs from the occupation fund. In a written affidavit the three Bulgarian politicians agreed to abide by the wishes of the Russian government, and promised that their attitude would not change should they return to power in Bulgaria.[21] With the acceptance of the subsidy, *Svetlina* became an organ of the Russian government. Its articles repeatedly emphasized that the interests of Russia in Bulgaria were such that the tsarist government could not look with indifference on the developments within the principality. As tension between the states mounted, the paper even suggested that if Russia were forced to occupy Bulgaria, it would be a second liberation. As could be expected, the Turko-Bulgarian treaty was severely criticized on the grounds that it would neither aid Bulgaria nor lead to a reconciliation with Russia. It would only satisfy the "self-seeking" ambitions of the prince.[22]

The arguments of Tsankov and his supporters fell on fertile ground. The Bulgarian economy was not strong. The war with Serbia, although short and victorious, had taxed Bulgarian resources. The heaviest burden fell on the Bulgarian peasant, who had always felt a greater admiration for Russia than had the more prosperous classes.

The dissatisfaction within Bulgaria was reflected in the division

---

[20] Bogdanov to Giers, *Avantiury*, tel. no. 5, Dec. 24, 1885/Jan. 5, 1886; Giers to Bogdanov, *Avantiury*, tel. no. 6, Dec. 26, 1885/Jan. 7, 1886.

[21] Bogdanov to Giers, *Avantiury*, tel. no. 7, April 5/17, 1886; *ibid.*, no. 8, April 5/17, 1886; Radev, I, 790–791.

[22] Lascelles to Rosebery, *FO*, 78/3892, no. 68, Sofia, Feb. 23, 1886; *ibid.*, 78/3893, no. 128, Sofia, May 1, 1886.

which had developed in the Liberal party. One faction, recognizing the sentiment in the country and the obvious advantages of Russian aid, supported Tsankov's position. The other remained firm in its adherence to the prince's policy. Karavelov, although unwilling to coöperate with Tsankov, began to make overtures to the Russians, for which he was strongly criticized by the Russophobe wing of the party. The latter attacked Karavelov's action in yielding to the Ottoman Empire two small areas inhabited by Bulgarians. Thus, even the ruling party in Sofia was not unified, nor did it give unqualified support to the prince's defiance of Russia.[23]

Russian partisans and Russian officials were active in Eastern Rumelia also. Since this province had not experienced direct Russian rule, its inhabitants were inclined to be less critical of Russian activities. Moreover, its people had discovered that union with Bulgaria was not an unmixed blessing. After the unification, Karavelov proceeded to introduce much-needed reforms in civil administration, including a reduction in salaries and administrative posts. Those who lost their jobs or had their salaries reduced naturally looked with disfavor on the regime in power.[24] Russia found adherents in this group, as well as in the political circles hostile to Alexander. In investigating reports that the Russian consulate had distributed money for political ends, the British consul in Plovdiv noted that the leaders of the parties opposed to the prince were now living in comfort, although they were without employment.[25] The success gained by the Russian cause was attested by Igel'strom, Russian consul in Plovdiv, who, on May 19/31, 1886, wrote to Giers that Alexander had lost the support he had enjoyed as a result of the unification and the victory over Serbia. The Bulgarian opposition, he noted, had now taken the position that a Russian occupation of Bulgaria was both inescapable and desirable.[26]

Alexander was well aware of the mounting antagonism to his rule. In the spring and summer of 1886 two plots against his life were uncovered: the first, a threat to poison him; the second, a plan for his abduction and possible assassination. The leader of the second plot was a Russian officer, Captain Nabokov.[27] Although neither plan succeeded, the

[23] Radev, I, 784–790; Stanev, *Istoriia na Nova Bulgariia*, pp. 63–70.

[24] Thornton to Rosebery, *FO*, 78/3870, no. 166, Constantinople, April 3, 1886, enclosing Jones to Thornton, Philippopolis, March 29, 1886; Lascelles to Rosebery, *FO*, 78/3893, no. 128, Sofia, May 1, 1886.

[25] Jones to Thornton, Philippopolis, April 19, 1886, in Thornton to Rosebery, *FO*, 78/3870, no. 203, conf., Constantinople, April 23, 1886.

[26] Igel'strom to Giers, *Avantiury*, no. 9, Plovdiv, May 19/31, 1886.

[27] Corti, *Alexander*, pp. 294–295; Lascelles to Rosebery, *FO*, 78/3893, no. 136, Sofia, May 19, 1886; *ibid.*, no. 154, conf., Sofia, June 15, 1886; Welsersheimb to Kalnoky, *HHS*, X 76, no. 27B, geheim, June 4/16, 1886.

prince knew that his life was in danger, and that his failure to achieve a real union of the Bulgarias and its recognition by the powers was responsible for the uncertainty and turmoil in Bulgarian political life.

An opportunity for Alexander to advance one step farther toward his objectives and to strengthen his prestige was offered after the elections of 1886. In these the government candidates won by an overwhelming victory both in Bulgaria and Eastern Rumelia. Although in theory the two assemblies should have met in separate sessions, Alexander decided to present Europe with another *fait accompli*. He invited the representatives of both assemblies to meet jointly in Sofia on the pretext that the provinces had common problems, even though they were separately administered. This arrangement was in direct violation of the Treaty of Berlin and of the April, 1886, agreement with the Porte. Despite the fact that Russia protested and accused Alexander of having used illegal means to obtain his majorities in the assemblies, the two bodies met on June 2/14 as a single unit.[28]

In his address at the opening of the united assembly, Alexander praised his subjects for their bravery and sacrifices in behalf of the union. He emphasized that the war had united the Bulgarian people and had won the respect of Europe. Though the two provinces were technically separated, they were in fact united through the joint session of the assemblies. Nowhere in his speech did he mention the name of the tsar or Russia, as had been the custom in the past.[29] When the text of the speech was received abroad, the great powers assumed the positions taken on previous issues. Great Britain was sympathetic toward Alexander's declarations, but would not give him unqualified support. Austria-Hungary and Germany were unwilling to sacrifice the Dreikaiserbund. Russia, openly hostile, declared that the prince had again defied the powers and that, if he were not reprimanded, the Balkan states might again revolt. The Russian government tried to persuade the Porte to take measures against this development, but, although the Turkish government expressed concern, it could only benefit from the hostility between Sofia and St. Petersburg.[30]

In its reply to the prince, the assembly approved Alexander's

[28] Corti, *Alexander*, p. 295; London *Times*, June 15, 1886, p. 7; Rosebery to Morier, *FO*, 65/1255, no. 149A, Foreign Office, June 26, 1886; Thornton to Rosebery, *FO*, 78/3872, no. 323, secret, Therapia, June 23, 1886; Flesch to Freycinet, *DDF*, VI, no. 260, Sofia, June 14, 1886.

[29] Corti, *Alexander*, pp. 295–296; Lascelles to Rosebery, *FO*, 78/3893, no. 150, Sofia, June 14, 1886; London *Times*, June 15, 1886, p. 3; Marinov, *op. cit.*, pp. 267, 270–271.

[30] Thornton to Rosebery, *FO*, 78/3872, no. 330, secret, Therapia, June 25, 1886; *ibid.*, no. 334, Therapia, June 25, 1886; London *Times*, June 28, 1886, p. 5; June 30, 1886, p. 9.

declarations, with one exception. Unlike the prince, the delegates concluded their address with an expression of devotion to the tsar as the liberator and protector of Bulgaria[31]—a significant indication of the strength of Russian influence despite the Russian stand on the unification issue. Notwithstanding this rebuff, Alexander had succeeded in further uniting the administrations of his two states and again he had acted without the support of the powers.

Since Bulgaria was now isolated diplomatically, Alexander sought support from among his fellow monarchs of the neighboring Balkan states, and for a brief time became an advocate of Balkan union. He went to Bucharest to discuss the matter with King Carol. In Rumania, according to Corti, Alexander "allowed himself to be carried away by over-confidence."[32] He advocated joint action not only against Russia but also against the Ottoman Empire, with the aim of acquiring Macedonian territory and the recognition of complete Bulgarian independence from Ottoman control. Perhaps his most foolhardy remark was that "Bismarck knows and approves of my plans and will help me; I do nothing without consulting him."[33] Carol immediately relayed this information to Radowitz, the German ambassador in Constantinople, who was a close friend of Bismarck and who shared the latter's dislike for the prince. As a result of this episode, the prince was discredited and Bismarck became even more convinced of the necessity of supporting the Russian stand.

When Rumanian support thus failed to materialize, Alexander envisaged the possibility of a Balkan league under the protection of the Dual Monarchy. According to Biegeleben, Alexander had stated that his "political ideal" was an Austrian overlordship of the peninsula "wherein the internal sovereignty of each country was guaranteed." If Russia and Austria were to divide the Balkans into spheres, Alexander concluded that "every Bulgarian patriot would ten thousand times rather have the mild and just rule of Austria."[34]

By July, 1886, the internal situation in Bulgaria was generally recognized as dangerous and unstable. One of the few who challenged this conclusion was Lascelles, British minister in Sofia, who commented, "I do not see anything in the internal state of Bulgaria to justify the belief that we are on the eve of a serious crisis."[35] In contrast, the London *Times* correspondent in Constantinople reported in June that

[31] London *Times*, June 23, 1886, p. 7.
[32] Corti, *Alexander,* p. 296.
[33] *Ibid.,* p. 297.
[34] *Ibid.,* pp. 298–299.
[35] Lascelles to Rosebery, *FO,* 78/3893, no. 173, very conf., Sofia, July 10, 1886. Rosebery wrote on the report "a good despatch."

a high Turkish official had jokingly remarked, "It is the season of volcanic eruptions; and it is possible that we shall see one in the Balkan Peninsula."[36] The events of August, 1886, confirmed his judgment.

In Bulgaria, as in the other Balkan states, the army held the balance of power in internal politics. From 1879, Russian officials had recognized that their control in Bulgaria rested on the influence they held through their officers in the Bulgarian army. The withdrawal of those officers in 1885 was intended to be the trump card which would force the prince's downfall. Instead, Alexander had been able to assume real command of his troops for the first time and to use them against foreign invasion and intrigue. It appeared, thereafter, that the bonds of allegiance between the prince and his troops were firm. Alexander himself was convinced of this; he trusted his officers and men, the majority of whom enthusiastically supported and admired him. The power of the military was now greater than ever and thus potentially more dangerous.

The opposition to the prince centered in a small, dissatisfied element, which, however, was so placed that it could wield an influence superior to that of the loyal majority. Alexander's alienation of some of his officers was a product of the Serbo-Bulgarian war. In their enthusiasm to defeat the Serbs, certain officers became overconfident and exposed their troops to unnecessary dangers, or acted contrary to orders and thus threatened the success of the campaign. Alexander was forced to reprimand them, and thereafter a number of these officers nursed grievances against him. The prince had offended other officers when, at Kaulbars' suggestion, he had attributed part of the Bulgarian success against Serbia to the training given by Russian officers. Still others in the army believed that they had not been sufficiently rewarded with medals or promotions after the victory. These conflicting emotions were exploited by the Bulgarian opposition, and the Russian agents lost no time in approaching the disaffected elements.[37]

Although not all the details of the resulting conspiracy are known, there is sufficient evidence to present a fairly detailed description of what took place. Colonel Sakharov, Russian military attaché in Sofia, undertook the primary steps in organizing the opposition. The first officer to respond to his overtures was Captain Radko Dimitriev. An enthusiastic Panslav, he believed that Bulgaria, as a member of the Slavic world, should concentrate on preparing for the eventual reckon-

---

[36] London *Times*, June 14, 1886, p. 5.

[37] Stanev, *op. cit.*, pp. 63–67; Radev, I, 795–796; Thornton to Rosebery, *FO*, 78/ 3871, no. 239, conf., Constantinople, May 17, 1886.

ing with the Germans. For this purpose he was willing to see his country fall under Russian control. Sakharov also approached Captain Benderev, an officer whom Alexander had reprimanded for over-zealous conduct in the Serbian campaign. Benderev at first refused to participate and informed Captain Nikiforov, Bulgarian minister of war, who brushed the report aside as unimportant.[38]

At the beginning of 1886 Alexander's popularity was still high, but in the next few months the failure of the powers to agree to a real union, together with the growing economic crisis, led other officers to join the conspirators. The opposition leaders and the Russian agents impressed upon these men that it was solely the fault of the prince that the union had not been fully realized.[39] The Bulgarians had to choose between Alexander and personal union, on the one hand, and actual union, the support of Russia and a new ruler, on the other. Once the officers were convinced that the welfare of the nation was at stake, they willingly joined the plot. Even Captain Benderev, who had previously reported loyally to the war minister, now joined. Major Gruev, com-mandant of the military academy, agreed to participate. Because of his position he had influence on the young cadets. The web of conspiracy was now so widespread that even Captain Nikiforov, minister of war, was included. He, like the others, felt that Alexander would have to be sacrificed for Bulgaria.[40]

Once the conspirators had been organized, practical steps were un-dertaken. In the summer it was falsely reported that Milan was pre-paring for a new campaign against the Bulgars. The probability of such an attack and its outcome were widely discussed, particularly in the army. The opinion was freely expressed that the recent Bulgarian vic-tory would not be repeated. Taking advantage of these fears, Sakharov informed the officers that, if Alexander were overthrown, Russia would defend Bulgaria against Serbia, and she would recognize the union.[41]

The renewed threat from Serbia was used not only to bring further pressure on the officers, but also as a pretext to secure the removal from Sofia of the officers loyal to the prince. At first Alexander was not dis-turbed by the reports of Serbian activity, but he was pressed to take positive steps to meet the supposed danger.[42] The cabinet even wished

---

[38] Radev, I, 796–798; Corti, Alexander, pp. 302–303.

[39] Lascelles to Rosebery, FO, 78/3893, no. 152, Sofia, June 14, 1886; Radev, I, 769–771.

[40] The details of the plot are related in Radev, I, 795–835; Marinov, Stefan Stambolov, pp. 276–299.

[41] Radev, I, 799–802.

[42] In actual fact, Serbia, because of her domestic difficulties, was no imminent threat. Radev, I, 806–808; Corti, Alexander, p. 303; Jovanović, Milan, III, 362–363.

to have it recorded in the minutes that he refused to take precautions.[43] Finally, he consented to send an officer to the front to confirm Nikiforov's reports. The officer subsequently joined the conspirators and brought back a report favorable to their cause. Alexander thereupon sent the loyal officers and their regiment to the front.[44]

Besides military personnel, the evidence confirms that Prime Minister Karavelov and Foreign Minister Iliia Tsanov were implicated. Tsanov carried on discussions with Bogdanov concerning the plans for the prince's removal.[45] Bogdanov reported that both Karavelov and Tsanov asked whether Russia would protect Bulgaria from attack by either Turkey or Serbia if Alexander were removed. Without official authorization Bogdanov gave them this assurance, and reaffirmed that the union would be recognized.[46] At the last moment, both men evidently decided not to coöperate with the conspirators, although neither did anything to protect the prince.[47] Thus the prime minister, the foreign minister, and the minister of war all betrayed the prince and prepared the way for his abduction.

The Russian government was fully informed on the progress of the conspiracy. Unlike previous episodes in which Russian agents had presented their government with *faits accomplis,* in this affair the responsible members of the government knew exactly what was to happen and the complicity of their agents. Thus, on July 3/15, 1886, Zinoviev wrote in a private letter to Giers, "In such ticklish matters it is necessary to be extremely cautious." If the plan to overthrow the prince took on a serious character, it would be "difficult for us to avoid participation in it." Zinoviev even speculated that, since it might lead to a war, Russia should make certain that she had a means of escape. From Bogdanov's telegram Zinoviev concluded that the agent was not involved, but was merely transmitting what he had learned from Colonel Sakharov. However, Zinoviev continued, Sakharov, as a member of the Russian agency, should be no less cautious; his participation in the intrigue could "compromise us."[48]

About three weeks later, in a telegram marked "very secret," dated July 27/August 8, 1886, Bogdanov informed Giers that the participants in the conspiracy intended to carry out their plans with the assistance of the second infantry regiment. The first regiment, which was stationed in Sofia and was loyal to the prince, would be sent to Slivnica

[43] Corti, *Alexander,* p. 303.
[44] *Loc. cit.*
[45] Radev, I, 810; II, 7; Vlangali to Giers, *NKG,* Aug. 1/13, 1886.
[46] Vlangali to Giers, *NKG,* Aug. 1/13, 1886; Radev, I, 810.
[47] Goriainov, "Razryv," p. 186; Corti, *Alexander,* p. 308; Radev, II, 7.
[48] Zinoviev to Giers, *NKG,* July 3, 1886.

on the pretext that the Serbian border needed to be strengthened. The
conspirators would give the prince a false impression of the imminence
of war with Serbia. A memorandum to this effect would be given to
Alexander on July 29/August 10; a shift of the regiments could be
expected by August 1/13. The appropriate moment for the revolution
would then be at hand, since all the high-ranking officers loyal to the
prince would be absent from Sofia. If the revolt succeeded, mobilization would be immediately proclaimed to protect Bulgaria from a Serbian or Turkish attack. Because of the shortage of money and military
supplies, the conspirators expected assistance from Russia. The last
paragraph of this report consisted of one sentence: "Sakharov asks that
you transmit the above to Obruchev," Russian chief of staff. In the
margin of the telegram the tsar wrote, "I am afraid that nothing decent
will come of this."[49] Thus it is obvious that the tsar, Giers, and Obruchev
each received a blueprint of the intended revolt before it took place.
Despite his avowed hatred of revolutionary activity, Alexander III was
implicated through the association of his agents in the removal of the
prince.

Two days later, Bogdanov sent another "very secret" telegram to
Giers stating that Alexander had agreed to the plan for strengthening
the Serbian frontier. The prince would be seized either before he left
for Slivnica or upon his return to Sofia. Once he was removed, the
conspirators planned to form a provisional government composed of
all parties, which would appeal to the tsar to recognize the results of
the revolution. It would ask that an imperial commissioner, either
Ignatiev or Dondukov-Korsakov, and other Russian officers be sent to
head the government. Again Sakharov asked that Obruchev be informed of these developments.[50]

The next published telegram from Bogdanov to Giers, dated August
9/21, 1886, stated simply: "Today at 3:30 in the morning the army
and the people overthrew the prince, who signed his abdication. The
prince and his brother were taken to a monastery. There was no bloodshed. Telegrams by foreigners are not being allowed."[51]

Alexander of Battenberg had thus been removed from the throne of
Bulgaria with the direct participation of the Russian agents in Bulgaria
and with the full knowledge of the highest officials in Russia. The Bulgarian army had played the role which Russia had originally assigned
to it in Bulgarian internal politics—the instrument by which control

---

[49] Bogdanov to Giers, *Avantiury*, tel. no. 11, very secret, July 27/Aug. 8, 1886.
[50] *Ibid.*, tel. no. 12, very secret, July 29/Aug. 10, 1886.
[51] *Ibid.*, tel. no. 13, Aug. 9/21, 1886. Vlangali had originally reported to Giers that
the plan was to take effect on August 2/14. Vlangali to Giers, *NKG*, Aug 1/13, 1886.

could be maintained over the fate of the prince. For the moment the revolution appeared to mark the success of the Russian plans and a triumph over Alexander of Battenberg. It remained to be seen, however, whether Russia could exploit her temporary advantage.

The details of the abduction are obscure and confused. Four different persons are reported to have informed the prince that a group of officers was planning to depose him.[52] Although he was urged to take precautionary measures, the prince tended to discount all these warnings, since he could not believe that the army would turn against him. One of those who informed him of the plot later wrote that Alexander had replied, "I do not wish to remain prince of Bulgaria by force; if they do not want me, then let them tell me so and I will go voluntarily."[53]

The abduction, on the night of August 8/20–9/21, 1886, proceeded according to plan, although with much noise and confusion. Alexander was awakened by his valet, who urged him to flee, but all the exits were blocked by the conspirators. Alexander finally made his way to the palace gate, where he was met by Gruev and Dimitriev. They presented the prince with the abdication papers, which he signed. The prince and his brother Francis Joseph, who was visiting him in Sofia, were placed in separate carriages and driven outside the city to a monastery. During the next three days the prince was moved from place to place. He was finally taken to Silistria on the Danube, and then by ship to the Russian port of Reni in Bessarabia. Once ashore he was permitted to return to his native Germany.[54]

While the prince was held hostage, he remained in complete ignorance of the Bulgarian developments which were to decide his fate. The conspirators understood that the success of their venture depended on prompt action, the preservation of peace and order, the response of the electorate, and support from Russia. Consequently, a government was needed which not only would enjoy popular support, but also would be strong enough to cope with the difficulties of the days ahead. The revolutionary group therefore selected Metropolitan Kliment to head the new administration. The other members of the government were to be D. Tsankov, R. S. Burmov, K. H. Stoianov, K. Radoslavov, K. Velchikov, and Major Gruev.

---

[52] Radev, I, 828; Golovine, *Fürst Alexander von Bulgarien*, pp. 405–406; Corti, *Alexander*, pp. 309–310.

[53] Golovine, *op. cit.*, p. 406.

[54] Descriptions of the abduction are numerous. See especially Corti, *Alexander*, pp. 310–314; Goriainov, "Razryv," pp. 186–187; Radev, I, 799–835; Koch, pp. 267–272; Hajek, *Bulgariens Befreiung ...*, pp. 334–340; von Huhn, *The Kidnapping of Prince Alexander of Battenberg*, pp. 29 ff.; Stephen to Iddesleigh, *AP*, XCI:1, no. 261, Sofia, Aug. 22, 1886.

Although Metropolitan Kliment apparently played no part in the abduction itself, he did consent to form the government. His previous record of devotion and loyalty to Russia made him the logical candidate for the position. His Russophil sympathies were demonstrated by his actions after the abduction, when, after offering a prayer in his church blessing the abduction, he implored his fellow worshipers to seek the forgiveness of Russia and the tsar for the insults cast upon them by Bulgaria's ungrateful prince. When the name of Russia was mentioned, a demonstration began and the assembled crowd shouted, "To the Russian consulate! Long live Russia!"[55]

Kliment's government turned first to the task of obtaining immediate tangible support from Russia in order to strengthen its own position and to forestall the formation of a countermovement. It was reported that Serbia was mobilizing and that the events of the past year might be repeated. The Turkish attitude, too, was in doubt. Bogdanov sent another telegram to Giers, on August 9/21, transmitting the plea of the provisional government that the tsar take the Bulgarian nation under his protection. The southern and western frontiers were regarded as particularly vulnerable. The official Russian views on the union were urgently requested. Since the Bulgarian treasury was empty, Bogdanov suggested that a loan in excess of a million francs be granted from the occupation fund. He had already provided the conspirators with 55,000 francs to defray the expenses of escorting Alexander out of Bulgaria. In conclusion, Bogdanov reported that the new government wished to avoid mobilization, which might lead to internal difficulties. The public had received the intial act with favor, but signs of unrest were now appearing. The situation could be saved only by strong and immediate support from Russia. When a crowd had assembled before the consulate, Bogdanov could do no more than assure them, in general terms, that Russia would not desert Bulgaria in her hour of need.[56]

The news of the abdication evoked tremendous enthusiasm in St. Petersburg. Russia's avowed enemy had been removed by his own subjects. Telegrams were soon received from Bogdanov and Kliment asking for the tsar's blessing and protection. Since Giers was away at the time, his assistant A. Vlangali was in charge of the foreign office. Like Giers, Vlangali was a cautious and judicious official who sought to prevent a crisis. He, however, had little influence on the tsar. The major decisions for the next two weeks were made by Alexander III, who was guided chiefly by personal feelings. Upon receiving Bogdanov's request

---

[55] Trifonov, *V. Drumev-Kliment*, pp. 131–132; Radev, II, 10.
[56] Bogdanov to Giers, *Avantiury*, tel. no. 14, Aug. 9/21, 1886; Radev, II, 10–12.

for aid, the tsar replied that the consul could inform the Bulgars that they would be protected from all external dangers, but that Russia had no intention of occupying the country, as had been rumored. Bogdanov was to advance the provisional government 800,000 francs from the occupation fund.[57]

Having received the endorsement of the tsar and financial assistance, Kliment's government was confronted with the task of securing the approval of the Bulgarian nation. Throughout 1886 both Bogdanov and Sakharov had been under the impression that Alexander's popularity was waning fast and that the elements opposing him were powerful and numerous. The conspirators, relying on a similar appraisal of the situation, had concentrated on one objective—the removal of the prince. Even the Russian agents had emphasized only this aspect of the problem. The difficulty of establishing a new regime and of gaining popular support had not been fully appreciated. The leaders of the revolt appear to have believed that, once the prince abdicated and the Russian government expressed its approval, everything else would work out automatically. The provisional government was soon to discover that its major opposition came not from the prince or from the outside powers but from the Bulgarian people.

Alexander's abduction had taken the Bulgarian nation by surprise. For a brief interval after the coup, many considered it inevitable and were ready to accept it. However, within a day it was evident that Alexander's popularity, particularly in the army, was greater than had been realized. News soon reached Sofia that garrisons in various parts of the country had reaffirmed their loyalty to the prince.[58] The provisional government through Major Benderev promptly issued a circular asking all the officers to pledge their allegiance to Kliment's government. The Russian promise to aid but not to occupy Bulgaria was widely circulated. Nevertheless, the government's appeal did not produce the desired response.[59]

Whereas the opposition to Alexander centered in Sofia, the loyal forces concentrated in Plovdiv, capital of Rumelia. There Stefan Stambolov became the leader of those who opposed the provisional government and supported the prince. Although Stambolov had never held a ministerial post, he was a prominent member of the Liberal party. His career had taken somewhat the same course as that of Tsankov. In the

[57] Goriainov, "Razryv," p. 187; Radev, II, 17–18; Morier to Iddesleigh, *FO*, 65/ 1260, no. 298, conf., St. P., Aug. 25, 1886; d'Ormesson to Freycinet, *DDF*, VI, no. 292, St. P., Aug. 23, 1886.

[58] Stanev, *op. cit.*, p. 74; Thornton to Iddesleigh, *AP*, XCI:1, no. 156, Therapia, Aug. 23, 1886.

[59] Radev, II, 32–33.

early 1880's he had come to dislike Russia because she supported the prince and endorsed his abrogation of the constitution. Later, Stambolov sided with the prince when the Russian government turned against him. By 1885 he had again reversed himself, and regarded Alexander as the principal obstacle to better relations with Russia, which he believed were necessary for Bulgaria. In fact, in the same year he suggested to the Russians that Alexander could be removed only by force.[60] In 1886 he again changed his mind, and was reported to have initiated overtures in July for a reconciliation between Alexander and Russia. When approached on this matter, Bogdanov replied that as long as Alexander remained on the throne, Russia would not make peace with Bulgaria.[61]

The news of Alexander's abduction caused the crystallization of Stambolov's political program. Three considerations determined his final stand. First, he judged the underlying sentiments of the Bulgarian people more accurately than did his adversaries. Second, he was politically ambitious, and an opportunity had arisen which he could use to advance himself. Third, he was a strong Bulgarian nationalist and saw little advantage in the establishment of a Bulgarian government completely subservient to Russia. In the abdication crisis, Stambolov emerged as the one strong man who knew what he wanted to achieve, planned his objectives far in advance, and carried them out with vigor and determination. In comparison with the original conspirators, and with those who now undertook to run the provisional government, he was resolute and clearheaded.[62]

Stambolov's first act was to ascertain the attitude of Karavelov, former prime minister, who was also his very good friend. Like Stambolov, Karavelov, in 1885, had believed that it was necessary to get rid of Alexander by force. In 1886 he, too, had tried to effect a reconciliation between the prince and the Russian government. Unlike Stambolov, he became involved in the preliminary steps of the conspiracy, although he took no part in its final stages.[63] After the event, when questioned by Stambolov, Karavelov replied that he could not participate in a deed in which he heard only shouts of "Long live Russia" and none of "Long live Bulgaria." Nevertheless, he did not wish to do anything to make the situation more difficult. Peace and order had to be achieved in the interest of the nation. He believed that events had gone

[60] Koiander to Zinoviev, *Avantiury*, no. 1, Jan. 18/30, 1885. Marinov, *op. cit.*, p. 271; for Stambolov's early career see pp. 93–226.
[61] Radev, II, 67 n. 1.
[62] Marinov, *op. cit.*, pp. 290–309; Radev, II, 67–70.
[63] Goriainov, "Razryv," p. 186.

so far that the *status quo ante* could not be restored.[64] Unable to obtain support from Karavelov, Stambolov thereafter formulated his plans alone.

Stambolov's first objective was to establish a government which would support the prince against the provisional government in Sofia, and to organize strong military backing for it. Second, he sought to persuade the prince to return to Bulgaria. Stambolov was able to convince the brigade commander in Plovdiv, Lieutenant Colonel Mutkurov, not only that he should remain loyal to the prince, but also that he should assume command of the entire Bulgarian army. Mutkurov soon found that the Plovdiv unit over which he had direct command was able to draw reinforcements from other military installations. On the same day on which Benderev sent his circular requesting the officers to support Kliment's provisional government, Mutkurov sent a telegram to Sofia ordering that government to step down within twenty-four hours or its members would face the death penalty. Simultaneously, Stambolov proclaimed the establishment in Plovdiv of a second government, loyal to Alexander, and called upon the nation to sustain it. Thus, on August 11/23, two days after the abduction, the counterrevolution had begun. A Russophil regime held sway in Sofia; Alexander's supporters were concentrated in Plovdiv.[65]

Faced with reports of growing discontent in the country, Kliment's government felt that it was not strong enough to defend itself against this new threat. Frightened and unprepared, Major Gruev and those directly responsible for the abduction informed Bogdanov that they had failed and would have to leave the country. Only one man, in their opinion, could save the situation, and that was Karavelov.[66] Following their advice, Bogdanov asked the Liberal leader to form a new government, but told him that Alexander was not to be permitted to return to Bulgaria. Karavelov, who had gained a high reputation because of his integrity in financial matters, did not hesitate to place his political activities on an entirely different plane. His actions in 1885 and 1886 were motivated by a mixture of *Realpolitik* and opportunism. He accepted the Russian agent's terms and concurred in the opinion that Alexander's return would not be accepted peacefully by Russia. Bogdanov assured him that Russia would protect Bulgaria from any external threats, notably from Serbia or the Ottoman Empire. The Russian government thereafter warned the Turks not to take advantage of Bulgaria's plight. Under these conditions, Kliment's provisional gov-

[64] Radev, II, 16–22.
[65] *Ibid.*, pp. 33–34.
[66] *Ibid.*, pp. 102–114; Goriainov, "Razryv," p. 187.

ernment was disbanded on August 12/24 and Karavelov took command.[67]

Stambolov, who was invited to join the new government, refused because of the conditions imposed by the Russian representative. During the next two days, Karavelov and Stambolov exchanged a series of telegrams. Karavelov could not agree to Alexander's return, since it would precipitate disorders within the country. He feared that Serbia would again attack, which could lead to a Russian occupation of Bulgaria. He begged Stambolov, on the basis of their long friendship and the welfare of the nation, not to act rashly but to come to Sofia.[68]

Meanwhile, Bogdanov, who was acting in concert with Karavelov, became convinced that a Russian occupation of Bulgaria was the only solution, despite the fact that the Russian government had given assurances to the contrary. He appealed to his government for authority to announce that if Alexander returned, Russian troops would enter Bulgaria. The tsar's comment to this was "nonsense." On another telegram from Bogdanov, he wrote, "All this is nonsense and all in Sofia don't know what they are doing and Bogdanov is included."[69] The refusal of the tsar to take a firm hand in the crisis left Bogdanov and Karavelov in an impossible position.

Stambolov, on the contrary, found his government growing stronger by the hour. The majority of the troops now joined his forces; the regiment, which had been sent to the Serbian front just before the abduction, was marching back to Sofia. Nachevich, the Bulgarian representative in Bucharest, reported to Stambolov that the agents of the great powers had assured him that Russia would not be permitted to occupy Bulgaria if Alexander returned.[70] Stambolov, moreover, did not share Karavelov's apprehension over a Serbian attack. With these points in his favor, Stambolov refused to compromise with Karavelov, and on August 15/27 the latter abandoned his attempts to form a government. Stambolov had triumphed; the prince's return was now unopposed.

On August 16/28 Stambolov announced that a regency had been established composed of himself, P. R. Slaveikov, and G. Stranski. Colonel Mutkurov became the commander-in-chief of all the armed forces. Having established its position as the sole governing authority, the regency sought the return of the prince. On August 13/25, Stambolov had sent a message requesting the tsar's endorsement of Alexan-

[67] Goriainov, "Razryv," p. 187; Thornton to Iddesleigh, *AP*, XCI:1, no. 210, Therapia, Aug. 27, 1886; Thornton to Iddesleigh, *FO*, 78/3879, tel. no. 154, Therapia, Aug. 27, 1886.

[68] Radev, II, 123–150; Marinov, *op. cit.*, p. 271.

[69] Goriainov, "Razryv," pp. 188–189; Radev, II, 154; Stephen to Iddesleigh, *FO*, 78/3899, no. 145, Sofia, Aug. 27, 1886.

[70] Radev, II, 154, 169.

der's return.[71] Although the tsar made no reply to this telegram, he informed Bogdanov, on August 16/28, that he was sending Prince Dolgorukii as his personal emissary to Sofia to study the situation, advise the Bulgarian government, and attempt to improve the relations between the two countries.[72]

Meanwhile, Alexander of Battenberg remained in ignorance of what had happened in Bulgaria. After landing at Reni on August 13/25, he telegraphed his father that he was proceeding by train to Lemberg, where he arrived on August 15/27. Alexander of Hesse had been able to follow the situation in Bulgaria with greater facility. On August 12/24 he had received a telegram from Stambolov and Mutkurov announcing that the provisional government had been overthrown and that the entire nation "begged" the prince to return.[73] Overjoyed by the news, Alexander of Hesse was convinced that his son should return to his principality, and sent a message advising him to do so. At Lemberg Prince Alexander received his father's message, a telegram from his brother Henry, son-in-law of Queen Victoria, and the personal greetings of his brother Louis.[74] All three offered the same advice.

Alexander was urged to return by Princess Victoria of Prussia, to whom Alexander had been secretly engaged, by her mother the crown princess of Prussia, and by Queen Victoria. The crown princess was still intent on arranging a match between her daughter and Alexander, partly because her daughter was in love with the prince and partly to outwit Bismarck. Queen Victoria was interested chiefly in the effect that the developments in Bulgaria would have on British interests in the Near East. Her judgments on Russia and Alexander III were sharp and bitter. In a letter to Salisbury she wrote that the results of Russian activity in Bulgaria were "without parallel in modern history." "A general conflagration," she believed, could be averted only by "maintaining the strength and efficiency of Prince Alexander's rule." She told Henry, Alexander's brother, that "open hostility to Russia was the best solution," and to Alexander himself she wrote, "My indignation and fury against your barbaric semi-Asiatic tyrannical cousin are so great that I can hardly trust myself to write about it."[75]

Overwhelmed by this deluge of optimistic advice, Alexander agreed,

---

[71] *Ibid.*, pp. 157–158.

[72] Goriainov, "Razryv," p. 188; Radev, II, 177–178. In fact the tsar had decided on August 7/19, two days before the abduction took place, that if Alexander were removed he would send Dolgorukii. Vlangali to Giers, *NKG*, Aug. 7/19, 1886.

[73] Corti, *Alexander*, p. 317.

[74] *Ibid.*, pp. 317–320.

[75] Buckle, *Victoria*, III, 179–187; Corti, *Alexander*, pp. 322–323; Staal to Giers, *Staal*, no. 28, Sept. 8/20, 1886.

although he had been disillusioned and shaken by his recent experiences. On August 16/28 he sent a telegram to Stambolov: "Inform the people and the troops that I shall arrive at Ruschuk early on Sunday morning and will go straight to Sofia to take over once again the power granted to me by God through the will of the people."[76] In so acting, Alexander realized that again he was challenging the Russian government.

Leaving immediately for Bulgaria, Alexander had a brief meeting with Stambolov at Giurgievo in Rumania. On August 17/29, eleven days after the abduction, Alexander again set foot in Bulgaria. Cheered by an immense and enthusiastic crowd, the prince was carried on the shoulders of his officers. Despite the sincerity of the welcome, the prince was exhausted by his ordeal, and was in no condition to face the strain of the moment or to make the necessary vital decisions.

Greeting the prince at Ruschuk were the representatives of all the major powers. To Alexander's surprise, Shatokhin, the Russian vice-consul, appeared also. The prince mistakenly interpreted his presence to mean that the Russian government had endorsed his return.[77] On the contrary, when St. Petersburg learned of the prince's decision, Bogdanov was instructed not to meet the prince and to relay this information to the other Russian agents.[78] Since he had not yet received the message, Shatokhin had acted on his own initiative and in conformity with the attitude of the representatives of the other powers. The presence of the Russian agent no doubt precipitated the disastrous course of action then adopted by the prince. Overwrought with the excitement of the day and confused by the situation in which he found himself, Alexander decided to take advantage of what he considered a sign of Russian approval. With the aid of his brother Louis, the prince composed a telegram to the tsar which read in part:

I thank Your Majesty for the attitude taken by your representative in Ruschuk. His very presence at my reception showed me that the Imperial Government cannot sanction the revolutionary action taken against my person. I beg Your Majesty to instruct General Dolgorukii to get in touch with me personally as quickly as possible; I should be happy to give Your Majesty the final proof of the unchanging devotion which I feel for Your Majesty's illustrious person. As Russia gave me my crown, I am prepared to give it back into the hands of its Sovereign.[79]

The last sentence lost for Alexander the throne of Bulgaria. Contrary to his previous declaration in the telegram to Stambolov that he was returning "to take over once again the power granted to me by

---

[76] Radev, II, 194; Hajek, *op. cit.*, p. 382.
[77] Corti, *Alexander*, pp. 332–334; Radev, II, 215; Goriainov, "Razryv," p. 189.
[78] Goriainov, "Razryv," p. 189. Bogdanov was also told to persuade the German and Austrian representatives to follow his example.
[79] Corti, *Alexander*, p. 334; Radev, II, 216–217.

God," he now admitted that "Russia gave me my crown." By a stroke of the pen Alexander had thus cut the ground from under the party which desired his return to power, and, at the same time, delivered himself into the hands of his personal enemy the tsar.

The extent of the damage done was not immediately apparent. Both the prince and his brother considered that the telegram had been "masterly in conception" and a "golden bridge for the tsar."[80] Full of confidence, they continued their journey to the capital amid wild acclaim. Alexander learned to his satisfaction that Colonel Mutkurov had marched into Sofia and had arrested Kliment, Tsankov, and Karavelov.[81]

When Alexander's telegram reached St. Petersburg, Giers was away and the tsar was at Tsarskoe Selo. Vlangali, therefore, again took charge. Since he was of Giers' opinion that a crisis should be avoided, he advised that Russia should accept the verdict of the Bulgarian nation and come to terms with the prince.[82] However, once more Alexander III took matters into his own hands. Rejecting repeated drafts presented by the Russian foreign office, the tsar finally wrote his own reply, which was released to the press before it had time to arrive in Sofia. It stated:

I have received Your Highness's telegram. I cannot approve your return to Bulgaria in view of the disastrous consequences which it may entail upon the country, already so severely tried. It will not be advisable to dispatch Dolgorukii; I shall refrain from doing so during the unhappy condition to which Bulgaria is reduced as long as you remain there.

Your Highness will understand what devolves upon you. I reserve judgment upon the course I am bidden to take by the honored memory of my Father, the interest of Russia, and the tranquillity of the East.[83]

Neither Vlangali nor Jomini approved of the message.[84] The British ambassador Morier wrote that there could be no doubt that the message came from the tsar himself in view of "the characteristic *brusqueness* of the form."[85]

The tsar's reply fell like a bombshell in Sofia, where the government had not even been informed of the existence of the original telegram. In despair Stambolov stated:

This is the man for whom we have roused the whole of Bulgaria, have put our necks in the noose and brother has raised sword against brother and he takes such

---

[80] Corti, *Alexander*, p. 338.

[81] Goriainov, "Razryv," p. 190; Corti, *Alexander*, p. 334.

[82] Lamzdorf, *Dnevnik, 1891–1892*, p. 62.

[83] Koch, pp. 276–278; Hajek, *op. cit.*, p. 387 n. 3; Montebellow to Freycinet, *DDF*, VI, no. 305, St. P., Sept. 3, 1886.

[84] Cyon reports that Jomini told him he had drafted several dozen replies which in essence accepted Alexander's return but the tsar had rejected all of them. Cyon, *Histoire de l'entente franco-russe, 1886–1894*, p. 158.

[85] Morier to Iddesleigh, *FO*, 65/1261, no. 305, St. P., Sept. 3, 1886.

a momentous decision without even telling us beforehand; he throws his crown at the feet of a foreign ruler and keeps us in the dark about it.[86]

Although Alexander subsequently regretted his hasty action and his failure to consult Stambolov, the damage had been done. The prince now had no choice but to leave Bulgaria, with the sole consolation that he was departing by his own choice and not under escort. He had, however, lost much of his desire to remain on the Bulgarian throne. He had been deeply hurt by the fact that "three-fourths" of the officers in the army had been involved in the abduction plot,[87] and could never forget how his faith in them had been betrayed. Many whom he had considered loyal to his person had stood with folded arms while the coup was carried out. He believed that the clergy had been deeply implicated also. Although he considered his Bulgarian subjects faithful, he knew that they wanted a reconciliation with Russia. As long as Alexander remained in Bulgaria, this would be impossible. The prince foresaw a renewal of civil war which would lead to a Russian occupation.[88] Finally, he was afraid that if he remained he would be in constant danger of assassination. When this last consideration was placed before Queen Victoria, whose government had hoped to persuade Alexander to remain, she realized that Alexander had little choice, "for what would our position be were such a dreadful event to take place?"[89] Alexander's father also telegraphed, "I am in complete agreement with a voluntary and honorable retirement."[90]

As soon as Alexander had made his decision, Stambolov took steps to secure an understanding with Russia. Viewing the situation realistically, he saw that it was highly desirable that amicable relations be reestablished, although he was not willing that Bulgaria become a Russian satellite state. On August 23/September 4 the Russian government was asked if Russia would respect the Bulgarian constitution, work for the success of the union, assist in the selection of a new prince, and support the provisional government. Suggestions on possible means of healing the breach between the states were solicited also.[91]

On the following day, I. Kartsov, Russian consul in Plovdiv, who was temporarily in Sofia, presented the reply. The Russian government agreed to support the provisional government under Stambolov as long as it represented all the parties and worked for the welfare of the na-

---

[86] Radev, II, 227–228; Hajek, *op. cit.*, p. 388. See also Marinov, *op. cit.*, pp. 310–312.
[87] Buckle, *Victoria*, 3d ser., I, 199 ff.; Corti, *Alexander*, pp. 339, 341–342.
[88] Radev, II, 250; Corti, *Alexander*, pp. 341–342.
[89] Buckle, *Victoria*, 3d ser., I, 200.
[90] Corti, *Alexander*, p. 340.
[91] Radev, II, 253; Goriainov, "Razryv," pp. 191–193.

tion. The selection of a new prince could be discussed only after peace and order had been restored in Bulgaria. Russia would support the union, but only on the condition that the Bulgars abandon force as a means of achieving their goals. The message concluded that Russo-Bulgarian relations would depend directly on the attitude and behavior of the provisional government.[92]

Before Alexander left Bulgaria, he notified the tsar that he would abdicate if Russia would recognize the regency which would have to be formed before his departure, and would respect Bulgarian independence. When a favorable reply was received, Alexander telegraphed his father on August 26/September 7:

Since Russia has guaranteed to respect the independence of the country as well as the rights granted to it by the Constitution and not to interfere in the internal affairs of the country, I have decided in agreement with all parties to abdicate in order to facilitate the reëstablishment of good relations between Russia and this country. I am informing all the powers of my decision and shall leave tomorrow [the 8th] or the day after [the 9th].[93]

The only matter left to be settled was the composition of the regency. It was to be expected that Stambolov and Mutkurov would be included, because of their roles in the counterrevolution, but the choice of the third member was difficult to make. Stambolov's biographer, Marinov, wrote that Stambolov favored Tsankov because of his Russian connections, but that the prince opposed him and advocated Karavelov. Corti disagrees and maintains that Stambolov, to the surprise of the prince and many officers, supported Karavelov because he could thereby control the former prime minister. Recognizing the wisdom of this suggestion, Alexander endorsed it and Karavelov became the third member of the regency.[94]

With the feeling that he had abdicated by free choice and retained the good will of the Bulgarian people,[95] Alexander, on August 28/ September 9, left the principality to which, as he later said, he had given the seven best years of his life. In Russia his departure was greeted with outright rejoicing. On August 26/September 7, the day on which Alexander made public his decision to abdicate, Giers spoke with Morier on the Russian attitude.

That unfortunate young man [*ce pauvre jeune homme*]—for I cannot but sincerely pity him and regard him even more as a victim of circumstances than of his own faults, though these have been many—has become in the eyes of the Russian

[92] Radev, II, 255; Goriainov, "Razryv," pp. 192–193.
[93] Corti, *Alexander*, p. 340.
[94] *Ibid.*, p. 344; Marinov, *op. cit.*, p. 315; Radev, II, 267–271.
[95] As a parting gesture Alexander told his officers that he would be ready to join them when the battle for Macedonia began. Radev, II, 271.

people, the incarnation and embodiment of everything which most deeply stirs the national indignation. He represents, in the first place, the untold ingratitude of the Bulgarians for their deliverers, and reminds them of the losses in blood and treasure incurred in a war which yielded no other results but disappointments. In the second place, he reminds them of all the humiliations submitted to in the Constantinople conference and since. Lastly, he represents the hopes and desires of Russia's enemies. Never, therefore, could there be peace between him and the Russian people.[96]

The tsar had thus succeeded in ridding Bulgaria of his cousin, whom he blamed for the unhappy course of Russo-Bulgarian relations. Although Russia had apparently emerged the victor after a seven-year struggle, it was still not clear on what basis Russo-Bulgarian friendship would be reëstablished. The tsar had informed Stambolov that the actions of the Bulgarian government would determine the path of the future. One of the first acts of the regency was to dispatch a telegram to the tsar expressing the hope that the differences of the past would be forgotten and that Russia would offer her protection to the principality and approve the union.

The reply from St. Petersburg was not cordial: Russia had agreed to recognize the regency appointed by the prince, but, since she had obligated herself also to defend the constitution, the appointments of Stambolov and Mutkurov could not be accepted. Although the constitution was ambiguous in this regard, all the regents should have been appointed from the previous ministerial council. By this maneuver the Russian government hoped to discredit Stambolov and Mutkurov, and perhaps secure the appointment of its own candidate, Tsankov, for one of the vacancies. Stambolov, rejecting the protest, argued that he and Mutkurov had been chosen under revolutionary conditions not foreseen in the constitution. Their appointments had been confirmed by the national assembly. Although the matter was not pressed by either side, it was an indication that the road ahead would not be smooth.[97]

The first national problem facing Stambolov and the regency was the election of a new prince. The constitution offered guidance only if the prince died without an heir. Following the procedure outlined for this emergency, Stambolov issued orders that elections be held for the Grand National Assembly, which was to meet to select the prince. Stambolov thus acted contrary to the Russian desire that no new ruler be chosen until the unrest and tension in the principality had subsided.

On September 13/25, General N. V. Kaulbars, Russian military attaché in Vienna, arrived in Sofia. His purpose, according to Giers, "was

[96] Morier to Iddesleigh, *AP*, XCI:1, no. 295, St. P., Sept. 7, 1886.

[97] Radev, II, 302–315; Goriainov, "Razryv," p. 197; Lascelles to Iddesleigh, *FO*, 78/3894, no. 247, Sofia, Sept. 14, 1886; d'Ormesson to Freycinet, *DDF*, VI, no. 308, St. P., Sept. 8, 1886.

to take charge of the agency and Consulate-General on the same footing as the other agents and Consuls-General."[98] Kaulbars, brother of the former Bulgarian minister of war, had been sent to Bulgaria by the tsar in 1883–1884 and again after the Serbo-Bulgarian war. On both visits he had achieved success and had won the respect of his colleagues and the Bulgarians. When his name came up again, Zinoviev wrote, "It is not possible to dispute his abilities."[99] Since he had the reputation of being judicious and careful, not prone to hasty action, his appointment was greeted with satisfaction not only in Bulgaria but also in Europe. His instructions, which were reasonable and appropriate, were "to study the situation and by his counsel assist the Bulgarians in putting an end to the present crisis in their affairs."[100] Kaulbars' third mission to Bulgaria, however, was destined to come to an entirely unforeseen conclusion.

According to all the available evidence, Kaulbars' tone and his treatment of the Bulgarian government reflected the ideas of Alexander III.[101] Throughout the episode, Giers and the foreign office were placed in the difficult position of defending a policy of which they obviously disapproved. The tsar's intention of controlling the Bulgarians with an iron hand was apparent in the first message which Kaulbars presented, on September 14/26, to the Bulgarian national assembly. The tsar thanked the assembly for its previous message and indicated that in the future he expected it to take no action that was not in agreement with the Russian views. General Kaulbars was being sent to work out an understanding between the two nations. Should he be successful, Russia would again undertake the defense of the principality.[102] On the same day Kaulbars presented a more specific note to the regents. First, the military precautions taken during the present state of siege were to be abandoned. Second, all persons arrested in connection with the abduction should immediately be released. Third, the elections for the Grand National Assembly should be postponed until conditions in Bulgaria returned to normal. Kaulbars emphasized that any action taken by the Grand National Assembly would now be regarded by Russia as illegal.[103]

[98] Morier to Iddesleigh, *AP*, XCI:1, no. 335, Sept. 16, 1886.

[99] Zinoviev to Giers, *NKG*, Aug. 29, 1886.

[100] Morier to Iddesleigh, *AP*, XCI:1, no. 357, St. P., Sept. 18, 1886.

[101] Zinoviev to Giers, *NKG*, Aug. 29, 1886; Paget to Iddesleigh, *AP*, XCI:1, no. 340, Vienna, Sept. 17, 1886.

[102] Radev, II, 332–333.

[103] Goriainov, "Razryv," p. 197; Radev, II, 333; Tatishchev, *Iz Prozhlago Russkoi Diplomatii*, p. 459; Marinov, *op. cit.*, p. 333; Panaiotov, *Russiia, Velikitie Sili i Bulgarskiiat Vupros sled Izbora na Kniaz Ferdinanda, 1888–1896*, p. 78; Lascelles to Iddesleigh, *AP*, XCI:1, no. 369, Sofia, Sept. 26, 1886.

The Russian note produced a new political crisis in Sofia. Despite the fact that the tsar had assured Alexander of Battenberg that he would respect the Bulgarian constitution and not interfere in Bulgarian internal affairs, his agent was now acting in a very different manner. Only on the first point would the regency make concessions. It agreed that, one week before the elections for the Grand National Assembly, the state of siege would be lifted in order to give the electorate the maximum freedom. With regard to the second and third points, the government cited the constitution. The prisoners could not be summarily released by the regency, since they were under the jurisdiction of the courts; the elections could not be delayed, for the constitution provided that they be held within a month.[104]

The determined attitude of the Bulgarian government pushed Kaulbars one step forward. Two days after he had delivered his first note he distributed a twelve-point circular in an attempt to go over the heads of the government and appeal directly to the electorate. The circular expressed the desire of the tsar that the Bulgarian people should turn to him in full confidence and rely on their "elder brothers" during the crisis. The Russian grievances against the Bulgarian government were listed next. The fact that the national assembly had sent a telegram of appreciation to Alexander of Battenberg after his abdication was called

... ridiculously illogical and [it] casts a deplorable shadow on the deputies. . . . the burning of the colors of the mutinous regiments produced a painful impression. When troops show themselves unworthy, the colors are taken away from them and placed in a cathedral, but the burning of a flag is unheard of in the military history of the world, and can only produce a deleterious effect on the cadets in whose presence it was performed.

The circular presented the three conditions previously sent to the government, and concluded: "All true patriots are advised to forget the past and look forward to the future with full confidence in Russia."[105]

Kaulbars' strong actions drew an immediate protest from the British government, which had been informed that the general would offer only "friendly counsel." Since the reports from Bulgaria were alarming, the British demanded an explanation from Giers. The Russian foreign minister denied any direct knowledge of the general's note, but admitted that he had heard of it through the press. He repeated that Kaulbars was instructed only to give "friendly advice," but he was forced to

---

[104] Goriainov, "Razryv," pp. 198–199; Marinov, *op. cit.*, p. 335; Radev, II, 333–335; Lascelles to Iddesleigh, *AP*, XCI:1, no. 371, Sofia, Sept. 28, 1886.

[105] The full text of the circular is in Lascelles to Iddesleigh, *AP*, XCI:1, no. 419, Sofia, Oct. 4, 1886. See also Radev, II, 344–345.

acknowledge that the tsar had allowed "great latitude" in the negotiations.[106] When this report reached Lord Iddesleigh, foreign secretary, he replied that Kaulbars had certainly "exceeded his instructions."[107]

From the published Russian sources available, it appears that Kaulbars indeed was not working in coöperation with the foreign office. The first report that Giers received was evidently that of September 25/ October 7, ten days after the messages to the assembly and the regency had been delivered. In this report, moreover, Kaulbars specifically stated, "I call attention to the words, 'I advise'; because I did not demand of, but only advised the Bulgarian minister [of foreign affairs]."[108]

Although, in his conversations with Morier, Giers did not attempt to justify the tone which Kaulbars had adopted, he did support the general's attitude in regard to the elections to the national assembly. He argued that only if peace and calm ruled in the principality could a truly representative and free assembly be elected. Now "the creatures of a government violently hostile to Russia" would take measures against the elements sympathetic to Russia.[109] When Giers defended the demand concerning the prisoners, Morier asked the Russian minister to look at the issue as an Englishman or a European might view it. If the Russian government insisted on this point, there "could be no other inference" but that Russia was determined to protect her agents, no matter what their actions.

> This participation by the friends and allies of Russia in one of the blackest political plots of the century had been boldly claimed by Monsieur Katkov as a title of honor for its authors, and if the Imperial Government now sought, through its agent, to shield the criminals, an indelible impression would be produced that official Russia inspired herself with the views of the "Moscow Gazette." ... Do you not see how completely this attitude is at variance with the general character of your policy and the antirevolutionary ideas which the Emperor, and all Russian society with him, pride themselves on representing?[110]

Giers could only reply that Kaulbars was not acting on orders. The foreign office had told him not to demand the release of the prisoners, but only that their trial be delayed until "passions have calmed down and there was no risk of the prisoners being condemned *ab irato*."[111]

The harshness of the Russian demands and the attitude adopted by Kaulbars intimidated some of the leading Bulgarian statesmen, who,

---

[106] Morier to Iddesleigh, *AP*, XCI:1, no. 378, St. P., Sept. 30, 1886.

[107] Iddesleigh to Morier, *AP*, XCI:1, no. 398, Oct. 6, 1886; Staal to Giers, *Staal*, no. 33, Sept. 24/Oct. 6, 1886.

[108] Kaulbars to Giers, *Avantiury*, no. 20, Sept. 25/Oct. 7, 1886.

[109] From Morier, *FO*, 65/1264, cypher tel. no. 154, St. P., Oct. 1, 1886.

[110] Morier to Iddesleigh, *FO*, 65/1261, no. 353, secret, St. P., Sept. 30, 1886. See also Staal to Giers, *Staal*, no. 34, London, Oct. 3/15, 1886.

[111] From Morier, *FO*, 65/1265, cypher tel. no. 154, St. P., Oct. 1, 1886.

fearing that a Russian occupation was at hand, began to consider whether they should not back down. Karavelov, in particular, felt strongly on the subject. Even Stambolov was impressed. On September 17/29, the day after the circular to the Bulgarian people had been distributed, Stambolov asked the British agent, Lascelles, if it would not be wise to follow Karavelov's advice and postpone the elections. Although the British government had finally acquiesced in the "forceful" abdication of the prince, it took a strong stand on the Kaulbars mission. Lascelles advised Stambolov to continue to abide by the constitution.[112] Heartened by the support of the British, as well as the European press, the Bulgarian government, on September 20/October 2, informed Kaulbars that Russia's advice would be accepted only when it did not conflict with the constitution. The general refused to accept this reply and repeated his previous demands.[113]

Aware of the British attitude, Kaulbars spoke with Lascelles, who reported:

> With regard to the release of prisoners, General Kaulbars at first argued that the government, being a party government, had not the right of judging members of another party. But on my observing that I thought he did the conspirators too much honor in raising them to the rank of a political party, he changed his ground, and argued that it would be unjust to keep these men in prison so long as many who were known to be equally guilty were still at liberty and that if the government refused to release those who had been arrested, he would be justified in demanding the imprisonment of several other persons. To this I replied that it did not appear to me that the fact of some criminals being at large was sufficient reason for releasing those who were in prison.[114]

On another occasion Kaulbars complained to Lascelles that all the ministers were ready to follow the Russian suggestions, but they were being advised to the contrary, presumably by Great Britain. When Stambolov was informed of this conversation, he and his ministers went to Kaulbars and again insisted that the Russian demands were in conflict with the constitution. The general's reply was, "The tsar knows the Bulgarian constitution better than you do."[115]

Having failed to secure the postponement of the elections, which were scheduled for September 28/October 10, the general decided that the only solution was a direct appeal to the electorate. He therefore asked the tsar for permission to travel through the principality before the election in order to inform the Bulgarian people of his mission and

---

[112] Radev, II, 347–348; Lascelles to Iddesleigh, *AP*, XCI:1, no. 418, Oct. 4, 1886; *Staal*, p. 315.

[113] Radev, II, 352; Lascelles to Iddesleigh, *AP*, XCI:1, no. 384, Sofia, Oct. 3, 1886.

[114] Lascelles to Iddesleigh, *AP*, XCI:1, no. 417, Sofia, Oct. 3, 1886.

[115] Radev, II, 353–354.

to persuade them to repudiate the policy of their government. The tsar wrote on the dispatch, "Absolutely agree to this and it is also necessary."[116]

The "state of siege" had been lifted two days earlier, as the government had promised. In Sofia, where Kaulbars began his personal campaign, he repeated the demand that the prisoners be released and the elections postponed. The crowd which had assembled voiced its disapproval and shouted for Bulgaria's freedom and independence. Because of this interference, the general was unable to finish his address. In reporting on the incident, Lascelles commented:

[it] may be taken as a proof of his personal courage and his disregard of diplomatic usage. It is, I presume, the first time that the representative of a foreign power has harangued a popular meeting in a sense hostile to the government to which he was accredited, and the question might arise whether such conduct would be covered by the diplomatic immunities to which foreign representatives are entitled.[117]

It is to be hoped that the general's journey may convince him that Bulgaria, however grateful she may be for her liberation from Turkish rule, has no wish to become a Russian province, and will do her utmost to maintain her liberty and independence. As, however, General Kaulbars was able to persuade himself that the meeting yesterday was a triumph for Russia, I am afraid that no evidence however strong will be able to shake the conviction he apparently entertains, and which seems to prevail throughout Russia, that it is impossible that Bulgaria should be anything but Russian.[118]

The general's stormy reception in Sofia was repeated throughout the country, in part because the government had organized the opposition. Wherever the general went, he was asked about Russian policy in regard to the union, Russia's favored candidate for the throne, and other questions designed to embarrass him. Although he sought to impress upon the people that it was the tsar himself who advocated the present policy, Kaulbars made little headway.[119]

The general did, however, influence some elements of the army. On September 20/October 2, the day before Kaulbars' tour began, the Bulgarian government received a report from the Shumen garrison advising it to accept the measures presented by Kaulbars or "independent action" would be taken.[120] Without the support of the army the regency was in a hopeless position. Stambolov, however, was able to persuade the garrison not to act. When Kaulbars arrived in Ruschuk, he found

---

[116] Kaulbars to Giers, *Avantiury*, tel. no. 18, Sept. 8/20, 1886. The date of this telegram is obviously wrong. See also Raindre to Freycinet, *DDF*, VI, no. 320, Berlin, Oct. 5, 1886.

[117] Lascelles to Iddesleigh, *AP*, XCI:1, no. 419, Oct. 4, 1886.

[118] Lascelles to Iddesleigh, *FO*, 78/3895, no. 277, Sofia, Oct. 4, 1886.

[119] Goriainov, "Razryv," p. 199; Radev, II, 370–402.

[120] Radev, II, 371–380.

the garrison in that city divided in its sympathies and on the verge of outright rebellion.[121] In Svischov, Shatokhin was able to inform the general that he had only to give the word and the troops there would revolt.[122] Although no military coup took place, an uneasy peace reigned throughout the country. Kaulbars' tour certainly increased the tension on the eve of the elections. The trip nevertheless failed in its main purpose and ended on an ominous note. When the general arrived in Varna, only the Russian consul was on hand to greet him, but no Bulgarians.[123]

Even on election day the Russian representatives continued their efforts to influence the outcome. In Sofia the acting Russian consul, A. V. Nekliudov, addressed a group of sympathizers assembled before the consulate and informed them that the tsar desired the postponement of the election. Thereupon the people marched to the polling place and tried to disrupt the election procedures. The police arrived, skirmishes occurred, and the rioters withdrew to the Russian consulate, where the injured were treated and all were given nourishment.[124] The next day, in what appears to have been a fit of anger, Nekliudov informed the Bulgarian government that he was severing diplomatic relations because of the punishment administered to those who opposed the elections. Even Kaulbars saw the folly of his act and instructed Nekliudov to retract his statement.[125]

On election day Kaulbars had ordered Nekliudov to deliver the following note to the Bulgarian government: "By the order of General Kaulbars, I have the honor to inform you that the Imperial Russian government declared today's election illegal, and as having no value in their eyes."[126] The unfavorable results of the election, instead of deterring Kaulbars, spurred him to more vigorous action, and on October 1/13 he delivered another note:

... as the elections have been proceeded with in opposition to the friendly advice given by Russia, he must formally declare that any action taken by those who govern Bulgaria, unless such action should be in accordance with the advice of Russia, will be considered illegal by the Imperial Government. [127]

Kaulbars maintained, logically enough, that if the elections were illegal, then so was the Grand National Assembly, which was to convene

---

[121] *Ibid.*, p. 388.

[122] *Ibid.*, p. 391.

[123] *Ibid.*, p. 402.

[124] Nekliudov to Kaulbars, *Avantiury*, no. 22, Sept. 30/Oct. 12, 1886.

[125] Tatishchev, *op. cit.*, pp. 468–469.

[126] Nekliudov to Nachevich, *AP*, XCI:1, no. 463, incl. 2, Sofia, Sept. 28/Oct. 10, 1886; Radev, II, 409.

[127] Radev, II, 437; Lascelles to Iddesleigh, *AP*, XCI:1, no. 457, Sofia, Oct. 19, 1886.

on October 15/27.[128] The Bulgarian government and the representatives of the great powers were so informed. Moreover, the general now adopted a new tactic. He told the British representative that he had become convinced on his journey that "the vast majority of the Bulgarian people were opposed to the present government, but that they dared not express their opinion in consequence of the organized terrorism of the government."[129]

Having seized upon the theme of "terrorism" to justify his failure, the general dispatched numerous reports to St. Petersburg emphasizing that the "terror" was directed not only against the Bulgars who supported Russia, but also against Russian citizens. In particular, Kaulbars judged that the Russian vice-consul and the Russian citizens in the port of Varna were in grave personal danger and needed protection. In response, the Russian government announced on October 12/24 that it was sending two warships to Varna to protect its nationals.[130] The Russian government thus made the most drastic move yet against the Bulgarian government.

In Sofia a veritable panic ensued. Karavelov felt, as did others, that the first step toward the occupation of Bulgaria had been taken. He now insisted that the Grand National Assembly not be convened and the officers be released.[131] Although Stambolov and Mutkurov realized the seriousness of the situation, they still refused to yield. To avoid the creation of an excuse for an occupation, they ordered the army not to engage the Russian troops should a landing be made from the ships.[132]

Kaulbars, meanwhile, attempted to exploit the advantage presented by the obvious alarm of the Bulgarian government. On October 14/26 he renewed his demand for the release of the prisoners, warning that if they were brought to trial it would be taken as a direct challenge to Russia and that she would be obliged "to use extreme measures." The Russian consulate gave wide publicity to this statement in order to create the impression that this was the last chance for a peaceful solution of the Russo-Bulgarian difficulties.[133] Kaulbars received able assistance from the Russian consul in Varna, who informed the local officials that if additional terrorism were directed against the Russians in the city, it would be bombarded. The two warships had in the meantime arrived, one on October 13/25 and the other four days later.[134]

---

[128] Lanel to Freycinet, *DDF*, VI, no. 332, Sofia, Oct. 24, 1886.
[129] Lascelles to Kaulbars, *AP*, XCI:1, no. 475, Sofia, Oct. 23, 1886.
[130] Radev, II, 437–438; Staal to Giers, *Staal*, no. 36, London, Oct. 13/25, 1886; Fane to Iddesleigh, *AP*, XCI:1, no. 482, Constantinople, Oct. 25, 1886; Süreya to Grand Vizir, *BD*, no. 138, Oct. 14, 1886.
[131] Radev, II, 441; Lascelles to Iddesleigh, *AP*, XCI:1, no. 493, Sofia, Oct. 26, 1886.
[132] Radev, II, 440.
[133] *Ibid.*, p. 441.
[134] *Ibid.*, pp. 442–446.

Thus, on the eve of the opening of the Grand National Assembly at Tyrnovo, Kaulbars had succeeded in frightening the Bulgarian government and people into believing that an occupation was at hand. Karavelov, as a result, refused to go to Tyrnovo, and thereby terminated his participation in the regency. Stambolov, in an attempt to appease Russia, offered the vacant seat to Tsankov. The latter refused on the excuse that the regency should be composed of men favorable to Russia.[135] The news of further unrest in the army, together with the repeated urgings of his colleagues, finally induced Stambolov, on October 17/29, to release the officers implicated in the abduction.[136] Kaulbars had thus through force and intimidation gained two of his three objectives. The state of siege had been lifted and the prisoners were free.

The success achieved by the threat of occupying Bulgaria impressed Kaulbars. On October 18/30 he informed Giers that a delegation of pro-Russian Bulgars advised what he described as the "half-occupation" of Bulgaria. In the opinion of the delegation, only the army officers were hostile to Russia, whereas the lower ranks were favorable to her. Russia should send a brigade to Varna to seize the Bulgarian officers and replace them with Russians. Although Kaulbars did not wholeheartedly endorse this plan, he did not reject it. He believed that agreement would first have to be reached with the European powers. If this proved possible, it would be best to send a large number of troops.[137]

As the general had realized, occupation in any form would be difficult without the consent of the powers. With each passing day the Kaulbars mission created greater apprehension in Europe. The election tour, the reports of a possible occupation, and the dispatch of Russian warships caused particular uneasiness in London. The Russian foreign office officials, scarcely concealing their own opinions, did what they could to explain Kaulbars' conduct. Jomini informed Morier that Russia was determined "not to be drawn into material intervention or occupation," but he warned that if Kaulbars should be murdered, "which was quite in the cards," it would be morally impossible not to intervene.[138] After the election had been held, Morier found Giers

... in a state of deepest depression. In the course of a long conversation he allowed me to infer, though he did not say so in so many words, that the mission of General

---

[135] Tatishchev, *op. cit.*, p. 469; Lascelles to Iddesleigh, *AP*, XCI:1, no. 529, Sofia, Nov. 3, 1886.

[136] Lascelles to Iddesleigh, *AP*, XCI:1, no. 513, Sofia, Oct. 30, 1886.

[137] Kaulbars to Giers, *Avantiury*, no. 27, Oct. 18/30, 1886; Goriainov, "Razryv," pp. 199–200.

[138] Morier to Iddesleigh, *FO*, 65/1261, no. 363, conf., St. P., Oct. 10, 1886.

Kaulbars had proved a total failure, and he fairly admitted that he did not see how the matter was to end, or how Russia was to extricate herself from the position she had got into.[139]

Giers also told the British ambassador that the tsar was taking the matter calmly: "Il envisage la situation en vrai philosophe."[140]

When the reports of terrorism were followed by the sending of the warships, Giers defended the action: "The Russian consulate was virtually in a state of siege and that not by the mob but by the Bulgarian gendarmes"—a situation for which he blamed the military commandant. Although Giers tended to "acquit" the Bulgarian government, he emphasized that it was powerless to deal with the anarchy prevailing in Bulgaria.[141]

Despite the fact that Giers could not openly condemn the actions of a Russian representative in his conversations with Morier, he could express his opinion within his own government. When Kaulbars' message concerning the "half-occupation" arrived, the foreign minister at once drew up a memorandum to the tsar in which he advised that under the existing circumstances neither a military occupation nor a military demonstration would be possible without the consent of the powers. At least the Russian ambassador in Berlin should discuss the issue with Bismarck. After the tsar had read the report, he wrote, "In my opinion it [the occupation] is not practical."[142] Subsequently, Zinoviev informed Kaulbars that the tsar did not approve of an occupation, since he considered it an "extraordinarily serious step."[143]

Deprived of the threat of an occupation of Bulgaria, Kaulbars tried another method of forcing compliance. On October 17/29 he issued an ultimatum demanding that all his conditions be met and that all acts against Russian subjects cease, or he and the entire Russian staff would leave the principality.[144] Upon receiving this declaration, Nachevich very cleverly requested Kaulbars to cite specific instances of maltreatment of Russians. The general refused to do so, since, he claimed, there were "so many instances having come to his personal knowledge during the time that he has been in Bulgaria."[145]

The new step was approved by Giers, who in a further conversation with Morier commented, "No country with self-respect would continue

---

[139] *Ibid.*, 65/1262, no. 366, most conf., St. P., Oct. 13, 1886; Giers to Bouteneff, *Staal*, no. 44, St. P., Nov. 19/28 [*sic*], 1886.
[140] Morier to Iddesleigh, *FO*, 65/1262, no. 366, most conf., St. P., Oct. 13, 1886.
[141] Morier to Iddesleigh, *AP*, XCI:1, no. 500, St. P., Oct. 28, 1886.
[142] Giers, memorandum to Alexander III, *Avantiury*, no. 28, Oct. 25/Nov. 7, 1886.
[143] Zinoviev to Shatokhin, *Avantiury*, no. 29, n.d.
[144] Radev, II, 448.
[145] *Ibid.*, p. 449; Lascelles to Iddesleigh, *AP*, XCI:1, no. 518, Sofia, Oct. 31, 1886.

to submit to the indignities to which the Russian officials and Russian subjects were daily exposed, and there was only one way to meet such a case, that of breaking off all communications and withdrawing from the country."[146] Giers added that he would recommend to the tsar that he approve the general's request that he "be authorized to declare that the ultimatum would take effect on the occurrence of the first new case," but that "he [Giers] did not contemplate such an eventuality and that he thought that the threat would suffice to bring about a discontinuance of the conduct complained of."[147]

Meanwhile, despite the general's warnings, the Grand National Assembly convened and elected Prince Waldemar of Denmark, brother-in-law of the tsar, as the new prince.[148] Although, on the advice of Russia, he rejected the offer, the regency had again successfully defied the general. The elections to the assembly had been held, and a prince had been chosen. It was apparent that Russia did not intend to occupy the country. Despite this optimistic outlook, the ultimatum on the withdrawal of Russian personnel still hung over the head of the Bulgarian government. If one more incident occurred, the regency would have to face the alternative of resigning or of having Russia sever diplomatic relations. Since tension was high and the number of Russian citizens in Bulgaria great, a new incident was certain to take place soon.

On October 30/November 11 the kavass (courier) of the Russian consulate in Plovdiv became involved in a street skirmish. According to one version, favorable to the Bulgarian side, the kavass was on the way to the telegraph office on official business at 10 P.M., although the city was under a 9 P.M. curfew. When he refused to heed the challenge of the police, a struggle ensued and he was forcibly returned to the consulate. A second account was that he was attacked by a crowd, beaten, and brought back to the consulate unconscious. No matter which version was correct, the overt act had occurred.[149]

As soon as Kaulbars was informed of the event, he demanded that those responsible for the failure to maintain order should be removed from office, and the participants in the incident should be imprisoned.

---

[146] Morier to Iddesleigh, *AP*, XCI:1, no. 521, St. P., Nov. 1, 1886.

[147] *Loc. cit.; ibid.*, no. 528, St. P., Nov. 3, 1886; Giers to Shuvalov, *GP*, V, no. 995, St. P., Nov. 11/23, 1886.

[148] Tatishchev, *op. cit.*, p. 470. The tsar's candidate for the throne was Prince Mingrelskii. Pressure was exerted on the Bulgars to accept him, but they categorically refused. See Lamzdorf, *Dnevnik, 1886–1890*, pp. 5–7; Marinov, *op. cit.*, pp. 366–375; Stanev, *Istoriia na Nova Bulgariia*, p. 89; Süreya to Grand Vizir, *BD*, no. 143, Nov. 13, 1886; *ibid.*, no. 144, Nov. 17, 1886; *ibid.*, no. 145, Nov. 14, 1886; Iddesleigh to Morier, *FO*, 65/1264, tel. no. 273, Foreign Office, Dec. 10, 1886.

[149] Lascelles to Iddesleigh, *FO*, 78/3896, no. 380, Sofia, Nov. 15, 1886, incl. Jones to Lascelles, Philippopolis, Nov. 14, 1886; Goriainov, "Razryv," p. 200.

If he did not receive satisfaction by November 5/17, he would leave the country. The Bulgarian government explained the circumstances of the incident, but refused to yield to the ultimatum. Left with no alternative, the general informed Nachevich on November 6/18 that he considered that his further presence in Bulgaria would serve no useful purpose. The Bulgarian government had now lost the confidence of Russia, and diplomatic relations could no longer be continued as long as the former was "composed of its present members."[150] Kaulbars left Sofia on November 8/20, followed soon thereafter by the other Russian agents. Diplomatic relations were thus severed eight years after the formation of the Bulgarian state, for whose existence the Russians had waged a costly war.

The motives behind Kaulbars' individual actions are difficult to fathom. The general was described by his acquaintances as a quiet, modest man, sound in judgment and discreet in his actions. Yet overnight he had changed into an arrogant, unyielding representative of Russian interests. He threatened, cajoled, and plotted against the government to which he was accredited. Whether he adopted these tactics on the instructions of the tsar, by whom he was appointed and to whom he reported, or whether he considered these the only methods which would succeed, cannot be ascertained. Bismarck believed that his conduct could not be attributed to his personal characteristics, since he behaved like a gentleman with all except the regents and their adherents. To them he acted "like a ruffian ... and this bearing was the result of direct instructions from the Emperor, who regarded the Regency as the legacy of the prince of Bulgaria."[151] Certainly, Kaulbars did not lose the esteem of the tsar. It is reported that when he returned to St. Petersburg, Alexander III greeted him warmly: "You are a soldier obeying the orders of your superior officer; you have acted to my full satisfaction."[152]

Despite the approval of the tsar, the tactics adopted by the general were recognized as mistakes by his contemporaries. In reviewing the episode four years later, Tatishchev, a prominent Russian historian and publicist, described the Kaulbars mission as the last episode in a "tragic comedy." Russia, he pointed out, had missed a golden opportunity. After the abdication of Alexander of Battenberg, the Bulgarian people had been eager for a reconciliation; they knew that without Russian assistance they would probably never achieve their national aims. The op-

[150] The text of Kaulbars' declaration is in Lascelles to Iddesleigh, *FO*, 78/3896, no. 384, Sofia, Nov. 18, 1886.
[151] Malet to Iddesleigh, *FO*, 364/3, no. 455, most conf., Berlin, Nov. 12, 1886.
[152] Morier to Iddesleigh, *FO*, 65/1263, no. 433, conf., St. P., Dec. 6, 1886.

portunity thus offered to Russian diplomacy had been compromised by the maladroit actions of the Russian representative.[153] Even Nekliudov, who had been more arrogant than Kaulbars in his dealings with the Bulgars, is reported to have admitted that if the general "had from the very offset adopted a friendly and conciliatory tone toward the Bulgarian government he would have in all probability readily obtained not only everything which has now been conceded almost by force, but also other concessions which are now being stoutly defended."[154] Nelidov, from his post as Russian ambassador in Constantinople, expressed a similar judgment. Protesting against the general's activities and their effect in Europe, he advised that Russia should put an end to "the diplomatic period which will carry the name of Kaulbars."[155]

The fate of the Kaulbars mission was a fitting climax to seven years of Russo-Bulgarian relations. The Russian government and its agents had come to rely increasingly on force and pressure. The attitude and actions of the general had marked the extreme of this policy; the result had been the departure of Russia's representatives from Bulgaria. Thereafter, Russia could interfere in Bulgarian affairs only in an indirect manner. She could sponsor groups and individuals who sought to overthrow the Stambolov regime or she could organize the opposition of the great powers to Bulgarian interests. However, no longer could she dictate the composition of Bulgarian ministries or control the army through her officers.

Although Alexander had proved anything but a submissive ruler, he had been designated by Russia and he had close ties with the imperial family. A new prince of Bulgaria, who would under the circumstances assume the throne in defiance of Russia, would neither rely upon nor ask aid from St. Petersburg. The policy adopted by Russia in regard to Bulgaria after the Congress of Berlin had thus met with complete failure.

---

[153] Tatishchev, *op. cit.*, pp. 457, 472.
[154] White to Iddesleigh, *FO*, 78/3876, no. 540, conf., Constantinople, Nov. 1, 1886.
[155] Nelidov to Giers, *NKG*, personal and very secret, Pera, Nov. 9/21, 1886.

XI

CONCLUSION

BY 1886 Russia's position in the Balkans was radically different from that of the period 1878–1883. Bulgaria, the theoretical outpost for an attack on or the defense of the Straits, was lost; only the Serbian people, whose nation had been abandoned to the Austrian camp, retained their strong pro-Russian sentiments. The Dreikaiserbund, based on the united determination of the three great conservative empires to preserve the peace and the *status quo,* had proved its value in the emergency of 1885–1886; but in the next year, 1887, it was to dissolve permanently. With the breakdown of the arrangement of the Treaty of Berlin, involving Russian domination in Bulgaria and Austrian control in Serbia, two issues which had their origin in the period under discussion thereafter dominated the Balkan diplomatic scene: the partition of Macedonia and the fate of Bosnia-Hercegovina. The national conflicts inherent in these problems were ultimately to involve Europe in the First World War.

Despite the fact that diplomatic ties between Bulgaria and Russia were severed in 1886, the Russian government kept a careful eye on events in Sofia in the hope that Russian influence could be restored. A Russian candidate for the throne, Prince Mingrelskii, was supported. When the Bulgarian government, led by Stambolov, categorically rejected his candidacy, Russia determined to force the regency from office. In this endeavor the Russian government used the diplomatic support which it could command, and also the services of the Bulgarian emigrants abroad who desired the downfall of the Stambolov regime. Both means failed.

The fate of Russian influence in Bulgaria was taken as a personal affront by Alexander III. As one observer remarked, "He is furious because even now that his archenemy Battenberg has been turned out, things are still going contrary to his expectations and wishes."[1]

Like most Russians, the tsar never lost the conviction that at heart the Bulgarian people were intensely pro-Russian and that they had been misled by their selfish, office-seeking leaders. His views were apparently confirmed by reports of the activities of the Bulgars in exile who sought his assistance. In 1887 the tsar personally gave his blessing, as well as financial and military assistance, to groups of rebels who made

---

[1] Bülow to Holstein [?], *GP,* V, no. 990, St. P., Nov., 1886.

three separate attempts to overthrow the government in Sofia.[2] After
the regency selected Ferdinand of Coburg as prince, despite Russian
protests, the intrigues against the Bulgarian government became increasingly numerous. None of the attempts to overthrow the regime
succeeded.

The vast majority [of Bulgars] is made up of those who desire to prevent the
country being made a lucrative farm for Russian officers and capitalists and who
hold their savings with the tenacity of a French peasant, which they believe and
probably know from experience would be impossible under Russian as well as
Turkish supremacy.[3]

Illegal and violent means of overthrowing the Stambolov government
had never had the enthusiastic approval of Giers. In 1888 he persuaded
the tsar that such methods should be at least temporarily abandoned.
Nevertheless, the Russian government refused to recognize Ferdinand
or his prime minister Stambolov. Russian influence was thus completely
removed from the official circles in Bulgaria.

In the achievement of Bulgarian emancipation, the role played by
the remarkable young prince, Alexander of Battenberg, had been of
the utmost importance. Although he can hardly be drawn as a heroic
figure, in the light of his servile telegram to the tsar after the abduction,
and the circumstances of his abdication, he did, in the course of his brief
career, become the prince of Bulgaria in more than name. A German
prince, called to the throne of a Slavic country, ill prepared to rule
under the constitutional regime established, he yet was to unify Bulgarian national sentiment against Russian domination. In this regard
his very youth and inexperience were of service to his country. When
he came to Bulgaria, he was determined to rule as an independent
prince. He ignored the hard facts of power politics—namely, that
Russia, because of her overwhelming military strength and the recognition of the great powers, was dominant in Bulgaria. Through his opposition to Russian dictation and, at times, through blind stubbornness,
Alexander prevented Bulgaria from becoming a Russian province. By
the time of the union, Alexander had succeeded in solidifying national
sentiment. Although he was finally forced to abdicate, the circumstances
under which he did so, while humiliating for him personally, were
factors in strengthening Bulgarian national independence.

The seven-year period under discussion, which marked a gain for
Bulgarian nationalism in the achievement of unification and freedom
from foreign control, was a period of loss for Serbia. Milan not only

---

[2] See *Avantiury*, chaps. iv, vi, vii; see also Zinoviev to Giers, *NKG*, Dec. 17,
1886.

[3] O'Conor to Iddesleigh, *FO*, 78/3897, no. 450, Sofia, Dec. 26, 1886.

failed to secure territory in the fatal war with Bulgaria; he was un-willing and unable to throw off Austrian tutelage. His failure abroad further weakened his position, and his pro-Austrian course was steadily opposed by his people. As one observer commented, "It would be no exaggeration to say that beyond a dozen or so of exceptionally well-educated and far-seeing Serbians, there is scarcely a native of this country, except His Majesty, who at heart is not Russian."[4] Recog-nizing the hopelessness of his position, Milan in 1887 attempted to abdicate, but through Austrian persuasion this move was postponed.

When the welcome news of Milan's abdication, in March, 1889, reached St. Petersburg, the tsar exclaimed, "Thank God!"[5] For two and a half years Russia had been without influence in either Sofia or Belgrade. With the assumption of the throne by Milan's son Alexander, and the return of Mihailo as metropolitan, Russian counsels again pre-vailed in Serbia. That state could now be used also as a base against Austria; no longer was it a weapon against Russian influence in the Balkans.

The fate of Milan offers an interesting contrast to that of Alexander of Battenberg. Despite the advantages enjoyed by Milan, who was a native prince from a national dynasty, he, unlike Alexander, failed to identify himself with the sentiments of his people or to win their sympathy. Although submission to Vienna was forced upon him, the enthusiasm with which he embraced vassalage to the northern power estranged him from the Serbs. The temper of Balkan nationalism was resistance to and not acceptance of foreign domination. Acquisitions in Macedonia would have helped to win him favor, but Bosnia-Herce-govina was very close to Serbian sentiments. Since Russian officials did not hold important positions in Serbia, since Russian territory did not border on Serbia, and since Russia held no unredeemed Serbian lands, the Serbian people could cling to the illusion that Russia remained the champion of the oppressed Orthodox Slavs.

The disastrous effects of the relations of the liberated Bulgarians with Serbia in this period are still apparent in the Balkans. Although the two peoples were united by history, race, language, culture, and religion, they worked thereafter in opposite camps, largely as a result of the events previously described, but it cannot be said that their subsequent fate was undeserved. As the Balkan states obtained their independence from Moslem rule, the problem of their mutual relations had to be settled. The ideal solution would have been a type of Balkan union, with each state organized on a national basis as nearly as was

---

[4] St. John to Salisbury, *FO*, 105/87, no. 41, Belgrade, April 22, 1888.

[5] Lamzdorf, *Dnevnik, 1886–1890*, p. 151.

geographically and ethnically possible. Another solution, that of national independence but mutual antagonism, finally prevailed. Once each of the small powers became free, each had irridenta and frankly imperialistic endeavors. As such they nullified each other and made great power interference in Balkan internal affairs much easier. Together, Serbia and Bulgaria might have had weight in international diplomacy; apart they became pawns in the historic struggle of Russia and the Habsburg empire.

The price for which they bartered their position was the fatal territory of Macedonia. After the Serbian defeat of 1885, the entire nation became emotionally involved in the issue. Whereas Serbia hitherto had pressed her claims without a well-organized plan, she now adopted an aggressive policy to further her interests and prepare the inhabitants for union with Serbia. The newly formed society of Sveti Sava, named after the patron saint of the Serbs, was the chief agency of propaganda and educational activities. Its Bulgarian counterpart, the Cyril and Methodius society, worked in opposition. As a result of the Macedonian problem, which Russia helped to precipitate, Serbia and Bulgaria were on opposite sides of the battlefield, not only in 1885 but also in 1913, 1915–1918, and 1941–1945. The present-day Communist regimes in Bulgaria and Jugoslavia also have been unable to reach an acceptable solution of the problem.

The period 1878 to 1886 had proved unfortunate for Russian policy also. Certain concrete successes, nevertheless, had been achieved. The short-term policy formulated in the fall and winter of 1879 had been carried out. At that time the leaders of the government, Miliutin, Giers, Saburov, Gorchakov, Jomini, and Alexander II, had all been obsessed by fear of the consequences of Russian isolation. They were concerned also over the British threat to the Straits and a possible Turkish occupation of the Balkan mountain garrisons. The Dreikaiserbund agreement was an endeavor to meet these problems, and in this limited sense it had proved its worth to Russia. By 1883 the danger of an immediate British seizure of the Straits or of a Turkish march into Rumelia was no longer acute. Moreover, the alliance had done much to prevent the Bulgarian union and the Serbo-Bulgarian war from becoming major international crises. Despite their mutual distrust, Austria and Russia, under the moderating influence of Germany, had worked together to seek a satisfactory solution. The immediate goals of Russian diplomacy as formulated by the Russian foreign ministry after 1878 had thus been attained.

The losses suffered by Russia in this period lie primarily in her long-range policy. The alienation of Bulgaria, which halted the Russian advance to the Straits, was the most serious. The creation of Bulgaria, the only real gain of the Russo-Turkish War, had in fact proved detrimental to Russian interests. The responsibility for this failure of policy must be shared by many branches of the Russian government, but the principal burden falls on Alexander III.

One of the most glaring weaknesses of the Russian handling of the Bulgarian problem was the failure to formulate and enforce a single line of action. The violent fluctuations in policy have been described in the previous pages. Russia first sponsored a liberal constitution and the election of Alexander of Battenberg. In 1881 she reversed her stand on the constitution and supported the prince's *coup d'état*. When Alexander failed to act to the satisfaction of Russia, the military dictatorship of Sobolev and Kaulbars was instituted. When the two generals did not achieve the desired results, the Russian government used the Russian officers in the Bulgarian army to put pressure on the government, and condoned forceful measures directed against Alexander. After the removal of the prince, Kaulbars, with a policy based on threats and intimidation, was sent to try to reëstablish the dominant influence of Russia. Russian policy thus shifted back and forth from the support of the Liberal party and the Tyrnovo constitution to the authoritarian rule of the prince, from aid to the prince personally to attempts to force his abdication, and from allowing the Bulgarian government free sway to attempts to dictate its principal activities.

To carry out these divergent policies Russia sent an ill-chosen succession of agents, none of whom held office for much longer than a year. In the British foreign service, holding a position in the Balkans was a part of the regular tour of duty. If an agent performed unusually well, he could hope to continue in a more distinguished position. Consequently, most of the diplomatic and consular assignments were held by men of ability. In contrast, the caliber of the Russian representatives was much lower. The Russian diplomats preferred appointments in western European or German capitals. As a result, the Balkan states received men who were less well qualified and had less influence in the government. This condition held true also for those appointed by the war ministry.

Moreover, Russian military and diplomatic representatives in Bulgaria quarreled with each other and supported contradictory policies, as did Parensov and Davydov, Ernrot and Kumani. Often they supported programs in direct contradiction to their orders. Dondukov-Korsakov, Kumani, Ernrot, Khitrovo, Sobolev, Koiander, and Bogdanov each on occasion acted against instructions and to the detriment of Russian interests. Russia lost prestige in Bulgaria, and her position in international diplomacy was compromised.

The Bulgarian question led directly to the rupture of the Dreikaiserbund, which after 1879 had been the basis of Russian foreign policy. After 1883, when the British threat had diminished, Austria-Hungary by slow stages replaced Britain as the chief Russian opponent, despite the fact that the Dual Monarchy was an ally. The basis of the growing estrangement was the historic suspicion which each felt for the other's activities in the Balkans. The Habsburg officials saw deceit and intrigue in every Russian action. The failure of the Russian government to curb the activities of its agents increased the Austrian fears.

On the Russian side, similar sentiments existed. The nationalist press, led by Aksakov and Katkov, saw Austrian activities as responsible for the compromising of the Russian position in Bulgaria. The old suspicion of the German powers thus received new impetus. Alexander III, who had never been a convinced proponent of the Austrian alliance, was strongly influenced by nationalist currents. In 1887 he therefore refused to renew the Dreikaiserbund. Shortly thereafter, the Reinsurance treaty with Germany was concluded so that Russia would not be isolated. Nevertheless, despite the latter agreement, Russia had in some degree returned to her dangerous position of 1878. Britain and Austria-Hungary, her chief opponents, were both left without treaty obligations to her. It could be expected that they would unite their efforts where possible. Although they did not become formal allies, they did embarrass and harass Russia in international diplomacy.

The rupture of the Dreikaiserbund had one added significance for Balkan affairs. Russian policy since 1870 had been based on the creation of a strong satellite Bulgaria. In return, Austria was to annex Bosnia-Hercegovina and dominate Serbia. With the loss of Bulgaria by Russia, the entire situation shifted. Russia either had to give up all hope of influence in the Balkans, which she would never do, or shift her support to Serbia. Her adoption of the latter course led to the abandonment of the exclusive support hitherto given to the Bulgarian exarchate and its Macedonian policy. Serbian aspirations in Macedonia were now for the first time officially acknowledged; moreover, Serbian claims to Bosnia-Hercegovina were viewed in a different light. The fate of Macedonia and Bosnia-Hercegovina thereafter became the center of conflict and led to the Bosnian crisis of 1908, the Balkan Wars of 1912–1913, and the First World War.

In the formulation and carrying out of Russian foreign policy two men, Alexander III and N. K. Giers, stand out. For the interests of both Europe and Russia, it was fortunate that Giers, not his competitors, such men as Ignatiev or Saburov, directed foreign affairs. Even though Russian policy in the three years after the Congress of Berlin was greatly influenced by Miliutin, Giers after 1882 succeeded in gaining the primary position with the tsar. In every major crisis in the period under study he was ultimately able to win acceptance for his opinions. His position was consistently moderate and conciliatory. In foreign policy he stood for peace, and was correctly recognized by his contemporaries as a strong supporter of the German alliance.

Because of his non-Russian ancestry and adherence to the continuation of the Dreikaiserbund, Giers incurred the enmity of the national school. In 1886 the nationalist press, led by Katkov, launched a concerted attack upon Giers and the Dreikaiserbund, whose terms had been divulged by Saburov.[6] The immediate cause of the campaign was the Bulgarian crisis of 1885–1886. In this struggle, some of the most influential men in Russia were ranged against Giers: Katkov, whose reports and editorials were read by Alexander III; Tolstoi, minister of the interior; Pobedonostsev, procurator-general of the Holy Synod; and, of course, Saburov. After a period of uncertainty, Alexander III gave his approval to the policy advocated by Giers. Katkov and Saburov thereafter disappeared from public life.[7]

Although Giers had won a signal victory, the major obstacle with which he still had to contend was the influence on the tsar of those outside the Russian foreign office. For, in the last analysis, it was the tsar and the tsar alone who made the final decisions. As Jomini wrote in 1888: "There will always be brawlers. When one is defended from above against their recriminations from below, one can be indifferent. In the contrary case it is intolerable."[8]

Thus the responsibility for the events described rests on the shoulders of Alexander III. In major policy decisions the tsar eventually supported the position of the foreign office; in less important matters, however, he often acted impulsively and with violence. Many of his actions were in direct opposition to the principles on which his conduct of Russian internal affairs was based. In the last years of his father's reign, repeated attempts were made on the lives of the members of the imperial family and their officials. The assassination of 1881 left an indelible impression on Alexander III, and in large part determined the

---

[6] The Katkov-Giers crisis is discussed in "M. N. Katkov i Aleksandr III v 1886–1887 gg.," *Krasnyi Arkhiv*, XXXIII (1933), 58–85.

[7] Soon after Katkov was reprimanded by the tsar, the famous publicist died.

[8] Jomini to Giers, *NKG*, July 4, [1888].

fate of the Loris-Melikov reforms. Thereafter, the entire state apparatus of Russia was directed toward stamping out revolutionary activity and suppressing liberal or socialistic agitation. Yet in the Balkan Peninsula, in Bulgaria in particular, the tsar supported policies which made it necessary for the Russian government to work with and aid those who had much in common with the assassins of his father.

Once Russia supported the cause of Bulgarian nationalism, an association with liberal groups was inevitable. Since Ottoman rule had deprived the Balkan states of a national aristocracy in the real sense of the word, the national idea was preserved by the relatively small educated middle class. From Serbia many students went to Vienna or Paris to study, from Bulgaria to Moscow or St. Petersburg. Those who attended western institutions were influenced by liberal, constitutional ideals; those who went to Russia were thrown with reform or radical elements among the student groups. All returned with liberal or socialistic, not conservative or monarchical, political programs. The revolutionary tendency in Balkan politics was further emphasized by the fact that national independence had been gained or would have to be won by war or revolution against the Ottoman Empire. Resistance to authority and the right to self-rule were thus accepted principles.

It was to be expected that the Russian government would have to deal with groups which did not share its autocratic principles, but what is remarkable is that Alexander III was willing to allow Russian activity to go so far beyond the bounds of legality. Although the tradition of assistance to the Christians against Moslem rule was established in the Christian states, Alexander departed from the past in personally condoning or actually assisting those who sought to overthrow a legally established government by violence. The Bulgarian government had been set up by an international act at the Congress of Berlin; yet the tsar lent Russian arms and financial aid to subvert it. In doing so, he worked within the same frame of reference as the nihilists and revolutionaries of Russia. A reactionary in Russia, he yet condoned and supported revolutionary activity in the Balkans when it served his purposes.

Alexander III was first and foremost a Russian nationalist, not in the definition of the Moscow school and its policy of a "free hand," but in the sense that Russian policy should be dictated solely by Russia's interests as a great power and not by political or religious ideology. "Orthodoxy," "autocracy," and the Panslav dreams of Slavic unity under Russian guidance were ideals to be applied only where they did not conflict with the practical demands of Russian strategy. The

German alliance was maintained, despite its unpopularity with influential circles, because it prevented Russian isolation; later an agreement was contracted with France, whose clericalism and radicalism had hitherto discouraged closer relations. Certainly, few sentimental visions of Slavic solidarity lingered on. "The Slavs must now serve us and not we them," Alexander III had written in 1885. Jomini in 1886 gave the opinion that perhaps Russia's Balkan policy should be based on the Greeks, who were "more intelligent and more consistent."[9]

Although guided by the interests of Russian nationalism, Alexander III remained blind to the forces of Bulgarian nationalism. Prior to 1878 no conflict had been apparent; to be a Bulgarian nationalist had been to be pro-Russian, since only with Russian aid could the Bulgarian people hope to throw off Turkish control. Thereafter the Bulgarian leaders had their own distinct national aims. As long as Russian policy led in the direction of the union of Bulgaria and Eastern Rumelia and eventually to the re-creation of the San Stefano state, the Bulgarian government could coöperate with Russia. When, however, it became apparent that Russia regarded Bulgaria chiefly as an outpost toward the Straits, and the Bulgarian army as a useful auxiliary force for the furtherance of Russian policy in the Near East, the Bulgarian political leaders were no longer willing to accept Russian domination.

The Russian diplomats recognized that their country's policy in Bulgaria was a mistake. The reaction to the Kaulbars mission, the culmination of Alexander III's policy, has been noted. Similar disapproval was expressed over the widespread use of force, intimidation, and bribery. Although these measures had at times enjoyed some local success, the affront to Bulgarian national pride had proved disastrous in the long run. In 1887 M. K. Onou commented on the bribes which Russia had distributed:

As for the money which has been spent in order to win over some influential Bulgars—I believe that money has been paid out at a complete loss. Sometimes much can be done with money, but not everything. I have often noticed that this money remains in the hands of intermediaries. It is a very delicate weapon and difficult to manage. We claim that the Bulgarians of the party at present in power are paid by the Austrians and the English. I doubt that—they are paid otherwise, by the support given to their thirst for domination and to other passions.[10]

Against the force of Bulgarian nationalism, the policy finally adopted—that of intimidation—could have succeeded only if Russia had backed her decision with a military occupation of Bulgaria. This, however, would have run the danger of reopening the entire eastern ques-

---

[9] *Ibid.*, April 25, 1886.
[10] Onou to Giers, *NKG*, Sept. 10/22, 1887.

tion on a European basis and perhaps of ultimate war. Throughout the period under discussion, Russia was never in a position in which she could hope to achieve victory either at the conference table or on the battlefield. She had neither completely reliable allies nor the necessary military power.

The charge that Bulgarian defection was caused by British and Austrian influence was the chief argument used by those seeking to excuse the Russian failure. In fact, although Britain and Austria-Hungary both gave moral support to Bulgarian resistance, particularly after 1885, neither country gave or offered material assistance. The wise view on Russian policy was expressed in a letter written by Jomini to Giers in 1888:

Let us rest on our *non possumus* and *laissons faire*. All things come to him who waits for the opportunity, prepares for it and seizes it. What happened in Serbia proves it. It is a moral success for our policy of patience and moderation. It will be the same in Bulgaria. If we have had painful failures it is we who have brought them upon ourselves in acting out of order. You will not make people like you by using force. It is time to finish with that system.[11]

The period 1878 to 1886 had buried the hopes which the Russian government had placed in the Bulgarian cause after 1860. Bulgaria was no longer a point of Russian strength but of Russian weakness. The situation was favorable in Serbia, but the use which would be made of this opportunity remained for the future. Bulgaria was now in the camp of Austria-Hungary, whose conflict with Russia henceforth dominated Balkan diplomacy.

---

[11] Jomini to Giers, *NKG*, July 4, [1888].

SELECTED BIBLIOGRAPHY

SELECTED BIBLIOGRAPHY

Only those books which were found most helpful for an understanding of this problem are listed below.

DOCUMENTARY SOURCES

Dorev, Pancho, ed. *Dokumenti za Bulgarskata Istoriia: Dokumenti iz Turskitie Durzhavni Arkhivi, 1863–1909* (Documents for Bulgarian History: Documents from Turkish State Archives, 1863–1909). Sofia, 1942. Vol. IV.

Hertslet, Edward. *The Map of Europe by Treaty, 1875–1891*. London, 1891. Vol. IV.

Leonov, R. *Documents secrets de la politique russe en orient, 1881–1890*. Berlin, 1893.

Lepsius, J., *et al. Die grosse Politik der europäischen Kabinette, 1871–1914*. Berlin, 1922–1926. Vols. III–VI.

Miiatev, Petur, ed. *Iz Arkhiva Konstantin Irechek* (From the Archives of Konstantin Irechek). Sofia, 1953.

Nikolić, Milan M., ed. *Timočka Buna, 1883* (The Timok Uprising, 1883). Belgrade, 1954–1955. 2 vols.

Pavlovich, P., ed. *Avantiury Russkogo Tsarizma v Bolgarii* (The Adventures of Russian Tsarism in Bulgaria). Moscow, 1935.

Pribram, Alfred F. *The Secret Treaties of Austria-Hungary, 1879–1914*. Cambridge, Mass., 1920–1921. 2 vols.

"Reikhshtadt" (Reichstadt), *Krasnyi Arkhiv*, I (1922), 36–61.

MEMOIRS, AUTOBIOGRAPHIES, BIOGRAPHIES, AND LETTERS

Aksakov, Ivan S. *Slavianofil'stvo i Zapadnichestvo, 1860–1886* (Slavophilism and Westernism, 1860–1886). Moscow, 1886.

———. *Slavianskii Vopros', 1860–1886* (The Slavic Question, 1860–1886). Moscow, 1886.

Buckle, George Earle, ed. *The Letters of Queen Victoria*. London, 1926–1930. 2d series, Vol. III, 3d series, Vol. I.

Cecil, Lady Gwendolen. *Life of Robert Marquis of Salisbury*. London, 1931–1932. Vols. III–IV.

Danilevskii, N. Ia. *Rossiia i Evropa* (Russia and Europe). St. Petersburg, 1888.

Hansen, Jules. *Ambassade à Paris du Baron de Mohrenheim, 1884–1898*. Paris, 1907.

Holborn, Hajo, ed. *Aufzeichnungen und Errinerungen aus dem Leben des Botschafters Joseph Maria von Radowitz*. Stuttgart, 1925. 2 vols.

Kartsov, Iuri. *Sem Liet na Blizhnem Vostoke, 1879–1886: Vospominaniia Politicheskiia i Lichnyia* (Seven Years in the Near East, 1879–1886: Political and Personal Remembrances). St. Petersburg, 1906.

Lamzdorf, V. N. *Dnevnik, 1886–1890* (Diary, 1886–1890). Moscow, 1926.

———. *Dnevnik, 1891–1892* (Diary, 1891–1892). Moscow, 1934.

Meyendorff, A. *Correspondence diplomatique de M. de Staal*. Paris, 1929. 2 vols.

Mijatovich, Chedomille (Mijatović, Čedomil). *The Memoirs of a Balkan Diplomatist*. London, 1917.

Nelidov, A. I. "Zapiska A. I. Nelidova v 1882 g. o Zaniatii Prolivov" (The Memorandum of A. I. Nelidov in 1882 Concerning the Seizure of the Straits), *Krasnyi Arkhiv*, XLVI (1931), 179–187.

Parensov, P. D. "V Bolgarii: Vospominaniia Ofitsera General'nago Shtaba" (In Bulgaria: The Remembrances of an Officer of the General Staff), *Russkaia Starina*, CI (1900), 107–127, 359–381, 593–602; CXXV (1906), 62–74, 272–

287, 509–527; CXXVI (1906), 62–78, 324–340; CXXXI (1907), 435–455; CXXXII (1907), 27–44, 599–619; CXXXIII (1908), 257–270; CXXXIV (1908), 17–47, 257–282.

Pobedonostsev, K. P. *L'autocratie russe: mémoires politiques, 1881–1894.* Paris, 1927.

———. *Pis'ma Pobedonostseva k Aleksandru III* (The Letters of Pobedonostsev to Alexander III). Moscow, 1925. 2 vols.

———. *K. P. Pobedonostsev i Ego Korrespondenty: Pis'ma i Zapiski* (K. P. Pobedonostsev and His Correspondents: Letters and Memoranda). Moscow, 1923. Vol. I.

Saburov, P. A. "Besedy P. A. Saburova s Kn. Bismarkom v 1879 g." (Talks of P. A. Saburov with Prince Bismarck in 1879), *Krasnyi Arkhiv,* I (1922), 62–91.

Schweinitz, Hans Lothar von. *Denkwürdigkeiten des Botschafters General v. Schweinitz.* Berlin, 1927. Vol. II.

Simpson, J. Y. *The Saburov Memoirs, or Bismarck and Russia.* Cambridge, 1929.

Vogüé, Vicomte E. M. de. *Journal: Paris-Saint-Petersbourg, 1877–1883.* Paris, 1932.

Zaionchkovskii, P. A., ed. *Dnevnik D. A. Miliutina, 1878–1882* (The Diary of D. A. Miliutin, 1878–1882). Moscow, 1950. Vols. III–IV.

GENERAL WORKS

Akademiia Nauk SSSR. *Istoriia Bolgarii* (History of Bulgaria). Moscow, 1954. Vol. I.

Arnaudov, M. *Eksarkh Iosif i Bulgarskata Kulturna Borba sled Suzdavaneto na Eksarkhiiata, 1870–1915* (Exarch Iosif and the Bulgarian Cultural Struggle after the Creation of the Exarchate, 1870–1915). Sofia, 1940. Vol. I.

Baddeley, John F. *Russia in the 'Eighties.* London, 1921.

Beaman, A. Hulme. *M. Stambuloff.* London, 1895.

Belić, Vladimir J. *Ratovi Srpskog Naroda u XIX i XX Veku* (Wars of the Serbian People in the Nineteenth and Twentieth Centuries). Belgrade, 1938.

Black, C. E. *The Establishment of Constitutional Government in Bulgaria.* Princeton, 1943.

Burmov, Aleksandr. *Bulgarski Revoliutsionen Tsentralen Komitet, 1868–1877* (The Bulgarian Revolutionary Central Committee, 1868–1877). Sofia, 1950.

Corti, Egon Caesar Conte. *Alexander von Battenberg.* London, 1954.

———. *Alexander von Battenberg: Sein Kampf mit den Zaren und Bismarck.* Vienna, 1920.

———. *The Downfall of Three Dynasties.* London, 1934.

———. *Leben und Lieben Alexanders von Battenberg.* Graz, Salzburg, Vienna, 1950.

Čubrilović, Vaso, and V. Ćorović. *Srbija od 1858 do 1903* (Serbia from 1858 to 1903). Belgrade, 1938.

Cyon, Elie de. *Histoire de l'entente franco-russe, 1886–1894. Documents et souvenirs.* Paris, 1895.

Djordjević, Vladan. *Crna Gora i Austrija, 1814–1894* (Montenegro and Austria, 1814–1894). Belgrade, 1924.

Driault, Édouard, and Michel Lhéritier. *Histoire diplomatique de la Grèce de 1821 à nos jours.* Paris, 1926. Vol. IV.

Edwards, H. Sutherlund. *Sir William White, His Life and Correspondence.* London, 1902.

Erdmann, Ada von. *Nikolai Karlovich Giers, russischer Aussenminister, 1882–1895.* Berlin, 1936.

Fishel, Alfred. *Der Panslawismus bis zum Weltkrieg.* Stuttgart and Berlin, 1919.

Fortunatov, P. K. *Voina 1877–1878 gg. i Osvobozhdenie Bolgarii* (The War of 1877–1878 and the Liberation of Bulgaria). Moscow, 1950.

Fuller, Joseph Vincent. *Bismarck's Diplomacy at Its Zenith.* Cambridge, Mass., 1922.

Genov, Georgi P. *Iztochniiat Vupros: Politicheska i Diplomaticheska Istoriia, 1856–1919* (The Eastern Question: Political and Diplomatic History, 1856–1919). Sofia, 1926.

Georgevitch, T. R. *Macedonia.* London, 1918.

Geshov, Ivan Evstratiev. *Spomeni i Studii* (Remembrances and Studies). Sofia, 1928.

Gitermann, Valentin. *Geschichte Russlands.* Zurich, 1949. Vol. III.

Golovine, A. F. *Fürst Alexander von Bulgarien.* Vienna, 1896.

Goriainov, Serge. *Le Bosphore et les Dardanelles.* Paris, 1910.

——. *La question d'orient à la veille du traité de Berlin.* Paris, 1948.

Grüning, Irene. *Die russische öffentliche Meinung und ihre Stellung zu den Grossmächten, 1878–1894.* Berlin, 1929.

Hajek, Alois. *Bulgariens Befreiung und staatliche Entwicklung unter seinem ersten Fürsten.* Munich and Berlin, 1939.

Huhn, A. von. *The Kidnapping of Prince Alexander of Battenberg.* London, 1887.

Iotsov, Dimitur. *Diplomaticheski Studii po Nasheto Osvobozhdenie* (Diplomatic Studies Concerning Our Liberation). Sofia, 1909.

Jakšić, Grgur. *Iz Novije Srpske Istorije* (From Recent Serbian History). Belgrade, 1953.

Janković, Dragoslav. *O Političkim Strankama u Srbiji XIX Veka* (Concerning Political Parties in Serbia in the Nineteenth Century). Belgrade, 1951.

Jovanović, Jovan M. *Južna Srbija od Kraja XVIII Veka do Oslobodjenja* (Southern Serbia from the End of the Eighteenth Century to the Liberation). Belgrade, 1938.

Jovanović, Slobodan. "Srpsko-Bugarski Rat" (The Serbo-Bulgarian War), *Političke i Pravne Rasprave.* Belgrade, 1933. Vol. III, pp. 1–237.

——. "Svetozar Marković," *Političke i Pravne Rasprave.* Belgrade, 1932. Vol. I, pp. 59–289.

——. *Vlada Aleksandra Obrenovića* (The Government of Alexander Obrenović). Belgrade, 1934. Vol. I.

——. *Vlada Milana Obrenovića* (The Government of Milan Obrenović). Belgrade, 1934. 3 vols.

Karosseroff, Iwan. *Zur Entwicklung der bulgarischen Eisenbahn.* Erlangen, 1907.

Kesiakov, B. D. *Prinos kum Diplomaticheskata Istoriia na Bulgariia, 1878–1925* (Contributions to the Diplomatic History of Bulgaria, 1878–1925). Sofia, 1925–1926.

Koch, A. *Prince Alexander of Battenberg.* London, 1887.

Kohn, Hans. *Panslavism: Its History and Ideology.* Notre Dame, 1953.

Kosev, D. *Novaia Istoriia Bolgarii* (Recent History of Bulgaria). Moscow, 1952.

Krachunov, Kristno. *Velikite Durzhavi i Bulgariia (1886–1887)* (The Great Powers and Bulgaria, 1886–1887). Sofia, 1928.

Kratchounov, K. *La politique extérieure de la Bulgarie, 1880–1920.* Sofia, 1932.

Lameroux, Jean. *La politique extérieure de l'Autriche-Hongrie.* Paris, 1918.

Langer, William L. *European Alliances and Alignments, 1871–1890.* New York, 1950.

Lowe, Charles. *Alexander III of Russia.* London, 1895.

Madol, Hans Roger. *Ferdinand of Bulgaria.* London, 1933.

Madzharov, M. I. *Istochna Rumeliia* (Eastern Rumelia). Sofia, 1925.

Marinov, D. *Stefan Stambolov i Noveishata Ni Istoriia* (Stefan Stambolov and Our Recent History). Sofia, 1909.

Medlicott, W. N. *Bismarck, Gladstone, and the Concert of Europe.* London, 1956.

————. *The Congress of Berlin and After: A Diplomatic History of the Near Eastern Settlement, 1878–1880.* London, 1938.

Milioukov, Paul, *et al. Histoire de Russie.* Paris, 1932. Vol. III.

Milošević, Raša. *Timočka Buna, 1883 godine* (The Timok Uprising, 1883). Belgrade, 1923.

Mousset, Jean. *La Serbie et son église, 1830–1904.* Paris, 1938.

Nechkina, M. V., ed. *Istoriia SSSR* (History of the USSR). Moscow, 1949. Vol. II.

Nolde, Boris. *L'alliance franco-russe.* Paris, 1936.

Novaković, Stojan. *Balkanska Pitanja, 1886–1905* (Balkan Questions, 1886–1905). Belgrade, 1906.

Ocherk Istorii Ministerstva Inostrannykh Diel, 1802–1902 (Sketch of the History of the Ministry of Foreign Affairs, 1802–1902). St. Petersburg, 1902.

Panaiotov, Ivan. *Russiia, Velikitie Sili i Bulgarskiiat Vupros sled Izbora na Kniaz Ferdinanda, 1888–1896* (Russia, the Great Powers and the Bulgarian Question after the Election of Prince Ferdinand, 1888–1896). Sofia, 1941.

Petrovich, Michael Boro. *The Emergence of Russian Panslavism, 1856–1870.* New York, 1956.

Pokrovskii, M. N. *Diplomatiia i Voinyi Tsarskoi Rossii v XIX Stoletii* (Diplomacy and Wars of Tsarist Russia in the Nineteenth Century). Moscow, 1923.

Ponsonby, Sir Frederick, ed. *Letters of the Empress Frederick.* London, 1929.

Popović, Vasilj. *Evropa i Srpsko Pitanje u Periodu Oslobodjenja, 1804–1918* (Europe and the Serbian Question in the Period of Liberation, 1804–1918). Belgrade, 1937.

Potemkin, V. P., ed. *Istoriia Diplomatii, 1872–1919* (History of Diplomacy, 1872–1919). Moscow, 1945.

Prodanović, Jaša. *Istorija Politički Stranaka i Struja u Srbiji* (History of Political Parties and Currents in Serbia). Belgrade, 1947. Vol. I.

Pržić, Ilija. *Spoljašnja Politika Srbije* (The Foreign Policy of Serbia). Belgrade, 1939.

Radev, Simeon. *La Macédoine et la renaissance bulgare au XIXᵉ siècle.* Sofia, 1918.

————. *Stroitelite na Suvremenenna Bulgariia* (The Founders of Contemporary Bulgaria). Sofia, 1911. 2 vols.

Riasanovsky, Nicholas V. *Russia and the West in the Teachings of the Slavophiles.* Cambridge, 1952.

Ristić, Jovan. *Diplomatska Istorija Srbije za Vreme Ratova za Oslobodjenje i Nezavisnost, 1875–1878* (Diplomatic History of Serbia during the Wars for Liberation and Independence, 1875–1878). Belgrade, 1896–1898. 2 vols.

Rupp, George Hoover. *A Wavering Friendship: Russia and Austria, 1876–1878.* Cambridge, 1941.

Shoob, Leo. "Konstantin Petrovich Pobedonostsev: A Study in Reaction." Unpublished doctoral thesis, Berkeley, California, 1947.

Shopov, A. *Dr. Stoian Chomakov: Zhivot, Deinost i Arkhiva* (Dr. Stoian Chomakov: Life, Work, and Archives). Sofia, 1919.

Simeonoff, Iwan. *Die Eisenbahnen und Eisenbahnpolitik in Bulgarien.* Halle, 1909.

Skazkin, S. *Konets Avstro-Russko-Germanskogo Soiuza* (The End of the Austro-Russian-German Alliance). Moscow, 1928. Vol. I.

Skerlić, Jovan. *Svetozar Marković: Njegov Život, Rad i Ideje* (Svetozar Marković His Life, Works, and Ideas). Belgrade, 1910.

Slavianskoto Druzhestvo v Bolgarii. *Proslava na Osvoboditelnata Voina, 1877–1878* (Celebration of the War of Liberation, 1877–1878). Sofia, 1929.

Smith, Colin L. *The Embassy of Sir William White at Constantinople, 1886–1891*. Oxford, 1957.

Sosnosky, Theodor von. *Die Balkanpolitik Oesterreich-Ungarns seit 1866*. Stuttgart, 1913–1914. 2 vols.

Stählin, Karl. *Geschichte Russlands von den Anfängen bis zur Gegenwart*. Berlin, 1939. Vol. IV, no. 1.

Stanev, Nikola. *Istoriia na Nova Bulgariia, 1878–1929* (History of New Bulgaria, 1878–1928). Sofia, 1929.

Stavrianos, L. S. *Balkan Federation: A History of the Movement toward Balkan Unity in Modern Times*. Northhampton, Mass., 1944.

Steinmann, Friedrich, and Elias Hurwicz. *Konstantin Petrowitsch Pobjedonozew, der Staatsmann der Reaction unter Alexander III*. Berlin, 1933.

Stojanović, Mihailo D. *The Great Powers and the Balkans, 1875–1878*. Cambridge, 1939.

Sumner, B. H. *Russia and the Balkans, 1870–1880*. Oxford, 1937.

Tatishchev, S. S. *Imperator Aleksandr II: Ego Zhizn' i Tsarstvovanie* (Emperor Alexander II: His Life and Rule). St. Petersburg, 1911. 2 vols.

——. *Iz Prozhlago Russkoi Diplomatii* (From the Past of Russian Diplomacy). St. Petersburg, 1890.

Trifonov, Iurdan. *V. Drumev-Kliment: Branitski i Turnovski: Zhivot, Deinost i Kharakter* (V. Drumev-Kliment: Of Branitsa and Tyrnovo: Life, Work, and Character). Sofia, 1926.

Wilkinson, H. R. *Maps and Politics: A Review of the Ethnographic Cartography of Macedonia*. Liverpool, 1951.

Windelband, Wolfgang. *Bismarck und die europäischen Grossmächten, 1879–1885*. Essen, 1942.

Zhigarev, Sergei. *Russkaia Politika v Vostochnom Voprose* (Russian Policy in the Eastern Question). Moscow, 1896. 2 vols.

Živanović, Živan. *Politička Istorija Srbije u Drugoj Polovini Devetnaestog Veka* (Political History of Serbia in the Second Half of the Nineteenth Century). Belgrade, 1924. Vol. II.

ARTICLES

Anonymous. "Bolgarskiia Diela i Ot'ezd Barona Kaul'bars v Peterburg" (Bulgarian Affairs and the Return of Baron Kaulbars to St. Petersburg), *Viestnik Evropy*, XXI (Dec., 1886), 896.

Anonymous. "M. N. Katkov i Aleksandr III v 1886–1887 gg." (M. N. Katkov and Alexander III in 1886–1887), *Krasnyi Arkhiv*, XXXIII (1933), 58–85.

Anonymous. "Vostochnyia Diela i Pis'mo Gen. Kaul'barsa" (Eastern Affairs and a Letter of General Kaulbars), *Viestnik Evropy*, XXV (Nov., 1890), 47.

Anuchin, D. G. "Kniaz V. A. Cherkaskii i Grazhdanskoe Upravlenie v Bolgarii 1877–1878 gg." (Prince V. A. Cherkaskii and the Civil Administration in Bulgaria, 1877–1878), *Russkaia Starina*, LXXXIII:2 (1895), 1–34; LXXXIII:3 (1895),

1–27; LXXXIII:4 (1895), 43–55; LXXXIII:5 (1895), 1–36; LXXXIV:2 (1895), 41–69; LXXXIV:3 (1895), 53–104; LXXXIV:4 (1895), 1–32; LXXXIV:5 (1895), 47–67; LXXXIV:6 (1895), 1–50; LXXXV:1 (1896), 55–78; LXXXV:2 (1896), 285–313; LXXXV:3 (1896), 449–470; LXXXVI:5 (1896), 225–266; LXXXVII:7 (1896), 45–81; LXXXVII:8 (1896), 231–254.

Bakalov, G. "Russkaia Revoliutsionnaia Emigratsiia sredi Bolgar" (Russian Revolutionary Emigrants among the Bulgars), *Katorga i Ssylka*, LXIII (1930), 114–137; LXIV, 105–120; LXVI, 109–147.

Blackstock, Paul. "The Occupation Fund Documents: A Reassessment of 'A Crude and Ignorant Forgery,'" *American Slavic and East European Review*, XIII:4 (1954), 535–548.

Byrnes, Robert F. "Pobedonostsev as an Historian," in H. Stuart Hughes, ed., *Teachers of History: Essays in Honor of Laurence Bradford Packard*. Ithaca, N.Y., 1954. Pp. 105–121.

———. "Pobedonostsev's Conception of the Good Society," *Review of Politics*, XIII (1951), 169–190.

Eftimii, Arkhimandrit. "Bulgarskata Eksarkhiia v Tsarigrad" (The Bulgarian Exarchate in Constantinople), *Godishnik na Sofiiskiia Universitet: Bogoslovski Fakultet*, X (1932–1933), 1–32.

Ernrot, K. G. "K Noveishei Istorii Bolgarii" (On the Recent History of Bulgaria), *Russkaia Starina*, LII (1886), 475–483.

Erusalimskii, A. "Borba Derzhav za Balkany i Prolivy v Kontse XIX Veka" (The Struggle of the Powers for the Balkans and the Straits at the End of the Nineteenth Century), *Voprosy Istorii*, Sept., 1947, pp. 83–104.

Firsov, N. N. "Aleksandr III" (Alexander III), *Byloe*, XXIX (1929), 85–108.

Goriainov, S. M. "The End of the Alliance of the Three Emperors," *American Historical Review*, XXIII (Jan., 1918), 324–350.

———. "Razryv Rossii s Bolgariei v 1886 godu" (Russia's Break with Bulgaria in 1886), *Istoricheskii Viestnik*, CXLVII (Jan., 1917), 173–201.

Grim, E. "K Istorii Russko-Bolgarskikh Otnoshenii" (Concerning the History of Russo-Bulgarian Relations), *Novyi Vostok*, V (1924), 68–85.

Jacktschitch (Jakšić), Grégoire. "Le traité secret austro-serbe du 28 juin 1881 et du 9 février 1889," *Revue d'histoire diplomatique*, LI (1937), 429–466; LII (1938), 65–105.

Jakšić, Grgur, and Vojislav J. Vučković. "Pokušaj Aneksije Bosne-Hercegovine 1882–1883" (An Attempt to Annex Bosnia-Hercegovina, 1882–1883), *Glas Srpske Akademije Nauke*, vol. 214 (1954), pp. 47–110.

Jelavich, Charles. "The Revolt in Bosnia-Hercegovina, 1881–1882," *Slavonic and East European Review* (London), XXXI (1953), 420–436.

Jelavich, Charles, and Barbara Jelavich. "Jomini and the Revival of the Dreikaiserbund," *Slavonic and East European Review*, XXXV (June, 1957), 523–550.

———. "The Occupation Fund Documents: A Diplomatic Forgery," *American Slavic and East European Review*, XII:3 (Oct., 1953), 343–349.

———. "The Occupation Fund Documents: Additional Evidence," *American Slavic and East European Review*, XIV:3 (Oct., 1955), 390–401.

———. "Russia and Bulgaria, 1879: The Letters of A. P. Davydov to N. K. Giers," *Südost-Forschungen*, XV (1956), 427–458.

Kapidžić, Hamdija. "Crna Gora prema Hercegovačkom Ustanku 1882 godine" (Montenegro and the Hercegovinian Uprising in 1882), *Godišnjak Istoriskog Društva Bosne i Hercegovine*, VI (1954), 25–63.

————. "Prilog Istoriji Hercegovačkog Ustanka 1882 godine" (Contribution to the History of the Hercegovinian Uprising of 1882), *Godišnjak Istoriskog Društva Bosne i Hercegovine*, II (1950), 207–216.

Khvostov, V. "Problemy Zakhvata Bosfora v 90kh godakh XIX Veka" (The Problems of the Seizure of the Bosphorus in the 'Nineties of the Nineteenth Century), *Istorik Marksist*, XX (1930), 100–129.

Koz'menko, I. V. "Pervonachal'nye Proekty Tyrnovskoi Konstitutsii" (The Original Plans of the Tyrnovo Constitution), *Osvobozhdenie Bolgarii ot Turetskogo Iga*. Moscow, 1953. Pp. 222–264.

————. "Peterburgskii Proekt Tyrnovskoi Konstitutsii 1879 goda" (The Petersburg Plan of the Tyrnovo Constitution of 1879), *Istoricheskii Arkhiv*. Moscow, 1949. Vol. IV, pp. 184–324.

Lascaris, M. "Greece and Serbia during the War of 1885," *Slavonic and East European Review* (London), XI:3 (July, 1932), 88–99.

Matveev, P. A. "Bolgariia i Vostochnaia Rumeliia posle Berlinskago Kongressa" (Bulgaria and Eastern Rumelia after the Berlin Congress), *Istoricheskii Viestnik*, XXIV (1886), 329–359, 567–597; XXV (1886), 57–89, 235–268.

Medlicott, W. N. "Bismarck and the Three Emperors' Alliance, 1881–87," *Transactions of the Royal Historical Society*, 4th series, XXVII (1945), 61–83.

————. "The Powers and the Unification of the Two Bulgarias, 1885," *English Historical Review*, LIV (1939), 67–82, 263–284.

Meyer, Henry Cord. "German Economic Relations with Southeastern Europe, 1870–1914," *American Historical Review*, LVII:1 (Oct., 1951), 77–90.

Molchanov, A. N. "Prints Batenbergskii: Iz Nedavnikh Vospominanii" (Prince Battenberg: From Recent Recollections), *Istoricheskii Viestnik*, XXV (1886), 90–101.

Nikitin, S. "Vozniknovenie Moskovskogo Slavianskogo Komiteta" (The Creation of the Moscow Slavic Committee), *Voprosy Istorii*, Aug., 1947, pp. 50–65.

Penson, Lillian M. "The Principles and Methods of Lord Salisbury's Foreign Policy," *Cambridge Historical Journal*, V (1935), 87–106.

Popov, A. "Ot Bosfora k Tikhomu Okeanu" (From the Bosphorus to the Pacific Ocean), *Istorik Marksist*, XXXVII (1934), 3–28.

Popović, Dimitrije. "Naše Držanje prema Bugarskoj" (Our Attitude toward Bulgaria), *Srpski Književni Glasnik*, II (1921), 41–49.

————. "Uspomene na Stevana Stambolova" (Remembrances of Stevan Stambolov), *Srpski Književni Glasnik*, XV (1925), 259–276.

Popović, Vasilj. "Sukobi izmedju Mitropolita Mihaila i Vlade" (Disputes between Metropolitan Mihailo and the Government), *Letopis Matice Srpske*, 342:2 (1935), 167–188.

Pribram, Alfred F. "Milan IV von Serbien und die Geheimverträge Oesterreich-Ungarns mit Serbien, 1881–1889," *Historische Blätter*, I (1921–1922), 464–494.

Shcheglov, A. N. "Russkoe Ministerstvo v Bolgarii: Vremia Aleksandra Battenbergskago" (A Russian Ministry in Bulgaria: The Time of Alexander of Battenberg), *Istoricheskii Viestnik*, CXXVI (Nov., 1911), 552–590.

Skobelev, N. V. "Rech' Gen. Skobeleva v Parizhe v 1882 g." (The Speech of General Skobelev in Paris in 1882), *Krasnyi Arkhiv*, XXVII (1928), 215–223.

Sobolev, L. N. "K Noveishei Istorii Bolgarii" (Concerning the Recent History of Bulgaria), *Russkaia Starina*, LI (1886), 703–752.

Stavrianos, L. S. "L'institution de l'Exarcat bulgare: son influence sur les relations interbalkaniques," *Les Balkans*, XI (1939), 56–69.

Trivanovich, Vaso. "Serbia, Russia and Austria during the Rule of Milan Obreno-vich, 1868–78," *Journal of Modern History*, III (1931), 414–440.

Troubetskoi, Grégoire. "La politique russe en orient," *Revue d'histoire diplomatique*, XXI (1907), 161–198, 394–426.

Tsankov, Stefan. "Konstitutsionnitie Printsipi za Otnoshenieto mezhdu Durzhava i Tsurkva v Slavianskitie Durzhavi" (The Constitutional Principles for the Re-lations between State and Church in the Slavic States), *Godishnik na Sofiiskiia Universitet: Bogoslovski Fakultet*, X (1932–1933), 1–18.

———. "Mezhdutsurkovnato Polozenie na Bulgarskata Tsurkva sled Osvobozh-denieto na Bulgariia" (The Interchurch Position of the Bulgarian Church after the Liberation of Bulgaria), *Godishnik na Sofiiskiia Universitet: Bogoslovski Fakultet*, X (1932–1933), 1–122.

Uebersperger, Hans. "Zur Vorkriegsgeschichte Serbiens," *Berliner Monatshefte*, XI (1933), 15–54.

Vasiliev, K. S. "Bor'ba Bolgarskago Naroda protiv Reshenii Berlinskago Kongressa 1878 goda" (The Struggle of the Bulgarian People against the Decisions of the Berlin Congress of 1878), *Voprosy Istorii*, Aug., 1955, pp. 119–129.

Wren, Melvin C. "Pobedonostsev and Russian Influence in the Balkans," *Journal of Modern History*, XIX:2 (June, 1947), 130–141.

INDEX

INDEX

Abaza, A. A. (Russian minister of finance), 82, 83

Aegean Sea, 5, 7

Agura, D. (Bulgarian minister of education), 116

Aksakov, Ivan S. (Russian Panslav writer): supports Russian policy in Bulgaria, 15, 93 ff., 104, 218; on Alexander of Battenberg, 84, 141; on Mihailo, 175; on Bosnian revolt, 189

Aleko Pasha (governor-general of Rumelia), 93, 210, 212–213

Alexander of Battenberg, Prince of Bulgaria: described by Corti, 40; military career, 40–41, 42–43; election of, 42; dislikes Russians, 42–43, 49; arrives in Bulgaria, 45; clash over title, 47 ff., 62; constitutional *coup d'état*, 49 ff.; appoints regency, 61; needs financial aid, 107, 110; abdication, 129, 260, 261; marriage plans, 154–155; plots against, 237, 241 ff., 249; abduction of, 249 ff, 260; deposed, 250, 251; returns to Bulgaria, 257 ff.—*Alexander of Battenberg:* and Alexander II, 55–56, 74 ff.; and Alexander III, 83 ff., 100, 107, 122, 135, 138–139, 145, 156, 219, 221, 225, 238, 241, 250, 258–259, 261, 275; and the army, 95, 101, 110, 144, 147 ff., 217, 225, 231, 233, 247 ff.; and Austria, 87, 131; and Bismarck, 86–87, 124, 131, 154, 246; and Bosnian revolt, 190; Bulgarian unification, role in, 215 ff., 237, 246, 276; and Conservatives, 117, 119 ff., 131–132; and Grand National Assembly, 56, 85, 89, 95, 98; and Great Britain, 131, 148, 246; and Katkov, 123; and Kaulbars, 103, 237–238; and Khevenhüller, 232; and Khitrovo, 86, 95, 97, 99, 101, 190; and Koiander, 157, 214–215; and Liberals, 73, 123, 132, 133; and Nachevich, 97, 110, 117; and Ottoman Empire, 219, 238, 241; and Parensov, 51 ff., 57; and the press, 86, 93, 141; and Rumania, 246; and Rumelia, 240; Russians in cabinet, 93, 102 ff., 114; and Serbo-Bulgarian war, 234 ff.; and Sobolev, 103, 113–114; and Stambolov, 216, 253, 259–260; and Tyrnovo constitution, 46, 54, 58, 74, 76, 133–134

Alexander of Hesse (father of Alexander of Battenberg), 40 ff., 257

Alexander Obrenović, Prince of Serbia, 201, 203, 277

Alexander II, Tsar of Russia, 15–16, 18, 55–56, 74 ff., 91, 177, 207

Alexander III, Tsar of Russia, 81–82, 90 ff., 131, 281 ff.; and Alexander of Battenberg, 83 ff., 100, 107, 122, 135, 138–139, 145, 156, 219, 221, 225, 238, 241, 250, 258–259, 261, 275; and Mihailo affair, 202; policy on Bulgaria, 235, 252–253, 256, 271

Andrassy, Count Julius (Austrian foreign minister), 4, 18, 66

Arsen'ev, S. V. (Russian diplomatic agent in Sofia), 108, 123

Austria-Hungary: and Alexander of Battenberg, 87, 131; and Bosnia, 3, 4, 8, 15, 24, 26, 206; and Bulgaria, 24 ff., 77, 78, 284; and Dreikaiserbund, 23 *et passim;* and Great Britain, 7, 19; and Macedonia, 24, 172; and Milan Obrenović, 173, 224, 231 ff.; and Orthodoxy, 174, 179, 180, 181; and Ottoman Empire, 166; and Rumania, 11, 13; and Rumelia, 213, 224; and Russia, 19, 23 *et passim,* 233; and Salonika, 24, 206; Serbia dominated by, 13, 164, 170 ff., 187, 188, 196; and Serbo-Bulgarian war, 232 ff.; treaties with Serbia, 3, 27, 166, 170 ff., 185, 203–204; Treaty of San Stefano, 6. *See also* Andrassy; Biegeleben; Haymerle; Kalnoky; Khevenhüller; Railways; Wolkenstein.

Balabanov, M. D. (Bulgarian minister of foreign affairs), 142, 148, 149, 242

Benderev, Captain (Bulgarian army officer), 248

Bessarabia, 4, 9, 10, 11

Biegeleben, Freiherr von (Austrian minister in Sofia), 102, 130, 231, 246

Bismarck, Prince Otto von, 7, 18, 20, 21, 23, 82, 84, 223, 233; and Alexander of Battenberg, 86–87, 124, 131, 154, 246

Bogdanov, P. M. (Russian consular agent in Sofia), 242, 249, 252

Bontoux, E., 169, 184. *See also* Railways.

Bosnia-Hercegovina: and Austria, 3, 4, 8, 15, 24, 26, 206; revolt in, 188–190; and Russia, 12, 189, 190

Date Due